Canadian Women in Print
1750–1918

Canadian Women in Print
1750–1918

CAROLE GERSON

Wilfrid Laurier University Press

This book has been published with the help of a grant from the Canadian Federation for the Humanities and Social Sciences, through the Aid to Scholarly Publications Programme, using funds provided by the Social Sciences and Humanities Research Council of Canada. We acknowledge the support of the Canada Council for the Arts for our publishing program. We acknowledge the financial support of the Government of Canada through the Book Publishing Industry Development Program for our publishing activities.

Canada Council for the Arts   Conseil des Arts du Canada   ONTARIO ARTS COUNCIL   CONSEIL DES ARTS DE L'ONTARIO

Library and Archives Canada Cataloguing in Publication

Gerson, Carole
    Canadian women in print, 1750–1918 / Carole Gerson.

Includes bibliographical references and index.
Issued also in electronic format.
ISBN 978-1-55458-220-4 (cloth)
ISBN 978-1-55458-304-1 (pbk.)

    1. Canadian literature—Women authors—History and criticism. 2. Women and literature—Canada—History. 3. Women authors, Canadian—Social conditions. I. Title. (cloth)

PS8089.5.W6G473 2010   C810.9'9287   C2010-900643-7

ISBN 978-1-55458-239-6
Electronic format.

    1. Canadian literature—Women authors—History and criticism. 2. Women and literature—Canada—History. 3. Women authors, Canadian—Social conditions. I. Title.

PS8089.5.W6G473 2010   C810.9'9287   C2010-900644-5

Cover image from iStockphoto. Cover design by Martyn Schmoll. Text design by Catharine Bonas-Taylor.

CONTENTS

ILLUSTRATIONS

ACKNOWLEDGEMENTS

VERY FEW BOOKS ARE CREATED by just one person, and this one owes its existence to the assistance of many. Over the years I have gratefully drawn on the research of other scholars, including Gwendolyn Davies' ground-breaking work on Maritime women writers, Michael A. Peterman's extensive knowledge of the Strickland family, Marjory Lang's fabulous book on Canada's first female journalists, Mary Rubio's expertise on L.M. Montgomery, and Veronica Strong-Boag's ongoing collaboration on Pauline Johnson. Other researchers have participated as students and as colleagues, beginning in the 1980s and 1990s when Carol McIvor, Marjory Lang, Deborah Blacklock, Sandra Even, and Katrina Harack helped to locate and record information on little-known writers for the database, Canada's Early Women Writers. I'm indebted to eagle-eyed Janet B. Friskney for sending me many details regarding Canada's literary history that I otherwise would not have found. As this book neared completion, Lian Beveridge pored over microfiche and Alison McDonald organized the bibliography. Many others have contributed directly or indirectly through numerous modes of academic discourse, ranging from informal conversations and email queries to invitations to contribute to conferences and publications. I'm grateful to David Bentley, Diana Brydon, Sandra Campbell, Mary Chapman, Leith Davis, Misao Dean, Nancy Earle, Michael Everton, Janice Fiamengo, Irene Gammel, Greg Gatenby, Sherrill Grace, Leslie Howsam, Karyn Huenemann, Peggy Kelly, Eve-Marie Kroller, Tracy Kulba, Benjamin Lefebvre, Mary Lu MacDonald, the late Lorraine McMullen, Heather Murray, W.H. New, Ruth Panofsky, George L. Parker, Betty Schellenberg, Christl Verduyn, Tom Vincent, and Gillian Whitlock for their ongoing generosity in providing insights, answering questions, and sharing information. This book owes much of its scholarly perspective to my editorial colleagues in the *History of the Book in Canada* project: Fiona A. Black, Judy Donnelly, Patricia Fleming, Yvan Lamonde, and Jacques Michon, who educated me about the wider field of print culture. I would like to thank SSHRC (the Social Sciences and Humanities Research Council) for several decades of continuing research support and the Killam program of the Canada Council for the Research Fellowship, which gave me the time to pull it all together.

Research for this book was enabled by the assiduous interlibrary loan staff at Simon Fraser University and by librarians and archivists across Canada, beginning with those who responded to my first queries more than twenty-five years ago. Grateful thanks are due to Anne Goddard and Linda Hoad at what is now Library and Archives Canada, Sandra Alston and Rachel Grover at the University of Toronto, Susan Saunders Bellingham at the University of Waterloo, Apollonia Steele and Joanne Henning at the University of Calgary, Nancy Sadek at the University of Guelph, Cheryl Ennals at Mount Alison, Mary Flagg at the University of New Brunswick, Carl Spadoni at McMaster, Patricia Townsend at Acadia University, Karen Smith at Dalhousie, Nellie Reiss and Richard Virr at McGill, Leon Warmski at the Archives of Ontario, and Kenneth G. Aitken at the Regina Public Library. I regret that I have not recorded the names of the staff who assisted at many additional institutional and public libraries, large and small, and at most of Canada's provincial archives, from Nova Scotia to British Columbia.

Some of the material in this book first saw the light of day in my contributions to proceedings of the conferences of HOLIC/HILAC (History of the Literary Institution in Canada/Histoire de l'Institution Littéraire au Canada) at the University of Alberta, *Context North America: Canadian–US Literary Relations* (Ottawa: University of Ottawa Press, 1994), and the first two volumes of the *History of the Book in Canada*, as well as in my monograph, *Canada's Early Women Writers: Texts in English to 1859* (Ottawa: CRIAW, 1994).

Abundant thanks to all my family for their continuous support, and to Martin for his patient assistance with the evolving technology of scholarly communication. This book is dedicated to my mother, who reads everything, and to my granddaughter, who has yet to learn to read.

INTRODUCTION

MOST BOOKS ABOUT THE LITERARY past focus on selected major authors and the contents of their works, examining their sources, topics, styles, influences, reception, and canonization. Some sections of *Canadian Women in Print* cover such ground, but in general my primary focus is the context in which writers worked, rather than detailed analysis of their words. Considering women's published writing as an intervention in the public sphere of national and material print culture, this book traces the broad field of publication by early Canadian women by calling attention to the various social, cultural, and material conditions that propelled them onto the printed page, whether they were professional writers or one-time authors. While I cannot claim complete linguistic inclusiveness, I pay some attention to women who wrote in French and note those who published in other languages. Writing in English inevitably predominates—not only because my own context is anglophone, but also because before 1918, the literary culture of francophone Canadian women was less prominent than it subsequently became.

The narrative arc of this book is implicitly progressive and celebratory as it documents the increasing involvement of Canadian women in the world of print, from Marie de l'Incarnation's writings about New France in the seventeenth century to the thousands who were active at the end of the First World War. There are different ways to approach this story: by focusing on the repression of women under patriarchy, or by focusing on how women created their own agency within the private and public spheres available to them. This book integrates the two. While I fully acknowledge the historical marginalization of women, I try not to dwell on victimization and erasure. Instead, using approaches from book history and print culture, I address the actual working and living conditions of women writers in order to reconstruct their engagement with print within the terms of their lived experience. In large part, the approach that structures this book derives from my involvement with the three volumes of *History of the Book in Canada*, a project that situates literary and other writing within the larger cycles of authorship, production, dissemination, and reception of print, in line with the scheme articulated in Robert Darnton's communication circuit. Book historians will recognize that my approach includes the modifications to Darnton's diagram later proposed by Thomas R. Adams and Nicolas Barker, who demonstrate the need for greater attention to the larger historical, social, religious, and economic contexts that shape the creation and reading of written works.[1] Many aspects of *Canadian Women in Print* respond to the call of Leslie Howsam, Simone Murray, and other feminist book historians to recognize the varied historical roles that women have played in the world of the book, and to examine "the gender identity of the book itself, both as physical object and as cultural product."[2] In essence, *Canadian Women in Print* looks at the history of Canadian women writers as participants in a "field" of cultural production (to adapt the terminology of Pierre Bourdieu).[3] As is the case elsewhere, that field has been shaped by gender; perhaps more than in other places, it has been overdetermined by nationalism, given the propensity of Canadian writers of both genders to immigrate, emigrate, and publish abroad.[4] By frequently situating anglophone Canadian women writers in relation to those in England and the US, this book engages with Linda Hutcheon's querying of national models of literary history;[5] while it is not possible to devise an alternative framework, my discussions consistently demonstrate the need to situate the national in relation to the international.

This is not to say that the traditional literary genres of poetry, drama, and fiction do not deserve attention in themselves; studies of specific writers or texts will continue to enlighten us, according to the disciplinary norms of literary studies. At the same time, this book implicitly argues that the practice of plucking poets and novelists from the broader contexts of women's writing offers a restricted view of a larger picture whose assembly remains a work in progress. Despite the endurance of some star figures, cultural authority is a matter of ongoing negotiation, as is the literary canon that it creates. While the metaphor of mapping might be appealing, it also risks being inaccurate, in that the terrain is not stable but depends on many variables, including the serendipitous survival (and recovery) of texts and the sparsity of knowledge about so many writers.

Collage is perhaps more a more accurate image, in that this book arranges many separate snapshots of specific individuals and scenes of writing in order to present larger composite stories.

Readers will meet many familiar names—not in separate chapters, but in discussions where their stories illuminate the history of Canada's print culture—as well as many more they will not recognize. Susanna Moodie, L.M. Montgomery, Nellie McClung, Pauline Johnson, and Sara Jeannette Duncan appear frequently, contextualized by writers whose names will be known to some (such as Agnes Maule Machar, Madge Macbeth, Marshall Saunders, and Agnes Laut) and by many more whose writings and biographies have vanished into the recesses of history. Like all representations on paper, this one is inevitably two-dimensional. If the printed page could be turned into hypertext, readers would be able to click on a name to find studies that deepen their understanding of specific writers, such as recent book-length studies dedicated to some of the better-known individuals (Johnson, Duncan, Moodie) or the chapters on specific early women novelists in *Silenced Sextet,* and on early women journalists in Janice Fiamengo's *The Woman's Page.*[6] I cite these two fine volumes because their authors chose to approach a collective situation through chapter-length studies of individual writers.[7] In a sense, I have done the opposite, with my chapters providing studies of collective situations in which individuals operated and which they helped to shape. Hence this book is not a Canadian parallel to Elaine Showalter's new history of American women writers, *A Jury of Her Peers* (2009), which charts an American female tradition from Anne Bradstreet to Annie Proulx by examining individual authors in relation to their literary works. The sheer magnitude of Showalter's study reminds us of the proximity and complexity of American print culture, in which women's bold and varied participation consistently offered inspiration for Canada's female writers.

Most of the writing produced by Canadian women before 1918 touched on the literary—broadly defined to include travel, biography, and cultural journalism—as well as the usually privileged genres of fiction, drama, and poetry. The few quantitative studies of Canadian writing published before 1918 demonstrate that among women writers of non-fiction, literary or proto-literary genres such as history prevailed. In the 1890s, it was the literary authors and journalists who caught the attention of commentators who included women writers in their assessments of Canada's cultural scene. The late nineteenth-century desire to foster a national cultural identity yielded a spate of newspaper and magazine articles, public addresses, and contributions to reference works that demonstrated the durability of E.H. Dewart's early statement that "A national literature is an essential element in the formation of national character."[8] While not losing sight of the broadened literary field that such publicity created for women, this book also calls attention to women who turned to print to voice social causes, such as temperance and missionary work.

Such activities did not occur in a vacuum, and women participated in the production of print in many capacities, including the material realm of print shops and publishing houses. Hence my first chapter opens with an examination of women's work in the book trades, from those who set type as printers' daughters and widows in the eighteenth century to the female bookbinders who sought unionization in the nineteenth century. This chapter then slides from the material side to the social context by considering many ways that women were involved in both fostering and controlling access to print. In the early nineteenth century, educated immigrants like Anne Langton helped to organize pioneer reading groups. Many women who lived in established communities participated in middle-class literary societies for the entertainment and enlightenment of their own social circles, while some residents of cities regarded the establishment of public reading rooms for the underprivileged as a route to social reform. Early in the twentieth century, women's literary groups were dedicated advocates for public libraries, and professional librarianship became an attractive area of employment for women. Recognizing that not all women writers sought affirmation in print, I conclude this chapter with a brief discussion of manuscript culture.

The second chapter, an overview of Canadian women writers from initial settlement until the 1850s, summarizes many "firsts" in Canadian women's literary history, beginning with the first European publication of writing from women of New France in the seventeenth century. In the pre-Confederation period, books were difficult to publish and many women were involved with periodicals as editors as well as contributors. After the American Revolution, nodes of female authorship developed at three specific sites in the remainder of British North America. In the Maritime colonies, Loyalist Deborah How Cottnam, Canada's first notable woman poet, was followed by a later generation of writers that included Sarah Herbert. In Montreal, literary interests occasionally enabled French and English women to cross paths, but not in the pages of the era's most significant periodical, the *Literary Garland*. The city's major pre-Confederation writers included Rosanna Leprohon, Mary Anne Sadlier, and the American-born Foster sisters. Upper Canada, the third region I discuss, was also marked by a pair of ink-stained immigrant sisters, Catharine Parr Strickland Traill and Susanna Strickland Moodie, whose literary community included Frances Stewart and Rhoda Ann Page. No overview of Canadian women writers of the pre-Confederation era can omit Maria Monk, whose notoriety for her supposed authorship of stories of abuse in a convent set her apart from other literary communities and provides a fitting conclusion.

The next three chapters situate Canadian women writers within the social, economic, and cultural conditions that prevailed through the nineteenth century and into the twentieth, thereby tackling the way the book is "intrinsically, though invisibly, 'marked' as masculine."[9] Chapter 3, "Strategies of Legitimation," analyzes women writers' self-representation in prefaces—primarily to poetry—and contrasts the negativity of tropes of apology with positive claims of moral and national value. While the diffidence of one-time authors seems sincere, professional writers, from Anne Jameson to Sara Jeannette Duncan, played ironically with the convention of affected modesty. Chapter 4 examines various genres of women's writing in relation to their motives and the financial side of authorship, writing being one of the few areas where women could hope for economic equality. While book publishing was seldom financially viable in nineteenth-century Canada, women writers who first built their audiences through journalism achieved some economic success and public acclaim. Many books were financed by authors; others were issued posthumously to commemorate a deceased writer. Toward the end of the century, ambitious young women who sought professional literary careers sold their work in the United States. Chapter 5 examines the careers of those who migrated there, in contrast with those who exploited American literary markets while staying home in Canada.

Fully half this book falls into its third section, "Breaking New Ground after 1875." Chapter 6 shows how the rise of women's journalism offered specific opportunities that coalesced in the founding of the Canadian Women's Press Club in 1904. In conjunction with their entry into professional journalism, women also became prominent authors of non-fiction, specializing in domestic education, botanical writing, and stories about animals, as described in Chapter 7. History proved the most attractive non-fiction genre, reflecting the era's conviction that historical awareness underpinned national identity. The expanded presence of women in print served many interests, and large groups of women entered the public sphere in the name of causes that were not equally progressive. Chapter 8, "From Religion to Reform," recognizes the many women who were active in denominational writing and publishing. The linking of temperance with women's suffrage shows the difficulty of applying later notions of advancement to earlier social movements: two of the major reformers of the era, Agnes Maule Machar and Nellie McClung, were drawn to radical social analysis through their commitment to conventional Christian values of service.

While the figure of the New Woman hovers over much of this book, it is in Chapter 9 that she is fully addressed in two incarnations—as living author and as fictional character. Historical New Women abounded in Canada's relatively flexible social structure, proving their mettle as undaunted journalists and intrepid travellers, yet few such adventurers appeared in fiction by Canadian women and most of these characters suffered for their daring. The final chapter looks to the twentieth century through writers who addressed the margins of race. Beginning with Mary Ann Shadd Cary, Canada's first significant Black woman writer, discussion then turns to Aboriginal writers—represented most prominently by Pauline Johnson—and concludes with the different modes of identification developed by the part-Asian Eaton sisters, Edith and Winnifred. Winnifred Eaton Reeve, like L.M. Montgomery and other career writers of her generation, cannily exploited her personal history and the popular genres of her era to prosper as an internationally successful celebrity.

Many years and miles separate Canada's professional women writers of the initial decades of the twentieth century from the first nuns to publish about New France in the seventeenth century. By 1918, women writing in both French and English had drawn the blueprints for the rooms they would occupy in the nation's cultural edifices that arose through the twentieth century. These structures would undergo frequent renovation as tastes altered; during the mid-twentieth century era of high modernism, the hegemony of the men's smoking room would relegate most women to the hallways and closets from which they would burst forth in second wave feminist writing in the 1960s. But their grandmothers had staked their right of occupancy to the parlour and the study as well as to the kitchen and the nursery, and would not be evicted.

Contexts: Women and Print in Canada, to 1918

ONE

❧❦❧

Women and the Broader Contexts of Print

WHEN WE CONSIDER THE RELATION BETWEEN Canadian women and print during the years before 1918, we are most likely to think of writers, particularly those known for their poetry, fiction, travel narratives, or memoirs of pioneer life. Such women dominate subsequent chapters of this book, in which I examine various facets of the social and material construction of authorship. As the activities of writing and publication necessarily take place within a larger framework of cultural activity, my study begins by outlining the broader context of women's participation in the infrastructure of Canada's early print culture. This chapter opens with an overview of women's work in material production, followed by consideration of their engagement with book culture through libraries and literary societies. It concludes with a discussion of women's manuscript culture in relation to the authority of print.

Women and the Material Creation of Print: Printing, Publishing, Bookbinding

In the eighteenth and nineteenth centuries, Canadian women often engaged in the business and commerce of books and print as members of their family enterprise, thereby replicating patterns of shared labour that were common in England and France.[1] Hence it is not surprising that women were associated with printing from the time the first press began operation. There was no printing in New France or the northern British colonies that would become Canada until Bartholomew Green shipped a press from Boston to the recently established settlement of Halifax in 1751. After Green's sudden death, John Bushell, Green's former partner, ran the enterprise and was appointed King's Printer in 1752, a position he held until his own death in 1761. A drinker and an uncertain businessman, Bushell relied on the assistance of his daughter, Elizabeth, to produce Canada's first newspaper, the Halifax *Gazette*, from 1752 until 1761 as well as government documents and various forms of job printing. Unfortunately, Elizabeth disappeared from the historical record after her father's partner, Anthony Henry, took over the business, and it is not known if she remained long in Nova Scotia or joined her brother, also a printer, who relocated to Philadelphia, where he died in 1797.[2]

It was not uncommon for printers' wives to work alongside their husbands, as did Marie Mirabeau, the first spouse of the pioneer francophone printer Fleury Mesplet, who set up shop in Montreal in 1776. During her husband's imprisonment from June 1779 to February 1783, Mirabeau kept the enterprise afloat, albeit in a reduced fashion. Such women sometimes continued the printing business following the death of a mate, as was briefly attempted by Mesplet's second wife, Marie-Anne Tison, after Mesplet died in 1794.[3] In both Europe and North America, the participation of women in printing was seldom formally acknowledged until they became widows and were identified as such by their imprint; this pattern was notable in the pre-revolutionary American colonies, where eight of the ten known female printers took over the family business from a deceased or incapable spouse.[4] The same model was followed by Elizabeth Gay in Halifax in 1805, Ann Mott in Saint John in 1814, Sophia Simms Dalton in Toronto in 1840, and Anne Lovell, also in Toronto, in 1868. Some widows' ventures proved fairly brief: Elizabeth Gay and Ann Mott each lasted barely a year as printers. However, Sophia Dalton continued for eight, successfully publishing Toronto's *Patriot* newspaper until she sold it upon her retirement.[5] Sometimes widows chose to maintain just one of their husbands' ventures in the book and printing trades. For example, in Quebec City, Louise Ledroit closed her husband's printing shop after his death in 1829, but kept his bookstore open.[6]

In Canada, as the production of newspapers, magazines, and books became increasingly mechanized through the nineteenth century, the proportion of women employed in printing and publishing grew from 11 percent in 1871 to 20 percent in 1921,[7] the vast majority working in commercial enterprises in Quebec and Ontario. Because prevailing social norms allowed women to be paid less than men, the women who worked in the industrial book trades were usually restricted to tasks that required less training than those reserved for men, and received lower wages. Unionization then fostered the entrenchment of a gender-based hierarchy in which male labourers, in the words of labour historian, Christina Burr, "defended their status in the workplace against industrial capitalist incursions and the increasing mechanization of the production process."[8]

Bookbinding was one of the first and most enduring areas of book production to employ women, in part due to their traditional skill in sewing. Canada's census of 1871 shows that about half the women in the book trades worked in binding and most of the others in printing offices, with a few in engraving and lithography shops.[9] In the following census of 1881, the proportion of female employees in binding was even higher.[10] Data from 1921 show that female staff continued to dominate binderies and the offices of companies in the book trades, and were also numerous in the category of undesignated employees.[11] Unionization reached women bookbinders when they were recruited by the Knights of Labor in the 1880s, followed by the founding of the International Brotherhood of Bookbinders in 1892 and the establishment of women's locals in Toronto in 1901,[12] yet women who worked in commercial binderies continued to receive a third to a half of the wages earned by men.[13] In union shops, they remained confined to the lower status "forwarding tasks" defined as women's work,[14] which involved the preparation and sewing of the pages, while men performed the more complex tasks of "finishing" the process by fitting and decorating the bindings (with the exception of the application of gold leaf, which remained a women's specialty). Hence it is not surprising that some women avoided union restrictions by opening their own businesses: the census of 1891 recorded a one-woman shop in New Brunswick, several woman-owned binderies in Nova Scotia and Ontario, and in Sainte-Hyacinthe, Quebec, a business operated by four women.[15]

In 1895, the Victoria *Daily Times* published an extensive survey of local employment opportunities for women, that included a detailed summary of work at a busy press:

> In the bookbinding, job printing, and also the colored label department of the Colonist Printing and Publishing Co. girls are found busily engaged. Two young women feed the colored label presses. The work is heavy, as the girls lift the paper up to the press, a height of about six or eight feet from the floor. It takes some time to learn to feed quickly and accurately, many sheets of paper being spoiled before proficiency is attained. The hours are from 8 to 6; wages $7.50 and $8.50 per week. In the bookbinding and job printing departments one girl does colored stamping work, such as envelopes, letter heads, etc. Another does ruling and folding, and a third, as well as assisting with ruling and folding, does such extra work as sewing,

running paging machine, etc. The wages are from $4 to $8 per week. Nine hours per day, excepting Saturday, when the day's work ends at noon. Some girls pick up the work very quickly, but as a rule it takes two or three years of practice to become "fairly expert." Women of artistic taste and delicacy of touch can, in this department, obtain better wages than at almost any other manual employment.[16]

In the late nineteenth century, the appeal of bookbinding crossed class boundaries. While the women employed in the commercial binderies were working-class labourers, middle-class women in Britain and the US were attracted to fine binding, partly as a hobby and partly as a profession. Marianne Tidcombe has documented the history of European women's involvement in bookbinding, both as a material art and as a business, noting that "[t]hroughout the 18th and 19th centuries, a fair number of women were in charge of bookbinding establishments."[17] A new trend arose in the 1870s when wealthy Englishwomen began to cover their books with attractive papers brought back from Italy. Interest spread as the craft of fine hand-binding appealed to those like William Morris and members of his circle, who saw it as not only a new and accessible art that built on existing women's skills in embroidery, painting, designing, and leatherwork, but also as a potential means of support for distressed gentlewomen. Classes in leatherwork and bookbinding proliferated in England over the turn of the century, such that "it seemed that almost every other woman was learning bookbinding, or knew someone who was a bookbinder,"[18] from royalty to women rescued from the streets by the Salvation Army. The work of women bookbinders was shown regularly by the Arts and Crafts Exhibition Society and sold through the Guild of Women Binders, established in 1898. A number of American women sailed to England to study bookbinding, including Evelyn Hunter Nordhoff, who subsequently established the Elephant Bindery in New York. In 1897, Minnie Sophia Prat from Wolfville, Nova Scotia, became Nordhoff's first apprentice and was soon joined by her younger sister, May Rosina. Remaining in New York, the Prat sisters opened their Primrose bindery in 1899, and were soon written up in *Harper's Bazaar*. Minnie's work earned medals "for artistic design and workmanship" at the Paris Exposition of 1900 and the Pan-American Exposition in Buffalo in 1901, but that same year she succumbed to typhoid. A third Prat sister, Annie Louisa, helped to keep the New York bindery active until 1903, when Rosina returned to Nova Scotia to marry. She brought her equipment home to Starr's Point, near Wolfville, where she continued to bind books privately for many decades and trained her niece as her assistant.[19] Despite considerable activity in England and the

US, there is little evidence of other Canadian women practising fine book-binding during its heyday.[20]

The pattern of gender categorization evident in bookbinding permeated all major areas of the print trades. Typographers' unions led the labour movement in Canada during the second half of the nineteenth century, resulting in increased pay scales and reductions in the standard work week. Yet they systematically discriminated against women, a practice deemed acceptable because women were not seen as family breadwinners and therefore were not entitled to equal pay, regardless of the level or quality of their work. The hand-setting of type, at which some women proved very able, was identified as a masculine domain that was rigorously preserved, especially as composition—particularly for newspapers—became increasingly mechanized following the invention of the linotype machine in the 1880s. In 1854, an article from a Cincinnati newspaper extolling the prospect of typesetting becoming "one of the regular employments for women" and declaring its intention to "avail ourselves of the labor of female

FIGURE 1.1 Composing room staff of the *King's County Record,* Sussex, New Brunswick, c. 1900, showing women setting type in the production of this weekly newspaper. (Provincial Archives of New Brunswick, Don Smith Collection: P446-6)

printers" was reprinted in the *Canadian Son of Temperance* (Toronto). The latter then concluded that "[t]he Canadian women are also thinking of becoming printers,"[21] a prediction that proved incorrect as female compositors were discouraged from learning and performing the highly skilled, specialized tasks that were strictly regulated by an apprenticeship system. According to Chris Raible, "George Brown's employing of women— 'Brown's harem' male journeymen derisively dubbed his establishment— was a major reason for the first strike at the *Globe*."[22] As larger and faster presses prevailed, "[b]y the turn of the century, the concept of the male breadwinner was used by the male unionists to attempt to exclude women from the pressroom and from the [International Printing Pressmen and Assistant's Union]."[23] Women who persisted in the trade often ended up in non-union shops, where wages were lower. We don't know how many learned to print outside the sphere of organized labour, as did teen-aged Ethelwyn Wetherald in the early 1870s. Because her father had been given a "small printing outfit which neither he nor I had been able to use," she went to work in the office of the *Welland Tribune* to learn to set type and enjoyed her time in the office of this small newspaper.[24]

The Victoria *Daily Colonist*'s 1895 assessment indicated that for a woman, a career in typesetting was more myth than reality. "There are only one or two women typesetters in Victoria," it noted, even though

> typesetting is one of the most desirable employments [a woman] can select, especially upon a daily newspaper. The work of actual typesetting is light, the stint is not long (usually from six to seven hours). The art is not easily acquired, however, and demands close application and a good memory, while a thorough knowledge of grammar and orthography is almost indispensable. There has been a great outcry against women invading this craft because so many of them will not take the trouble to master it thoroughly.... But if a woman goes into a printing office with the determination to master the craft so far as her opportunities permit she will find the calling productive of much good mentally and socially as well as financially.

Although few women gained union membership, those who managed to do so clearly benefitted: "The recognition of women by the International Typographical Union gives a certain dignity to the trade which no other employment for women has. Union women are paid the same wages as men for similar work."[25]

A broad snapshot of women's employment in printing and publishing in 1900 is given in *Women of Canada*,[26] based on responses to their own survey rather than on the census data usually used by scholars:

TABLE 1.1: Occupations and Numbers of Women Employed in Printing and Publishing Houses Heard From

	P.E.I.	N.S.	N.B.	QUE.	ONT.	MAN.	N.W.T.	B.C.
Establishments reported	2	7	8	32	95	3	2	4
Sub-editors	1	1		8	14			
Contributors and correspondents	3	24	34	49	248			
Proof-readers	1	1		13	20			
Typesetters	5	20	11	24	32			
In Bindery		2	2	132	468	6		6
Book-keepers, clerks, saleswomen, type-writers, stenographers, etc.	3	10		115	97	1		1

Source: *Women of Canada*, 1900

Of the 153 establishments heard from, very few give the same wages to women as to men.

In London, England, the high wages of printers and compositors, along with women's reputedly nimble fingers, inspired the Society for Promoting the Employment of Women (whose board included Anna Jameson)[27] to develop women's opportunities in the printing trades. In 1860, board member Emily Faithfull set up the Victoria Press to train and employ female compositors. This venture caught the attention of Queen Victoria, who appointed Faithfull as Printer and Publisher in Ordinary to Her Majesty in 1862. During its twenty years of existence the press produced, among other items,[28] thirty-five volumes of the *Victoria Magazine*, which advocated the right of women to gainful employment. Subsequently, Emma Paterson established the Women's Printing Society in London in 1876. Similar ventures in the US included Mary Nolan's *Central Magazine*, which claimed in 1873 that it was the first American magazine entirely produced by women, from authors and editors to compositors and proofreaders.[29]

While Faithfull's life and work are well documented, much less is known about a Canadian undertaking that followed her model, even though one of its founders, Henrietta Muir Edwards, later acquired renown as one of the "Famous Five" whose efforts eventually led to the formal recognition of women as legally "persons" eligible for appointment to the Canadian Senate in 1929. In 1878, two unmarried feminist Baptist sisters, Amelia and Henrietta Muir, opened the Montreal Women's Printing Office on Bleury Street. This enterprise grew out of the Working Girls' Association, founded in 1873, whose first projects included a public reading room and a self-supporting boarding house for young women. Few specific titles are attributed to the press, whose history is difficult to pin down. Its productions included *Women's Work in*

Canada, founded in 1878, a newspaper whose size and longevity remain uncertain because no copies survive[30] and two extant texts, both dated 1879. *Agnes Harcourt; or "For His Sake,"* whose preface is signed "A.M." [Amelia Muir], was issued by the Montreal Women's Printing Office and is further identified as "Reprinted from *Women's Work in Canada.*" *Scripture Catechism, Intended for the Instruction of Children,* whose preface is signed "E.M.H.," was "Printed at the W.G. [Working Girls'] Association 73 Bleury St." According to Patricia Roome, by 1882 the Montreal Women's Printing Office had become job printers whose range of services included "'bill heads, business circulars, promissory notes, receipt forms, and all kinds of business printing,' such as 'reports, pamphlets, programmes, cards.'"[31]

It is virtually impossible to identify other items produced by female printers in Canada before 1919. Nor is it easy to locate those that can be regarded as published by women, if by publication we mean the production of texts intended for an audience beyond the specific memberships of women's organizations that issued annual reports, minutes, programs, constitutions, and similar forms of self-documentation, which, before the development of mimeography, were often produced in small quantities by job printers. Of the items intended for wider distribution that have been preserved in the Canadian Institute for Historical Microreproductions (CIHM) microfiche collection of Early Canadiana, the majority are church related and focus on such issues as temperance or missionary work, a subject to which I return in Chapter 8. Secular texts were produced by women's historical associations, art associations, or service organizations, including many branches of the National Council of Women. For example, in Halifax, from 1906 to 1916 the local Council of Women regularly prepared an elegant illustrated catalogue for the art exhibit at the Nova Scotia Provincial Exhibition. In Winnipeg, in 1914 the civic committee of the University Women's Club issued a report on the work of women and girls in the department stores of Winnipeg.[32] Cookbooks abounded, as documented in Elizabeth Driver's recent bibliography, with the worthy causes that prompted their production visibly proclaimed. Typical were *The YWCA Cook Book,* compiled by the ladies of St. Thomas, Ontario, in 1908 to raise money for their building fund and *Cook Book: Economical Recipes for the Women of Canada During the War,* produced in 1915 by the Longfellow Chapter of the Imperial Order of the Daughters of the Empire in Waterloo, Quebec, whose profits went toward "work for the soldiers."[33]

Women and the Access to Print: Libraries and Literary Societies

During Canada's early years, formally organized subscription or private libraries were often founded by prominent men in government or the military, with women participating through the membership of spouses or male relatives. Historian Mary Lu MacDonald has identified some thirty French and English literary societies that were active in Upper and Lower Canada between 1824 and 1850, none of which had female members, "although women were usually allowed to attend the lectures and debates as guests."[34] Despite such exclusion from elite libraries, during this period there were several women among the many operators of commercial circulating libraries that loaned books for a fee: Miss Read in Kingston, and Mary Davis in Halifax.[35] As well, some educated women who settled in the Upper Canadian bush during the 1820s became active organizers of social libraries, which used members' fees to purchase reading materials. Shortly after arriving in the Cobourg region in 1822, Frances Stewart recorded her pleasure in discovering that the people of nearby Port Hope "have a *book society* among themselves. Each member pays four dollars per annum."[36] The diaries of Thornhill settler, Mary Gapper O'Brien, record that in 1829 she enlisted her sisters-in-law to help establish a Book Society, an effort she repeated in 1835 when she moved to Shanty Bay on Lake Simcoe.[37]

In the early 1840s, at Sturgeon Lake near Peterborough, Anne Langton similarly established the first local library when she made her family's collection available to the public. Charging a "quarterly sixpence," she wryly noted that she had "but four" subscribers, charitably attributing their sparsity to "scarcity of cash" rather than lack of interest.[38] Heather Murray's research reveals that at this time "women would often be the prime movers behind such organizations, although they and the format they favoured would be displaced at mid-century, as men's organizations formulated grander plans for reading rooms and other early forms of civic libraries."[39] In both French and English Canada, "For most of the nineteenth century, Euro-Canadian women could be admitted only to the fringes of men's organizations"[40] ranging from patrician associations, such as the enduring Literary and Historical Society of Quebec, to the educationally oriented mechanics' institutes that sprang up to enlighten labourers in towns and cities across the country.

Nevertheless, women persisted in their involvement with print, often at the margins of mainstream culture. Black women established "the first women's literary society in Ontario and perhaps in all of Canada" with the founding of the Windsor Ladies Club by Mary Bibb in 1854, quickly followed by the Ladies Literary Society of Chatham.[41] Dr. Emily Howard Stowe and Canada's early suffragists exploited the respectability of literary societies when they founded the Toronto Women's Literary Club in 1875 to mask the true purpose of their group, which became apparent in 1883 when they renamed themselves the Toronto Women's Suffrage Club. The last decades of the nineteenth century saw "an explosive growth" in historical and literary societies as "middle-class women and their daughters, weary of rejection by the men's societies that monopolized the cultural terrain," set up their own clubs.[42] *Women of Canada* provides a valuable inventory for the year 1900 with a list of three dozen Literary Societies and Clubs, a third of whose names specified a female membership.[43] Among those with a membership described as "mixed" was the Eclectic Reading Club of St. John, New Brunswick, whose establishment in 1870 rendered it one of the oldest such organizations. For many years its executive included Frances Elizabeth Murray, an occasional author who was well known for her charitable and church work.[44] During her residence in Halifax from 1878 to 1897, Anna Leonowens, famous for her Boston-published books about her experience as governess to the large royal family of Siam, organized a Pioneer Book Club, followed in 1895 by a Shakespeare Club for young women.[45] An interesting sidebar to the association of women with reading appears in William Notman's portrait photographs of Montreal girls from the 1860s through the 1880s. Art historian Loren Lerner has documented how the posing of well-dressed middle- and upper-class girls and young women with their attention statically focused on books signalled their intellectual and social status, along with their commitment to domestic propriety.[46]

In addition to looking to their own self-improvement, middle-class reformers and club members also established reading rooms for working women, such as the one set up by the Muir sisters in Montreal in 1873. In her novel, *Roland Graeme: Knight* (1892), Agnes Maule Machar describes how the factory owner's daughter and other service-minded young ladies of a mill town prepare a refuge for female workers that contains "a neat bookcase, filled for the most part, with story-books for which their former owners had no further use."[47] More rigorous would have been the contents of the Girls' Reading Room in Montreal, run since 1886 by the Evangelistic Hall, which offered "industrial and educational classes" as well as a library that was "very much used."[48] Organizing libraries for rural women was an early goal of many Women's Institutes.[49] Moreover, many of Canada's public libraries owe their existence to the dedicated advocacy of women's literary associations, as demonstrated by two Alberta organizations that both began in 1906. Soon after its founding, the Calgary Women's Literary Club became involved in their city's successful request for a Carnegie library, which was completed in 1912. The Women's Literary Club of Medicine Hat likewise advocated the establishment of a municipal public library, which, without Carnegie support, opened its doors in 1915.[50] In Quebec, Robertine Barry's *Journal de Françoise* supported the growth of public libraries during the same period.[51] Women's desire to create publicly accessible collections of reading material can be explained not only by their marginalization in the realm of men's literary organizations, but also, among the wealthier classes, in relation to their exclusion from the traditions of private book collecting. Women certainly owned some of the materials they read, as demonstrated by Elizabeth Mauger's bookplate printed in Halifax in 1756 and affixed to her copy of volume five of the *Spectator*.[52] Yet the corpus of over one thousand catalogues of private libraries created for *History of the Book in Canada* yields only four entries that refer to collections of books owned by women, the earliest in 1813 in Halifax, and the latest in 1920 in Montreal.

In line with their interest in the public good, women of late nineteenth-century Canada not only sought to provide books, but also attempted to regulate their use. In 1893, a significant motive behind Joséphine Marchand Dandurand's founding of her groundbreaking women's magazine, *Le Coin de feu*, was to promote the presence of books in the home while guiding women to read only those whose morality suited the female mind.[53] Prominent was the National Council of Women, to whom Lady Schultz read her paper on *How to Provide Good Reading for Children* before it was issued as a ten-cent pamphlet in 1895.[54] The following year, the council's subcommittee on literature prepared a report on "the circulation of impure literature and pictures" and warned that "a far greater amount of objectionable literature is being circulated amongst children than the general public has any idea of." Its authors claimed that offensive pictures and salacious magazines were easily obtained from railway porters and through the mail, sometimes in the guise of religious papers, and they offered no distinction between "cheap, trashy, sensational literature" and the works of Émile Zola. To attain its goal of distributing "cheap, attractive, healthy literature" to young people, the council recommended the establishment of school and public libraries, formalized reading groups, and the circulation of lists of recommended books. Its appended list of publications whose transmission by mail in Canada was prohibited were mostly American in origin, from such evidently naughty titles as the *Climax* (Chicago) and the *Detective Library* (New York), to many that seem innocuous such as the *Home and Fireside* (New York) and the *American Farmer* (Portland, Maine). Signed by Ishbel Aberdeen and adopted by the National Council of Women at its annual meeting in Montreal in May 1896, the report was ordered to be printed and circulated, at the price of twenty-five cents per dozen.[55] Also in 1896, Madge Merton (Ella S. Atkinson) and John A. Cooper, editor of the *Canadian Magazine*, co-authored an article on "Our children and their reading" that was divided into two sections according to the gender of the authors. While Cooper concentrated on luring boys away from penny dreadfuls by offering titles by Henty, Ballantyne, and other authors of adventure stories, Atkinson argued that "a girl should read the same books her brother should read" because "[m]en and women will be more companionable when they absorb thought from the same sources."[56]

As the nineteenth century turned into the twentieth, the identification of women as handmaidens to mainstream literary activity became particularly evident in their expanding role as library staff, usually in cataloguing and other work that required attention to detail. For example, when author Félicité Angers was hoping to receive a job with the Quebec government, she confided that "cela me serait bien avantageux surtout si l'on me place dans un bibliothèque."[57] The development of library services for children early in the twentieth century created another marginal sphere characterized by a concentration of women, as it was deemed "quite natural that the library workers set apart to care especially for the children should be women." While many concurred that "Library work is a great field for women, and in it they have proved especially successful,"[58] female librarians remained in subordinate positions. In 1900, *Women of Canada* commented that "A large percentage of those employed in Library work are women; but not many women are heads of Libraries excepting in the smaller institutions.... The Public Library of Toronto, the largest circulating Library in the Dominion, gives employment to 25 persons, of whom 22 are women."[59] James Bain, the Toronto Public Library's first chief librarian, earned an annual salary of $2,000, while the women's salaries ranged from $300 to $600.[60] One of the first women to rise to a senior position in library management was Mary Sollace Saxe, who headed the Westmount Public Library from 1901 to 1931. An author as well as a public servant, Saxe published a children's book in 1919 and turned to playwriting after retirement.

FIGURE 1.2 Staff of the Reference Library, Toronto Public Library, c. 1895 (Toronto Public Library, T 12007)

Privacy or Print: Women's Manuscript Culture

While publication is one useful criterion for discerning Canada's early literature, much was initially penned for more limited dissemination, some of which later found its way into print. Julie Roy makes the case that the women of New France and post-Conquest Quebec enjoyed a rich epistolatory culture in which the letter became "un véritable laboratoire où explorer l'écriture et parfois même s'adonner à des genres plus canoniques. L'espace épistolaire devient pour elles une sorte d'alternative à l'espace public dans lequel s'inscriront les champs politique et littéraire des hommes."[61] One important such archive is the letters that Élisabeth Bégon wrote to her son between 1748 and 1753. Discovered in 1932 and published in 1935, they are now valued as a window into the daily life of New France. Moreover, such letters often performed major interventions, affecting careers, military operations, and, in the case of Madeleine Jarret de Verchères, later construction of the national historical narrative. De Verchères recounted the story of her heroic defence of the family fort in 1692 in two influential letters that petitioned for financial assistance. Published at the end of the nineteenth century, they contributed to her veneration from the 1880s to the

1920s as the Canadian Joan of Arc.[62] In the 1830s, according to Julie Roy, the growing popularity of albums, in which well-born young francophone women collected poems, music, drawings, and the like, created "une forme qui se rapproche étonnamment du phénomène de la publication."[63]

Manuscript culture flourished in late eighteenth-century Nova Scotia, where Deborah How Cottnam's poetry reached its intended audience of friends and students in copies carefully written out by hand.[64] In a similar fashion, many early settlers and visitors recorded their experiences for family and friends in order to circulate their words in manuscript. Written "neither as strictly personal, private narrative, nor an openly public one," these writings belong to what historian Barbara Williams describes as the "liminal domain of semi-private/semi-public expression."[65] Such shared documentation was a long-standing practice of female diarists and correspondents, as exemplified by Elizabeth Simcoe. During her five years' residence in Upper Canada, where her husband served as lieutenant governor from 1791 to 1796, Simcoe maintained a diary (eventually published in different editions in 1911 and 1965), sections of which she frequently sent to her children and friends back in England. Simcoe's words, like those of many other administrators' wives temporarily domiciled in Canada, were often regarded as auxiliary to the official record and were therefore composed in full awareness of their authors' public status. Illumination of the role of audience is nicely provided by the diaries of Lady Durham and Jane Ellice, which present complementary accounts of the same 1838 journey. Ellice, the lively young wife of Lord Durham's private secretary, recorded her Canadian experience at the behest of her father-in-law, who gave her the blank book with the inscription: "to be kept faithfully and fully on her American expedition by Janie for her affectionate Edward Ellice."[66] Lady Durham's restrained style befitted her official role as Lord Durham's consort, whereas Ellice's unbuttoned narrative recounts an entirely personal response to the individuals, events, and insects encountered during her travels. It is Jane who tells us about "luncheon at the horrid little *Mr. Moleson's*, who would hold Ly. Durham *tight* under his arm all the time we were walking thro' his garden, to her great annoyance."[67] That Lady Durham perceived her diary as potentially a public document becomes particularly evident in the edition prepared by Patricia Godsell, which intersperses diary entries with Durham's letters home to her mother. Only when writing in the more private mode of the personal letter did she openly voice her opinions and discomforts, such as having to endure "the dreadful dinners & the dreadful ladies"[68] of Quebec City in the overpowering heat of a Canadian June.

Frances Monck, who was married to the brother of Lord Charles Stanley Monck, Governor General of British North America from 1861 to 1867, likewise kept a journal of her year-long visit in 1864–65. After her return to England, she maintained the practice of restricted circulation when she had just ten copies printed for private distribution as *My Canadian Leaves* (1873). Fuller publication occurred in 1891, but the edition issued by Richard Bentley was trimmed of some twelve thousand words of "candid comment on Canadian people and affairs." However, Lady Monck not only retained her own copy of the first edition but also added further annotations, and it was this unexpurgated version that was reproduced in a facsimile edition by the Canadian Library Service in 1963. In a similar fashion, Lady Hariot Dufferin, whose husband served as Governor General from 1872 to 1878, also waited until her Canadian experience was long past to publish the book she titled *My Canadian Journal* (1891), which derived from weekly letters she had sent to her mother. Ever the professional wife, in editing her private words for public consumption she maintained a diplomatic posture: "The Governor-General and his wife belong to no party; and we met with such universal kindness from all persons with whom we came in contact in the Dominion, that I, at least, never wanted to remember that people differed from each other in their political views, and was only too glad to leave politics to those whom they necessarily concerned."[69]

Women in private life, on the other hand, wrote only for their families, often composing what critic Kathryn Carter describes as "journal letters" in her study of those sent back to Britain by Mary Gapper O'Brien.[70] Typical of the genre are the journals of newlywed Lucy Peel, sent to her family in England during her three and half years of residence in the Eastern Townships (1833–36),[71] and the better-known writings of Anne Langton, an unmarried woman who joined her extended family in the Peterborough area in 1837. Langton's copious letters were saved by relatives, as were the journals that were meant to be read by those who remained in England. "Did you ever write a journal with the intention of sending it to any one? I think it would be difficult to do it with simplicity," she recorded in 1838. This journal was composed with great self-consciousness regarding the documentation of daily life, as when she reflected that "[o]ne is tempted to act sometimes with the page in view that has to be written, and a day's proceedings would often be diverted from their ordinary course by the recollection that they were to be recorded." Langton's surviving journals, like those of L.M. Montgomery, were secondary documents, shaped from the elements first recorded in a

FIGURE 1.3
Anne Langton, self-portrait,
1840 (Archives of Ontario,
F 1077-71-0-17, image
number 10008574)

"sort of Diary" that was essentially a household log documenting the
weather, visitors, and daily toil.[72]

Private writers such as these women become known as published
authors after their correspondence and journals appear in print.
Although often perceived as a doorway into the public sphere, the
medium of print could be carefully contained with small print runs and
restricted distribution. Langton's entry into the public realm occurred in
generational stages, beginning with *The Story of Our Family*, prepared from
letters and journals at the request of her young "Nephews and Nieces"
and printed "for private circulation" in Manchester in 1881. This book
was followed by *Langton Records: Journals and Letters from Canada,
1837–1846* (Edinburgh, 1904), edited by her niece, Ellen Josephine
Philips, a fulsome volume again designated "for private circulation only."
The general public was not invited to share Langton's story until her last
surviving nephew, Hugh Hornby Langton, severely truncated the preceding volume for the book he issued as *A Gentlewoman in Upper Canada: The
Journals of Anne Langton* (Toronto 1950, 1967). This text presents a more
optimistic version of Langton's story than the one she chose to tell in her
first narrative. Although Anne published *The Story of Our Family* with

"great diffidence,"[73] her journals record her growing enjoyment in documenting the details of daily life. On 1 January 1839, she wrote:

> I am presuming that my October journal was interesting to you before I receive any assurance to that effect, and purpose giving you a January one, not, however, I must confess, solely with a view to the pleasure of my brother and sister, but also of my own, for I had great enjoyment in a little daily converse with you. I find there are many little things one can mention the very day they occur without fearing that they will appear trifling, which after the lapse of a week one would not think of recording, and just these trifles bring us more before you than more important, but more occasional events.[74]

Anne Langton, like several other women whose historical significance was recognized late in their lives (including Lydia Campbell, who appears in Chapter 10), participated in her own entrance into print. The same can probably also be said of the illiterate escaped slaves whose stories were recorded by Benjamin Drew in 1856. Seventeen of the 117 contributors to his volume of fugitive slaves' personal narratives were women, ranging from the well-known Harriet Tubman, who declared "I grew up like a neglected weed,—ignorant of liberty, having no experience of it" to the unidentified "Mrs. ── ," described as "a very intelligent and respectable" resident of St. Catharines who preferred to remain anonymous.[75]

Other women joined Canada's print culture only after death. Irish-born Frances Stewart, who settled in Douro Township in 1822 and became a close friend of the Moodies and especially of the Traills following their arrival in the mid-1830s, entered the public arena when her letters were issued posthumously as *Our Forest Home: Being Extracts from the Correspondence of the Late Frances Stewart* (1889; enlarged ed. 1902). Prepared by her daughter, Ellen Dunlop, this volume offers a dialogic narrative, with Ellen's commentary inserted between selections from her mother's many remarkable letters. As well, Ellen's recollections sometimes replace lost correspondence about important family events. Intimate with the literary Edgeworth family in Ireland and many writers in Canada, the intensely private Stewart declined to write her autobiography and worried about her letters being "sent round" to readers for whom they were not intended.[76]

Stewart is one of a handful of women categorized in the *Dictionary of Canadian Biography* as a memoirist or diarist, whose journals or other personal manuscripts appeared in print when their historical value was recognized long after their death. Posthumous publication turns such writers into authors and their manuscript remains into durable texts. It also transforms their readers from a controlled audience to the general public. In many cases, women's manuscript writing was intended for fairly wide consumption, such as settlers' letters that were shared with an extended family. As well, wives of public figures such as colonial administrators or officials of the Hudson's Bay Company—notably Frances Simpson and Isobel Finlayson—wrote journal-letters that functioned as semi-official documents and from the start were seen as informal contributions to the public record.[77] Nonetheless much was also written for only a few special eyes. For example, Kathleen Venema describes how Letitia Hargrave discovered "early in her career that private letters made public can be dangerous things," and quickly learned the self-censorship required to secure her family's future with the Hudson's Bay Company.[78] Yet the very act of preservation renders personal documents accessible to others, who may regard posthumous publication as an obligation or an honour rather than a betrayal. The delicacy of this distinction between private and public is particularly noticeable in relation to prolific authors like Susanna Moodie and Catharine Parr Traill, who carefully chose which components of their lives were to be written up for public consumption, and which were to remain private. Subsequent publication of their personal letters—even many decades after the deaths of all involved—sometimes raises discomfort. For example, Susanna Moodie would not be pleased to learn of the eventual publication of her letters to her husband, which, among other private concerns, reveal her sexuality, as when she wrote to him in 1839: "these long separations are most painful to me. A state of widowhood does not suit my ardent affections."[79] Several generations later, L.M. Montgomery faced a similar dilemma with regard to her private account of her infatuation with Herman Leard when she was in her mid-twenties. Later preparing her journals for her sons and posterity in general, she retained her florid depiction of her youthful throbbing passions, choosing to preserve a self-representation quite different from the proper mother and minister's wife that her family and acquaintances knew in daily life.

In Quebec, the leaching of private writing into the public realm is demonstrated by popular pioneer journalist Henriette Dessaulles ("Fadette"), who became one of the most visible francophone women journalists in the first decades of the twentieth century. From 1914 to 1922, she reprinted her newspaper columns in five separate volumes, followed by several children's books in the 1930s. In her younger years, from the age of fourteen until her marriage at twenty-one (1874–81), she maintained a private journal that she would not even show to her best friend: "Je refuse en disant: 'Oh! moi j'écris pour moi toute seule!' Je ne lui explique pas que c'est mon âme qui tient la plume et qu'il m'est impossible de lui laisser lire mon âme."[80] But fame can make a difference, and it now appears that after her husband's death in 1897, Fadette (like Montgomery) edited her youthful journals, discarding several notebooks and altering the remainder so that her courtship by her future husband provides a unifying narrative thread. In 1908, a modified extract appeared in her column in *Le Journal de Françoise*.[81] Whether or not she contemplated further publication, no other portions appeared in print before her death in 1946. Nonetheless, a number of critics have noted the unusually novelistic tenor of the journal that her granddaughter approved for publication in 1971, followed by numerous subsequent editions in French and translation into English in 1986.

Sometimes it is difficult to discern whether or not a private diary was ultimately intended for public consumption. For example, Eliza Ann Chipman, wife of a Nova Scotia Baptist minister, kept a secret spiritual diary for some thirty years, from 1823 to 1853. She revealed its existence to her husband only a few days before her death, with a request that it not be "committed to the flames, for she had enjoyed much comfort in reading christian Diaries, and therefore, if there could be a selection of gleanings from her own, which might be useful to others, she was willing that her friends and the public should have the benefit."[82] Similar is the case of Lydia Clark Symmes of Aylmer, Quebec, whose journals of 1857–59, recounting the last years of her life, remained in manuscript until they were printed for private circulation by her son in 1902. *My Mother's Journal* proved sufficiently popular to merit a second edition "on the understanding that all profits from its publication, if any, shall be used in the extension of the cause of Christian Endeavour."[83] Posthumous publication was not reserved for authors of diaries and letters; memorial volumes of poetry receive attention in Chapter 4.

Languages and Ethnicities

English and French were not the only tongues in which Canadian women wrote and published before 1918. As noted in the next chapter and further elaborated in Chapter 10, Indigenous women were involved in the creation of texts in Mohawk, Cree, Ojibwe, and other Aboriginal languages, whether translations of religious works or their own compositions. The linguistic landscape was further shaped by immigrants who wrote letters, kept diaries, and sang songs in their home languages. They also produced newspapers in an array of tongues, which by 1918 included German, Gaelic, Icelandic, Yiddish, Swedish, Finnish, Danish, Ukrainian, Chinese, Japanese, Arabic, and Bulgarian.[84] While it is difficult to determine the extent of women's involvement in these transplanted print cultures, it is likely that unnamed wives, sisters, and daughters followed the pattern of English and French women by assisting in print shops and with the writing of anonymous material.

Long before a number of Canadian Jewish women became known as literary authors in both Yiddish and English following the First World War, several appeared in print in connection with the publication of cookbooks. In 1865, Constance Hart became the first Jewish woman to produce a book in Canada with *Household Receipts or Domestic Cookery*.[85] Half a century later, the Ottawa Ladies Hebrew Benevolent Society sponsored *The Economical Cookbook* (1915), the first collection of Jewish recipes published in Canada.[86] While cookbooks were important focal points in immigrant culture, most of those published in Canada were written in English and French.[87]

Immigration to the West accounts for a visible cluster of allophone women writers. Torfhildur Þorsteinsdóttir (1845–1918) lived in what is now Manitoba on an irregular basis for nine years, thereby earning a berth in the *Dictionary of Canadian Biography*. She wrote only in Icelandic and published in Reykjavik, where she is now recognized as Iceland's first woman novelist and "the first Icelander to make a living as an author."[88] More directly engaged with Canada was Margret Benedictsson (1866–1956). While residing in Selkirk, Manitoba, she founded a feminist newspaper, *Freyja* (1898–1910), for which she wrote much of the literary and other content, and she campaigned actively within Manitoba's Icelandic community for women's suffrage before she moved to the US in 1912. Mrs. Arvie Queeber qualified to join the Canadian Women's Press Club for the column in Swedish that she contributed to her husband's paper, the *Wetaskiwin Alberta Tribunen*.[89] In Winnipeg, Florence Randal Livesay took the unusual step of applying her literary talent to the lyrics sung by her Ukrainian housemaids to produce *Songs of Ukraina, with Ruthenian Poems* (1916), which also includes translations of work by several major male poets. This volume of folk lyrics and wistful reflections can be seen as a tribute to an immigrant culture that was not widely appreciated by the Anglo-Canadian mainstream. As well, it was an example of the modernist engagement with primitivism, evidenced by the previous publication of some of its contents in such literary magazines as *Poet Lore* (Boston), *Poetry* (Chicago), and the *University Magazine* (Montreal).[90]

Before 1918, Canadian women were involved in many facets of textual culture: they worked in the material realm as printers, compositors, and bookbinders; they shaped the cultural realm as facilitators, gatekeepers, and translators; and they recorded the social realm as documenters of private and public life. Within this framework, it was through their literary activities that the significance of women's voices and experiences was most consistently recognized, as the scattered colonies of the early nineteenth century consolidated into a self-confident national culture during the decades following Confederation.

TWO

Beginnings to the 1850s

IN CANADIAN HISTORY, THE YEAR of Confederation—1867—is frequently identified as a significant turning point. However, when we examine the presence of women in Canada's English-language print culture, it becomes evident that the early 1850s represent a distinct threshold. The reasons are many. Substantial growth in population during the previous three decades contributed to improvements in education, the rise of literacy, the spread of newspapers, and increasing numbers of local imprints.[1] The establishment of literary societies, libraries, and mechanics' institutes also helped to expand the audience for local literature. As well, a number of experienced writers immigrated to the colonies that would become Canada and attempted to transplant the literary milieu of Edinburgh, London, or Boston to their new homes, where most of their work appeared in newspapers and cultural periodicals. Particularly significant was the longevity of the *Literary Garland* (Montreal, 1838–51), which welcomed women's writing and created a lasting textual literary community for dispersed authors who could never hope to meet in person. It was here, for example, that Susanna Moodie read the early work of Rosanna Mullins (later Leprohon) and discerned that her "power and vigor" marked her as "[o]ne of the gifted" who "may become the pride and ornament of a great and rising country."[2] Other periodicals called attention to the prominence of women's literary activities in the US. In 1843, when the *Amaranth* of Saint John, New Brunswick, reprinted a long article on "Literary Ladies in America," it implicitly established a goal for the colonies that had remained loyal to Britain.[3]

Women and Print in the Canadian Colonies

The participation of women in the print history of the Canadian colonies can be seen as a pyramid. Its base is composed of thousands of anonymous women whose work as custodians of culture and transmitters of literacy occurred in family kitchens, schoolrooms, and religious organizations, in busy municipal centres and on the remoter frontiers of settlement in British and French North America. Seldom named as individuals, few ordinary women are to be found in early records of the creation, content, and consumption of Canadian print culture, but some exceptions exist. Women of Lower Canada who were involved in legal claims saw their names printed in statements of case; similarly identifiable are those who placed advertisements in newspapers, joined benevolent associations that issued printed reports, or became known in death as subjects of newspaper obituaries, broadside death notices, or the rare printed elegy. Yet even when a woman's social standing merited a separately published funeral sermon, the historical record usually reveals more information about the clergyman who authored the text than about the woman whose demise occasioned it. For example, the printed funeral sermons for Mrs. Abigail Belcher and Mrs. Jane Chipman, who died in Nova Scotia in 1771 and 1775, are described in Marie Tremaine's bibliography of early Canadian imprints with accompanying notes that offer capsule biographies of the officiating clerics but no information about the deceased women.[4]

In Lower Canada, where the literacy rate for women remained below that for men,[5] girls who were able to obtain an education attended the convent schools run by the major teaching orders of the Ursulines in Québec and Trois-Rivières and the Congrégation de Notre Dame in Montreal. Here they received one or two years of intense instruction, sometimes using texts specifically prepared for Canadian use.[6]

The Catholic Church emphasized mothers' duty to instruct their children, a responsibility that required reading aloud to them. This role received iconographic emphasis in the recurring image of Sainte Anne, mother of Mary, who was not only particularly popular in Quebec, but was "most often seen in her role as the Educatrix of the Virgin with the emphasis placed on reading."[7] In urban English-speaking areas, educated women established reading schools for children. One of the first in the northern British colonies was Elizabeth Render, whose advertisement appeared in the second issue of the Halifax *Gazette* (30 March 1752). From 1790 through 1840, as populations increased, the same pattern of women engaged in domestic or private teaching soon prevailed in Upper

Canada until it was replaced by the establishment of the province's public school system.[8] The role of women as teachers led to their early involvement in writing for children, a topic taken up in Chapter 4.

In the minds of most inhabitants of British North America, education was inseparable from religion; in women's daily lives, whatever their creed, religion was a principal locus of print culture, and religious works comprised much of their reading. The funeral sermon delivered in Halifax in 1778 on the death of Mrs. Margaret Green noted that "Books of meer Amusement (Plays, Romances, Novels &c.) she seldom looked into, esteeming Time too precious to be trifled away in Vanity."[9] In all the Canadian colonies, from the late 1810s onward, Protestant women joined Bible societies, which proliferated in small and large communities, where their promotion of individual access to the scriptures included local distribution of texts and fundraising for larger missionary efforts abroad. In several instances, religion was a primary motive for an author's involvement with Canada at all. American evangelist Nancy Towle wrote about the execution of a criminal in Montreal in 1833,[10] and during the winter of 1833–34, Quaker minister Hannah Backhouse included Upper Canada in her extended trip from Britain to North America to lend support to struggling congregations, an experience later recorded in *Extracts from the Journals and Letters of Hannah Chapman Backhouse* (1859).

Hence it is not surprising that women frequently cited the religious and moral significance of their writing as justification for its publication. Whatever the faith of the author and the genre of her text, it is virtually impossible to draw clear distinctions between religious and secular writing in most early Canadian poetry, biography, fiction, drama, or life-writing. For example, Mary Anne Sadlier's voluminous output in fiction, drama, translations, and catechisms consistently expressed her strong Catholic faith. As well, the preparation of religious works in First Nations languages brought underacknowledged Native and Métis women into the sphere of print culture. In the 1820s, at Oka (Kanesatake), Charlotte de Rocheblave taught Algonquian dialects to Catholic missionary authors;[11] in Upper Canada, Christiana Brant, eldest daughter of Chief Joseph Brant (Thayendanegea), assisted her husband, Henry Aaron Hill (Kenwendeshon), with his Mohawk translations of the Bible published during the 1830s.[12] On the Prairies, Angélique and Marguerite Nolin, Métis sisters based in St. Boniface, opened the first school for girls in the West in 1829 and in the following decade enabled Father Georges-Antoine Bellecourt to prepare texts in Ojibwe.[13] This pattern continued into the 1850s with Sophia Thomas Mason's involvement in translating the Bible into

Cree syllabics, her work unacknowledged on the title pages of the resulting volumes although her missionary husband gave her personal credit.[14]

Recognition of women as consumers of imaginative literature was confirmed in 1789 by a newspaper advertisement addressed to Quebec's "Ladies and Lovers of Elegant Poetry," which solicited subscriptions for a proposed "Collection of original poems, written in elegant stile by various ingenious Ladies and Gentleman, who favoured a friend of the Printer with copies."[15] This book's failure to appear illustrates the fragility of literary culture in the colonies, although occasional Canadian editions of popular American and European novels (whose readership the world over was largely female) attested to the faith of a few printer-publishers in a growing domestic market. One of the over two hundred editions of the first bestselling American novel, Susanna Rowson's *Charlotte Temple* (1791), was issued by J. Wilson in Hallowell, Upper Canada in 1832.[16] However, most surviving early Canadian print materials aimed at women were more pragmatic in nature, such as commercial notices for "The British lady's diary and pocket almanack" and the services of "Mrs. Ward's scouring business."[17] Cookbooks, a genre usually associated with women, were first produced in Canada in local editions of work previously published elsewhere: Menon's *La cuisinière bourgeoise*, originally published in Paris in 1746, was issued in Quebec in 1825, and *The Cook Not Mad; or, Rational Cookery*, first issued in New York State in 1830, was reprinted in Kingston in 1831. Canada's first locally authored cookbooks appeared in 1840, both with titles naming women as their primary audience: the anonymous *La cuisinière canadienne* in Montreal, and in Toronto, *The Frugal Housewife's Manual*, credited to "A.B., of Grimsby."[18]

Midway up the print culture pyramid are the women who participated in the business and commerce of books and print as members of their family enterprise, as described in the preceding chapter. At the apex reside the women who became publicly visible as authors, especially those who developed a continuing presence as literary figures. Regardless of gender, before the 1850s authorship brought little reward. In the words of Mary Lu MacDonald, "All writers in the Canadas in the first half of the nineteenth century were amateurs who made their living in some other activity";[19] the same was true for residents of the Maritime colonies, with the exception of Thomas Chandler Haliburton, whose Sam Slick books garnered handsome sums from his British publisher. Did this state of compulsory amateurism make it easier or more difficult for women to get published? On the one hand, there was little competition for profit; on the other, if writers had to pay to produce their work, women usually owned less economic capital. Hence authorship for Canadian women was restricted to the few possessing sufficient time, determination, and funding to get their words into print, and was accomplished more easily in English than in French. The vast majority of those who proved successful were White middle-class immigrants from the British Isles or the United States, or their recent descendants.

Not surprisingly, patterns of authorship for Canadian women reflect the different cultural histories of the two country's dominant language groups. Women's writing about the colonies that would become Canada was printed in French a good century before anything appeared in English, and was closely affiliated with the Catholic Church. Marie Guyart, better known as Mère Marie de l'Incarnation (1599–1672), arrived in New France in 1639, where she established the Ursuline order. She remained in Quebec for the rest of her life, writing copious spiritual texts and letters that were later published in Paris. Following her lead, several nuns documented the early history of their congregations. Marie Morin, the first writer born in New France, recorded the annals of the Hôtel Dieu of Montreal in 1697, while Marie-Andrée Regnard Duplessis and Jeanne-Françoise Juchereau de la Ferté collaborated on *Les annales de l'Hôtel-Dieu de Québec, 1636–1716* (1751). This pattern of documentation continued in the nineteenth century when Catherine Burke and Adèle Cimon anonymously co-authored the four-volume history of the Ursulines in Quebec (1863–66). The case of eighteenth-century Parisian dramatist Madame de Gomez shows how the writing of a secular French author could be incorporated into a religious paradigm when republished in Quebec. Her *Histoire de Jean de Calais, roi de Portugal* appeared anonymously in Quebec City in 1810, with illustrations and added editorial material indicating that the purpose of this edition was to instruct young French-Canadian readers in wisdom and virtue.[20] Women in both cultures wrote copious letters and personal memoirs that sometimes circulated extensively in private family and social circles. As noted in the previous chapter, many such manuscripts did not appear in print until decades or even centuries after their original composition, once they acquired the status of historical documents. Early examples include the 1698 memoirs of Marguerite Bourgeoys, the eighteenth-century letters of Élisabeth Bégon of New France and Rebecca Byles of Nova Scotia, and, from the 1830s, the diaries of Lady Durham, Jane Ellice, Frances Simpson, and Mary O'Brien.

A number of English-speaking women wrote from relatively brief experience of the various colonies that would become Canada. Some were literary novices, while others were authors who had established

careers in Britain before arriving as visitors or immigrants and were therefore quick to exploit the fresh material offered by the New World. Frances
Brooke was already well known in London when she penned the first
novel set in Canada, her four-volume *History of Emily Montague* (1769),
after several years' sojourn in British North America during her husband's tenure as chaplain to the British garrison in Quebec. Likewise,
intellectual Anna Jameson's visit to Upper Canada during her husband's
posting resulted in her travel account, *Winter Studies and Summer Rambles*
(London, 1838). One young woman was inspired into authorship by her
father's administrative position in British North America; Henrietta
Prescott's first book, the lively *Poems: Written in Newfoundland* (London,
1839), appeared during her father's term as governor of the colony. Harrowing Atlantic voyages and shipwrecks incited two other women to publish narratives that now belong to Canada's print heritage: *Narrative of the
Shipwreck and Sufferings of Miss Ann Saunders* (Providence, 1827), who survived the disaster in which her fiancé died only by resorting to cannibal-
ism, and Lady Louisa Aylmer's *Narrative of the Passage of the* Pique *across the
Atlantic* (London, 1837). So appealing was Canadian material that many
minor English writers used second-hand sources without ever crossing the
Atlantic, among them British religious author Henrietta Maria Bowdler,
who cites Brooke's *History of Emily Montague* as the source of her Canadian
material in her moral novel, *Pen Tamar* (1830), when she sends her heroine to New France for two chapters. Catharine Parr Traill likewise drew on
the experience of others for her children's tale, *The Young Emigrants*
(1826), whose superficial description of settler life contrasts tellingly with
the books and letters she wrote after her own emigration in 1833.

During the pre-Confederation era, some of the colonies' literary journals were very hospitable to women writers and, like an increasing proportion of women's magazines in the United States,[21] a number had
female editors. These include the *Montreal Museum* (1832–34), edited by
Mary Graddon Goselin, with Miss Elizabeth Tracey as co-editor for the
first two numbers;[22] the *Literary Garland* (Montreal, 1839–51), which was
edited for its last two years by Eliza Lanesford Cushing; Mrs. Leonard's
the *Child's Bible Expositor*, published in Toronto, 1840–42; the *Olive Branch*
(Halifax), a temperance paper edited by Sarah Herbert in 1844–45; the
Mayflower, or Ladies' Acadian Newspaper (Halifax, 1851–52), edited by Mary
Eliza Herbert; and the *Provincial, or Halifax Monthly Magazine* (1852–53),
edited by Mary Jane Katzmann. Many writers of both sexes published only
in such periodicals and newspapers; typical female examples include
Emily Coxon, who in 1833–34 had twenty-six poems in the *Canadian*

Courant and one in the Montreal *Gazette*, Mary Graddon Gosselin, whose verses appeared in the *Montreal Museum* during her editorship; and Elizabeth Mary Maclachlan ("E.M.M."), who consistently contributed poetry and fiction to the *Literary Garland* from its first number in 1838 until her death in 1845.[23] Also typical is the pattern of Emma Donoghue Grant (Mrs. John P.) whose poems in the *Literary Garland* and other periodicals of the 1840s were collected many years later in a volume appropriately titled *Stray Leaves* (1865). In her exhaustive analysis of literary writers in both languages whose work appeared in books and serials in Upper and Lower Canada from 1817 to 1850, Mary Lu MacDonald identified 108 authors of whom eighteen were female and just one, Odile Cherrier, was a francophone woman writer.[24]

In Canada's early newspapers, the widespread practice of publishing anonymously or under pseudonyms or initials, and of casually reprinting unattributed items from other sources, makes it difficult to identify the versifiers—male or female—whose work appeared in their "Poet's Corner" columns. It is equally difficult to pin down many authors of prose, including the creator of the delightfully ironic "Patty Pry" letters, set in Halifax, that appeared in the *Novascotian* through the summer of 1826.[25] Nor is it always possible to determine whether the rare full name of a woman was indeed genuine and, if it was, whether she had ever set foot in British North America. While no guarantee of female authorship accompanied a feminine pseudonym, men are presumed not to have employed the internationally ubiquitous signature of "A Lady," some of whose Canadian users have since been identified as Sarah French, Mrs. Fales, and Hannah Pickard. However, the anonymous lady who authored the children's book, *A Peep at the Esquimaux* (1825), still remains masked.[26]

Fortunately, authors of monographs tend to leave deeper tracks. Although a number of items discussed in this book were originally issued anonymously or pseudonymously, particularly before Confederation, creators of only a few woman-authored texts in English remain unknown. Among them are Nobody Knows Who, several of whose poems are tantalizingly dated Halifax, 1852,[27] and A.B. of Grimsby, the "Canadian lady" credited with producing "the first English-language cookbook compiled in Canada."[28] In the periodical press, the practice of publishing under pseudonyms persisted much longer and picked up toward the end of the nineteenth century as women who established their presence as journalists often adopted a transparent alias, a topic pursued in Chapter 6. Women's pen names tended to be more opaque in French Canada, where many feminine signatures remain unidentified. For example, it took nearly a century to pin down Marichette, who in 1895–98 published a series of provocative letters written in Franco-Acadien dialect in the weekly *Evangeline*, as teacher Emilie C. LeBlanc.[29]

Because books were expensive to produce, no publisher could afford to take a risk on literary works. Authors either paid the cost themselves or raised the required funds by subscription, a practice that was common in Europe for books with a limited market and endured in Canada until the end of the nineteenth century. Two important books of 1824 were published this way: the first novel by a native-born Canadian, Julia Beckwith Hart's *St. Ursula's Convent; or, the Nun of Canada* (Kingston), and one of the first woman-authored books of poetry to appear in Canada, Margaret Blennerhassett's *The Widow of the Rock and Other Poems* (Montreal). In a similar fashion, the publisher of Catharine Parr Traill's very successful second-to-last book, *Pearls and Pebbles; or Notes of an Old Naturalist* (1894) required her to collect two hundred subscriptions before going into production.[30]

Several women in distress took advantage of the elevated cultural status of both books and poetry to employ their literary talent to create publications that served as fundraisers. In 1833, "Widow Fleck" issued a slim pamphlet of verse in Montreal, begging her purchasers to support a widowed mother left destitute by her husband's death from cholera. Seven years later, Ethelind Sawtell published *The Mourner's Tribute*, a more robust volume with a similar appeal. She swiftly won the advocacy of the *Literary Garland*, which commended the author, "one whom misfortune only has tempted to cultivate the field of literature," for her efforts to maintain "an honourable independence."[31] The sheer volume of this book (271 pages, compared to Fleck's twelve) suggests that widowhood may have granted Sawtell the opportunity to get previously written material into print.[32] Mary Anne Madden Sadlier's lengthy literary career began with a similar plea to the public when, as a young unmarried woman recently arrived in Montreal, she published her first book by subscription. Her preface apologizes that "necessity rather than choice brings me before the public," an act that would never have occurred "had it been my fate to belong to that fortunate class which is happily exempt from the necessity of working."[33]

Three Sites of Literary Activity

Before 1855, literate women were involved with textual communication in manuscript and print wherever they lived or travelled in British North America. Examples span the terrain, from the woman in eighteenth-century Newfoundland, known only as D.O., who requested that religious books be sent from London,[34] to the journals and letters of fur-trade wives like Frances Simpson, who documented her exhausting 1830 canoe journey in Rupert's Land, to Mary Ann Shadd, who became the colonies' first Black woman editor when she founded the *Provincial Freeman* in Windsor in 1853. However, there were few locales where women achieved a sufficient critical mass to create an identifiable regional literary culture. Following the Conquest of New France and the American Revolution, different patterns of immigration to separate British North American colonies led to three significant sites, each associated with a pair of sisters: the Herbert sisters in Halifax, the Foster sisters in Montreal, and the Strickland sisters in eastern Ontario. These nodes were created by the immigration of New England Loyalists to Nova Scotia and New Brunswick in the late eighteenth century, the development of Montreal as a centre of English-language culture and publishing during the first half of the nineteenth century, and the settlement of the Strickland family and other literary-minded British immigrants in eastern Ontario in the 1830s and 1840s in a triangle created by Peterborough County, Cobourg, and Belleville. While the cultural life of Upper and Lower Canada involved considerable interaction between the two colonies, which shared a major waterway and, after 1841, a common legislature, it scarcely touched residents of the Maritime regions, whose primary social and political links were to old Britain and New England. In all three regions, women's published writing tended toward genteel poetry and prose aiming to refine the colonies' rough edges, tempered by the social conscience of writers with a strong commitment to Christian service, and by the occasional realism of those who wrote about their own experiences of settlement.

Maritimes

While the educated Loyalists who relocated to Nova Scotia and New Brunswick brought with them the literate culture they had enjoyed in New England, subsequent publication of some Maritimers' books in Boston emblematized the ongoing ties between the two regions, despite the fractures caused by the American Revolution. A number of male Loyalist writers developed a distinct public voice in satiric and lyric poems that circulated in manuscript and sometimes appeared in newspapers, establishing a tradition subsequently confirmed in the prose satire of Thomas McCulloch's *Stepsure Letters* of the 1820s and Thomas Chandler Haliburton's series of Sam Slick books, which began in the 1830s. The literary culture of Loyalist women has been vividly documented in Gwendolyn Davies' accounts of the correspondence of Rebecca and Eliza Byles, young sisters who moved to Halifax and wrote regularly to their aunts in Boston for more than fifty years, and in her reconstruction of the life of their teacher, Deborah How Cottnam ("Portia," 1728–1806), "probably Canada's first anglophone woman writer."[35] Born and raised in Canso, Nova Scotia, Cottnam put her unusually rigorous education to good use when she needed to support her daughter and herself. She opened a series of schools, beginning in Salem, Massachusetts, before moving in 1777 to Halifax, where her ailing husband died in 1780, and then to Saint John, New Brunswick, in 1786. Her surviving poems place her in the eighteenth-century tradition of occasional literature, with verses that mark important events. Some are contemplative reflections presenting her own thoughts; others follow the mode of courtesy writing addressed to specific individuals.[36] Circulating her poetry in manuscript rather than in print, Cottnam created a literary legacy for her students who copied her verses in their exercise books and for her descendants, culminating in her great-granddaughter, Grizelda Tonge, who was viewed as one of Nova Scotia's most promising poets when she suddenly died in 1825 at the age of twenty-two.[37] Another Maritime teacher who was also a writer, Mrs. S.K.P.[38] Fales, had been a student of Susanna Rowson in New England.[39] She advertised her Halifax school from 1829 to 1833, and in 1834 published *Familiar Letters of Subjects Interesting to the Minds and Hearts of Females*, in Boston, under the pseudonym "A Lady."[40]

Although narratives of settlement experience were a significant genre among the women authors of Upper Canada, only one such volume emanated from the Maritime region. Emily Shaw Beavan published *Sketches and Tales Illustrative of Life in the Backwoods of New Brunswick, Gleaned from Actual Observation and Experience during a Residence of Seven Years in That Interesting Colony* in London in 1845, following her return to Britain. While in New Brunswick, Beavan regularly contributed stories and poems to the *Amaranth* of Saint John, several of which reappeared in her book. A more consistent literary presence, in Gwendolyn Davies' analysis, was forged by female writers who belonged to the Methodist church, which "created an evolving role for women" and in whose prose there runs a "strong sense of social conscience that is inextricably linked to their Methodist backgrounds."[41] Yet Methodism was not sufficiently liberal for Mary Coy Bradley, of Gagetown and Saint John, who recorded her frustration at the Church's restriction of women to teaching when she would have preferred to preach, "going abroad to proclaim salvation to a dying world."[42] Briefer was the presence of Hannah Maynard Pickard

(1812–44), who moved from Boston to Saint John upon her marriage to a Methodist clergyman in 1841 and died in Sackville less than three years later. Her Boston-published stories for children, one of them set in Saint John, invoke the expected values of piety and Christian service.

Of this group, the Halifax-based Herbert sisters had the greatest impact. During her brief life, Sarah Herbert (1824–46) published religious poems and stories in Maritime journals, some of them specifically Methodist, such as the *British North American Wesleyan Methodist Magazine* of Saint John. Her serialized fictions suited the temperance ideology of the magazine in which they appeared, the *Olive Branch* (Halifax), which she herself edited for a year, from 1844 to 1845. Sarah's posthumous reputation is largely indebted to her half-sister, Mary Eliza Herbert (1829–72), with whom she shared a volume of poetry, *The Aeolian Harp* (Halifax, 1857), which "became a popular gift book in the Maritimes and did much to enhance the reputation of the sisters as writers of genteel verse."[43] In 1851, Mary optimistically founded the *Mayflower, or, Ladies' Acadian Newspaper*, a monthly compendium of domestic advice, poetry, reflective sketches, and sentimental fiction. In addition to writing the lead serial story that opened each issue, Herbert included some of her own poems and sketches under different signatures,[44] a common practice of authors or editors who felt it strategic to dilute their presence. Despite general support from the Methodist Church, the *Mayflower* proved less hardy than its botanical namesake, and lasted only nine numbers. Her literary ambitions still intact, Mary Herbert went on to publish three novels at her own expense, but, according to Gwendolyn Davies, her best work, "Lucy Cameron," remains in manuscript in the archives at Dalhousie University.[45]

The ephemerality of the *Mayflower* was soon repeated by the *Provincial, or Halifax Monthly Magazine*, launched by Mary Jane Katzmann in January 1852, which lasted just two years despite being aimed at the wide readership accessible through her genteel Anglican milieu. In 1866 Katzmann was operating the Provincial Bookstore in Halifax, a position she relinquished to her younger sister when she married businessman William Lawson in 1868. As Mary Jane Katzmann Lawson ("M.J.K.L."), she developed a reputation for writing local history and in 1888 she collaborated with Alice Jones to issue the *Church of England Institute Receipt Book*, whose poetic "Introduction" is signed M.J.K.L.[46] The historical record shows no interaction between Lawson and Herbert, even though they lived in the same small city and were nearly the same age. Davies notes that "In looking at Herbert's writing environment, there is no sense of any solidarity among the women publishing at the time except, perhaps, among the

women of Methodist persuasion."[47] Under these circumstances, it should
not be surprising to find even less connection between the pre-Confederation women writers of the Maritimes and those residing in the Canadas.

Montreal

During the first decades of the nineteenth century, Montreal's rapid growth
in population and economic significance established its prominence as a
rival to Quebec City in the literary culture of French Canada, and as the
centre of English-language literary activity for both Lower and Upper Canada.
Despite a flourishing intellectual culture among francophone men, francophone women with public literary ambitions were not numerous and
found few outlets for their writing. In the analysis of Manon Brunet, women
in Quebec were sufficiently educated to produce publishable work but were
socially conditioned to engage with print as readers rather than as writers.[48]
Those who produced creative work retained it for the private realm of salon
culture and epistolary communication. For example, in 1809 Marie-Mar-
guerite La Corne composed an elegant love song that she sent in a letter to
her second husband, Jacques Viger, but she is not known to have submitted
anything for publication, even though Viger was at the time the editor of *Le
canadien.*[49] The climate for female writers was not improved when the author
of several poems published in 1837 under the pseudonym "Marie-Louise"
was unmasked as a man.[50] The second volume of *La vie littéraire au Québec*
lists fifty "agents littéraires" for the period 1806–39 and the third cites 100
"acteurs littéraires" for 1840–69; of these 150 names, just four are women
(two in each volume). Active in the first decades of the nineteenth century,
Louise-Amélie Panet-Berczy circulated her verse only in manuscript and
apologized for being "une espèce de bas-bleu";[51] many of the poems that survive in her notebooks demonstrate her appreciation of the Irish poet, Thomas
Moore.[52] According to critic Julie Roy, Panet declined the publicity of print,
preferring the legitimation of élite salons, letters, and the manuscript albums
of her friends.[53] In the same period, Odile Cherrier, under the wing of her
better-known brother, André-Romauld, issued three poems in 1838 using the
pseudonym Anaïs. Not yet identified is "Améla," who claimed to be a fif-
teen-year-old girl when she published the first of four sentimental poems that
appeared in the *Aurore des Canadas* from October 1839 to October 1840.[54]
The lineup for the middle of the century remains, comprising an author of
one book of family history (Eliza Anne Baby Casgrain) and Rosanna Mullins
Leprohon, whose works, originally published in English, enjoyed greater
longevity when translated into French. Hence it is not surprising that when

Mary Graddon Gosselin attempted to create a bilingual journal, the *Montreal Museum, or Journal of Literature and the Arts* (1832–34), "the first periodical in British North America specifically intended for female readers by a female editor," she found herself editing a magazine that, with the exception of two poems, was entirely in English, with some French writing appearing in translation.[55]

For English-speaking writers, a major source of encouragement was the entrepreneurial spirit of John Lovell, a shrewd and very successful printer/publisher who issued most of the English and many of the French cultural works that appeared in Montreal before Confederation, including the crucial periodical, the *Literary Garland* (1838–51). Edited by Lovell's brother-in-law, John Gibson, the *Garland* was the same size and price as the *Montreal Museum*.[56] While some of its contents were reprinted from British and American sources, the vast majority originated in the Canadas, with a few items arriving from New Brunswick. In a region where many authors were recent immigrants from England, Ireland, Scotland, and the US, the *Literary Garland* became a site of convergence that helped forge a sense of common social, aesthetic, and political values. It not only paid its contributors but also provided names or initials for many; a page count of work by identified authors shows that women produced 55 percent of its poetry and 70 percent of its fiction, much of it in the form of serialized novels by a core group of writers. In addition to providing an important venue and income for Susanna Moodie, the *Garland* nurtured the initial phase of Rosanna Leprohon's remarkable career, which began with two poems published in 1846 when she was just seventeen. Over the next four years these were followed by another thirteen poems, one story, and five serialized novels of manners and morality. All set in an England that she had probably not visited, the latter nonetheless demonstrate Leprohon's growing mastery of social fiction that would blossom in the 1860s with her three novels of French Canada. The magazine also sustained young Mary Anne Madden, who became a contributor upon her emigration from Ireland in 1844. After her arrival in Montreal she published in a number of periodicals, including the *Garland*, first as "M.A.M.," then as "M.A.S." following her marriage to James Sadlier. His publishing business both supported and profited from her spectacular rise as the popular Irish-American Catholic novelist, Mrs. Sadlier, who would go on to publish more than thirty novels, mostly in New York after the family relocated there in 1860.

The *Literary Garland*'s list of contributors also included two daughters of the bestselling American novelist Hannah Foster, whose 1797 novel, *The Coquette*, rivalled Rowson's *Charlotte Temple* in popularity. Harriet

Vaughan Foster Cheney and Eliza Lanesford Foster Cushing had each published a pair of novels in Boston during the 1820s before moving to Montreal, where their husbands established their careers (as merchant and medical doctor, respectively) during the following decade. Their elderly mother joined them in her last years, and died in Cushing's home in 1840. Once in Montreal, the Foster sisters quickly integrated into the local literary community, contributing regularly to the *Garland*, which Cushing edited in 1850–51 after the death of John Gibson, and founding the *Snow Drop* (1847–53), Canada's first significant juvenile periodical. From Montreal, Cheney issued two additional children's books that were published in Boston in the 1840s. Cushing's *Esther, a Sacred Drama; with Judith, a Poem* (Boston, 1840) enjoys the distinction of being the only dramatic work published by a Canadian woman during the entire pre-Confederation period.

Eastern Ontario

While the development of women's literary culture in the increasingly cosmopolitan environment of Montreal may have been predictable, more surprising was the successful transplantation of literary activity to eastern Ontario with the arrival of the Strickland sisters and like-minded immigrants from England and Ireland. After the death of their father in 1818, Susanna and Catharine Strickland followed their eldest sister, Agnes, into London's genteel literary circles where, during the 1820s, they eked out a living by writing children's books and contributing poetry and prose to literary periodicals and annuals. In the early 1830s, after rather late marriages to fellow half-pay army officers, Thomas Traill and John Wedderburn Dunbar Moodie, the sisters immigrated to Douro Township in Peterborough County. On the shores of Lake Katchewanooka, the Moodies and Traills took up adjoining grants of uncleared land beside the lot already occupied by Samuel Strickland, their younger brother who had been sent out in 1825 to learn farming. Some of Susanna's poems preceded her arrival, appearing in the Cobourg *Star* in September and October of 1831, well before the Moodies crossed the Atlantic the following summer.[57] During the 1830s, the sisters continued to write in order to supplement their families' declining fortunes as the two couples proved more successful at producing children than at generating income from their agricultural ventures (Susanna bore seven babies, of whom five survived, as did seven of Catharine's nine). Before she became a major contributor to the *Literary Garland*, Susanna developed a prominent profile in the colonies' newspapers and magazines, including two poems that

FIGURE 2.1
Susanna Strickland Moodie,
c. 1860 (Library and Archives
Canada, C-007043)

found their way to the New Brunswick *Amaranth* in 1841. Shortly after her arrival, Catharine issued the first of her many pioneer guidebooks: *The Backwoods of Canada: Being Letters from the Wife of an Emigrant officer, Illustrative of the Domestic Economy of British America,* published in London in 1836 by the Society for the Diffusion of Useful Knowledge. During the 1840s, after moving to Belleville, Susanna published the sketches of pioneer life that proved the genesis of her most famous book, *Roughing It in the Bush* (1851). As well, Agnes Strickland occasionally helped to facilitate the publication of her emigrant sisters' writings in English periodicals.

The Stricklands' milieu included other middle-class settlers who shared their values and friendship. Particularly important were Frances and Thomas Stewart, who had emigrated from Ireland in 1822. Not a published author herself, Frances retained significant connections with the Edgeworth family, who sent Maria Edgeworth's new novels in annual boxes of books that were widely shared. Maria Edgeworth in Ireland and Agnes Strickland in London joined the roster of exemplary female authors, initiated by Susanna Rowson and Hannah Foster in the US, who had close personal connections with aspiring women writers scattered across the British North American colonies. This pattern of networking

FIGURE 2.2
Catharine Parr Strickland
Traill, c. early 1890s (Library
and Archives Canada, C-067325)

would continue with the Moodies' and Traills' interaction with the Page
family of Cobourg and with Traill's later connection with the young
Isabella Valancy Crawford.

Following their 1840 move to Belleville, Susanna and John Moodie
became more deeply involved in colonial literary life with their editorship
of the *Victoria Magazine* in 1847–48. Styled "A CHEAP PERIODICAL for the
CANADIAN PEOPLE," the magazine aimed to induce "a taste for polite literature among the working classes" in order to stimulate "the mental improvement of the masses."[58] Other than a few pieces that Agnes sent from
England and several compositions from local authors, the majority of the
contents, whether signed or not, were penned by the Moodies themselves,
on topics ranging from classical Rome to current humour. Unable to sus-
tain the role of "literary philanthropists,"[59] the Moodies gave up the journal
after its first year. The *Victoria Magazine*'s published list of 781 subscribers
shows that it was supported primarily by residents of Belleville, with surprisingly few readers in Montreal despite Susanna's prominence in the *Literary
Garland*. Nonetheless the *Victoria Magazine* did come to the attention of the
Garland's editors, who commended a story by one of its contributors,
Rhoda Anne Page ("R.A.P."). She was a daughter of Thomas Page, editor of
the Newcastle *Farmer* in the late 1840s, who published a story in the *Victoria*

Magazine as "Thomas Page, Esq." The Pages had arrived in Cobourg in 1832 at the same time as the Traills; after her marriage to William Falkner in 1856, Rhoda moved to the Rice Lake plains, where she resumed her friendship with Catharine Parr Traill. A more prolific writer than her sister, Elizabeth Agnes ("E.A.P."), who also appeared in the *Victoria Magazine*, Rhoda issued a pamphlet of her verse, *Wild Notes from the Back Woods*, printed by the Cobourg *Star* in 1850. Her brief life poignantly underscores her many poems about the transitory nature of material experience: Rhoda Anne Page Falkner died seven years after marriage, after bearing eight children (including two sets of twins). Four of her children survived, but all copies of her booklet seem to have vanished.[60]

Maria Monk

Apart from these supportive and often happy literary communities stands the lonely figure of Maria Monk. In view of the many women who struggled for recognition as authors, it is ironic that the best-known female figure in the book history of pre-Confederation Canada was essentially a hoax and a victim of national, religious, and gender-based prejudices. Born in 1816 in Saint-Jean-sur-Richelieu, Monk first came to public attention on 14 October 1835 in a New York penny paper, the *Protestant Vindicator*, claiming to have been impregnated by a priest while attending the Hôtel Dieu nunnery in Montreal. Several months later an account of her abuse, the *Awful Disclosures of Maria Monk* (New York, 1836), became an instant and enduring bestseller. A sequel, *Further Disclosures*, quickly followed, and by 1860 some 300,000 copies of Monk's misadventures were in circulation in various editions. Through 1836 and 1837, refutations and affirmations of Monk's reliability churned from presses on both sides of the Atlantic, including affidavits denying the validity of her story from her mother and from the matron of the Montreal Magdalen Asylum, a refuge for wayward women where Maria had briefly resided.

Current scholarship attributes principal authorship of Maria Monk's horrific tales to two unscrupulous American Protestant ministers, George Bourne and J.J. Slocum, who exploited a vulnerable, unstable woman in order to fuel their anti-Catholic nativism. Quickly abandoned by her sponsors, Monk remained in New York, where she eventually turned to petty crime and prostitution, and died in prison in 1849.[61] Unlike many fraudulent texts, the narratives of Maria Monk refuse to subside into the recesses of history, and received renewed attention when her daughter's autobiography was published in 1874. At the beginning of the twenty-first century, the new medium of electronic dissemination stimulated a fresh phase of controversy when Monk's texts became available through Early Canadiana Online.[62] In light of the research conducted on Monk, it is surprising that no information has been forthcoming about Sara J. Richardson, "An escaped nun" and author of a later account of abuse by the Catholic Church. Her *Life in the Grey Nunnery at Montreal. An Authentic Narrative of the Horrors, Mysteries, and Cruelties of Convent Life*, published in Boston in 1858, would have appealed to the audience for anti-Catholic sensationalism that had credited Maria Monk.

After 1855

The consistent rise in women's literary and publishing activity up to the 1850s was followed by a contrasting plateau in the two subsequent decades. Reasons for this change in momentum include the economic and social disruptions caused by the American Civil War (1861–64), which reduced publishing opportunities and affected cultural production beyond the northern border of the republic. Bibliographies of cultural periodicals in the colonies that would become Canada reveal a dip in start-ups until the late 1870s (particularly outside of Montreal) that suggest a dearth of energy and commitment. As well, the literary immigrants who had accounted for much of the early activity—some of whom remained productive, such as Moodie and Traill—had not yet been invigorated by the next generation of locally born authors. Rosanna Leprohon stands virtually alone as Canada's principal female author of the 1860s. In an effort to generate a sense of national literary identity, Rev. E.H. Dewart, a Methodist minister in Canada East, issued his groundbreaking anthology, *Selections from Canadian Poets*, in 1864. This collection of 172 poems by forty-eight poets in the Canadas (no Maritimers were represented) includes fifty poems by eleven women. Dewart's introductory essay, arguing that "A national literature is an essential element in the formation of national character,"[63] quickly become a landmark document in the annals of Canadian criticism.

Also significant was the rise of New York as the major centre of North American publishing, following the Civil War. Symptomatic was the path followed by May Agnes Fleming: after sending her bestselling fiction to Boston and New York in the 1860s, Fleming moved from her home of Saint John, New Brunswick, to New York City in 1870. In Gwendolyn Davies' succinct analysis, "With the women writers who stayed at home in a pocket culture such as the Maritime area was before 1867, there was no distribution and no lasting fame."[64] American opportunities would tempt many Canadian writers born in the 1860s, a trend examined in Chapter 5.

A turning point in both the literature of French Canada and the valorization of its women writers came in 1881 with the serialization of the opening chapters of Félicité Angers' *Angéline de Montbrun*, Quebec's first psychological novel. The following decades saw a surge in the publication of books by francophone women. In the late 1880s, short novels were issued in *feuilleton* format by Adèle Bibaud in Montreal and Mme Duval-Thibault in Fall River, Massachusetts. Collections of women's prose soon began to appear with Joséphine Marchand's *Contes de Noel* (1889) and Robertine Barry's *Fleurs champêtres* (1895). The first volume of poetry from "une plume canadienne, acclimatée par delà nos frontières"[65] was Duval-Thibault's *Fleurs du printemps*, printed in Fall River in 1892. The first volume containing poems by a woman to be issued within the borders of Quebec was Éva Circé's *Bleu, blanc, rouge* (Montreal, 1903), a book that included some prose, while the first book by a woman dedicated entirely to poetry was *Fleurs sauvages* by Léonise Valois, published by Librairie Beauchemin in Montreal in 1910.

Canada takes pride in the prominence of its women authors, noting the first Canadian-born author was a woman (Marie Morin), the first novel set in Canada was written by a woman (Frances Brooke), and the first native-born author of a novel was likewise female (Julia Catherine Beckwith Hart). Yet other data belie the notion that the country's print culture has particularly favoured women. Numeric tabulations quickly reveal that women cast a sliver-thin shadow on the pre-Confederation literary field where they attained some visibility as authors and translators of fiction, poetry, memoirs, and travellers' tales, but remained absent from the weightier genres grounded in the formal education that conferred cultural substance: history, sermons, science, philosophy, political discourse, and similar forms of serious writing.

PART B

Women Writers at Work

THREE

Strategies of Legitimation

HOW AND WHY DID EARLY Canadian women writers get their words into print? Many of their books open with prefaces that now offer us a valuable corpus of texts in which to study their justification and self-representation. My discussion of the prefaces to literary works issued by Canadian women from 1800 to 1918 inevitably focuses on books written in English, which vastly outnumbered those written in French. This difference was evident in 1900, when *Women of Canada*'s compilation of the country's female writers listed sixty novelists, three of whom wrote in French, and eighty-seven poets, of whom again just three were francophone. Although their numbers were small, the prefaces to books by French-Canadian women demonstrate that patterns of justification and endorsement were similar in both cultures. Regardless of language, the vast majority of Canada's early women writers were occasional authors who couched their entry into the public sphere in rhetoric that combined the familiar tropes of authorial apology and female modesty. In contrast, a distinctive handful of professional authors played with these conventions of legitimation in ways that slyly supported both their individual narrative styles and their intellectual accomplishments.

Prefaces and Self-representation

In general, what do prefaces tell us about the complex relationship between the female writer, her work, and her audiences when the author often felt herself doubly marginalized, as a woman and as a Canadian? Occasional tribute was paid to literary women in survey articles such as Thomas O'Hagan's essay of 1896, "Some Canadian Women Writers"[1] and in introductions to poetry anthologies, nearly all produced by men. While some anthologists, like W.D. Lighthall, commended the sweetness of Canada's "lady singers" and complimented their "masculinity,"[2] it was quite acceptable for J.E. Wetherell to acknowledge the existence of Canada's female poets by placing them at the back of his collection, *Later Canadian Poems* (1893), in a cogent representation of their marginality, a feature of the book that went unnoticed in a long, laudatory review in the *Canadian Magazine*.[3] Such public statements performed the dual function of overtly extolling the presence of women writers in Canada while covertly revoking the artistic seriousness granted to their male counterparts. More private and often more revealing are prefaces to individually authored works, where the writer briefly speaks in a personal (albeit ritualized) voice about her sense of her self and her audience.

However, the voice in the preface may not belong to the author of the text. A more complex picture emerges when we distinguish two separate discourses of introduction, each with its own set of conventions and expectations. The woman who composed her own preface usually assumed that the normal purpose of a self-introducing writer was explanation and apology, and the normal tone humility. In contrast, externally authored introductions—"allographic" in Gérard Genette's terminology[4]—issued from authority figures who were usually male. Their role was to intercede between the author and her public, confidently proclaiming her significance, often in a landmark first volume or final publication such as an author's collected works or a posthumous memorial edition. Rather conveniently, the two divide along chronological lines. Authors' apologies, especially to poetry, prevailed until the 1890s and almost disappeared in the twentieth century, an indication, perhaps, of increasing confidence and acceptability. External introductions, on the other hand, were just as frequent after the turn of the century as before; greater changes occurred in the sociological makeup of the introducers than in their purpose and language.

While an explanatory introduction is all but obligatory for the anthologist, this is not the case for the author of poetry or prose. Despite Rosanna Leprohon's claim to have composed the preface to her novel, *Antoinette de Mirecourt* (1864), only because she was advised that "it is usual to do so" and she had "no wish to deviate from the established custom,"[5] the majority of books published by nineteenth-century Canadian authors lack such introductions. Hence the presence of a preface signals that the author is requesting visibility for herself as well as for her work and has something distinctive to impart, however briefly or obliquely she may express it. Written last but strategically placed to be read first, the preface may record the author's final thoughts, yet it preconditions the reader's first encounter with the principal text. As Gayatri Spivak notes, "the question of the preface" calls attention to the "shifting and unstable" nature of readings and texts.[6]

In her sweep of non-fiction books by anglophone Canadian women, Anne Innis Dagg found examples of apologetic prefaces in all the major genres practised by women in the nineteenth century.[7] In most instances, these authors of travel narrative, local history, autobiography, biography, and instructional materials were first-time or one-time authors, who claimed reluctance or minimized either their literary abilities or the significance of their book. In some cases, a woman's entry into authorship was entirely due to historical accident. For example, Theresa Delaney and Theresa Gowanlock, who found themselves unexpectedly thrust into the limelight when they were "captured" during the North-West Rebellion, prepared *Two Months in the Camp of Big Bear* (1885) because it was their "bounden duty to give the public a truthful and accurate description" of their experience. Delaney claimed that "Outside my limited correspondence, I never undertook to compose a page, much less a book." While Gowanlock's brothers happened to own the Parkdale *Times*, which published the little volume in order to capitalize on the publicity generated in the press, she claimed that she desired only to withdraw to "wished for seclusion from which I never would have emerged but to perform a public duty."[8] More common were explanations such as that offered by schoolteacher Jennet Roy to account for her *History of Canada for the Use of Schools and Families*. When the book appeared in 1847, she explained that her "little work" (of 231 pages) had been "composed to meet a real want," and "[pleaded] as her excuse the absolute necessity of providing such a source of information for British American Youth."[9] Authorized for school use in Upper Canada and widely taken up in Lower Canada as well, this text proved a valuable property for her publishers, who nonetheless retained the author's prefatory apology through six further editions during the next two decades.

In linking her apology to a national purpose, Roy deployed a rhetorical strategy favoured by the majority of Canadian literary writers in the first half of the nineteenth century, according to Mary Lu MacDonald.[10] Typical was the hope of Julia Beckwith, author of the first novel by a native-born Canadian, that the publication of *St. Ursula's Convent* (1824) might contribute to "the slow progress of improvement in British North America."[11] In a corpus of prefaces written mostly by men, MacDonald found that moral imperatives followed nationalism as a frequently stated motivation for creating Canadian books. During an era when "[a]ll writers in the Canadas ... were amateurs who made their living in some other activity,"[12] the third most common approach was "the stance of the apologetic amateur" who followed the convention that "[l]iterature was perceived as an appropriate leisure occupation for ladies and gentlemen who, of course, had no interest in money."[13] However if we examine only the prefaces written by women, we find that apologies override statements of both national and moral purpose; moreover, no male authors ever "craved indulgence because of their sex."[14] In constructing their apologies, women invoked moral and national imperatives to justify their temerity in stepping into print.

Prefaces to Poetry

A review of critical and editorial statements issued in Canada from 1824 to 1924 shows that poetry was consistently regarded as the highest literary calling.[15] Poetry was also the genre most likely to be introduced by a preface. While apologetic prefaces to women's poetry had declined in Britain over the previous two centuries,[16] they continued to prevail in Canada's colonial environment. Prefaces written by female poets are distinguished by a recurring note of diffidence, characterized by negative and passive phrasing. Their work was not intended for publication, these women often claimed, but, yielding to the "urgent solicitations" or "kind encouragement" of friends, they were "induced" to offer it to the public.[17] In addition to denying her own agency in seeking publication, the female poet frequently denied as well her capacity for authorship, speaking of her "timidity" and "unfeigned diffidence," her "inability" and "incapacity," while describing herself as "untaught" and her work as "feeble," "unstudied," or mere "immature verses" from her schooldays.[18] This self-diminution was often intensified by calling attention to the physically small size of her book. While a few writers, like Margaret Blennerhassett, ironically noted her unavoidable use of the "hackneyed expressions" associated with these conventions of authorial modesty,[19] their ubiquity also demonstrates the writers' internalization of the social values couched in the advice offered by Robert Southey to Charlotte Brontë in 1837, when he informed the woman who was to become one of the greatest authors of the nineteenth century that "[l]iterature cannot be the business of a woman's life, and it ought not to be."

In Victorian Canada, economically speaking it was almost impossible for literature to be the business of anybody's life, male or female. More insidious was the notion underpinning Southey's "ought not," that writing unfitted a woman for normal life:

> The day dreams in which you habitually indulge are likely to induce a distempered state of mind; and in proportion as all the ordinary uses of the world seem to you flat and unprofitable, you will be unfitted for them without becoming fitted for anything else. Literature cannot be the business of a woman's life, and it ought not to be. The more she is engaged in her proper duties, the less leisure she will have for it, even as an accomplishment and a recreation.[20]

Hence it is not surprising to find that early Canadian prefaces lend support to Suzanne Juhasz's later declaration that "[t]o be a woman poet in our society is a double-bind situation, one of conflict and strain, for the words 'woman' and 'poet' denote opposite and contradictory roles."[21] In 1859, Augusta Baldwyn begged not to be regarded as "unwomanly"; nearly half a century later Sarah Sherwood Faulkner claimed that in publishing her "stray bits of verse" she was not presuming to "aspire to the rank and title of *poet*," and as late as 1935 Ethel Ursula Foran declared, "[i]t is not my intention to take even the most humble place among authors."[22]

Such self-deprecation was equally common among francophone women. As their work began to appear in periodicals in the late nineteenth century, they requested the indulgence of editors and readers and begged for kindness from their critics.[23] In her preface to *Fleurs sauvages* (1910), Léonise Valois deftly managed to invoke the familiar tropes of publishing at the behest of friends and pleading for indulgence, while also demonstrating her poetic technique in a rhyming "Offrande" whose last verse repeats the first:

> Mes vers, vous les voulez, à vous donc je les donne
> Avec mon amitié,
> Et que votre indulgence, amis, me les pardonne
> S'ils vous font trop pitié.[24]

Male poets, both famous and obscure, also wrote apologetic prefaces in a long-standing tradition of "authorial reluctance" and "affected modesty,"[25] but usually with a distinct difference in style. An illustrative contrast between masculine assertion and feminine hesitation may be found in the prefaces to the first books written by William Thomas Carroll Ryan and Mary McIver, two Canadian poets who married in 1870. His preface to *Oscar: and Other Poems* (1857) confidently announced:

In presenting the following Poems to the public, I would first say a few
words, not to point out my own faults or errors, which is the fashion now;
nor to apologise: the former I leave the reader to find out, and the latter to the circumstances under which the Poems were written,—the
greater portion being composed at different times, and in positions the
most unfavorable.... Without asking for indulgence, or praying for for-
giveness, I leave the work to be judged according to its merits. That it
may please the public is the earnest hope of

THE AUTHOR[26]

In contrast, her preface to her *Poems* (1869) demurred:

Although some of my occasional contributions to the Press have met with
kind and considerate criticism, I feel it would be presumptuous to expect
a continuance of the same should my writings, viewed as a whole, fail
to attain that standard to which every poetical work should aspire. I will
not seek to defend the many imperfections perhaps but too evident in
this, my first venture into the field of literary labour; but may I not hope
that the earnest love and reverence which I have ever borne to the
divine art of poetry, and which has brightened ways dark and narrow
enough at times, may in some measure atone to the reader for any defi-
ciencies of style or expression?[27]

Men were more likely to argue for the significance of their work than
simply to excuse its defects. Both Isidore Ascher and Rev. Edward Hartley
Dewart, for example, composed brief prefatory essays asserting the cultural
value of "minor poetry."[28] George E. Merkley expected his *Canadian
Melodies and Poems* (1893) to be well received because in Canada any stimu-
lus to a national literature ought to be encouraged, and Robert Awde
endorsed his new volume of *Jubilee, Patriotic and Other Poems* (1877) with
copious quotations from London reviews of this first book. Moreover, a
male author could excuse the crudity of his writing by situating it within the
context of other work that valorized his existence. Dewart reminded the
reader that he was a "minister of religion," Merkley mentioned that several
of his poems "were mere attempts to relieve the monotonous routine of college life,"[29] and in his introduction to his second book, William Thomas
Carroll Ryan discussed in some detail the connection between his poetry
and his military career. Lawyer and newspaperman Dr. F.K. Foran outlined
a very purposeful life when he explained that his "rude verses" were "written at haphazard and in all manner of places, from the forests of the Black
River to the Halls of Laval, from the Indian wigwam to the House of Com-
mons; in newspaper offices, law offices, and government offices; in court
rooms and lumber camps; in monastic retreats and election campaigns."[30]

Few such strategies were available to female authors. With the exception of several widows who published poems to solicit charity, women referred obliquely, if at all, to the place of their writing in their daily lives, rarely offering more than a passing comment about their "few leisure hours."[31] Quite untypical was Susanna Moodie's confessional introduction to her 1853 novel, *Mark Hurdlestone,* which informed her readers that her periodical writing bought shoes for her children. Pamelia Vining Yule was relatively candid when she revealed that her verses were written "in brief intervals snatched from the arduous duties of teaching and the even more arduous ones of domestic life";[32] generally speaking, because women's domestic and family work seldom received public acknowledgment, it could not offer a legitimating context for their creative writing. While men's apologies tend to focus on their work and to be cast in terms of what they *do*, apologies from women focus more directly on themselves and are presented in terms of who they *are*. Hence critic Steven Totosy de Zepetenik describes as "preemptive" the "relatively frequent apology of women authors for being young and inexperienced."[33]

As women who dared "attempt the pen," in the well-known words of Anne Finch, Countess of Winchilsea, they were "intruders on the rights of men,"[34] directly challenging the norm of female self-effacement encoded in Annie Louisa Walker's 1861 poem, "Woman's Rights." This Canadian version of Southey's "ought not" idealized the limits of female life:

> To live, unknown beyond the cherished circle
> Which we can bless and aid;
> To die, and not a heart that does not love us
> Know where we're laid.[35]

It is quite consistent that the book in which these lines appeared was published anonymously, although Walker herself would later become a more public literary figure.[36] In the prefaces under discussion, the woman author's "anxiety of authorship," to borrow the phrase coined by Sandra Gilbert and Susan Gubar,[37] surfaces in her occasional use of courtroom language: the reader is often cast as judge, of whom the poet requests "forbearance" and to whom she "pleads" and "atones."[38] The ostensible object of these entreaties may be the poet's work, but when she presents her writing as her "child,"[39] she deflects the subject of concern back to her feminine self. In this spirit of self-effacement, Clotilda Jennings published her *Linden Rhymes* pseudonymously in 1854 and contrived to say as little as possible, erasing her authorial self in the negative language and denial of agency typical of this mode of discourse. Here is her entire preface:

In the way of Preface to this small book, I have not much to say. It is impossible for me to explain how it was written, or why it is now published;—else, perhaps I might disarm criticism. But I offer to my dear friends, without whose generous and effectual aid I could have done so little toward publishing, and to my numerous and kind subscribers, most grateful regard; from my countrymen and country women generally, I entreat a merciful verdict.[40]

Sixty-two years later, similar reticence characterized Jeanne-Lynne Branda's first pamphlet of religious poetry, *Vers le bien* (1916):

Ce livre est dédié à mon père et à ma mère en témoignage de ma reconnaissance et à toutes les jeunes filles en témoignage de mon dévouement. Puisse-t-il réaliser son but et porter quelques âmes vers le bien. C'est mon seul désir et ce serait ma seule récompense.[41]

Strategies of Justification

If the common tropes of apology and trepidation represent the sincere feelings of Canada's early female poets, how did these women validate their literary activity? Balancing their negative references to themselves are the moral and national values claimed for their work. Primary for many was the domestic value of writing destined "for the Home Circle," as Carrie Leonard titled her book, its goal not the gratification of personal ambition but the "moral uplift of humanity."[42] Clara Mountcastle offered her simple verses to satisfy Canadians' need for "poetry in the home, poetry that will give rest and pleasure."[43] The role of women's writing was to be nurturing and meliorative whether, like Caroline Hayward's poems, intended to comfort "the sorrowing relatives of the Heroes of the Crimea" while raising money for the "Patriotic Fund,"[44] or, like Kate Madeline Bottomley's Ottawa novel, *Honor Edgeworth* (1882), to improve the manners of local women. In Montreal, Joséphine Dandurand addressed her punningly titled collection of essays, *Nos travers* (1901), to "mes amies et fidèles lectrices," to promote her compatriots' dignity, moral improvement, and intellectual culture.[45] In Charlottetown, Mrs. W.W. Rodd overcame her "many misgivings" to issue her poems in the hope of "shedding a ray of comfort on some poor sorrowing soul who is passing through the deep waters of affliction."[46]

Further justification appears in these writers' awareness of their role in developing a national literature. A Canadian readership, they suggest, might be more forgiving than a British one when presented with work that was at the very least, in a phrase used by both Yule and Leprohon,

FIGURE 3.1
Joséphine Marchand
Dandurand ("Josette")
(MS Coll. 00450, Thomas
Fisher Rare Book Library,
F5156)

"essentially Canadian." Running as a subtext through the prefaces that refer to the growth of a national identity is Julia Beckwith Hart's notion that Canadian literature has to begin somewhere,[47] and because the country is still in its infancy, consideration might be given to imperfect work that would be rejected in a more mature culture. More purposeful nationalism motivated some of the more confident authors. Francophone writers shared a mission to preserve "les traditions, les touchants coutumes, les naives superstitions et ... pittoresques expressions des habitants de nos campagnes avant que tout cela n'ait complètement disparu,"[48] in "des productions canadiennes se rattachant à nos moeurs, à notre histoire."[49] On the anglophone side, Sarah Anne Curzon's challenge to "the inertness of Canadian interest in a Canadian literature" took a feminist turn in her efforts to set Laura Secord on "a pedestal of equality" with the more celebrated male military heroes of the War of 1812.[50]

Described as possessing "a masculinity and energy found in the work of no other Canadian woman,"[51] Curzon was one of the most self-assured female preface writers of her century. Focusing exclusively on its subject, her preface to *Laura Secord and Other Poems* ... (1887) anticipates the modern explanatory introduction whose lack of authorial self-reference signals the writer's assumption that the act of writing requires no personal excuse. In succeeding decades, female authors would increasingly ignore the tradition of the apologetic preface; rarer in Victorian Canada was its outright rejection. A delightful anti-preface penned by Mrs. John Crawford in 1890 opens boldly: "There are two things about a book which I always skip,—the preface and the moral." She continues: "A preface is either an explanation or an excuse," and denies the need for either: "To those who read it, the book will be its own explanation and apology. And the book which does not convey its own meaning and moral, should be neither written nor read."[52] Similar confidence imbues Clara Mountcastle's sprightly rhyming introduction to *The Mission of Love* ... (1882):

> Dear reader! whether old or young,
> It matters not I ween;
> Or grave, or gay, or dark, or fair,
> Or all the shades between,
> Thou'lt find some lines to fit thy case
> Within this volume's narrow space.[53]

Such assertiveness also characterizes the tone of the external preface writer who acts as counsel for the author, pleading her case before her readers. Appropriately, among the authors of prefaces to early Canadian women's books there are judges and lawyers, one of whom was better known as a prime minister. The sex and status of authors of external prefaces turns out to be as significant as their manner of discourse.

Externally Authored Prefaces to Women's Books

Before 1920, in both French and English Canada the external introducer to a woman's book was most often male and most likely to be a clergyman, followed by lawyers, men of letters, and similar claimants to expertise. The following examples demonstrate the magnitude of the masculine authority that was brought to bear on women's writings. Laure Conan's groundbreaking novel, *Angéline de Montbrun*, issued in book form in 1884, was introduced by Abbé Casgrain with a lengthy essay that was originally intended to be read at the first session of the Royal Society of Canada. Anne-Marie Gleason's first book (1902) was graced with "Un mot de préface" from a Jesuit priest and her second (1912) was prefaced by patriotic advocate Edouard Montpetit, while books by Blanche Lamontagne garnered laudatory endorsements from lawyer Adjutor Rivard (1913) and nationalist cleric Lionel Groulx (1917). Author Louis Fréchette introduced Josephine Marchand's *Contes de Noel* (1889) and historian Benjamin

Sulte did the same for Mme Duval-Thibault's *Fleurs du printemps* (1892). In English Canada, Mina Hubbard's *A Woman's Way through Unknown Labrador* (1908) opens with a brief preface by the author followed by an extensive introduction by William Brooks Cabot, an authority on Labrador; Frances Herring's novel of the North, *The Gold Miners* (1914), was introduced by Judge F.W. Howay.

If the role of external introducer was conferred on a woman, as with Ethelwyn Wetherald's 1905 introduction to the *Collected Poems of Isabella Valancy Crawford*, her status almost always derived from her fame as a writer, literature being one of the very few areas where a woman could achieve sufficient status. Hence the sense of lineage was acute, as in Gaé-tane de Montreuil's preface to Alcide Lacerte's *Contes et légendes* (1915), in which she exults, "Je suis marraine!"[54] Not surprisingly, woman authors of external prefaces in Victorian Canada were exceedingly rare, and the few instances reveal the importance of family and other personal connections. Among the Stricklands—nineteenth-century English Canada's most prominent female literary family—the women occasionally wrote prefaces for one another. Agnes Strickland's elevated English reputation underscored her introduction to Catharine Parr Traill's *Canadian Crusoes* (1852), which Agnes approached as a British author preparing a British readership for a rather exotic foreign tale. Traill's last book, *Cot and Cradle Stories* (1895), was edited and introduced by her niece, Agnes FitzGibbon (Susanna Moodie's daughter), known as an author of non-fiction. Before the turn of the century, the only women to preface another writer's poetry were Halifax literary journalist Constance Fairbanks, who co-edited the poems of fellow Haligonian Mary Jane Katzmann Lawson, and prominent Catholic novelist Mary Anne Sadlier, editor of the posthumous *Poems of Thomas D'Arcy McGee* (1869) and introducer of Jean Nealis's *Drift* (1884).

Two important questions arise regarding the contents of these externally authored prefaces: In what ways do they differ from those by the authors themselves, and do the two sexes develop different discourses of introduction? Nineteenth-century external prefaces echo the authors' own justification of their work for its national significance, commending early writers as distinguished pioneers and lauding later authors for helping to secure Canada's position in the British Empire. When they turn to the women writers' "salutary"[55] effects on the morals and manners of their readers, the Victorian introducers engage in what Elaine Showalter terms "*ad feminam*" criticism,[56] often dwelling on "the mission and power of women to ennoble and bless society."[57] Thus in the case of poetry, praise for the personality of the poet blended with assessment of her work. Rosanna Leprohon, we are told, was "in the highest sense a woman, a lady" whose poetry represented "the emotional record of a blameless and beautiful life."[58] In contrast to personal prefaces, externally authored references to the female poet's "devotion to religion and family," loving kindliness," and "useful Christian labour"[59] occasionally provide specific details about the woman's actual life (although in Leprohon's case, no mention is made of her thirteen children).

At the same time, the literary qualities for which a woman poet was praised usually referred back to her gender, the emotional qualities of her work receiving more attention than its intellectual or artistic aspects. Delicacy, beauty, simplicity, piety, purity, and closeness to nature were among the elements frequently lauded in nineteenth-century prefaces. In the prefaces to Pauline Johnson's books, the typically feminine qualities of emotionalism and closeness to nature were intensified as Indian passion and love of the wild. Yet to be praised for success in the female realm was to be implicitly downgraded as an artist. Hence we find some women undergoing a sex change in the words of their advocates, as when John

FIGURE 3.2
Isabella Valancy Crawford
(MS Coll. 00450, Thomas
Fisher Rare Book Library,
F5155)

Garvin assigned Isabella Crawford a "master muse."[60] As a term of appro-
bation, the word "virility" was applied to woman poets by female introducers as well as by men.[61] Living on the outskirts of civilization afforded no
protection from the dilemma of the female author described by Virginia
Woolf: if she was not to be dismissed as "only a woman," she had to be
shown to be "as good as a man."[62]

Given the small numbers of samples and the differing circumstances of
their composition, it is not possible to provide a generalized comparison
between the approaches of male and female introducers of woman
authors. However, one specific instance offers a telling contrast: the 1905
edition of *Poems of Isabella Valancy Crawford* was published with two prefaces.
John Garvin commended "Malcolm's Katie" for its "picturesque description, brave-hearted purpose, [and] tender, constant passion." This hardly
seems to be the same poem as the one praised by Ethelwyn Wetherald for
its "strong and coherent thought, imagery unhackneyed and unstrained,"
and "a diction as concise, ringing and effective as the blows of its hero's
axe."[63] Prefaces, like other commentary, may cast greater light on the pre-
suppositions of the speaker than on the writer and her work.

Self-legitimation of Professional Authors

The title of Andrée Levesque's 1989 book, *La norme et les déviantes*, offers
some insights into women writers' prefaces. Although her study deals with
sexual rather than literary behaviour, Levesque offers a concise dialectic
that suits a broader spectrum: "Le discours et le vécu. Les prescriptions et
les comportements. L'histoire des femmes se prête à l'étude de la
dichotomie ou de la coïncidence entre ces deux concepts."[64] While
women might have done much private writing, the norm was not to publish their work and the apologetic prefaces of first-time and occasional
authors may accurately convey their tremulous feelings regarding their
sense of deviance when they ventured into the public sphere. However,
apologies penned by seasoned female authors should be approached with
greater circumspection. For professional women writers, deviance was the
norm, and when they invoke apology, their overstatement of the conventions invites an ironic reading. For example, when Susan Frances Harrison, well on her way to a professional career as a musician and an author,
presented her 1886 book of stories "in all proper fear and humility to
[her] Canadian public,"[65] her use of the word "proper" resembles Sara
Jeannette Duncan's cheeky dedication of her first book to Mrs. Grundy,
with its mock-serious use of typographical variants. In the absence of a

preface, this gesture serves the same function by advising the reader of the tone of the text to follow:

This Volume

AS A SLIGHT TRIBUTE TO THE OMNIPOTENCE OF HER OPINION

AND A HUMBLE MARK OF PROFOUNDEST ESTEEM

Is Respectfully Dedicated

TO

MRS GRUNDY[66]

When an apologetic preface is read in conjunction with the book it introduces, its excessive humility may seem to be a strategic manoeuvre that underscores the assertiveness of the ensuing text. For an early example, let us consider how Anna Jameson, in the second paragraph of her preface to *Winter Studies and Summer Rambles in Canada* (1838), claims the novelty requisite of the travel genre: "While in Canada, I was thrown into scenes and regions hitherto undescribed by any traveller ... and into relations with the Indian tribes such as few European women of refined and civilised habits have ever risked, and none have recorded."[67] Her casual idiom—"thrown into"—belies her carefully orchestrated plan to travel as far as possible in order to satisfy her curiosity and produce a saleable book. The trope of modesty, which characterizes the preface in which the phrase appears, ironically highlights the substantial size of her "little book" (which ran to three volumes of more than 300 pages apiece), while the powerful intellect displayed in her discussion of German literature and analysis of the conditions of women renders her text far weightier than "'fragments' of a journal addressed to a friend." Such rhetoric serves several purposes. The direct antithesis between the casual, humble persona constructed in the preface and the authoritative voice of the main text effectively highlights the distinctiveness of Jameson's accomplishment as both author and traveller. At the same time, knowing the coziness expected of female literary culture, Jameson adopted the apparently private mode of writing to a close female friend (Ottilie von Goethe) in order to offer the reader a sense of intimacy within a very public medium. This strategy, which may have contributed to the book's commercial success, also informs Catharine Parr Traill's *The Backwoods of Canada* (1836), which purports to be a series of letters written to her mother, who had remained in England.

In contrast to Jameson's deviance as an independent, intellectual female traveller, Traill's normative position as a married settler underpinned her confidence in addressing "the wives and daughters of emigrants of the higher class who contemplate seeking a home amid our Canadian wilds." Arguing in her preface that successful immigration depended upon "the internal management of a domicile in the backwoods," a topic not yet developed by male writers, Traill declared that the intervention of "a woman's pen alone" was required to "honestly [represent] facts in their real and true light."[68] Hence much of her assurance derived from the novelty of her historical situation. Her ability to identify and then fulfill a gender-specific need did not invite the authorial modesty associated with more literary genres, as exemplified by Rosanna Leprohon's preface to her first free-standing novel, *Antoinette de Mirecourt* (1864).

Well known as a poet and author of serialized fiction by the time she published *Antoinette*, Leprohon was an experienced wordsmith when she penned her first preface, whose collection of negatives and diminutives is probably unsurpassed in the discourse of authorial modesty. In a statement of less than 250 words there are six appearances of "not" or "no" and an equal number of diminutives such as "simple," "merely," "little," and "smallest" (some couched in the litotes of "no little gratification" and "will not prove unwelcome"). At the same time, Leprohon argues that despite the abundance of "literary treasures of 'the old world'" and the inundation of cheap reading matter from the US, Canadians "should not be discouraged from endeavouring to form and foster a literature of their own." She concludes by claiming that the greatest merit of her book is that it is "essentially Canadian."[69] Such comments suggest that her over-stated modesty relates as much to her venture into public nationalist discourse as to her gender. The effect of this self-abnegating preface is to disarm the reader who is about to encounter a very different voice on the next page, as the story opens with a narrator who takes on the guise of a self-assured hostess. She conducts us into the D'Aulnay household in old Montreal "[w]ithout going through the ceremony of raising the ponderous knocker," while chatting about "our Canadian year" and "our modern ideas"[70] of style. This proudly Canadian narrator, whose frame of reference is more often English despite the French milieu that she penetrates, presents herself as a participant in the characters' social circle and intrepidly spies on the hapless heroine's private moments before applauding her final good fortune. Moreover, the story she tells doesn't quite embrace conventional norms of feminine behaviour. Misao Dean's linking of the novel's domestic romance with an overtly political analysis[71] suggests that like Jameson, Leprohon chose to use the tradition of "affected modesty" as a foil for the mettlesome text to follow.

Rather than using prefaces as the occasion for self-justification, Susanna Moodie placed her claims for legitimation within the texts of *Roughing It in the Bush* (1852) and *Life in the Clearings versus the Bush* (1853), where she performed some artful manoeuvres in her self-defence as "the woman that writes."[72] For narrative purposes, she cast her persona as an unhappy settler needing "to conceal [her] blue stockings beneath the long conventional robes of the tamest commonplace"[73] in order to obtain social approval in the Canadian backwoods. Yet at the time of publishing these words, the historical Susanna Moodie was actually a fulsome participant in a flourishing trans-Atlantic print culture, embarking on her most productive decade, which saw six books issued by Richard Bentley in London between 1851 and 1855. Moodie's self-deprecatory comments in *Life in the Clearings* nicely demonstrate her adeptness at demurring as a woman while asserting her power as a narrator when she requests her "[d]ear patient reader" to "[a]llow me a woman's privilege of talking of all sorts of things by the way.... [B]ear with me charitably, and take into account the infirmities incidental to my gossiping sex and age."[74] In addition to disclaiming narrative unity (creating what Misao Dean describes as "the structure of non-structure, of gossip and personal anecdote"),[75] Moodie evades responsibility for dry details of colonial administration by stating that "As a woman, I cannot enter into the philosophy of these things."[76] In the same vein, she later asserts that "Women make good use of their eyes and ears, and paint scenes that amuse or strike their fancy with tolerable accuracy," but it is up to "the strong-thinking heart of man to anticipate events, and trace certain results from particular causes."[77] Such comments appear to concede to the conventions of gender, while in effect cannily legitimating the casual style of Moodie's digressive, chatty sketches of characters and events in books whose appeal to the reading public added substantially to her household income.

At the end of the nineteenth century, similar self-confidence characterized L.M. Montgomery's youthful goal to make her name and fortune as a writer. Despite her later self-projection as the beleaguered young author-heroine of the Emily trilogy written in the 1920s, Montgomery's earlier diaries and correspondence reveal that she started out with few qualms: she felt born to write, she wanted to make money, and authorship was the obvious route to personal and material satisfaction.[78] Indeed there is an interesting coincidence in the way that, at the pinnacle of their literary careers, these two authors dwelt on the hardships of their earlier years: Moodie, writing in 1850 about the difficulty of establishing her

Canadian literary identity in the 1830s, and Montgomery, writing after the First World War about the obstacles to her start as a writer several decades earlier. While this material offered these writers an opportunity to appeal to readers' emotions, it also suggests that even the most successful women writers could be haunted by a sense of deviancy.

FOUR

꧁꧂

The Business of a Woman's Life

WHILE IT IS IMPOSSIBLE TO ENUMERATE all the Canadian women who published books before 1918, we can gather useful data from a few inclusive sources. "Canada's Early Women Writers," a database that now resides on the website of the Simon Fraser University library,[1] contains files on several hundred women who authored an English-language book of fiction or poetry before 1918 and about whom some biographical information has been found. Anne Innis Dagg's compilation of Canadian women authors of non-fiction books in English identifies another 125 from the same period.[2] One of the first questions posed by this accumulation of more than three hundred names is: Why? In a society not distinguished for its hospitality to literary activity, why did so many women put so much effort into presenting and preserving their writing in the form of a book? As demonstrated in the previous chapter, only a small proportion announced their motives in prefaces. In other instances, the author's purpose is evident within her text. Few openly admitted that they wrote to earn money. Some, like Catharine Parr Traill, wrote to instruct children, while others supported specific causes such as Sarah Anne Curzon's commitment to both feminism and patriotism, and Annie Charlotte Dalton's promotion of sympathy for the deaf. Advancement of moral reform motivated Margaret Murray Robertson. Agnes Maule Machar and Marie Joussaye both sought to improve the working and living conditions of the poor, while animal welfare inspired the stories of Marshall Saunders and Annie Gregg Savigny. But the majority of Canada's early women writers published their volumes and booklets, in many cases paying the costs themselves, without a deliberate reformist purpose and with little hope for financial reward.

A different situation obtained in Quebec, where, as in France, women began to publish significantly only when journalism became an acceptable way to earn money toward the end of the nineteenth century.[3] In the middle of the century, the popularity of translated versions of Rosanna Leprohon's social fiction demonstrated French-Canadian women's desire to read stories of their own culture in their own language. Following the positive reception of Laure Conan's *Angéline de Montbrun* (1884) and subsequent serious fiction, several Québécois women turned to novels, long established internationally as the most lucrative genre for anglophone women. In the 1880s Adèle Bibaud drew on the literary heritage created by her illustrious grandfather, poet and historian Michel Bibaud, when she issued several full-length historical romances as well as a number of shorter stories published in the pamphlet format known as the *feuilleton*. Across the border, in Fall River, Massachusetts, Anna Duval-Thibault's novel, *Les deux testaments*, was published in 1888 by *L'Indépendant*, the newspaper run by her husband. While a few other women wrote poetry and drama, fully half the Québécois women writers of the 1895–1918 period were described as journalists, in contrast to just 12 percent of the men, whose major genres included poetry, fiction, theatre, criticism, history, and scholarly writing.[4] Unable to progress in the traditional hierarchy of the masculine press, a number of women founded their own periodicals, beginning with Joséphine Marchand Dandurand's *Coin de feu* (1893–96) and followed by Robertine Barry's *Le Journal de Françoise* (1902–09) and Georgina Bélanger's *Pour vous mesdames* (1913–15). Extremely conscious of "the very slight part played by French Canadian women in the domain of literature," which Robertine Barry attributed to "a condition of intellectual society which is hostile to women in literature,"[5] these journalists cautiously advocated improvements in women's education to enable them to become discerning readers and capable writers.[6]

Journalism was not only appealing in its own right, but could also be a springboard to successful book publication. Barry's well-received *Chroniques du lundi* (1895) inspired other francophone women to publish collections of their periodical writings. The genre known as the *chronique*, similar to the English sketch or column in brevity and flexibility, and belletristic in tone, was popular in this period, which saw the publication of some twenty collections (by men as well as women) in Quebec between 1895 and 1918. Four of these were volumes of the *Lettres* (1914, 1915, 1916, 1918) of Fadette (Henriette Dessaules),[7] drawn from her enduring weekly column in *Le Devoir*. Viewed as particularly suitable for women, the *chronique* represented "la voie d'entrée principale des femmes in littérature."[8] An English-language counterpart would be Sara Jeannette Duncan's regular columns "Other People and I" and "Women's World" in the *Globe* (1885–87), "Saunterings" and "Afternoon Tea" in the *Week* (1886–88), and "Bric-a-Brac" in the Montreal *Star* (1887–88). Duncan's decision to turn to fiction, rather than attempt to publish her journalism in book form, demonstrates the strength of the international English-language fiction market during the 1880s. As the century turned, the readership of Canada's anglophone periodicals sufficiently expanded to support books by authors who built their audience through their journalism, a process exemplified by the popularity of Emily Murphy's travel sketches. Her first book, *The Impressions of Janey Canuck Abroad* (1902), became known when it was subsequently serialized in the *National Monthly of Canada*, where it was followed by a still uncollected series, "The Impressions of Janey Canuck at Home."[9] By the time Murphy issued *Janey Canuck in the West* (1910), her signature was familiar across the country, especially to readers of the Winnipeg *Tribune*, which published her book reviews, and the Winnipeg *Telegram*, where she was literary editor from 1904 to 1912.[10] Hence the ground was well laid for the success of *Open Trails* (1912), which "sold over 60,000 copies at a time when 5,000 copies was considered a good sale in Canada."[11]

Money, Motives, and Publishing

To be inferred from the publishing of Canadian women's writing before 1918 is a web of conflicting notions regarding relations between self and history, the private and the public, and author and text. The history of the book as a cultural icon carries strong connotations of religious sanctity and specialized scholarship, wafting from not so distant eras when book creation was implicitly a male domain and the book itself "a sign of culture and gentility."[12] As the medium is inseparable from the message, the physical form in which an author's words appear plays an important role in signalling their significance. The material book, which gathered an accretion of cultural and religious significations from the classical period through the Middle Ages[13] and into the modern era, is historically a more masculine medium than is publication in a periodical. The arrival of newspapers—and especially magazines—offered a secular, ephemeral, and relatively recent mode of textual communication that has more easily accommodated women for several centuries.[14]

When a woman publishes a book, the transition from the single handwritten manuscript to multiple publicly accessible printed and bound copies constitutes a leap out of the private sphere in which women's lives have traditionally unfolded into the public realm, where the author herself, especially if not shielded by anonymity or a pen name, becomes an object of general attention. Presenting her work in the shape of a book both valorizes an author and violates her, simultaneously giving her an enduring identity and subjecting her to discomforting public scrutiny. Hence the publishing of women's writing, in Canada as elsewhere,[15] has been enmeshed in conflict, such that the pleasure of seeing one's name in print is tainted by the discomfort of being turned into a "thing," as Margaret Atwood put in 1973, or the notoriety of being labelled "the woman that writes," in Susanna Moodie's earlier formulation, and suspected of belonging to another species.[16]

Hence also conflicting attitudes surrounding the notion of earning money from writing. Payment for literary production defines writing as work, an activity not traditionally sanctioned for "proper ladies," in Mary Poovey's phrase.[17] But payment also signals value: "Money dignifies what is frivolous if unpaid for," to quote Virginia Woolf.[18] Financial need could therefore justify a middle-class woman's recourse to literary labour to support herself or her children. The ambiguity of the situation that obtained well into the twentieth century is expressed in the phrasing of Susanna Moodie's 1851 comment to Louisa Murray when, in reference to John Lovell, publisher of the *Literary Garland*, Moodie wrote: "If you can afford to write for him gratis, you are more fortunate than I am."[19] This comment invokes the notion that money should not be of concern to ladies, who should be able to "afford" to indulge their artist inclinations without attention to cost or reward; yet over the past several centuries, writing has "afforded" women one of their few economically viable opportunities to work without blatantly transgressing their class status or their domestic commitments.

However they may wish to, authors who desire publication can seldom separate the pleasure of writing from the economics of getting into print. In 1892, Sarah Anne Curzon wrote to William Kirby: "Literature as far as I am acquainted with it has few enough rewards, and even if it had many I am not sure but the consciousness that one has made some mark on the mind of one's time would not transcend them all."[20] From first-hand experience, Curzon knew only too well the paucity of tangible rewards that awaited the late nineteenth-century Canadian poet. Three years earlier, Louisa Murray had appealed to readers of the *Week* on Curzon's behalf to rescue her from debts incurred from the publication of *Laura Secord and Other Poems*. Murray explained that Curzon had overestimated the patriotism of her fellow Canadians, "believing that the subject would appeal to all Canadian hearts as it did to hers, and [that] a ready sale [would] secure her from pecuniary loss, she undertook the expenses of its publication." Now Curzon was threatened by "loss and mortification." The terms of Murray's appeal construct a special pleading for the female author of a proto-feminist nationalist text: "all those who, whether they acknowledge woman's rights or not, acknowledge woman's influence, must allow that to inspire the future wives of our young men, with the spirit of patriotism through the teaching of a noble example, is no small contribution towards the making of the nation Canada is yet to be."[21]

While money was often to be made from periodicals, prestige and canonicity have been conferred by books; writers of both sexes well knew that powerful rhymes seldom endure without the reinforcement of sturdy binding. Instructive is the fate of Louisa Murray, "the major Canadian prose writer of the 1870s."[22] Although her serialized novels and serious essays were much admired during her lifetime, and the readership for Canadian periodicals was generally much larger than that for Canadian books,[23] Murray's failure to issue her work in book form subsequently rendered her almost invisible. When teacher and journalist Florence Sherk published her only book of poems in 1919 at the age of sixty, her purpose was simple: "I do not want to be forgotten."[24] Less confident was the still unidentified elderly woman who wrote to Archibald MacMechan as "Mrs. Nobody" residing at "No. O Nowhere Street" who tried to arrange for an anonymous vetting of her book of poems, which "persistent friends" had persuaded her to publish, and about whose literary merit she was having second thoughts.[25] Such books were often self-published personal testaments to busy lives devoted to traditionally unrecognized women's work in the family or the classroom, on the farm, and occasionally on the newspaper—activities that would normally produce no monuments other than those standing in the graveyard. In a new country so obviously in a state of continual transition, the solidity of the book, an object both concrete and portable, may have seemed all the more attractive.

A number of literary books by Canadian women were memorial volumes assembled after the death of an established author. Rosanna Leprohon, highly respected in Victorian Montreal for her poetry and serialized fiction, saw some of her novels published as books, but not her poems; the latter appeared in 1881, two years after her death, to commemorate "a blameless and beautiful life."[26] This practice generated a third title for Hannah Maynard Thompson Pickard, who had published two volumes of fiction by the time of her premature death in Sackville, New Brunswick, in

1844. Selections from her correspondence, prose, and poetry were collected by a family friend in a single volume titled *Memoir and Writings of Mrs. Hannah Maynard Pickard, Late Wife of Rev. Humphrey Pickard, A.M. ...*, which was published in Boston in 1845 and distributed through the Wesleyan network in New England and the Maritime colonies. Half a century later, the only two books by Mary Jane Katzmann Lawson, well known for editing the *Provincial; or Halifax Monthly Magazine* (1852–53) and for her periodical writing, appeared three years after her death in 1890. With lesser writers, an early or sudden demise sometimes provided the necessary incentive for book publication. Such may have been the case with Miss M.A. Campbell, whose *Posthumous Poems* was issued in Woodstock, Ontario, in 1865 and about whom nothing further has been discovered.[27] The names of poets who published their verse in newspapers or magazines enter the bibliographical record because their untimely deaths prompted mourning relatives and friends to prepare memorial editions of their poems.[28] Such books fit the pattern of posthumous publications "edited by dutiful executors and relatives, and published privately or by subscription" that Samantha Matthews describes as a "sub-genre" of nineteenth-century literary culture in England. She explains that "Literary and poetical 'remains' flourished in the period: predicated on the author's death, they were composed of selections of poems and other fragments, typically accompanied by passages from letters, and a biographical introduction in which the poet's death-bed, last wishes, last words, and burial-place often featured conspicuously."[29] Examining an earlier era, Margaret Ezell notes that typically such posthumous volumes "are contained within a discursive framework where the printed text stands as a physical memorial monument to the author, erected by his or her friends and justly representing his or her literary merits." Posthumous editions addressed "specifically to those with whom the living author had had relationships" not only created literary authority, but also kept the writer's voice alive in "a continuation of that presence which survives destruction, that matter which the living are permitted still to embrace."[30] In Canada, the endurance of this impulse gave rise to *Figures et paysages* (1931) by Marie-Louise Marmette (pseud. Louyse de Bienville), a collection of thirty periodical pieces assembled by her daughter shortly after the author's death to give substance to a busy journalistic career that covered the first two decades of the twentieth century without producing a book.[31]

The iconic value of the printed word was also confirmed on less solemn occasions. During the 1890s, the Ottawa poets, Archibald Lampman and

Duncan Campbell Scott, shared new poems with their friends in elegantly printed Christmas cards. Among Canadian women, this practice was followed by prominent agricultural journalist E. Cora Hind, who sent her seasonal greetings in the form of pamphlets titled "Tales of the Road" in 1907, 1911, and 1913. Each recounted "some of the amusing, sad, and dramatic incidents which occur so frequently in travelling over the western prairies,"[32] thus establishing her interest in travel writing that would reappear in her later books about her experiences in Europe in the 1930s.

Many of the titles mentioned thus far have been described as self-published. The researcher who investigates archival collections of authors' and publishers' papers quickly learns that most volumes and booklets of poetry and literary prose issued in Canada before 1918 were financed by the author, male or female, a situation that endured well into the twentieth century. Title pages seldom indicate who paid the production costs, and the academy's bias against so-called "vanity publishing" has created the assumption that when a book appeared under a publisher's imprint, that publisher was financially responsible. This was not the case. While the evidence must be gleaned from the fragmentary remains of authors' and publishers' correspondence, it consistently reveals that few publishers ever risked their own money on literary genres (especially poetry) and few authors expected them to do so. In 1944, after producing over a dozen volumes of poetry and stories that spanned more than fifty years of writing, eminent author Duncan Campbell Scott told a fellow Ottawa poet that "he had published all of his books at his own expense."[33]

Such comments attest to the prevalence in Canada of the practice known as commission publishing. As explained in a British source of 1891, "A very large and profitable branch of the publishing business is that known as Commission business, in which the author defrays the whole expense of production, and pays the publisher for his services as agent between him and the public.... It is often the only method to be employed in dealing with philosophical, scientific, and technical works; it is nearly always the only method of publishing poetry; it is also responsible ... for at least three-quarters of modern fiction."[34] The standard arrangement was for the author to cover production costs in exchange for the publisher's reputation, distribution, and publicity. The author might also be expected to arrange for a substantial number of sales. Profits might return to the author after the publisher took his contracted commission on the selling price. In 1905, E.S. Caswell, of the Methodist Book and Publishing House, explained to Nellie McClung:

[O]ur general rule is not to purchase any manuscripts whatever and we may say that most of the stories published in Canada are issued at the entire risk of the author, that is the author pays for the manufacture of the book, that is the printing, binding, etc., and the publisher markets the book for the author at a commission of 50%. [...] The publisher of course does not receive all of this as most of these stories are sold through the trade who generally secure a discount of 30%. Then there is the general expense of running a business to be taken into account, and the advertising of the book in various publications so that it may be brought before the attention of the public. This costs a good deal of money and the publisher when receiving 50% does not receive any too much considering the outlay to which he is put.[35]

For Canadians, the best procedure was to arrange for co-publication with an American firm, as Caswell proposed to do with *Sowing Seeds in Danny*:

[T]he cost of setting the type and binding and placing the book on the market is so great that it does not pay us to publish a story from the original manuscript for the Canadian market alone. If an American publisher can be interested,—and we think you can write to interest one—that big market offers a very attractive field. The stories that we publish at our own cost are in reality reprints from imported plates of English or American books. We can procure the plates very much cheaper than we can set the type.[36]

Records of the Methodist Publishing House for books issued from 1894 to 1914 under the imprint of William Briggs (who held the position of book steward) indicate that the cost varied with the size of the book and the print run, the publisher's commission usually being 40 percent or 50 percent of the retail price.[37] This system protected the publisher and didn't necessarily impoverish the author. In 1905, Hannah Isabel Graham exulted that her booklet, *A Song of December and Other Poems*, issued by Briggs in 1904, was

a decided success in every way. After paying all expenses amounting to about $130.00 I am the happy possessor of a surplus to the amount of over one hundred dollars which is not bad for a first venture. Mr. Briggs says there are scores of Canadian writers who would be in transports if they could say the same. He says it sold better by far than any of the others they published.[38]

While there was no overt gender discrimination with regard to the willingness of a publisher to accept an author's money, the system was structurally discriminatory in that fewer women were wage earners with cash on hand or unconditional access to family coffers. Not many displayed the temerity of Susie Frances Harrison, who raised the two hundred dollars needed to produce *Pine, Rose, and Fleur de Lis* (1891) by actively soliciting subscriptions at a time when subscription publishing was a declining practice.[39] The story of Isabella Crawford's economically disastrous self-publishing venture with *Old Spookses' Pass ...* (1884) belongs to Canada's literary lore. She paid James Bain and Son of Toronto to produce a thousand copies of her little paper-covered book, of which only fifty sold at the price of fifty cents. Unlike the male poets with whom she is historically grouped, she had no recourse to the security of a civil service position like Lampman and Scott, or the safety net of teaching and/or editorial work like Roberts and Carman. Nor, like W.W. Campbell, did she have access to the political connections that, according to a prominent member of the literary establishment, constituted the only "road to preferment for a literary man" in Canada.[40]

Despite its obvious limitations, the marketplace usually had one stall reserved for indigent gentlefolk. During the middle decades of the nineteenth century, literary publication, which signalled education and gentility, offered a strategy that allowed impoverished members of the middle class to solicit charity. Men could raise money this way if sufficiently debilitated by age and illness: J.W.D. Moodie's *Scenes and Adventures of a Soldier and Settler*, published by subscription in 1866, cost five hundred dollars for a thousand copies and netted the elderly Moodies about six hundred dollars.[41] The practice was particularly suited to distressed women and widows, such as "Widow Fleck" and Ethelind Sawtell, whose early ventures are detailed in Chapter 1. By far the most enterprising Canadian woman to try her hand at charitable self-publishing was Sara McDonald, the author of the anonymous *Sabra, or the Adopted Daughter*, written to free her family from debt. In 1858 McDonald took the astounding step of ordering a first edition of five thousand copies; these she sold so successfully that she brought out a second revised edition in 1863, a third in 1867, and a fourth in 1873.[42] Literature was also a viable recourse for writers who were physically challenged. The *Book of Poems* of Euphemia Russell Bellmore, who had the misfortune to lose her sight and a hand, went into eight editions between 1869 and 1874; Blanche Elmore, "born blind," issued six or seven pastel-covered booklets of poetry during the 1890s, their author's disability announced on the title page of each one. Early in the twentieth century, the publication of Pauline Johnson's *Legends of Vancouver* in 1911 was organized by friends who sent out letters to solicit sales across Canada to establish a trust fund for the dying poet.

For women in less stringent circumstances, income from their books brought welcome pin money that gave them a little more control over their lives. Nina Moore Jamieson, whose "business [was] to be [a] farmer's wife" embroiled with "the cows and the children and the everlasting housework," described her writing as her "pleasure" whose profits allowed her to make donations to worthy causes.[43] Rhoda Sivell's *Voices from the Range*, printed by the T. Eaton Company in 1911, bought two stallions for her ranch.[44] Most spectacular was the success of the communally authored *Tried! Tested! Proven: The Home Cook Book*, originally assembled by the Ladies' Committee to raise funds for Toronto's Hospital for Sick Children. First issued by Belford Brothers in 1877, it had sold 100,000 copies by 1885, "said at the time to be the largest sale of any book ever published in Canada,"[45] and was into its 100th edition in 1918.

Writing for Children

As the most common "business" of a woman's life was homemaking and rearing children, the spread of literacy and compulsory schooling through the nineteenth century made it increasingly acceptable and profitable for women in Britain and English-speaking North America to write for young readers. According to one authority, "the first resident of Canada to write for children" was Diana Bayley, an established English author who continued to pen moral tales after immigrating in the 1830s.[46] That juvenile literature was one of the few areas where women could achieve distinction is demonstrated by the *Dictionary of Literary Biography*. Of all the genres and activities covered by this reference series, it was in writing for children that American and British women attained their greatest representation: half the authors in *British Children's Writers, 1800–1880* (vol. 163) are female, as are nearly 40 percent of the authors in *American Writers for Children before 1900* (vol. 42), 36 percent of those in *British Children's Writers 1880–1914* (vol. 141), and more than half of those in *American Writers for Children, 1900–1960* (vol. 22). Figures for Canada, while more recent and less systematic, suggest similar proportions among anglophones. In the Macmillan Company of Canada's list of books published by Canadian authors from 1921 to 1929, twenty of the thirty-six juvenile titles were authored by women, twelve by men (ten by Charles G.D. Roberts alone), and four jointly by a man and a woman.[47] Women's continuing dominance in this area was confirmed by Anne Innis Dagg's compilation of books published in Canada from spring 1984 to spring 1985, in which women wrote 57 percent of the texts classed as "juvenile and young adult."[48]

Francophone women followed a similar pattern, albeit along a steeper trajectory, as indicated in Claude Potvin's chronological inventory of French-Canadian children's literature. He lists fifty-one titles published before 1920, of which just five were by women, beginning with Mme Dandurand's *Contes de Noel* (1889), a collection of Christmas stories, many of which had appeared in newspapers between 1882 and 1884. However, the presence of women quickly consolidated with the advent of the landmark juvenile periodical, *l'Oiseau bleu,* launched in Montreal in 1921. Through the next two decades women wrote nearly half the children's books published in French,[49] and at the end of the 1960s, it was estimated that about 60 percent of French Canada's authors for children were female.[50]

Before Confederation, some anglophone women became writers for children through their commitment to education, even though they lacked the credentials of the schoolmasters and clergymen who dominated the field. These teachers' books, scattered across various disciplines, present an eclectic view of the period. One of the first such volumes was Mrs. Goodman's *First Step in History, Dedicated to the Young Ladies of Canada,* published by subscription in Montreal in 1827, which represents one teacher's determination to "cultivate the mind, improve the temper, and ... excite a *taste*" for history by presenting "extracts of as much of the History of England, as I think necessary for a young lady to commit to memory." Her rather idiosyncratic selections adulate General Wolfe, ignore the American Revolution, and inform students that the distinguishing events of the reign of Elizabeth I were: "Knives first made in England. The art of making paper, introduced. Telescopes, and the art of weaving stockings, invented. Watches first brought into England from Germany."[51] Another teacher, Ann Cuthbert Fleming, published two volumes of poetry in Scotland before she emigrated to Montreal, where she operated her first school from 1815 until 1820 and opened her second during the 1830s.[52] Here she developed a new approach to the teaching of reading and produced four textbooks for her own pupils, one aptly titled *First Book for Canadian Children* (1843). *Little Grace; or, Scenes in Nova Scotia* (1846), the first children's book published in that colony, was written by Miss Elizabeth P. Grove, for many years the proprietor of a girls' school in Halifax, to inform her students about the past and present of their current home. Several more titles appeared in the 1850s, when a Toronto teacher known only as Mrs. Gordon prepared *Outlines of Chronology for the Use of Schools* (1859); in New Brunswick, Sarah French issued *Letters to a Young Lady on Leaving School and Entering the World* in 1855, followed the next year by *A Book for the Young,* an anthology of original and selected verse and prose.

Among these early school texts, the most successful was Mrs. Jennet Roy's *History of Canada for the Use of Schools and Families,* first issued in Montreal in 1847 and praised by the Moodies as an "excellent little work" that would foster Canadian children's faith in the "future political greatness" of their rising country whose citizens were "governed by wise and just laws, and protected from insult and injury, by the maternal love and unconquered arms of Britain."[53] As the book passed through the hands of various publishers—mostly in Montreal, but sometimes with co-production in Toronto and Kingston—it was continuously reissued through the 1850s, reaching its seventh edition in 1864. The first two editions (1847 and 1850) cite the full name of the author as Jennet Roy, thereby indicating her gender. However, for the French version of 1854 it was shortened to "J. Roy," a name that could easily pass as both male and French. This illusion was supported by that edition's omission of the author's preface that accompanied all the English editions, along with the absence of any sign that the book had been translated. In all subsequent English editions, the author's name on the title page remained "J. Roy." The publisher's preface to the updated seventh edition refers to the book as "Roy's History of Canada," a phrase that suggests that the author was assumed to be male. Despite the durability and obvious value of her book, Jennet Roy's personal story remains unknown.

In Canada as elsewhere, women's work as the primary rearers and first entertainers of children also gave them authority as producers of imaginative literature for the young. In this genre, as with educational writing, immigrants played a significant role in establishing the presence of English-language female authors. Most visible before Confederation were two pairs of sisters from established literary families. In England, following the death of her father in 1818, Susanna Strickland published at least half a dozen children's books (mostly didactic fiction) before emigrating to Canada as Mrs. Moodie, and Catharine Parr Strickland (later Mrs. Traill) produced twice that number, her output including nature studies as well as fiction. Like several other British women writing for children at this time, including Priscilla Wakefield (*Excursions in America,* 1806) and Mary Martha Sherwood (*The Indian Chief,* 1830), Catharine Strickland created a story about North America based entirely upon her reading of travellers' narratives. In *The Young Emigrants* (1826), the ease with which the Clarence family settles in the New World contrasts ironically with the difficulties that Traill would herself experience when she undertook the same commitment six years later.

The other pair of immigrant sister writers were Harriet Vaughan Cheney and Eliza Lanesford Cushing, two daughters of Hannah Webster Foster of Massachusetts, author of the bestselling early American novel, *The Coquette* (1797). During the 1820s the Foster sisters wrote several books of fiction suitable for youthful readers before they emigrated to Montreal, within a few years of the Strickland sisters' settlement in Upper Canada. Slightly younger than the well-known American women of letters, Sarah Josepha Hale and Lydia Sigourney, who through the first half of the nineteenth century pioneered literary professionalism for women as authors for both women and children in the US, these four authors found that Canada offered comparatively few literary outlets. In juvenile literature as in general literary writing, periodicals proved a more hospitable medium than books.[54] While the work these women published in general periodicals such as the *Literary Garland*, the *Victoria Magazine*, and the Montreal *Family Herald* was suitable for older children, Cushing and Cheney took a particularly brave step with their founding of Canada's first cultural magazine for young readers, the *Snow Drop; or, Juvenile Magazine* (1847–53).[55] While they wrote some of their own material and published a few items by Moodie and Traill, most of their content was selected from American and British sources.

The *Maple Leaf* (Montreal, 1852–55), the *Snow Drop*'s rival, also featured a female editor when it was taken over by widowed Eleanor Lay after the death of her husband, the magazine's founding editor. This magazine contained additional work from Strickland pens and published Moodie's first piece of writing specifically directed toward the youth of the New World, whose welfare, she declared, necessarily involved her as "the mother and grandmother of Canadian children."[56] However, the appearance of these two periodicals did not generate a surge of local writing for young readers. Moodie's publisher and established market were in Britain, and her six subsequent novels, although not unsuitable for older children, reveal very little about their author's connection with Canada.

The publishing history of Traill's major contributions to the *Maple Leaf* cogently illustrates the problem of trying to develop a children's literature in a colonial society at the time when writing and publishing for children were beginning to flourish in larger centres. Through 1853 the *Maple Leaf* serialized Traill's "The Governor's Daughter; or, Rambles in the Canadian Forest." This sequence of nature lessons, set within the frame story of a newly arrived immigrant family, aimed to acquaint the children of Upper and Lower Canada with their own environment by using the "familiar format" of an ongoing conversation (in this case, between the little girl and her nanny), a mode long established in Britain for teaching science to children and women.[57] In its first incarnation, the story falls into the genre of settlement literature: much like Traill's *Canadian Settlers' Guide* and Moodie's *Roughing It in the Bush*, it offers useful knowledge to assist with the process of settlement and local cultural development. But the work received book publication only in England and the United States. The American edition, *Stories of the Canadian Forest; or, Little Mary and Her Nurse* (1857) removed many references to English class structure, while changes to the English title, from *Lady Mary and Her Nurse: or, A Peep into the Canadian Forest* (1856) to *Afar in the Forest; or, Pictures of Life and Scenery in the Wilds of Canada* (1869) suggest that strangeness rather than familiarity became its main attraction. This book has not endured, whereas Traill's *Canadian Crusoes* (1852), issued in a scholarly edition in 1988, is now the most canonical Canadian children's book preceding Marshall Saunders' *Beautiful Joe* (1894) and L.M. Montgomery's *Anne of Green Gables* (1908). Although its original London publication was arranged by Traill's sister, Agnes Strickland, for a British audience, the book was widely read by Canadian children who enjoyed this Robinsonade as an adventure tale, absorbing its factual details while engaged with its narrative.[58] Cautioning that children allowed a steady diet of fiction would suffer because "superstition, credulity, and a love of falsehood are by degrees established in the infant mind,"[59] Traill ensured that her New World story for children was imbued with useful and accurate information, and acknowledged *The Life, History, and Travels of Kah-ge-ga-gah-bowh (George Copway)* (1847) as an important source.

   Alongside the well-known Strickland sisters perch many obscure early Canadian writers for children, including some still shrouded in anonymity. Most tantalizing is the unknown author of *A Peep at the Esquimaux* (1825), the sole volume of poetry about Canada published for children during the entire pre-Confederation period, who followed the example of scores of her peers by identifying herself only as "A Lady."[60] We might also think of the books that were not written for Canadian children. Both Rosanna Leprohon and Mary Anne Sadlier, accomplished authors and busy mothers, seem to have produced no works for younger readers, an absence that might represent concession to the hegemony of imported books, a lack of opportunity to publish, or simply a lack of interest. In 1865, presumably at her own expense, Isabella Campbell brought out *Rough and Smooth: or, Ho! for an Australian Gold Field*, claiming that her book was merely "a journal written for the instruction and amusement of my own children, which I have thought of too egotistical and personal a nature to interest other little ones than them. My friends, however, think otherwise; and have urged the printing, on the plea, that children like *true* stories better than fictitious ones, and never tire of reading travels."[61] These remarks suggest that much writing for children may remain unpublished and might even be retrievable from archives, such as Amelia Frances Howard-Gibbon's *An Illustrated Comic Alphabet*, created in 1859 but not published until 1966.[62]

Many Canadian-authored titles for children were fictions with a distinct moral purpose. Candy Brown has documented the massive increase in evangelical publishing in the United States over the course of the nineteenth century and noted that purchasers tended to cross denominational boundaries.[63] In both Canada and the US, women became prominent authors of material destined for the shelves of Sunday school libraries (further discussed in Chapter 8), which included books and magazines with prose and poetry by such Canadians as Margaret Murray Robertson, Adeline Boardman Todd, Emma Louise Estey, Hattie Colter, Agnes Maule Machar, and Mary Eliza Herbert and Nellie McClung. In the later decades of the nineteenth century, women became visible advocates for animal welfare, another common theme in stories for children, which was represented in Canada by Annie Gregg Savigny before Marshall Saunders achieved renown with her series of animal stories initiated with *Beautiful Joe* (1894). It is illuminating to observe how the notion of separate spheres extends to the animal story, a genre often associated with children. Male writers such as Charles G.D. Roberts and Earnest Thompson Seton, who focused on adventures in the wilderness, were welcomed into the Canadian literary canon, whereas female writers, who stressed children's humanitarian treatment of domestic animals, were sidelined as sentimentalists.

Few Canadian women enjoyed the international reputations and blockbuster financial gains achieved by American and British writers like Louisa May Alcott and Frances Hodgson Burnett, who demonstrated that the golden age of children's literature, which they helped create on both sides of the Atlantic, was not just metaphorical. Despite selling over a million copies, Saunders' *Beautiful Joe* earned little for its author, whose royalty cheques were "always small and erratic."[64] Nonetheless, in the second half of the nineteenth century many Canadian women writers profited happily from the burgeoning production of family and children's periodicals. Some contributed to Canadian magazines like the *Family Herald & Weekly Star* of Montreal, which published more than a dozen serialized stories by Mrs. Cushing from 1859 to 1879 before turning largely to foreign authors for such material. More critical was the mass of Canadians who wrote for the major British and American juvenile periodicals from 1870 onward. The most common venues for women writers were *St. Nicholas Magazine*, edited in New York by Mary Mapes Dodge, and the *Youth's Companion* of Boston, whose notable proportion of Canadian content expanded further when it employed Canadian E.W. Thomson as revising editor from 1891 to 1901. Describing the latter as "perhaps the most prestigious children's magazine ever published," R.G. Moyles has enumerated some 565 Canadian-authored pieces that appeared in the *Youth's Companion* between 1882 and 1928, including some seventy poems by Ethelwyn Wetherald. Hence he argues the need to recognize the role of these magazines in Canada's literary history in order to appreciate "just how prolific and influential Canadian writers of children's literature really were.... [H]aving no outlet in their own country, they were accepted by such discerning writer-editors as Mary Mapes Dodge, and they gained an international reputation rarely accorded later writers of children's literature."[65] In the pages of these international magazines, English-speaking children around the world read stories and poems by Wetherald, Saunders, Isabel Ecclestone Mackay, Sara Jeannette Duncan, Marjorie Pickthall, and L.M. Montgomery, as well as work by Lampman, Roberts, Scott, Parker, and other Canadians. At the beginning of the twentieth century, Montgomery became the first Canadian woman to earn a substantial income from juvenile literature due to her strategic management of her entry into the large American periodical market.

Professionalism

To be differentiated from the charity cases and the hobbyists is a third category of Canadian literary women—the professionals. Driven by both financial need and a strong sense of commitment, they forged careers that achieved a degree of commercial success, defying the social strictures underlying Robert Southey's 1839 stipulation to Charlotte Brontë that "Literature cannot be the business of a woman's life," and joining the "d—d mob of scribbling women" by whom Nathaniel Hawthorne felt threatened.[66] During the nineteenth century, their models were primarily British and American. But in the first decades of the twentieth there emerged a group of financially successful, popular Canadian women writers who served as beacons to their aspiring sisters. Marshall Saunders, L.M. Montgomery, Marjorie Pickthall, Nellie McClung, Isabel Ecclestone Mackay, Madge Macbeth, and Mazo de la Roche showed that it was possible to earn money, sell their work abroad, and maintain their dignity while remaining in their homes in Canada. Moreover, the occasional windfall of producing a bestseller or winning a substantial prize offered the possibility of prosperity, an inconceivable prospect in the few other occupations open to middle-class women, such as teaching or nursing.

The first such exemplar in French Canada was Felicité Angers (pseud. Laure Conan). Unmarried and not attracted to the life of a nun, she turned to writing to earn her living and became "the sole instance of a French Canadian woman doing so in this field"[67] after bringing out her first book under the patronage of Abbé Casgrain. Following serialization in the *Revue canadienne* (Montreal) in 1881 and 1882, *Angéline de Montbrun* promised to earn its author three hundred dollars if its first edition of 1884 sold out.[68] Subsequent books and journalism, along with a five-year stint editing a religious periodical, led to Angers' financial solvency. Self-conscious about the personal exposure involved in attaching her name to a novel about a young woman's failed romance, Angers approached authorship with extreme diffidence. She explained to Casgrain: "Malgré vos bonnes paroles j'éprouve encore le besoin de me justifier d'avoir essayé d'écrire. Permettez-moi donc de vous dire que les circonstances ont tout fait où à peu près. Ma volonté, je vous l'assure, y a été pour bien peu de chose. La nécessité seule m'a donné cet extrême courage de me faire imprimer."[69] When the original draft of Casgrain's preface contained information that might expose her identity, Angers sent it back, stating, "J'ai déjà une assez belle honte de me faire imprimer. Peut-être, monsieur, ne comprendriez-vous pas ce sentiment—les homes sont faits pour la publicité.—Mais croyez-moi, dans ce que je vous dis il n'y a nulle affectation, c'est un sentiment aussi profond que sincère."[70] From the beginning, Angers declared "Jamais je n'ai permis de joindre mon nom à mon pseudomyme,"[71] and did her best to maintain her pseudonym as a disguise through a prolific career that included some 195 articles in Quebec publications and ten more books. However, this modesty didn't prevent her from lobbying Prime Minister Sir Wilfrid Laurier for government support, arguing, "Si j'étais homme, on me traiterait bien autrement."[72]

It is not easy to document the financial side of most writers' careers. History has favoured only a few with the preservation of their account books or royalty statements; moreover, because money was viewed as a sordid subject, acceptance letters from periodicals frequently announced that a cheque would follow without specifying the amount. Throughout the period under discussion, poetry was most likely to earn money if sold to newspapers or magazines, while fiction in any form was the more reliable commodity despite its lesser cultural value.

Among pre-Confederation woman writers, Susanna Moodie's experience is the most accessible. She came to Canada as an acknowledged author and promptly got her work into the local newspapers, likely without payment.[73] The first twenty-dollar bill earned by her *Literary Garland* writing elicited tears of joy because it signalled empowerment for herself and potential well-being for her children. During the 1840s and 1850s, the income from her writing considerably upgraded her family's standard of living, allowing them to purchase a piano, a concrete symbol of their restored social status, and later to send a son to medical school (from which he didn't graduate). Moodie's *Literary Garland* work, paid at the rate of £5 per sheet of sixteen pages of prose and £8 per sheet of poetry, brought her more than £25 annually over eleven years (1839–50), and from 1852 to 1856, sales of six books to Richard Bentley in London and to De Witt and Davenport in New York earned at least £350 more.[74] Although Moodie never met her English publisher in person, they developed a warm epistolary friendship that follows the model of the Gentleman Publisher outlined by Susan Coultrap-McQuin.[75] Moodie hosted the visit of Bentley's son, Horace, to Upper Canada in 1858 and he assisted her in obtaining a grant from the Royal Literary Fund in 1865.

However, Susanna Moodie's income seems to have suffered considerably from her position with regard to both gender and geography. A comparison may be made with London-based Anna Jameson, who agreed to a fee of £300, described by her biographer as "handsome by the standards of the 1840s," for a one-volume "Companion to the galleries of art."[76] Moodie's records, which are admittedly incomplete, suggest that for *Roughing It in the Bush* Bentley paid her an initial £50 for the copyright, followed by another £50 later in 1852 and £30 more in 1858. On a first printing of 2,250 copies priced at a guinea apiece, Bentley's profit must have been considerable.[77] Two North American male authors who also published with Bentley during this period struck much better deals. Thomas Chandler Haliburton, who had been accustomed to receiving £500 for a book, in 1851 settled for £300 for the copyright to *Sam Slick's Wise Saws and Modern Instances* because Bentley pleaded declining markets for "light literature."[78] Susanna's brother, Samuel Strickland, received £100 per thousand copies of his vastly inferior *Twenty-Seven Years in Canada West* (1853), instigated and edited by big sister Agnes in order to restore her family's dignity, which she felt had been affronted by the coarseness of *Roughing It.* Even more damaging was Moodie's inability to collect anything for pirated American reprints. The cheap Putnam edition of *Roughing It*, nine thousand copies of which were produced by 1854, brought her only ten free copies and an apology from the publisher for not being obliged to give her "a proper remuneration."[79] With subsequent books she attempted to arrive at better arrangements with American firms, but despite her practice of recycling her work whenever possible, she failed to negotiate substantial terms. By 1866 her earnings had dwindled to the point where she was painting flowers and writing to Bentley as a "bold beggar" seeking any kind of literary work. We don't know whether the 1871 edition of *Roughing It* brought her more than two hundred dollars, although she was supposed to receive an additional four cents per copy after the first twenty-five hundred.[80]

During the 1870s and 1880s, the briefer careers of Isabella Crawford, whose poverty was not relieved by the trickle of dollars Toronto newspapers paid for poetry, and May Agnes Fleming, who moved to New York where her agile pen achieved an annual income "well in excess of the ten thousand dollars estimated by literary historians,"[81] attest to the difficulty of sustaining literary activity while living in one country and relying upon the markets of another. The next chapter recounts how, as the century turned, professionals such as Lily Dougall and Sara Jeannette Duncan pursued their careers outside of Canada, their work aimed mostly at British and American publishers and readers. Indeed, so foreign is the notion of professional authorship to the Canadian mind that during the entire period under investigation, the Canadian census failed to distinguish authors as a unique category. In 1871 and 1881, "Artists and Littérateurs" were combined, with no distinction by gender. In 1891, the listing was for "Authors, lecturers, and literary and scientific persons" (the latter are *hommes de lettres* in French), of whom fifty-eight (21 percent) were women. In 1921, the category became "Authors and librarians" of whom 67 percent were women due to the predominance of female library workers.

George L. Parker dates the possibility of literary professionalism in Canada from the early 1890s, with the advent of a commercial and cultural infrastructure to support Canadian writers.[82] If we look beyond the more prominent women cited above we can find an earlier precedent in Jessie Kerr Lawson, whose profile is so subdued that she isn't even mentioned in the *Literary History of Canada* (1964) or the *Encyclopedia of Literature in Canada* (2002), although in 1894 the *Canadian Magazine* described her as "well-known in Canada."[83] A sterling example of Scottish fortitude, Lawson shouldered the burden of supporting her growing family when her husband's health collapsed, first by moving them all to Canada in 1866, and then by exercising her pen. The success of the commercial career launched from her home in Hamilton sent most of her ten sons and daughters to institutions of higher education. Lawson's skill lay in her ability to accommodate her literary products to the available markets. She sold popular sentimental serials to the *People's Friend* in Dundee, wrote a column for the Glasgow *Herald,* and in Toronto published several novels as well as contributing to the *Week* and *Grip.* For each portion of her output she adopted an appropriate pseudonym: "Mona Fife" and "Hugh Airlie" for Scottish material, "Barney O'Hea" for Irish topics, "J.K.L. Washington White" for "subjects related to Negro life," and variations on her initials for other items.[84]

That women could be literary professionals was clearly acknowledged when the Canadian Society of Authors, founded in 1899, announced that they would make "no distinction of sex" and considered it "a matter of congratulation that the feminine contingent of Canadian writers are with us to a woman."[85] Their meagre surviving records suggest that 15–18 percent of the members were women,[86] a proportion considerably better than the literary sections of the Royal Society of Canada, which admitted its first woman with the election of Gabrielle Roy in 1947.

The gender differentials in payment that Moodie endured were generally less overt by the turn of the century. It is difficult to obtain comparable data; the *Youth's Companion* in 1890–92 usually paid William Wilfred Campbell $10 or $15 a poem, a rate consistent with the $10, $12, or $15 paid to L.M. Montgomery, Isabel Ecclestone Mackay, and Marjorie Pickthall over the next two decades. At the *Canadian Magazine,* as with most periodicals, rates were variable and likely negotiable. For one year (1898–99) their highest paid contributor was Joanna E. Wood, who received $12 for each instalment of "A Daughter of Witches." However, this was less than the amount previously paid for a serial novel by Scottish author Ian MacLaren (whose "Kate Carnegie" cost up to $19 per instalment, depending on length) or for John George Bourinot's series on the "Makers of the Dominion of Canada" ($16.66 per chapter), or the $25 per poem that William Henry Drummond commanded.[87] Rates for literary products were based on reputation rather than explicitly on gender. Even though women were implicitly excluded from the academic and political networks and honours that conferred a portion of an author's literary capital, writing offered a fairer chance to achieve economic equality than teaching, where a woman was lucky to earn half the salary of a man.

The biographies of three successful Canadian women writers of the first decades of the twentieth century—who also left adequate records of their earnings—document very different motivational circumstances. Marjorie Pickthall was a single independent woman, Madge Macbeth was left a widow with two small children, and L.M. Montgomery was driven by her determination to protect her children from the poverty and denial of education that had marred her own youth. From the archival business records of each we can draw a few insights into how the interrelation of money and motive determined what and how they wrote and published.

Although etherealized by her admirers, Pickthall, as remembered by Arthur Stringer[88] and represented by her account book, was a hard-nosed businesswoman whose story of financial achievement is outlined in greater detail in the following chapter on the importance of American markets for Canadian women. After the First World War, Pickthall shifted her targeted audience from England (where she was born) to New York, where her American agent expertly nudged the price of her magazine stories up to $450 apiece. In 1920 she earned about $1,500; in 1921 her income was approximately $3,500; in 1922, the year of her unexpected death at the age of thirty-nine, her work earned more than $8,000.[89]

Figures cited by Pickthall and Montgomery indicate that the 1885–1929 period was very rewarding for professional authors who sold their work to mainstream American serials, and therefore especially good for Canadian women who wrote from home. The long-term financial security almost attained by Pickthall was achieved with a vengeance by Montgomery, whose account books tell a different motivational story. Pickthall diligently recorded the specific details of each transaction, but her annual totals are only approximate. Her concern was to assess the market value of each item and as profits from her fiction increased, she submitted fewer and fewer individual poems to periodicals, reserving her poetry to be collected in her books. Montgomery's "Price Record Book," on the other hand, documents more than her business activity. Every few years she tallied her total income and average earnings from each genre in a way that assessed her self-worth as well as her financial standing. During the 1920s, when her books of fiction brought well above $10,000 a year, she still relentlessly calculated her income per poem and per story going back to the "first three wonderful dollars of 1896."[90] Thus in 1929, when her accumulated earnings, now "representing 33 years," totalled over $213,000, she recorded that the average amount per poem over the entire time period was only $3.45 and per story was $26.32. There is an important contrast here that reflects each author's relation to her work.

While Pickthall and Montgomery both thought of themselves primarily as poets and valued their poetry above their fiction, Pickthall seemed quite willing to forego magazine publication of verse to earn more money from fiction, which would in turn buy her the time for poetry. Montgomery, on the other hand, even while earning bundles from her novels, continued to send out nickel and dime poems when it ceased to make good business sense to do so because she felt that she touched "a far higher note in my verse than in my prose."[91]

For Montgomery, making money was both goal and justification. In 1903 she claimed that "I am frankly in literature to make my living out of it.... I know that I can never be a really great writer. My aspiration is limited to this—I want to be a good *workman* in my chosen profession."[92] According to her journal, the relatives who sneered at her writing were silenced by "the *dollars*" she earned.[93] As well, the spectacle of her uncles trying to take over her grandmother's house reinforced her sense of a woman's need for property of her own to counter "the power of selfish, domineering men eaten up with greed."[94] Writing brought money and money brought empowerment: hence Montgomery's impatience with women who failed to make use of the agency that was available to them. In 1909, frustrated with conventional literary heroines, she declared, "The 'patient Griseldas' of women deserve all they get."[95]

Montgomery happily entered the busy realm of Sunday school periodicals and the burgeoning American market for popular family and children's serials, carefully ranking her publishing venues as she constructed and climbed her alpine path to success. In 1903, she had "about 70 different periodicals on [her] list."[96] She advised one correspondent that "The Youth's Companion of Boston, Mass. is the foremost paper of its class in America.... They pay $8 to $15 for good verse on acceptance and send complimentary copy. This is *high price* for verse in America,"[97] and told another that "*The National* of Boston" was "a good second-classer."[98] The *Preliminary Bibliography* of Montgomery's writings documents the tremendous range of serials that accepted her poems and stories, from the *American Agriculturalist* (New York) to *Zion's Herald* (Boston).[99] At the beginning of her career she sent stories to a few Canadian periodicals such as Montreal's *Family Herald* and poems to Toronto's *Ladies' Journal*; after 1915 the majority of her poems saw first publication in Toronto in the *Canadian Magazine, Saturday Night*, and *Maclean's*. However, the vast bulk of her prose went first to better-paying American periodicals before it was reprinted in Canadian magazines. Montgomery saw herself as a producer of commodity fiction, willing to write a "sensational" story if suffi-

ciently paid. In a moment of fatigue during the flurry of publicity following the unexpected success of *Anne of Green Gables*, she asked, "What shall
it profit a woman if she gain a big royalty and lose her own soul!"[100] But
such rhetorical flourishes never halted her pen.

Although her story continues beyond this book's cut-off date of 1918,
it is satisfying to conclude this discussion with the image of Madge Macbeth as a consummate professional woman author. Her career began in
1908, when widowhood suddenly transformed her from a middle-class
wife to a young single mother. It ended with her death in 1965, when she
left an estate worth over $727,000 and was crowned "A literary queen" by
the Ottawa *Citizen*. Although born in the US, Macbeth decided to remain
in Ottawa after her husband died of tuberculosis. Here she cultivated a
personality that was sufficiently polished and captivating to win her way
into the elite dining rooms, both literary and governmental, of the
nation's capital, and qualify for a dramatic portrait photograph by Yousuf
Karsh. As the first woman president of the Canadian Authors Association
(CAA) and the only president to serve three terms, she achieved a success
that was political as well as economic. By 1933, the majority of the members of the CAA were women,[101] yet with the exception of Macbeth, they
were conspicuously under-represented in the power structure of the
organization founded to advance authors' professionalism.

FIGURE 4.1
L.M. Montgomery, c. 1940
(Library and Archives Canada
C-011299)

FIGURE 4.2
Madge Macbeth, photographed
by Yousuf Karsh, 1938 (Yousuf
Karsh, Library and Archives
Canada PA-164252)

Poetry never attracted Macbeth, who claimed she wrote "everything but hymns" and concentrated on journalism, travel writing, fiction, and film.[102] As with most professional women authors, she was motivated less by notions of high art than by her children's growing feet, and she marketed some of her work under pseudonyms to expand her sales. By 1918, aspiring writers were seeking her advice, as "the experiences of those who have got up the ladder of fame are always the sign-posts for those who follow."[103] During the 1920s and 1930s, while Morley Callaghan hobnobbed with Americans in Paris and Frederick Philip Grove established his reputation by fabricating his biography and networking with the country's cultural king-makers (earning the Lorne Pierce medal [1934], membership in the Royal Society [1941], and two honorary degrees), Macbeth, who received none of the above, wrote several novels that have been undervalued because of the gender of their author or their subject. *Shackles* (1926), a "woman to woman"[104] novel about a female author unhappily married to a consummate egoist, presented a Canadian argument for a woman writer's room of her own three years before the appearance of Virginia Woolf's landmark book. *The Land of Afternoon* (1924), published under one of Macbeth's pseudonyms, Gilbert Knox, so effectively pilloried backstage Ottawa life that the few reviewers and critics who knew that the author was not a man assumed that she must have been assisted by one.

Far from enjoying the independent income and room of her own that Virginia Woolf considered essential for a woman author, most Canadian women writers turned to writing to secure both the money and the roof over their heads they required in order to live. Most of their books now slumber in storage in our university libraries; less tangible but no less culturally significant are the uncertain texts of their lives, which both reveal and conceal their authors' motives for getting into print.

FIVE

Canadian Women and American Markets

IN *MR. HOGARTH'S WILL* (1865), the Scottish-Australian feminist novelist Catherine Helen Spence portrays the frustration of educated women who needed to support themselves. Hoping to find work with a bookseller or publisher in Edinburgh, Jane Melville is shown "eight or ten nice-looking girls ... busily engaged in stitching together pamphlets and sheets to be ready for the bookbinder." Upon learning how little they are paid, she comments bitterly, "you have girls at low wages to do what is tedious, and men at higher to do what is artistic; that is a very fair division of labour." The publisher responds, "Nay, nay; I believe our profession, or rather trade, is more liberal to the sex than any other. Write a good book, and [we'll] give you a good price for it: design a fine illustration, and that has a market value independent of sex."[1]

Chronically undereducated, barred from professional training, and conditioned to remain within the home circle, middle-class women who needed to earn money or desired relatively respectable self-expression exercised their pens, whether in Europe or North America. Some who catered to the growing market for family-oriented fiction wrote their way into considerable wealth. American examples are particularly telling: by the 1850s, nearly half the popular books produced in the US were by women, and by 1872 they wrote nearly three-quarters of the novels.[2] *Uncle Tom's Cabin*, "the first of the great global best sellers that changed the marketing and influence of fiction," sold "305,000 the first year in the United States, and two million around the world,"[3] bringing Harriet Beecher Stowe $10,000 in royalties in the first four months after its publication in 1852. Mary Mapes Dodge's children's classic, *Hans Brinker*, sold 300,000 copies in 1865, thus classing her book, along with Dickens' *Our Mutual*

Friend, as one of the two top sellers of that year.[4] Louisa May Alcott, who had the foresight to retain the copyright to *Little Women* (1868) rather than sell it outright for $1,000, achieved financial solvency with her first royalty cheque for $8,500.[5] It is one of the ironies of women's literary history that Fanny Fern (Sara Payson Willis) began her career as one of America's highest-paid journalists with *Ruth Hall* (1855), her bestselling account of the tribulations of a desperate woman writer.

London or New York?

Angela Woollacott has recently shown that between 1870 and 1940, the vogue of attempting "to try her fortune in London" attracted "tens of thousands" of Australian women to the Imperial centre.[6] This trend was followed by far fewer Canadians, due to the proximity and prosperity of the US. The situation of the Canadian writer seeking economic success was aptly summarized in Sara Jeannette Duncan's 1887 assertion that "the market for Canadian literary wares of all sorts is self-evidently New York."[7] If we consider the six major anglophone Canadian poets of the late nineteenth century, we can see the role of gender in determining the possible trajectory of a writer's career. The two Ottawa poets, Archibald Lampman and Duncan Campbell Scott, who were both supported by secure civil service positions, published much of their work locally and mostly at their own expense.[8] The only way for the two New Brunswick poets, Charles G.D. Roberts and Bliss Carman, to indulge their penchant for rather bohemian literary lives was to jettison Canada (and the academic careers toward which their education had pointed) for New England and New York. But the opportunity to be a civil servant, poet-professor, or jaunty vagabond was unavailable to Canada's two leading female poets of the period, Isabella Valancy Crawford and Pauline Johnson. As unmarried, self-supporting women, both lived by their wits and their pens. From her home, first in Peterborough and later in Toronto, Crawford sold at least two serial novels and about two dozen stories to some of Frank Leslie's periodicals in New York between 1872 and 1885.[9] But her primary gift was for poetry, most of which appeared in Toronto newspapers where payment was meagre at best. The posthumous appearance of one poem in *Outing*,[10] the prominent New York recreation magazine that published many Canadian writers (including Pauline Johnson), suggests that Crawford's route to solvency may have been cut short by her sudden early death; in the following decades it would become possible for Canadians like L.M. Montgomery and Marjorie Pickthall to prosper from sales to American magazines, as outlined in Chapter 4. Whereas male poets like Roberts and Carman could enjoy bohemian personas that enlivened their appeal, Johnson's career, detailed in Chapter 10, was governed by a need to avoid any whiff of sexual impropriety, her economic success dependent upon her ability to maintain the purity of her wholesome image as a family entertainer.

Of the generation of Canadian literary writers born between 1855 and 1874, nearly half (regardless of gender) departed and remained outside the country for substantial portions of their professional lives.[11] The enormous attraction of the US stands in sharp contrast to the limited appeal of the UK. While a small but highly visible group of male Canadian authors, including Gilbert Parker, Robert Barr, and Grant Allen, successfully joined the teeming London literary milieu of the 1880s and 1890s, the Canadian literary women who crossed the Atlantic were less likely to blend into the British cultural community. Indeed Sara Jeannette Duncan's rather tragic Elfrida Bell, heroine of her novel *A Daughter of Today* (1894), can be read as a cautionary example to brash North American New Women who might attempt to penetrate the frigidly hierarchical and class-conscious London literary network. Given her journalistic and literary connections in North America, Duncan would likely have joined the Canadian expatriate community in New York or Boston had she not married an Anglo-Indian based in Calcutta. From 1892 until she retired in 1919, her extended regular visits to England facilitated communication with her London publishers and the frequent appearance of her work in English periodicals. But the often biting critique of English society that permeates her fiction (as in the caricature-like figure of Lavinia Tring in *Set in Authority*) suggests that Duncan did not replicate the integration enjoyed by her male colleagues. As she traversed the globe, she took advantage of the opportunities for international publication—in periodicals as well as books—made increasingly accessible through the evolution of the new figure of the professional literary agent, as recently documented in Misao Dean's account of Duncan's relationship with the American firm of A.P. Watt.[12] The one prominent Canadian woman writer who successfully relocated in England, Montreal-born Lily Dougall, represents a very different stream of activity. An intellectual who disapproved of the "modern woman" (the subject of her 1896 novel, *The Madonna of a Day*), Dougall left her native Montreal because the severity of her asthma left her unable to tolerate the city's extreme winters. With an LLA (Lady Licentiate in Arts) degree from the universities of Edinburgh and St. Andrews, she moved in circles devoted to religious and philosophical discussion, especially during her final years when she lived near Oxford (1912–23).

British family roots, preference for publication in England, and the desire to enhance their profiles in Canada account for the English sojourns of two other Canadian women writers of Duncan's generation, Pauline Johnson and Joanna Wood. Johnson's claim that she needed to visit London in 1894 in order to publish her first book belies the pattern of her male contemporaries (Carman, Lampman, Roberts, Scott) who issued many of their early volumes of poetry in the US, not Britain. The homeland of Johnson's Bristol-born mother, England likely beckoned due to Johnson's Imperialist sentiments and to its hospitable reception of fascinating mixed-race colonials like herself, in contrast to the discomfort she felt in the US. As well, London seems to have been the residence of the mysterious lover of her youthful Brantford canoeing days.[13] The plaudits that Johnson collected during this two-month sojourn provided cultural capital that enriched her publicity materials for the next decade. Joanna Wood, whose London visit in 1900–01 included acquaintance with Charles Swinburne and presentation at court, similarly exploited the cachet of her London experiences upon her return, issuing fulsome accounts in the *Canadian Magazine*.[14]

Southward Bound

This handful of Canadian literary women oriented toward Britain was vastly outnumbered by those drawn to the US. As Agnes Maule Machar explained to an English acquaintance from whom she sought assistance in placing her work with English publishers, "we Canadian authors have to choose between trying the United States or Britain, and the *first* is more accessible."[15] While geography was an obvious factor, even stronger were the copious new opportunities for women to work in journalism and publishing offered by the burgeoning American popular culture industry during the last decades of the nineteenth century. [16] Until this development, the usual respectable job outside the home for a middle-class young woman was to teach school, a profession so draining and unrewarding that it was quickly abandoned by almost every ambitious literary woman who set foot in a classroom, including Sara Jeannette Duncan, L.M. Montgomery, Nellie McClung, and Agnes Laut. Nick Mount's analysis of comparative census data shows that over the turn of the century, the proportion of women employed in the US as journalists or writers was almost double that in Canada.[17] Hence it is not surprising that many adventurous Canadian women with literary aspirations moved south to work as reporters, editorial assistants, or readers for American publishers of newspapers, periodicals, reference series, and books. Today we know only about those who retained some vestige of their Canadian identity and, in some cases, later returned. It is likely that many dozen more were simply absorbed into the US along with hundreds of thousands of other Canadian emigrants who, like Walter Blackburn Harte, denied "that there was any essential difference between Canadians and Americans.... The Canadian distinct type is yet to be evolved, if it is a possible evolution."[18]

The list of Canadian-born women who became prominent American journalists around the turn of the previous century includes Eve Brodlique (Summers), who claimed she "would rather be a poet than anything else in the world,"[19] but established her name as a very successful Chicago journalist, and Agnes Lockhart Hughes, also a poet, who became much better known as associate editor of the Seattle *Mail & Herald.* Journalists who returned to Canada after a period of employment in the American press include Lily Barry, Helen Gregory MacGill, Margaret Graham, and Irene Currie Love. Accounts of Canadians who lived in New York, such as Sophia Almon Hensley and the mysterious Countess Norraikow, are now available in Mount's *When Canadian Literature Moved to New York,* which shows that Sara Jeannette Duncan was not the only Canadian literary leaf to be "blown far," to cite the words on her tombstone. In the dissertation that preceded his book, Mount tracked 112 Canadian literary expatriates active in New York alone between 1880 and 1914, of whom more than one hundred resided in the US for extensive periods. (Canadian literary workers in Boston, Philadelphia, and other American cities have yet to be similarly enumerated.) While many were publishers, illustrators, or journalists rather than literary authors, their formal congregation in the Canadian Club of New York and informal meetings in restaurants, bars, and teashops created a critical mass that facilitated publication for Canadian prose writers and poets in the rapidly expanding American periodical and book market. Of the names on Mount's list, less than 10 percent of the men are known to have returned to Canada, whereas for women the repatriation rate was closer to 40 percent.[20]

Sara Jeannette Duncan is now the most prominent of those who spent time in the United States. In the fall of 1885, at the age of twenty-three, she was hired by the Washington *Post* as an editorial writer, a portion of her career that lasted less than a year. The biography of Ethelwyn Wetherald, another creative writer who put in some time doing uncreative literary work in the US, follows a common pattern. While living in Ontario and working for newspapers in London, Ontario, and Toronto, Wetherald earned her first dollars for poetry from *St. Nicholas Magazine* (New

York) and the *Youth's Companion* (Boston). Soon she followed her verses southward, spending the winter of 1895–96 in Philadelphia, where she worked as assistant to the editor of the *Ladies' Home Journal*. Her subsequent position, with the multi-volume *Library of the World's Best Literature*, was well paid at eighteen dollars a week. But fearing that editorial activity "must crush out whatever spontaneous growth of [her] own was still surviving,"[21] she returned to Canada to write poetry while working on her brothers' farm on the Niagara Peninsula. The career of Lily Barry, poet, essayist, and later an active member of the Canadian Authors Association, similarly included a stint of New York journalism in the 1890s. For Hamilton-born Jean MacIlwraith, New York represented a fresh start in middle age, after the death of her invalid mother. From 1902 to 1917 McIlwraith read manuscripts for Doubleday, Page. She enjoyed the excitement of Manhattan and New Jersey, but found that her own career languished in consequence: during the seven years preceding her move she published at least seven books,[22] but during her New York years just two. Her retirement to Ontario allowed her to write two more books and fulfill her craving for "pure air, a garden, leisure."[23]

The biographies of women writers born and raised in Canada who emigrated permanently to the United States present different relationships with their native land. Some, like novelist Hersilia Mitchell Keays, virtually disappeared from the historical or bibliographical record. Although Keays was born in Woodstock, Ontario, and was identified as a Canadian by the *Canadian Magazine* when her new book appeared in 1906, the sole Canadian reference source to include her name is the *Dictionary of Hamilton Biography*. Other writers remained more traceable as they blended into the American melting pot. While the nine books by Ontario-born Isabel Bowler Paterson appear in Watters' *Checklist*, the author was regarded as an American by the readers of her influential book review column in the New York *Herald Tribune* (1922–49); in her later books, Paterson herself adopted an American voice. In contrast, those who felt that their American residence was a matter of economics rather than ideology consciously strove to retain a Canadian identity. Mary Bourchier Sanford, for example, spent most of her adult life pursuing secretarial work and journalism in New York while writing several historical romances about Canada.[24] Still recognized today is Constance Lindsay Skinner, whose poems inspired by the culture of the Squamish people of the West Coast appeared in all three editions of A.J.M. Smith's *Book of Canadian Poetry*, erroneously described as "translations."[25] In 1920, after residing in the United States for more than twenty-five years (since her mid-teens) and after writing many volumes of American popular history, Skinner justified these books in a letter to one of her Canadian admirers: "Alas! Canada has, as yet, failed to provide a market for her writers; and writers must live—at least we *think* we must."[26] Agnes Laut also wrote extensively about the United States for American readers while maintaining a strong connection with Canada (further discussed in Chapter 9). With her income coming from American-published periodical articles and books, Laut found it economically advantageous to establish her residence in upstate New York; the "health" that she cited as one of the reasons for her expatriation may have related as much to her finances as to her physical condition.

Writing from Home

Most of the writers mentioned thus far are relatively obscure and, with the exception of Sara Jeannette Duncan, still quite uncanonical. It is when we look at some of the better-known Canadian women writers of the early twentieth century that we can see the significance of American publishers and audiences in shaping their careers. The women who spent time in the United States were all New Women, for the most part unmarried (Isabel Paterson had a husband who faded rather obscurely from her life), childless, and interested in working outside the home. Most of those who stayed in Canada had children and chose literary work because it allowed them to remain at home—in their own houses, and in their own country. L.M. Montgomery, Madge Macbeth, Mazo de la Roche, Nellie McClung, Isabel Ecclestone Mackay, Lily Adams Beck, and Marjorie Pickthall could achieve high profiles as Canadian women writers largely because the American market for books and magazine contributions enabled them to do so.

Until the establishment of international copyright guidelines with the Berne Convention (which took effect in the British Empire in 1887) and the American Copyright Law of 1891, Canadian authors had little hope of making a decent living from foreign publication of their writing while residing at home. As detailed earlier, the income of Susanna Moodie, who along with her sister, Catharine Parr Traill, pioneered literary professionalism for Canadian women, depended principally on the Canadian market for periodical literature (notably the *Literary Garland*) and the British market for the books of her London publisher, Richard Bentley. The payment Moodie may have received for her fiction from the New York firm of De Witt and Davenport remains unconfirmed.[27] What is known is that the pirated Putnam edition of *Roughing It in the Bush*, of which nine thousand copies had been printed by 1854, brought Moodie only ten free copies and an insincere apology from George Putnam for not being legally obliged to send her "a proper remuneration."[28] This problem was averted during the next two decades by May Agnes Fleming, who became Canada's first bestselling female author, earning well over $10,000 a year by supplying contracted serials to the American popular press. In 1868, she made an agreement with *Saturday Night* of Philadelphia to "write three stories annually at $666.66 each, or $2,000 annually." However, this pinnacle of success required her to relinquish her identity as a Canadian. Her fiction makes few references to Canada, and at the height of her career, in order to be near her publishers, she relocated her family to New York, where "the *New York Weekly* reportedly paid her fifteen thousand dollars for two novels."[29]

The first Canadian novel reputed to sell over a million copies, Marshall Saunders' *Beautiful Joe* (1894), similarly illustrates the need to compromise. In order to publish her story of an abused dog, which had received an award from the American Humane Society, Saunders' publisher demanded that she Americanize both her canine hero and her original Ontario setting. Like William Kirby before her, Saunders came to represent some of the perils of international publishing with regard to Canadian authors' inability to maintain control over their copyright in Britain and the US. Although *Beautiful Joe* was an international bestseller and gave rise to a sequence of popular books about animals, Saunders could not live by her pen. In the 1920s, she resorted to lantern slide lectures on such topics as "Marshall Saunders and Her Pets" and "Marshall Saunders: Her Life and Literary Adventures." She spent her last years in penury and received assistance through the Canadian Writers' Foundation.

Despite Saunders' experience, many turn-of-the-century American readers were quite receptive to Canadian content, or at least to that which satisfied their interest in local colour. Most popular were aspects of Canada that could be constructed as exotic: the customs and folklore of French Canada, tales of the northern and western frontiers (including often stereotypical Indians, Métis, and Mounties), historical romance, and, following the success of *Anne of Green Gables* (1908), Prince Edward Island. Periodicals and publishers catering to American readers were decidedly less enthusiastic about realistic representations of Canada's towns and cities. Hence the combination of American dollars, American receptivity toward popular women writers, American attraction to certain Canadian topics, and the urgent need for story content in the emerging American film industry, encouraged most professional Canadian literary

FIGURE 5.1
Marshall Saunders, 1920s
(Canadian Writers'
Foundation, Library and
Archives Canada, PA-135699)

women active after 1880 to aim their sights at the popular market rather than the loftier realms of high modernism.

Several specific examples retrieved from various archival sources illuminate the general career patterns of women determined to make money by writing for American magazines while remaining fully Canadian. Letters in the files of the *Canadian Magazine,* one of the country's leading cultural periodicals during the first decades of the twentieth century, indicate that many who wished to publish in Canada could not afford to do so. In 1906, Archibald MacMechan, gainfully employed as a professor of English at Dalhousie University, complained that the eight dollars he received for his researched article on James De Mille represented "starvation wages" and warned that Canadian magazines "will not be supported from motives of patriotism alone."[30] When offered the same sum for a story, Marjorie Pickthall withdrew it because she had expected at least fifteen dollars and published the item instead in the *Atlantic.* In a later letter concerning a poem, Pickthall explained that on this occasion, she had "acceded to your unusually low terms because I like to see my verse occasionally in a Canadian publication."[31]

As payment for literary products was based on reputation rather than explicitly on gender, it is illuminating to follow the growth of Pickthall's reputation and income over the last ten years of her brief life once she explicitly turned to American markets. The publication of her first book of poems, *Drift of Pinions* (Montreal, 1913), was personally financed by her mentor, Andrew Macphail (possibly assisted by Pelham Edgar), and would bring her $400 if the entire run of 1,000 copies sold out.[32] At the time of Pickthall's death in 1922 some of her stories were bought by major American periodicals such as *Red Book, Collier's,* and the *Delineator* for more than $400 apiece and her total income for that year exceeded $8,000. Substantial benefits continued to accrue to her estate (i.e., her father) for several decades.[33] Unfortunately, she never did sell anything to the *Saturday Evening Post,* which, according to fellow author Arthur Stringer, was then paying "one to two thousand dollars apiece for short stories." Like Charles G.D. Roberts before her, Pickthall didn't relinquish her sense of identity as a poet, but adapted to the pragmatics of the marketplace by living *for* poetry *by* prose. As well she relished "the feeling of handling money ... one has earned oneself."[34]

Pickthall's success can be attributed to several factors. First of all, the period immediately after the Great War was a time of considerable prosperity for authors publishing in the United States. For example, crime

FIGURE 5.2
Marjorie Pickthall, 1916
(Library and Archives Canada,
C-006724)

writer Frank Packard, creator of the Jimmy Dale books, maintained his residence in Canada as he enjoyed an almost tenfold growth in his income, from \$2,600 in 1912–13 to \$25,500 in 1927–28.[35] Secondly, although popularly characterized as an ethereal poetess, Pickthall was a hard-nosed businesswoman who knew the value of a good literary agent. In 1913, she began to submit her work to English periodicals through the well-known British agent J.B. Pinker, and to New York magazines through Paul Reynolds. Then in 1920 she changed to a more competent American agent who earned every penny of his commission, which rose from 15 percent to 20 percent as he expertly nudged up the price of her work. In 1922 he sold two stories to *Red Book* for \$450 apiece; less than four years earlier these same items had been bought by British magazines for £10 and £12.

L.M. Montgomery's "Bought and Sold Book" in the Guelph University Archives dramatically illustrates that for some Canadian women writers, the American book market could be as lucrative as that for periodical fiction. According to Montgomery, from 1908 to 1911 *Anne of Green Gables* sold about as many copies in England and in Australia as in Canada, but American sales were twenty-three times the Canadian sales in 1908, eleven and a half times the Canadian sales in 1909, and more than twelve times the Canadian sales in 1910 and 1911. With the next title, *Anne of Avonlea*, American sales outnumbered Canadian sales by a consistent ratio of ten to one for the first three years the book was on the stands.[36]

Writing for Hollywood

While good money was to be made from books and periodicals published in the US, Hollywood became a true gold mine at the beginning of the twentieth century. Fascination with a romanticized rural Canada characterized the American film industry as well as the popular fiction market. According to Pierre Berton, "There was a kind of vogue for Canadian pictures before the Great War. The country, to most Americans, was almost unknown and therefore exotic." In Hollywood, Canada's filmic identity was consistently constructed as a frontier environment: "Well over 90 per cent of the pictures made about this country were set either out of doors or inside log cabins or saloons."[37] Some of these scripts and scenarios were penned by Canadians. Two substantial opportunities were available to writers: to sell stories to the movies, or to work within the film industry as a salaried screenwriter. The track record of Canadian women, from what I have been able to discover, was disappointing on the first count. Madge

Macbeth seemed to be on the road to considerable success when she sold the movie rights to an early novel, *Kleath* (1917), for $680, of which she received 65 percent. Unfortunately, the resulting film appeared under the title of Robert Service's *The Law of the Yukon*, with no acknowledgment to Macbeth as author. Unsold copies of *Kleath* were remaindered and Macbeth was unable to interest filmmakers in any of her subsequent proposals. L.M. Montgomery, who should have profited substantially from Hollywood's interest in Anne Shirley, bitterly recorded that her publisher, L.C. Page, waited until 1919, after their relationship had fractured, to sell the film rights to *Anne of Green Gables* and kept the full fee of $40,000 for himself.[38]

More successful with the movies was the Montreal-born, Alberta-based novelist Winnifred Eaton Babcock Reeve, known for her bestselling faux-Japanese romances published under her pseudonym "Onoto Watanna" (discussed in Chapter 10). While living in New York she produced nearly a book a year from 1899 to 1912, the majority published by Harper. In 1903, the New York office of Macmillan paid her an advance royalty of $5,000 for *Daughters of Nijo*, and in 1915 *Hearst's Magazine* offered her $7,500 for the serial publication of *Marion*. That year she wrote her first film serial, and claimed to have won a $10,000 prize from the Chicago *Tribune* for a serial scenario;[39] her later career as an editor and writer for Universal Pictures and Metro-Goldwyn-Mayer began at a salary of $200 a week and progressed steadily upward.[40] As with the New Women of the previous generation, Reeve's aspirations necessitated residing outside of Canada. In 1924 she left her second husband in Calgary and moved her children first to New York and then to Hollywood, where she remained until the Depression cut deeply into the film industry.

When Toronto author Pearl Foley was told she would have to leave Canada to sell her work, she replied, "No, I like it here and I'm going to stay. I want to 'go over' in Canada without having to do it from across the line."[41] For many decades, the American magazine market made it possible for many Canadian women like Foley to have it both ways—to achieve commercial success abroad while continuing to live at home.

PART C

Breaking New Ground after 1875

SIX

Periodicals and Journalism

IN A LARGER SENSE, the title of this section, "Breaking New Ground," applies to this entire book, for the story of women's expansion into the masculine world of print is also a narrative of their increasing presence in the public sphere, a domain essentially defined and documented by print until the emergence of broadcasting and film after the First World War. In Canada as in Britain and the US, the last two decades of the nineteenth century saw a visible acceleration of print activity on many fronts as increases in literacy were accompanied by decreases in the cost of producing and distributing print materials. The more that print became accessible, the more it was used to advance women's visibility and views, not by only the bold New Women who asserted their right to the ballot, education, and careers, but also by women engaged in social reform and more traditional activities in church and missionary work. Women's increasing participation in and use of the primary medium of dissemination and preservation in Western culture involved their physical presence as well as their words: most Canadian women who wrote in English did so under their own names, while technological advances made it increasingly common to reproduce authors' photographs as frontispieces to their books and circulate images of their faces in the serial press. As well, writers in many genres not only gave interviews but also became well known as public speakers. Their oral texts intersected with their publications by providing opportunities to prepare new material and to build audiences for their books, whose sales were in turn enhanced by their author's public persona.

International Contexts

Discussion of the many different motives and causes that launched women into print needs to be grounded in the material realities of opportunities and production. Both before and after the paperback revolution of the mid-twentieth century, newspapers and magazines have been far more abundant than books because they were less expensive to produce and distribute, yet because they are more fragile and ephemeral, they have been less consistently preserved and are more difficult to track. In her analysis of the periodical as a publishing genre, Margaret Beetham points out the paradoxical nature of regular serial publications: from the eighteenth century into the twentieth, serials were at the core of disseminating ideas and change in social, political, and cultural realms (not to mention their relationship with developments in print technology), yet individual issues were discarded as soon as the next came out. In the few titles deemed worthy of preservation in bound volumes, much of the material that attracted readers was selectively removed in an effort to transform magazines into books.[1] Hence we may hypothesize that the impermanent nature of periodical publishing helped to make it an area that was particularly accessible to female authors and editors.

Sarah Jinner's almanacs, issued in London in the mid-seventeenth century, set the Anglo-American pattern of periodicals for women and children becoming the niche in which a critical mass of women first took on significant roles in editing and publishing. Tracing the rise of female editors, managers, and owners gives us a useful measure of women's agency in a realm of print whose purposes ranged from practical communication to social indoctrination to literary cultivation.[2] On both continents, in accord with Margaret Fuller's view that the serial was "the only efficient instrument for the general education of the people,"[3] women established periodicals as literary outlets and as instruments of advocacy in the many causes they took up, including the abolition of slavery, women's rights, temperance, religious advocacy, and suffrage.

In England, the pattern of women founding and/or editing periodicals for female readers was established in the middle of the eighteenth century. Because the extent of women's editorial involvement with the *Female Tatler* (1709–10) remains uncertain,[4] Eliza Haywood's the *Female Spectator* (1744–46) is often described as "the first English periodical written by women for women."[5] Haywood was scarcely alone: Elizabeth Beighton edited the *Ladies' Diary* from 1744 until 1753,[6] followed by Frances Brooke's *Old Maid* (1755–56). The 1760s saw the appearance of at least four new magazines addressed to women readers,[7] including Charlotte Lennox's *Lady's Museum* (1760–61). Examples swelled through the nineteenth century with such notable examples as *Eliza Cook's Journal* (1849–54); Charlotte Yonge's *Monthly Packet* (1851–99); the *English-woman's Domestic Magazine* (1856–64), edited for eight years by Mrs. Beeton; Barbara Bodichon's *English Woman's Journal* (1858–64); Emily Faithfull's *Victoria Magazine* (1863–80); Lydia Ernestine Becker's *Women's Suffrage Journal* (1870–90); and the *Englishwoman's Review* (1881–1903), edited by Helen Blackburn. A bibliography covering the period 1832–67 lists more than two dozen British women who edited nearly three dozen women's magazines and newspapers; this list is supplement by Barbara Onslow's research, which shows that nearly half the women in her appendix of one hundred nineteenth-century British women journalists worked for a time as editors.[8] As the century progressed, British women became serious contributors to the major mainstream magazines with writings on a wide range of political and social subjects, their presence sometimes concealed by the practice of anonymous journalism, which "enabled women to enter the field in greater numbers than was generally suspected [...] and allowed them to address topics not generally thought of as suitable to a woman's pen."[9]

In the United States, a similar pattern of female activity was consolidated in the 1820s. Patricia Okker has compiled a comprehensive list of more than six hundred American women who, over the course of the nineteenth century, were editorially involved in periodicals that ranged from daily newspapers to spiritualist journals.[10] Significant milestones include Sarah Josepha Hale's forty-year editorship (1837–77) of *Godey's Lady's Book*, a magazine of fashion, advice, and entertainment that was a staple in many Canadian homes, as was *Frank Leslie's Chimney Corner*, edited by Miriam Squier Leslie from 1865 to 1885. The enduring New York-based *St. Nicholas Magazine*, avidly read by children across the English-speaking world, was conducted by Mary Mapes Dodge from its commencement in 1873 until her death in 1905. In addition to editing general magazines for women and children, American women, like their British counterparts, founded and ran many periodicals to support both conventional and reformist causes, including Abigail Goodrich Whittelsey's *Mother's Magazine* (1833–48), which reached a circulation of 10,000 in 1837;[11] Amelia Bloomer's feminist *Lily* (1849–54); Lucy Stone's involvement with the suffragist *Woman's Journal* in the 1870s and 1880s; and Clare Bewick Colby's radical *Woman's Tribune* (1883–1909), which "for its entire twenty-six year run ... relied on neither economic nor intellectual support from men."[12]

Journalism and Canadian Women

Canadian women developed their presence in the periodical press along a somewhat different route from that taken by their British and American counterparts. The Canadian narrative is less tangible and, like so many features of our cultural history, follows different trajectories in English and in French. Of the country's *femmes de lettres*, the term favoured in 1920 by Georges Bellerive to describe the twenty-nine francophone writers covered in the first collective study of "nos auteurs féminins,"[13] a good half of those active from the 1890s to 1918 were journalists who appeared in newspapers and other periodicals in regular columns known as *chroniques*, a genre discussed in Chapter 4. Over the turn of the century, in a "véritable explosion du journalisme féminin,"[14] a number of female contributors to Montreal's daily and weekly press went on to establish separate periodicals addressed to women. The first was Joséphine Marchand, whose career began in 1878 with columns in her father's newspaper, *Le Franco-canadien*, and continued in many major newspapers before she established *Le Coin de feu* (1893–96). Robertine Barry's columns in *La Patrie*, notably her "Chronique du lundi" (1891–1900), led to her own magazine, *Le Journal de Françoise* (1902–09). After writing for the woman's page in *La Presse* from 1898 to 1903, Georgina Bélanger went on to establish *Pour vous mesdames* (1913–15), while Anne-Marie Gleason, who had taken over from Barry at *La Patrie*, founded the enduring *La Revue moderne* (1919–60).

On the anglophone side, the story is more diffuse. Following the efforts of several women to conduct literary magazines in the pre-Confederation era (detailed in Chapter 2), there was a decline in their visibility, as both editors and contributors, in English-Canadian cultural periodicals. Women contributed 55 percent of the fiction and 70 percent of the poetry by identified writers in the *Literary Garland* (1838–51), a proportion that soon slipped to 52 percent of the poetry and 30 percent of the fiction in the *Canadian Monthly and National Review* and its successor, *Rose-Belford's Canadian Monthly* (1872–82), and to 29 percent of both poetry and fiction in the *Week* (1883–96).[15] To some degree, this decline in writing for literary periodicals was balanced by a rise in newspaper journalism at the end of the century. Nonetheless, in 1891 Walter Blackburn Harte noted that "There has not been in Canadian journalism the same influx of women into the ranks, that is one of the interesting phases of American

FIGURE 6.1
Robertine Barry
("Françoise") (MS Coll.
00450, Thomas Fisher Rare
Book Library, F5157)

journalism, and the lingering English prejudice against the development of strong personalities, with its natural sequence of signed articles—a common feature of every Sunday paper in the United States to-day—has deterred many ambitious women from entering the profession."[16] Chapter 5 has already shown how the attraction of employment in New York, Boston, and other large cities lured many Canadian women to American magazines and newspapers. As Eve Brodlique explained, "Although my work was being accepted by my home papers and I was reasonably sure of ultimate success, yet the fact that in the States journalism was everywhere recognized as a profession as dignified and worthy as that of a teacher of mathematics or of morals; as equally dignified and honorable for women as for men [...] decided me to go into the Union and cross swords, or rather pens, with the women of the States."[17] As journalism slowly developed into a distinct profession for women in the 1880s, fresh attention accrued to several charismatic young women who achieved Canadian "firsts." In 1886 Sara Jeannette Duncan became the first full-time female writer for the Toronto *Globe*. Kit Coleman's success at the Toronto *Mail* in the 1890s culminated in 1898 in her fame as "the world's first officially accredited woman war correspondent"[18] when she went to Cuba to cover the Spanish-American War. Coleman had made her debut in Edmund Sheppard's upstart *Saturday Night*, launched in December 1887, which deliberately set out to attract women readers by highlighting female contributors and gave a significant boost to Pauline Johnson and Ethelwyn Wetherald, among many others. This weekly paper quickly established "an unusually brilliant social page under the direction of Lady Gay (Grace Denison), which featured commentary on Ottawa social life by Amaryllis (Agnes Scott)," two of Sheppard's many female protégées who went on to become well known in Canada.[19]

Before the 1920s, most of the notable women in English-Canadian journalism pursued their careers as columnists in the daily and weekly press, not in cultural periodicals or women's magazines, despite numerous attempts during the 1880s and 1890s to establish general periodicals for Canadian women. The staples of these various endeavours, most of which were produced in Ontario, were fashion, domestic advice (often with a section for children), and light fiction, which was usually imported. Often glossy and attractive, they failed to attract sufficient advertisers and subscribers to compete effectively with their more stable American counterparts such as the enduring *Ladies' Home Journal*, which was founded in 1883. Long regarded as lacking in cultural or historical value, these magazines survive in fragmentary holdings and have received scant scholarly attention. Little is known about their owners, editors, and many of their contributors.

Examples include the lavish *Canadian Queen* (Toronto, 1889–92), whose contests for readers, designed to generate subscriptions, led to its dubious self-congratulation as "an unprecedented success ... in the history of Canadian Magazines, since our subscribers are already numbered by fifties of thousands in Canada, the United States, and Great Britain."[20] Among the named contributors of texts designated "For the Canadian Queen," Jessie Kerr Lawson and Grace Denison were two established Canadian writers whose stories and poems would not have appeared without due remuneration. The *Ladies' Journal* (Toronto, 1884–96) was edited for three years (1892–95) by Jane Wetherald, who published a few items by her better-known elder sister, Ethelwyn, thereby adding some rare Canadian content to that magazine's usual diet of selections from American sources. Jane Wetherald's acceptance of some of L.M. Montgomery's first efforts gave her early important encouragement.[21] In her career

Figure 6.2
Ethelwyn Wetherald (MS Coll.
00450, Thomas Fisher Rare
Book Library, F5159)

choice, Jane was following the example of Ethelwyn, who had done "most of the editorial work"[22] on *Wives and Daughters* (London, Ontario, 1890–93), a monthly supplement to the London *Advertiser* that E.W. Thomson described as "far and away the ablest literary paper that Canada has ever had."[23] Less is known about Toronto's *Ladies' Pictorial Weekly*, edited in 1892 by Madge Robertson Watt, which ran a series on "Prominent Canadian Women" that included authors Pauline Johnson, Agnes Maule Machar, Maud Ogilvy, and Ethelwyn Wetherald. Fashion was the primary concern of the *Ladies' Bazar* (Toronto, 1887–91?) and of the short-lived *Ladies at Home* (Toronto, 1893), which became the equally ephemeral *Ladies' Companion* (Toronto, 1893).

Alongside these commercial journals emanating from the offices of Toronto's publishing entrepreneurs,[24] many women dedicated to various causes conducted specialized serials with little expectation of payment. Their subject areas reflect traditional areas of women's social and cultural activity, especially in the denominational press. The number of women involved in church-based authorship and publishing well exceeded those known for literary writing and secular journalism, yet few have been recognized outside their specific congregational spheres. Conditioned to regard themselves as handmaidens to their church, the thousands of women involved in the ubiquitous Sunday schools, ladies' aid organizations, and mission societies that proliferated across Canada from the 1870s onward wrote and edited reports, newsletters, and magazines issued under the names of their groups.[25] Some of these publications were local and some were national; titles changed as periodicals started, stopped, or merged over the years. A cognate category was temperance magazines; both are described in greater detail in Chapter 8. While such serials were important means of communication within Canadian organizations, in many respects national boundaries held little meaning. Ruth Compton Brouwer's comment that "A vigorous free trade in religious ideas and activities took place across the Canada–United States border during the nineteenth century" applies equally to the religious and temperance publications in which these ideas were expressed.[26] For example, Sharon Anne Cook found that "The Canadian WCTU distributed five American and one Ontario-produced leaflet series to its supporters," due to the organization's "limited market and financial resources."[27] Most large Canadian churches were affiliated with international denominations, and readers of pious magazines were quite content with material produced in the United States. By the same token, major Canadian authors of Sunday school materials, like Agnes Maule Machar and L.M. Montgomery, were happy to appear in American publications.

While Canada contributed its share to the rise in women's denominational publishing that percolated throughout the English-speaking world, the new wave of female-edited children's periodicals that flourished in Britain and the US in the latter part of the nineteenth century inspired few Canadian examples. Margaret Polson Murray's weekly, the *Young Canadian,* founded in Montreal in 1891, failed to survive its first year despite its initial inclusion of many well-known Canadian authors such as Charles G.D. Roberts and Archibald Lampman. Nor did Canada see the surge of suffrage periodicals generated by the women's rights movement in Britain and the US; Canadian feminists, like Canadian children, were mostly nourished by magazines from abroad.

Serials of regional interest fared better. This pattern began in 1853 when Mary Ann Shadd Cary became Canada's first female newspaper editor with her founding of the *Provincial Freeman,* in Chatham, Ontario, as a new voice for the region's Black community (further discussed in Chapter 10). In 1900, *Women of Canada* cited examples of female editors from coast to coast, from Miss M.E. Bissett, who published the *Cumberland News* on Vancouver Island, to Mrs. Mary McCormick, editor of the weekly Digby *Courier* in Nova Scotia.[28] In Charlottetown, Jessie Gourlie Hogg launched *Christmas Chimes*, an annual that lasted from 1901 to 1908, and in Nova Scotia, in 1905, a retired teacher teamed up with a widow to purchase the Windsor *Tribune*, which the two women ran successfully for more than a quarter of a century.[29] Marjory Lang describes how rural weeklies, often "the glue that held a community together,"[30] became a favoured domain of female journalists during the first years of the twentieth century, with their involvement increasing when the men went overseas during the First World War. On a smaller scale, newsletters issued by students at girls' schools, such as the *Almafilian*, from Alma College in St. Thomas, Ontario, served as training grounds for later print activity. This was clearly the case with *Sesame: The Annual Publication of the Women Graduates and Undergraduates of University College* (1897–1901), whose contributors included many names that would soon reappear in print, such as poet Evelyn Durand, journalists Madge Robertson and Mary Elizabeth McOuat, teacher Maud C. Edgar, and Shakespeare specialist Gertrude Lawler.

Although Elizabeth Hulse has identified the premises and proprietors of magazines published in Toronto before 1900, most editors of late nineteenth-century Canadian women's periodicals were unidentified and their contributors obscure; if named at all, the latter were usually American. As Emily Poynton Weaver noted in 1915, "Many of the press women of the Dominion are engaged in work that is at least partially editorial, but the line of work taken up in particular cases is difficult to trace on account of the fact that the workers are scattered through so vast a country. Moreover, much editorial work is done by women who are in charge of very important departments of publications, which, in the main, are edited by men."[31] One notable exception was the *Canadian Home Journal* (1895–1958), first edited by Faith Fenton (1895–97) and later by Jean Graham. Two of Fenton's articles profiled Canadian women writers Catharine Parr Traill and Agnes Maule Machar.[32] After the turn of the century, the pro-suffrage *Everywoman's World* (1909–22) also made a commitment to content relevant to Canadian women's lives, written by local authors. In 1914 and 1915, Mary Josephine Trotter (later Benson) contributed a series of articles on distinguished Canadian women in many walks of life, including authors Marshall Saunders, Katherine Hale, Jean Graham, Marjory MacMurchy, L.M. Montgomery, Kit Coleman, and E. Cora Hind.

Toward Professionalism

Most of the examples cited thus far demonstrate that while women often successfully ran small publications of local or special interest, their presence in the mainstream daily press remained circumscribed by gender. Hence the novelty of the "Women's Edition" of the Toronto *Globe* on 18 April 1895, an extended forty-page issue organized as a fundraiser for the YMCA that involved, in the words of Jane Wetherald, "All the leading women writers of Ontario, and in fact of the Dominion." For one day, women managed all features of the newspaper office while avoiding the coarse behaviour for which male reporters were notorious:

> [T]he night of the 17th ... upwards of 20 women took possession of the printing office on Richmond St., and literally ruled the roost. Of course they did not take their coats off and sit around in their —— sleeves, neither did they elevate their heels and expectorate indiscriminately.... An efficient staff of reporters, under the able leadership of Faith Fenton, looked after the city news, while telegraph editors and political news editors struggled bravely and succeeded well. At 2 a.m. the last proof had been read.... Then all hands went down below to watch the last form stereotyped, and the circular plates put on the press. It was an exciting moment, and when the papers came rolling off that marvellous piece of mechanism, a Potter printing press, at the rate of about six in a second, we all gave a cheer.... Thus ended the six or eight weeks of arduous labor; but all were content, for now it can no longer be said, "Oh, Canadian women have no business capacity."[33]

The entire project, including the circulation committee, canvassers, proofreaders, and illustrators, involved close to one hundred women, including two sporting editors (Miss Cawthra and Miss Grant Macdonald) and Wetherald's position as advertising editor.[34] Special items included a description of the Taj Mahal by the Countess of Aberdeen, a tribute to Catharine Parr Traill by Sarah Anne Curzon, and a witty account of "A Newspaper Woman's Day" by Emma Bill Buchan of Winnipeg. Marjory MacMurchy contributed extensive reviews of two new novels, Lily Dougall's *What Necessity Knows* and Sara Jeannette Duncan's *A Daughter of Today*, reading the latter as a study of character.

A rare event in a major newspaper whose normal engagement with women was relegated to the women's pages, this women's edition gave the intrepid Faith Fenton her day in the sun as city editor, otherwise a "bastion stormed only in wartime."[35] Such innovation arose because this special edition of the *Globe* partook in a popular American trend. American historian Ann Colbert has documented the phenomenon of women's editions of newspapers from 1894 to 1896, a fad that began in Rockford, Illinois, in March 1894 and quickly spread along the same lines as "stunt journalism and newspaper crusades."[36] Usually justified as philanthropic efforts, these special women's editions were typically much larger than the regular issues of the newspapers and often featured articles by well-known women's rights activists, sometimes with clever examples of gender reversal. Newspaper owners happily complied because the novelty of these editions generated handsome advertising and sales revenues.

Other Canadian newspapers soon followed the *Globe*'s example. The Halifax *Herald*'s advance announcement of a "Woman's Extra" for 10 August 1895, consisting of "eight pages of forty-eight columns, the entire contents of which will be specially written by Nova Scotia women, for women, about women," advised potential advertisers that "A first edition of 30,000 copies will be printed, thus ensuring it a constituency of at least 100,000 women readers alone; and there is no doubt that even a greater number of men than women will read every line of these articles and discuss them for weeks to come."[37] This venture attracted so many contributions that a second issue followed on 1 October. The *Herald*'s two "Woman's Extras" contained stories, poems, and articles on topics ranging from family life to higher education, signed by a roll call of Atlantic literary women and activists, as well as a few external celebrities such as Pauline Johnson.[38] In line with its general evocation of maternal feminism and moral uplift, this Halifax project included an account of "The Evolution of the Colored Woman." Contrasting "the class of negro women in our garrison city" with "the dignity, the talent, the finished manners" of the delegates at a recent convention of coloured women in Boston, the author argued that "the woman that offers the greatest development through the process of evolution is the colored woman."[39] In British Columbia, on the other side of the country, the two major Victoria newspapers overcame their rivalry to enable the Local Council of Women to produce a pair of special editions. The Woman's Edition of the Victoria *Daily Times* for 27 May 1895 included reports from every woman's association in the city and a detailed account of working girls' clubs. A series of interviews with working women described hours and wages in traditional occupations such as dressmaking and in newer areas of employment such as the telephone exchange and food-processing plants. Capstone was the mock solemnity of M. Grant's satire, "The Suffrage Question. Two Views: Fairly Stated from Both Standpoints," which proposed to remove men's right to vote because the responsibilities of the ballot interfered with their primary duties as breadwinners.[40] The eighteen columns made available in the Victoria *Daily Colonist* of 28 May 1895 included Agnes Deans Cameron on "Suffrage for Women," C.L. Davie on "Women in the Professions," and Dr. Mary McNeill on "Women in the Medical Profession." The *Daily Colonist* repeated the venture with its substantial Women's Edition of 6 November 1909, which included an inventory of "Women Writers of the Coast."

In this active climate of mainstream print for and by women, it comes as no surprise that the "Official Organ of the National Council of Women of Canada," *Woman's Century* (Toronto, 1913–21), made a highly visible commitment to women's involvement in multiple levels of print production. Founded in 1893 as the Canadian component of the International Council of Women,[41] under the initial presidency of Lady Aberdeen, the council was a coast-to-coast federation that gathered secular and church-based women's organizations whose interests ranged across art, horticulture, health, suffrage, temperance, social reform, professional status, and education. By 1916, the total membership of the council and its affiliated societies was estimated to be 150,000.[42] In its first decade, the National Council of Women of Canada supported the production of two substantial and wide-ranging compendia: *Woman: Maiden, Wife, and Mother* (1898) and *Women of Canada: Their Life and Work* (1900), the latter prepared for distribution at the Paris International Exhibition (and a significant resource for the book you are now reading). In addition to printing yearbooks, records of its annual meetings, and reports from committees struck to examine a multitude of topics, the council also facilitated the campaign for women's rights by publishing Henrietta Muir Edwards' groundbreaking *Legal Status of Canadian Women* (1908), a book that led to later publications by Edwards on the legal status of women in Alberta, and by Elsie Gregory MacGill on laws affecting the women of British Columbia. The council also inspired Minnie Smith's *Is It Just?* (1911), a story written to illustrate the plight of married women in British Columbia whose property was registered in the name of untrustworthy husbands.

The council's appreciation of the significance of print as the primary medium of first-wave feminism, especially in a country as dispersed as Canada, was bolstered when the Canadian Women's Press Club became an affiliate in 1909. *Woman's Century* self-consciously promoted the power of print, its cover frequently quoting from Psalm 68:11: "The Lord giveth the word: The women that publish the tidings are a great host." Different cover designs highlighted the council's nationalism and feminism. Centred on the cover of the issue for March 1915, in full caps, was the phrase

"MADE IN CANADA," while later covers proclaimed: "Edited by Women for Women." As well as identifying its editors and contributors—all female except for a few men on active service who wrote about the First World War—the magazine called attention to the material realities of publishing and asked its supporters to take responsibility for ensuring its survival. "The success of this Journal depends on the co-operation and support of every Canadian woman interested in the great reforms for which women are working," stated the contents page in September 1915, and listed these causes as "The Just and Humane Regulation of Child Labor; the Cause of Temperance; the Fight against White Slave Traffic; Proper and Sanitary Housing; Pure Milk, Food, and Water; the Care of the Feeble Minded and the Aged Poor; the Reform of the Laws relating to Women; the Franchise; the Crusade against Consumption; the establishment of a Minimum Wage." Printed in a bottom corner of the same page was the witty request: "Would the ladies who are receiving two papers, kindly hand one to a friend or enemy."[43] Later editorial comments asked readers to recruit subscribers, buy shares in the magazine's publishing company, and patronize advertisers. An article on the annual shareholders meeting of the Woman's Century Ltd. reported "very satisfactory progress for the year 1916"[44] and listed the names of its sixteen female directors. Accompanying photos of four of them substantiated the magazine's consistent claim that women were fully capable of succeeding in business and in securing a niche in the country's print culture: "This organ of progressive Canadian womanhood, conceived, published, and edited entirely by women, has now achieved in Canadian journalism, a position peculiarly its own, where it counts as a factor in the national life of the Dominion."[45] This concern with female participation, based on a middle-class awareness of women's progress, seems to have stopped short at the level of material production. Surviving issues of the magazine are silent about women setting type or otherwise working in the unidentified shop that printed and collated the physical journal. In an ironic reversal of patriarchy, it is entirely possible that women occupied the boardroom while men performed the manual labour of producing the magazine.

The Canadian Women's Press Club

Over the turn of the nineteenth century, a time when vastly more Canadian women were employed in schoolrooms than in newsrooms, journalism strongly appealed to young women with literary aspirations due to its greater flexibility, its hospitality to married women, and the romantic aura surrounding the notion of the "girl reporter." Despite the allure of the term "journalist," Canada's official census count of women employed as "journalists, editors, and reporters" was just thirty-five in 1891, fifty-two in 1901, sixty-nine in 1911, and 248 in 1921.[46] In 1900, *Women of Canada* fully identified fifty women working in journalism (three of them francophone) and mentioned knowledge of at least five more.[47] Journalism was generally understood to mean editing or regularly writing for a periodical, but the looseness of the term contributed to the unreliability of these numbers; Marjory Lang notes that they "probably excluded many women who were writing from home or working for family-owned newspapers."[48]

While journalism was believed to pay better than teaching, this was not necessarily the case. In 1884, when the average female teacher in Toronto made $342 and the average male $720,[49] the average salary for a newspaper reporter in Ontario, working sixty-two hours a week, was $550.[50] In other regions, the situation was worse. For example, in 1901, L.M. Montgomery enjoyed being "the only girl on staff"[51] at the Halifax *Echo*, but her meagre salary of $5 a week covered just her room and board. While salaries varied, at the turn of the century $20–$25 a week was probably the best a Canadian woman journalist could hope to earn. The top female journalist in New York, believed to be making $100 a week, actually received only $42.[52] In the lower ranks of newspaperdom women did not earn significantly less than men, but their incomes failed to increase because they were unable to secure the editorial and managerial positions that brought comfort and prestige.

Marjory Lang demonstrates that the remarkable rise of woman journalists at the end of the nineteenth century had less to do with advances sought by women as they entered many professions that had previously been closed to them than with the transition in Canadian newspapers from serving as organs of political or religious advocacy to functioning as commercial enterprises. Advertising overtook sectarian support as the economic mainstay of the periodical press at the same time as women were identified as significant consumers; hence, to build their budgets and their readerships, newspapers and magazines took on the goal of linking producers with purchasers. To attract advertisers, periodicals competed for female readers by hiring women to edit designated women's pages and to write suitable articles. With the remarkable exception of E. Cora Hind, who entered journalism as an agricultural reporter, most of the prominent women journalists of the last decades of the nineteenth century and the first of the twentieth established their identities in the women's pages of Canada's large daily newspapers. The list includes Sara

Jeannette Duncan, whose wit enlivened the *Globe's* "Woman's World" column in 1886 and 1887,[53] and Faith Fenton, who wrote the "Woman's Empire" column in the Toronto *Empire* from 1887 until 1894. Most notable was Kathleen Blake Coleman. She established her enduring identity as "Kit" when her "Woman's Kingdom" page, which began in the Toronto *Mail* in 1889, attracted a massive readership due to her lively wit and addition of science, business, and current events to the usual diet of fashion, housekeeping, and domestic advice.[54]

Although women represented barely 4 percent of the total number of journalists in the Canadian censuses of 1891 and 1901, rising to 6.8 percent in 1911 and 13 percent in 1921, many achieved high individual profiles. According to Marjory Lang, oddity worked to their advantage: in the English-Canadian press "there were comparatively fewer male than female bylines in newspapers, and it was probably easier to win fame as a female rather than male newspaper personality."[55] In both French and English, many of the era's best-known female journalists wrote under pen names. Generally serving to create identities rather than to hide them, these personas asserted professional status and established distance between the women's public and private lives. A few, like Mary Agnes FitzGibbon, who wrote for the *Globe* as "Lally Bernard," maintained the widest possible separation between their newspaper self-representation and their personal existence; others, like Kit Coleman, went out of their way to perform their public personalities.[56] Chantal Savoie's taxonomy of the pseudonyms of francophone women links generational patterns of nomenclature with women writers' struggle for recognition.[57] On the anglophone side, some pen names connoted seriousness, such as Agnes Maule Machar's "Fidelis" and Laura Durand's "Pharos." Those that were playfully alliterative, such as Sara Jeannette Duncan's "Garth Grafton," Lily Lewis's "Louis Lloyd," Kate Simpson Hayes's "Mary Markwell," and Alice Fenton Freeman's "Faith Fenton," implicitly followed the self-mocking advice of mid-century American writer Sara Parton, known as "Fanny Fern": "In choosing your signature, bear in mind that nothing goes down, now-a-days, but *alliteration*. For instance, Delia Daisy, Fanny Foxglove, Harriet Honeysuckle, Lily Laburnum, Paulena Poppy, Minnie Mignonette, Julia Jonquil, Seraphina Sunflower, etc. etc."[58] Ethelwyn Wetherald's poetic "Bel Thistlethwaite," used for her early newspaper work, was the actual name of her maternal grandmother, while irony inspired Susie Frances Harrison's "Seranus," derived from a misreading of her signature, "S. Frances."

Embodying the turn-of-the-century New Woman, female journalists became identified with women's progress not only due to the relative

unconventionality of their own lives, but also because women's achievements were newsworthy. Some members of the first generation of Canadian female journalists, like their American counterparts, not only
reported news but also created it with their exploits, such as Sara Jeannette Duncan's round-the-world trip, which began in 1888. This adventure was partly sponsored by the Montreal *Star,* where Duncan published
the first accounts of her travels, while her travelling companion, Lily
Lewis, sent her stories to the *Week* in Toronto. Such exposure proved a
mixed blessing. While stunts and adventures sometimes placed female
writers on the front pages of the newspaper, most were confined to the
limited realm of the society, children's, and women's pages, with little
opportunity to advance into other departments or into management
unless facilitated by the departure of the men during wartime.

   Women Who Made the News, Marjory Lang's superb study of English-language women journalists in Canada from 1880 to 1945, documents how
the expansion of the women's pages in Canada's major newspapers in the
1880s led to the 1904 founding of the Canadian Women's Press Club
(CWPC), "the first nationally organized women's press club to remain in
continuous existence in the world" and "the first national club of working
journalists in Canada."[59] As with so many Canadian women's organizations, this one was inspired by an American precedent—in this case, the
founding of the National Woman's Press Association in 1885, and the subsequent establishment of regional associations in many cities or states.[60] As
the CWPC quickly grew from the original group of sixteen women to the
forty-four who attended the Winnipeg convention in 1906, to 109 in 1910,
and then to 365 in the 1920s, its members declared that their primary purpose was "to maintain and improve the status of journalism as a profession
for women in Canada."[61] In its first decades the CWPC declared ethical
principles in line with the maternal feminism of the day, a moralistic
stance that subsequently declined as the twentieth century unfolded in all
its complexity. However, the restricted notions of professionalism that
maintained the status of doctors, lawyers, and similar specialists eluded a
group of ink-stained wage earners dependent upon the judgment of their
employers. In the absence of discernible educational qualifications, membership in the CWPC was limited to "women who could demonstrate their
status as paid journalists ... and every year they had to prove their continued activity."[62] Through the CWPC they built support networks and raised
the profile of women in the persistently masculine world of the pressroom,
yet some prominent female journalists, such as Mrs. Willoughby Cummings, were reluctant to join.[63] Nonetheless, the CWPC contributed to a

Figure 6.3 Founding members of the Canadian Women's Press Club, en route to the Saint-Louis Exhibition, June 1904 (Media Club of Ottawa, Library and Archives Canada, PA-138844)

growing sense of community among women writers that involved many who did not qualify for membership. For example, the enduring connection between Nellie McClung and Pauline Johnson, which began around 1898,[64] was symptomatic of the era's ethos of female solidarity. Marjory MacMurchy was particularly known for her generous mentoring, and Madge Macbeth warmly recalled how MacMurchy advised her to take advantage of her Ottawa location by interviewing parliamentary back-benchers before proceeding to better known members of the House.[65]

Whatever the nature of the work, the demands of the press seldom complemented the sustained creation of literature. Emily Poynton Weaver noted that "women often tend to undertake the more literary side of newspaper work,"[66] with book reviews and cultural gossip columns that likely brought some satisfaction. The Toronto branch of the CWPC asserted its literary side on several occasions. In 1911 it issued *Canadian Days*, a little book of "selections for every day in the year from the works of Canadian authors,"[67] and a decade later showcased its own members' work in a collection titled *Verse and Reverse*. The success of this effort inspired a second collection a year later, but the project failed to become the "institution" envisioned by its editor, Isabel Ecclestone Mackay.[68] The prevailing tension between journalism and literature found expression in poet Wilfred Campbell's regret that Ethelwyn Wetherald, who belonged in "the front rank of Canadian sonnet writers," had "given herself over to the drudgery of journalism."[69] Wetherald soon followed the path of Sara Jeannette Duncan in abandoning regular press work in order to concentrate on fiction and poetry. While some women, like Florence Randal Livesay, managed to juggle both realms of writing with moderate success, most who achieved prominence as full-time journalists relinquished their literary ambitions.[70] Kate Simpson Hayes directly addressed this problem in a 1910 article in the *Canadian Bookman* titled "Canadian Women Writers—Have They Arrived?" Of the 109 members of the CWPC, "of whom perhaps fifty depend upon the pen for a living," she found "only twenty who have reached the dignity of authorship, and only seven who may be said to have 'arrived.'" Not wanting to disparage the "poor laborers of the pen, whose 'Women's Page' demands a daily grind of words, mere words," Hayes credited workaday journalists as the foundation of Canadian women's literary activity: "these faithful toilers throughout the land are doing their little best in gathering together the materials, just as the brick-maker carries the clay, shaping it, and making ready for the fires the blocks which shall be used in construction a day later." Hayes declared that "first in order of excellence comes Madame Frechette [Annie Howells Fréchette],"[71] followed by Agnes Laut, and then adroitly avoided further specification of her enshrined seven. Instead, she found a way to compliment every one of the more than ninety women she named, some of whom long preceded the founding of the CWPC.

Whereas Hayes represented the women's page as a press ghetto and at best a stepping stone to distinctly literary writing, critic Chantal Savoie argues that in the French-Canadian press the women's pages functioned as "un salon littéraire public,"[72] where the leading female journalists corresponded openly with their readers regarding literary matters as well as domestic advice. At times their recommended reading contested the prevailing clerical restrictions of the era, but Savoie's compilation of all the writers cited in the women's pages of the major French newspapers between 1897 and 1904 shows a high level of compliance in their very strong orientation toward devotional and Catholic writing, while paying substantial attention to works by women.[73] These journalists also mentored aspiring writers, recommending revisions, and correcting poets' prosody.

Well before the founding of the CWPC, English-speaking women writers similarly promoted one another within the pages of the country's magazines and newspapers. In 1888, the *Week* published Ethelwyn Wetherald's series of five articles on "Some Canadian Literary Women," and Laura Durand consistently showcased Canadian women writers in her enduring "Circle of Young Canada" page in the *Globe,* to which she added the Saturday Book Club in 1905.[74] In 1893, the *Week* quoted Eve Brodlique to the effect that "The largest Canadian dailies have become more liberal, and following the American example have devoted a weekly supplement to literary articles, stories, and poems. This has been the women's opportunity."[75] This trend was exemplified in the *Globe.* Whereas the regular presence of women diminished in the 1890s as the paper reduced its women's section from a daily to a weekly offering,[76] women became increasingly visible in its *Saturday Magazine,* launched in 1889. The *Magazine*'s proportion of female authors, created by such contributions as Lally Bernard's travel sketches of Ireland, England, and France, which appeared in 1904–05, further expanded in 1906 when the editorship was given to M.O. Hammond, who accentuated the magazine's literary content and encouraged many women writers.

It is difficult to enumerate the *Saturday Magazine*'s absolute proportion of women writers due to its inclusion of unsigned columns and articles. In many single issues, named women outnumbered named men as contributors of poems, very short stories, and articles on Canadian history, travel, and human interest. Authors whose work appeared frequently included Jean Blewett, Amy Campbell, Katherine A. Clarke, Katherine Hale, Isabel Ecclestone Mackay, Marjorie Pickthall, Virna Sheard, Sarah A. Tooley, Emily Poynton Weaver, Ethelwyn Wetherald, and Lillian Zeh. During the course of Hammond's involvement, some of this literary content shifted from the *Saturday Magazine* to the Saturday issue of the paper itself.[77] While the magazine paid its contributors less than the big American periodicals, its rates were similar to those of other Canadian magazines, which offered $5 to $15 for a poem; authors of articles were lucky to receive $25.[78] More important for many writers of both sexes was Hammond's personal support, and the sense of belonging to a literary community.

SEVEN

Stretching the Range: Secular Non-fiction

WHILE GENERALIZATIONS ABOUT EARLY CANADIAN writing abound, there are few enumerative studies based on quantitative data, in large part because the bibliographic record remains uncertain. Given the mobility of Canadian writers and their propensity for foreign publication, it has always been difficult to define who counts as a Canadian author and what counts as a Canadian book. Such difficulties notwithstanding, two studies offer a good general picture of women's output in several specific areas. Anne Innis Dagg has identified and categorized a corpus of 965 non-fiction books issued by English-Canadian women before 1946. Her compilation shows that numbers vastly increased after 1885, with fifty-eight titles published up to that year, and 205 in the following three decades. The most prominent subject areas are those associated with the better-known literary writers of the period: travel and description (20.5 percent), history (18 percent), autobiography (13.5 percent), and biography (12 percent). Most of the remaining subjects are also inflected by gender: religion and morality (9 percent), social issues (9 percent), education, including textbooks (7 percent), and homemaking/advice (3 percent). Dagg found just eleven books issued before 1916 that she classified as "science and medicine," accounting for 4 percent of Canadian woman-authored titles published before 1916.[1]

A different classification scheme prevails in Clara Chu and Bertrum MacDonald's study of women's contributions to Canadian writing on science and technology before the First World War, which cites 248 works by 145 women: fifty-seven (23 percent) monographs and 191 (77 percent) journal articles. The larger size of this corpus is due to its inclusion of texts about Canada by foreign authors, and of sixteen travel narratives that contain somewhat scientific descriptions of the "natural history, geology,

anthropology, or geography of an area."[2] In their research, Chu and Mac-
Donald discovered several authors not noticed by Dagg, including Eliza
Maria Jones of Brockville, who issued two of their study's five monographs
on agriculture. Although 145 may seem a sizable number, Chu and Mac-
Donald note that most of the women in their study issued only one work,
and that women comprise just "1.4 percent of all currently-known authors
of works on Canadian science and technology"[3] active before 1915. They
found that women authors' favoured subject areas involved ethnographic
observations associated with travel and settlement, or topics that reflected
domestic life or common feminine pursuits such as botany, natural history,
and agriculture, including apiculture. Here too, literary authors prevail;
two of this study's most prolific writers are Catharine Parr Traill and Annie
L. Jack. The role of such writers was primarily to popularize science and
technology, sometimes for the public at large and sometimes specifically
for a female audience.

Dagg's data confirm that in the last two decades of the nineteenth
century, women maintained the foothold they had earlier established as
authors of memoirs and autobiography, genres that became increasingly
attractive to those with unusual stories to tell, ranging from Charlotte
Fuhrer's sensational *Mysteries of Montreal: Being Recollections of a Female
Physician* (1881) to Emma Albani's engaging and detailed account of her
international operatic career in *Forty Years of Song* (1911). As well, increasing numbers of books reflected women's accelerating involvement in
social issues and their wider range of travel (topics discussed in Chapters 8
and 9). Women's expanding intellectual and social spheres at the end of
the nineteenth century also yielded an enlarged print presence in such
fields as religion, history, and biography. While women were slowly entering traditionally "masculine provinces," their impact on the prevailing
"gender division of literary labor"[4] should be seen as an evolving adjust-
ment rather than an abrupt transformation, a pattern demonstrated in
their changing involvement in education. At the turn of the century,
women's writing of occasional textbooks, which they had been doing for
many decades (as discussed in Chapter 4), became more authoritative.
For example, well-educated Gertrude Lawler, who prided herself on
receiving the same salary as a man while teaching at the newly founded
Harbord Street Collegiate Institute in Toronto,[5] edited two Shakespeare
plays for high school use, with her credentials well displayed on the
books' title pages.[6] As well, women became influential in shaping pedagogical theory and practice. After Aletta E. Marty's book, *The Principles
and Practice of Oral Reading* (1904), was authorized for high school use by

Ontario's ministry of education,[7] Marty herself achieved distinction as the first female public school inspector appointed in Canada. Overall, however, earlier models prevailed. Very little impersonal non-fiction emanated from women's pens and most of their writing continued to draw upon their own experience.

Domestic Education

Adelaide Hoodless was impelled into her groundbreaking work in teaching both children and adults about health and sanitation after she was shattered by the 1889 death of her youngest child due to an infection from contaminated milk. Her dedication to reducing the high rate of infant mortality forged a new path in social education as she headed the movement to establish domestic science as a classroom subject. At the behest of Ontario's minister of education, she wrote the foundational textbook, *Public School Domestic Science* (1898). With the goal of reaching women in their homes as well as girls in school, Hoodless launched the first of Canada's enormously successful Women's Institutes in Stoney Creek, Ontario, in 1897; by May 1914, in Ontario alone there were nearly 25,000 members in 843 branches.[8] This model was quickly emulated in the British Commonwealth and northern Europe, leading to "the largest international rural women's movement ever established."[9] In Canada, each Women's Institute was paired with a district Farmer's Institute, bodies that "had existed since 1884 under the auspices of the provincial Department of Agriculture"[10] in order to provide information about scientific advances in agriculture. Women's Institutes offered courses and lectures on a wide range of subjects, including domestic economy, health, sanitation, child rearing, legal issues, and financial planning. In addition to preparing communally authored cookbooks,[11] their programs were bolstered by signed publications written by members of various branches, produced in collaboration with provincial departments of agriculture. One of the busiest such women was social activist Alice Ravenhill. Following her emigration from England to Victoria in 1910, Ravenhill authored at least seven pamphlets that were disseminated through the British Columbia Department of Agriculture on topics ranging from *Labour-Saving Devices in the Household* (1912) to *The Care of Young Children* (1914). In Quebec, a parallel movement to formalize the teaching of household science was spearheaded by Jeanne Anctil, who brought to Montreal the model of her training in Switzerland in order to open the Écoles Ménagères Provinciales in 1907. Alongside magazine articles, she published two influential texts: *350 recettes de cuisine*

(1912), whose title page proclaims her credentials as "Directrice ... Les Écoles Ménagères Provinciales," and *Livret d'enseignement ménager: méthodologie spéciale à l'usage des normaliennes: résumé du cours donné à l'École ménagère de Fribourg (Suisse)*, the latter issued by the Quebec Department of Agriculture in 1915.[12]

Writing to Inform

Most women who wrote to convey information operated at the intersection of the personal and impersonal. Those with a penchant for research tended to focus their curiosity on topics that touched their own lives and could be studied without institutional affiliation; those who acquired specialized knowledge usually positioned themselves as disseminators of information to the public at large, including schoolchildren. The interests of Canadian women differed somewhat from those of their sisters in England, where Jane Marcet published on chemistry and Harriet Martineau achieved a name in economics. Canadian women with intellectual aspirations became especially visible in the established field of natural history (primarily botany and gardening) and in the growing field of Canadian history, where their writings on many topics had a wider reach than the more limited histories of women for which British female historians like Agnes Strickland were best known.[13]

Along with her identity as a writer for children, Catharine Parr Traill brought to Canada an early nineteenth-century English education in botany that included experience in the collecting and labelling of specimens. Through six decades of publishing about the wildlife of her adopted country, her writings resound with her delight in decoding the Canadian pages of the book of nature, a medieval metaphor that she frequently deployed as she, in turn, captured the denizens of the North American forest in print. In her first Canadian work, *The Backwoods of Canada* (1836), Traill declared that she could make herself "very happy and contented in this country. If its volume of History is yet a blank, that of Nature is open, and eloquently marked by the finger of God; and from its pages I can extract a thousand sources of amusement and interest."[14] Unable to draw, she relied on a combination of denotative and connotative language to represent the plant life of the new world. For example, her description of the "plant in our woods, known by the names of man-drake, may-apple, and duck's-foot" includes its formal botanical name and classification, the size and colour of its petals, fruit and leaves, and the feminine simile likening its new leaves to "a folded umbrella or parasol." She concludes with the housewifely comment that "The fruit would make a delicate preserve with sugar."[15] Traill's magnum opus in this genre, *Canadian Wild Flowers* (1865), was illustrated by her niece, Agnes FitzGibbon, who taught herself lithography for the project. This volume was arguably the first "coffee-table book in Canada," according to the editors of Traill's letters, who point out that "*Canadian Wild Flowers* was a work of female initiative and talent, well calculated to appeal to members of genteel society in Canada West and East, many of whom were willing to buy a book for the high price of $5," albeit their primary interest was probably in its painstakingly hand-tinted plates.[16]

In her botanical work, Traill asserted both her own authority and that of her Indigenous neighbours: "I suppose our scientific botanists in Britain would consider me very impertinent in bestowing names on the flowers and plants I meet with in these wild woods: I can only say, I am glad to discover the Canadian or even the Indian names if I can, and where they fail I consider myself free to become their floral godmother, and give them names of my own choosing."[17] Over the decades, in her writings for children (*Canadian Crusoes*, 1852; *Lady Mary and Her Nurse*, 1856) and adults (*Studies of Plant Life*, 1885) she gave increasing attention to First Nations' knowledge of plants and their medicinal and other uses. Attuned to the contradictions inherent in the process of settlement and to her own complicity in irrevocably changing the ecology of Upper Canada, in 1874 Traill expressly regretted that "with the removal of the sheltering woods must also disappear most of the rare plants, indigenous to the soil, that derive their nurture from them."[18] For many years, critics approached Traill's nature writing in relation to the professionalization of science, and condescendingly described her as an eager but "distant and small player" whose "originality belongs to the gentle way in which she blended her scientific and literary interests."[19] However, the recent turn to ecological thinking now commends her "[insistence] on a holistic approach to the natural ecosystem,"[20] and inverts her position from the margins of Victorian science to the "forefront of natural history and conservation in Canada."[21]

Writing about gardening rather than wilderness made Annie L. Jack a familiar name in eastern Canada, where many households rejoiced when she adapted her "Garden Talks" weekly column, which began in the Montreal *Daily Witness* in 1898, into her book, *The Canadian Garden: A Pocket Help for the Amateur* (1903, reissued in 1910). The book's practical, sympathetic, and often wry style reflects its author's cumulative experience as a successful rural gardener in Châteauguay, Quebec, a contributor of poetry, fiction, and articles on horticulture to many American and Canadian

FIGURE 7.1
Carrie M. Derick (Catherine L.
Cleverdon, Library and Archives
Canada, C-068506)

periodicals, and a happy mother of twelve.[22] Across the country, Julia
Wilmotte Henshaw of Vancouver, who enjoyed a diverse career as a journalist and novelist, became best known for her authoritative books on
alpine flowers. *Mountain Wildflowers of America* (also issued as *Mountain
Wildflowers of Canada*) (1906) and *Wild Flowers of the North American Mountains* (1915) were both designed to appeal to the general public by organizing their contents according to the colours of the flowers, thereby
contravening scientific norms.

Given the accepted role of women in disseminating botanical information, it is not surprising that this was the field in which the first woman
was appointed to the rank of full professor in a Canadian university. Carrie Derick achieved this breakthrough when she was named professor of
morphological botany at McGill in 1912 after significant effort.[23] Befit-
ting her profession, most of Derick's publications appeared in scholarly
journals, except for a series of illustrated articles on Canadian plants written in 1900 for the *Star Weekly*, which reissued them the following year as
a ten-cent monograph, *Flowers of the Field and Forest*. Here Derick created
an appealing resource by softening the technical details of her descriptions with literary citations and folklore. Despite having done the necessary research at the University of Bonn, Derick did not receive a doctorate

because that university did not then grant Ph.D. degrees to women. In the cognate area of agriculture, the doctorate that E. Cora Hind received in 1937 was an honorary degree, the first conferred on a woman by the University of Manitoba, in recognition of her contribution to the development of western agriculture. A self-taught expert on wheat, Hind earned her berth on the Winnipeg *Free Press* by correctly estimating the size of the annual wheat crop. Beginning as an agricultural and market reporter in 1901, she built her reputation as a crop and stock expert so quickly that in 1909 she became the first woman agricultural editor of a North American newspaper.

Animals figure much less prominently than plants in Canadian women's writing about the natural world, even though many female authors dealt with farm and domestic animals in their everyday lives, and occasionally with wild creatures as well. Several late nineteenth-century male writers achieved renown for their semi-fictional informative tales of animal life in the wild—notably Charles G.D. Roberts and Ernest Thompson Seton—whereas women usually approached animals through a domestic lens. This pattern plays out in some of Traill's books for children, which include copious information about forest life. In *Lady Mary and Her Nurse*, Traill tamed the wilderness by creating indoor nursery dialogues between Lady Mary and her Canadian nanny to introduce her readers to harmless, curious creatures such as the flying squirrel and the chipmunk. Famous for her animal stories, Marshall Saunders wrote about the humane treatment of domestic animals such as dogs and ponies, beginning with her bestselling novel narrated by its canine hero, the mutilated dog known as *Beautiful Joe* (1894). This book's audience was astutely assessed by Saunders' London publisher, Jarrold's, which marketed *Beautiful Joe* as a companion piece to Anna Sewell's already classic *Black Beauty* (1877).[24] Saunders's only non-fiction book, *My Pets: Happenings in My Aviary* (1908), recorded her observations of birds and small animals in captivity. Animal welfare was a theme of many female reformers who, like Saunders, were active in the Society for the Prevention of Cruelty to Animals and local humane societies; typical were the two books that Annie Gregg Savigny wrote for the Toronto Humane Society in the 1890s to teach children to be kind to dogs and horses. Unlike most male-authored stories of wild creatures, women's writing aimed to reform human conduct rather than to describe animal life and behaviour per se.

In contrast to the quantity of stories about mistreated dogs and ponies that flowed from their pens, surprisingly few women wrote about their practical experience with farm animals. This sparsity illustrates the extent to which agriculture was a masculine topic, even though women bore much responsibility for the success of the family farm. The dairy was commonly a female domain, as demonstrated by Eliza M. Jones's pamphlet, *Dairying for Profit; or, The Poor Man's Cow,* published twice by John Lovell in Montreal (1892, 1894). It was also translated into French, and brought her an invitation to speak to "the first Congress of Farmers, in the City of Quebec."[25]

More avant-garde was Georgina Binnie-Clark, who wrote two books about homesteading in Manitoba. After her archly Edwardian travel narrative, *A Summer on the Canadian Prairie* (1910), was published in London, Binnie-Clark settled in Manitoba as a solo woman farmer. Her second book, *Wheat and Woman* (Toronto, 1914), recounts her dependency on horses and the obstacles she encountered in a patriarchal order that was not prepared to grant property and recognition to independent women.

The inequity of the legal system that many women like Binnie-Clark experienced inspired the books produced by a number of activists to inform Canadian women about the institutions that governed their lives. Under the aegis of the National Council of Women, Henrietta Muir Edwards compiled *Legal Status of Canadian Women as Shown by Extracts from Dominion and Provincial Laws* ... (1908) and then went on to produce a similar volume focusing on Alberta (1916). Elsie Gregory MacGill's *Daughters, Wives, and Mothers in British Columbia* (1913), produced jointly by the local branch of the council and the University Women's Club,[26] led to her appointment as a justice of the peace and judge of the juvenile court. In 1916, journalist Marjory MacMurchy issued her survey of Canadian women's lives and activities under the catchy title *The Woman—Bless Her. Not as Amiable a Book as It Sounds.* In separate chapters on women's organizations, the business woman, the college woman, the country woman, the woman at home, and women and the war, this little volume documents a period of major transition in the lives of Canadian women, as wartime shortening of their skirts anticipated further expansion of their horizons.

History

Although Catharine Parr Traill found Canada's volume of history "yet a blank" in 1836, within a few decades women began to fill those empty pages—independently at first, and in a more organized fashion toward the end of the nineteenth century. Women's historical societies were founded in Toronto in 1895, in Ottawa in 1898, and in Hamilton in 1899. In 1896, a women's branch of Montreal's Antiquarian Society was established with the principal mandate to restore and maintain the Château de Ramezay.[27]

At the turn of the century, historical societies with "mixed membership" existed across the country, from Halifax to Vancouver; Nova Scotia and Ontario were also home to associations dedicated to the history of the United Empire Loyalists.[28] The rising nationalism and imperialism of the post-Confederation era, which invoked heroic narratives of the past to shape the present ideology and future vision of the new Canadian nation-state, generated a flurry of historical interest on the part of concerned men and women whose enthusiasm produced what one historian describes as "the golden age of local history in Canada." From 1867 until 1920, amateur historians met regularly to read their research papers to one another, and thereby "preserved a vast amount of information which would otherwise most certainly have been lost."[29] Their subjects ranged from well-known figures to ordinary pioneers, and their goal was to celebrate both heroic military deeds and the everyday patriotism of Loyalist families. The relative novelty of the field enabled modestly educated middle-class anglophone women such as Sarah Anne Curzon, the Lizars sisters, Janet Carnochan, and Agnes Maule Machar to write with authority and achieve credibility. Their names, as well as those of journalists like Emily Poynton Weaver, frequently appeared as bylines to historical essays and columns in newspapers and magazines.

Several decades before these Ontario historians became recognized participants in the cultural landscape of late nineteenth-century Canada, two earlier efforts stand out. Female members of Catholic religious communities, like their male counterparts, maintained detailed annals that were sometimes published.[30] In Quebec, such records enabled two cloistered nuns, mères Saint-Thomas (Catherine Burke) and Sainte-Marie (Adèle Cimon), to produce their foundational four-volume work, which was issued anonymously as *Les Ursulines de Québec depuis leur établissement jusqu'à nos jours* (1863–66).[31] Elsewhere in the same province, Catherine Matilda Townsend Day embarked on a mission to record the past of her farming community in order to "bring to a more lively remembrance the hardships and privations suffered by the early settlers to these townships."[32] She collected official documents and personal anecdotes from older relatives and neighbours for two volumes, *Pioneers of the Eastern Townships* (1863) and *History of the Eastern Townships* (1869). Both were printed in Montreal and sold by the widowed author, whose long-term cultural capital as "the first historian of the Eastern townships" would exceed her meagre earnings from her books.[33] A similar initiative was later undertaken by Margaret McNaughton who wrote *Overland to Cariboo* (1896) to commemorate the 1862 trek from Fort Garry in Manitoba to British Columbia's Cariboo goldfields by a group of adventurers that included her now paralyzed husband, who had made the journey at the age of nineteen. In this general effort to establish identity by recording the past, memory itself acquired value, as in Elizabeth Lee Owen Macdonald's series of recollections, "Charlottetown Fifty Years Ago," published in the *Prince Edward Island Magazine* in 1900–01.[34]

Women who worked alone, like Day and McNaughton, tended to base their historical writing on family experiences and local anecdotes. Such writing typifies what Jean Barman terms the "experiential tradition." Lacking university degrees, these writers' "legitimacy as historians rested, at least in part, on their facility at generalizing their own life experiences."[35] Women who belonged to historical associations were more likely to venture beyond the personal in order to contribute to the self-conscious construction of a progressive national narrative that positioned Canada as a significant offspring within the larger family of the British Empire. A case in point is Matilda Ridout (Lady Edgar), whose first book was an edited collection of family letters published in 1890, prepared in the experiential tradition. A founding member of the Women's Canadian Historical Society of Toronto and one of its early presidents, she subsequently became involved in national history as the only female contributor to the twenty-volume *Makers of Canada* series (co-edited by her son, Pelham Edgar, and poet Duncan Campbell Scott) for which she wrote *General Brock* (1904), a heroic biography of the leader in the War of 1812.

It was the opportunity to participate in nation-building—to add the individual bricks of their specific knowledge to the ever-expanding edifice of an indisputably Christian, British-based, northern-spirited Canada— that generated an enduring commitment from an important cluster of Ontario women. Their senior member was Agnes Maule Machar, who sought to reconcile French and English Canada through both her non-fiction and her creative writing, including a poem requesting clemency for Louis Riel. Her heroic tales of Canadian history, aimed at young readers, promoted an imperialistic Canadian identity that was nonetheless in harmony with the United States. Whether writing about the nation as a whole or dwelling on the past of her hometown of Kingston, Machar's writing was characteristically shaped by a "providential view of history," in the words of critic Janice Fiamengo, with "emphasis on imperialism as a Christian enterprise."[36] Stratford-born sisters Kathleen and Robina Lizars began their collaboration by collecting local historical data on the settlement of the Huron tract. They characterized their first book, *In the Days of the Canada Company* (1896), as "pleasant reading" rather than "historical writing," renouncing any claim to learned analysis and justifying their work as a contribution to the need to capture the accounts of old settlers and eyewitnesses before "recollections, like colours, fade."[37] In the Niagara area, teacher Janet Carnochan became a noted figure, the region's role as a destination for fugitive slaves being one of her themes. Her thirty years of involvement with the Niagara Historical Society began when she served as its founding president in 1895 and continued as she led its construction of Memorial Hall in 1907, the first building erected as a dedicated museum in Ontario.[38] Based on extensive research, her writings "focused on Niagara as both the cradle of Canadian history ... and a place shaped by great national experiences."[39]

To the common goal of nation-building, suffrage activists Emma A. Currie and Sarah Anne Curzon added another—to write women into Canada's heroic national narrative. In the words of historian Beverly Boutilier, "it was in order to further the cause of women's rights, and thus to redefine the parameters of female citizenship, that Sarah Curzon initially turned to the writing and preservation of Canadian history."[40] For Curzon, "the Ontario local history movement was a point of access to the dominant male culture. First as an invited speaker and pamphleteer, and later as the founder of the Women's Canadian Historical Society of Toronto, she used the authority accorded to her as the champion of Laura Secord's claim on history to articulate an explicit link between the two political causes that animated her adult life: women's rights and imperial federation."[41] The recent research of several feminist historians demonstrates that their nineteenth-century predecessors' combination of maternalist and nationalist ideologies underscores Laura Secord's current status as one of Canada's few canonical heroines. Boutilier and Cecilia Morgan argue that such works as Curzon's verse drama, *Laura Secord, the Heroine of 1812* (1887), and Emma A. Currie's prose account, *The Story of Laura Secord and Canadian Reminiscences* (1900), constructed Secord as a feminine symbol of "Loyalist self-sacrifice and duty to country and Crown"[42] by celebrating her deed as an exemplary expression of womanhood. Thus "Secord was a heroine not because she transcended the bounds of woman's 'sphere,' but because she claimed the nation as part of it."[43] In Curzon's own words, "To save from the sword is surely as great a deed as to save with the sword; and this Laura Secord did, at an expense of nerve and muscle fully equal to any that are recorded of the warrior." Her desire to set Secord on "a pedestal of equality"[44] accorded with her own activism as a founding member of the Toronto Women's Literary Club, Canada's first suffrage association, and as recording secretary of the Dominion Women's Enfranchisement Association.

FIGURE 7.2
Sarah Anne Curzon, 1891
(Library and Archives Canada,
C-025817)

Now paired with Secord's characterization as the saviour of British interests in 1812 is Madeleine de Verchères, hailed as the Canadian Joan of Arc for defending the French colony in 1692. The lineage of Verchères's memorialization began with her own claim for recognition in two letters, the first written in 1699 and the second sometime after 1726.[45] Her story was preserved in the eighteenth century by historians La Potherie and Charlevoix, and taken up again after her letters were redis-covered in the 1860s, just in time to feed into the nationalist reconstruc-tion of New France as the heroic golden age of French Canada. Like Secord, Verchères became the subject of poems, stories, and dramas. While some of these issued from female pens,[46] Verchère's fame, in con-trast to that of Secord, did not depend upon the advocacy of women or serve as a feminist rallying point.

As the century turned, women produced other kinds of historical writ-ing, often in areas related to their own professional status or public activi-ties. Maude Abbott, one of Canada's first female doctors, researched the history of medicine at McGill University. Teachers and school principals, such as Lilian Hendrie, Maria Lawson, and Mary Ellen Spence, produced new textbooks on Canadian history. The long list of other authors who sought to entertain children with non-fictional and fictional stories about

Canada's past includes Jean Newton McIlwraith, Katharine Livingstone Macpherson, and Emily Poynton Weaver. Women writers' contributions to the late nineteenth-century popularity of historical fiction for readers of all ages both reflected and helped to legitimize their involvement in serious historical research and writing. Many of the female historians whose informative narratives have already been mentioned also wrote patriotic fiction, such as Agnes Maule Machar's *For King and Country. A Story of 1812* (1878), and the Lizars sisters' *Committed to His Charge. A Canadian Chronicle* (1900). Another mode of historical writing concerned women's documentation of their public activities. The appearance of a volume such as the forty-year history of the Ottawa Orphan's Home, a charity run by women since its establishment in 1864, signalled these women's perception of themselves as historical agents. It also gave an opportunity for the book's author, Maria Thorburn, to take public credit for her otherwise anonymous service work: "As nearly all the annual reports have been written by myself, I make no apology for quoting largely from them without acknowledgment."[47]

Most prolific in the sister genres of historical non-fiction and historical fiction was Agnes Laut. Her literary career began in 1895 after she left teaching for several years of editorial work and journalism at the Manitoba *Free Press*, followed by two more years of freelance "tramp life." Her travels through much of North America, including Newfoundland and Labrador, yielded articles for American, Canadian, and English periodicals, and enabled her to collect material and ideas that would fortify her subsequent historical work. Laut's great break came with the instant success of her first novel, *Lords of the North* (1900), which dramatized the lengthy struggle between the Hudson's Bay Company and the North West Company for control of the fur trade as a contest between feudal robber barons. Laut's profits from this book purchased a substantial residence in Wassaic, New York, whose location suited her health and her need to live near her American publishers. While she continued with fictional narrative in *Heralds of Empire* (1902), which was followed by three more novels, she also produced a dozen books of non-fiction, the majority based on historical research, and scores of periodical articles. Her third book, *The Story of the Trapper* (1902), a characteristic combination of history, biography, and folklore, reputedly earned $50,000. In 1908, Kate Simpson Hayes described Laut as "the only Canadian woman receiving 'a man's pay' for a woman's work; the reason of this is, she does a man's work for that pay!"[48] Laut took pride in first-hand archival research; in her foreword to *Pathfinders of the West* (1904) she chided the "slovenly methods" of "pseudo-historians" who had not properly credited the western ventures of Radisson and Groseilliers. Evidence of her status as an historian was her selection as one of just two women to contribute to the "Chronicles of Canada" series edited by University of Toronto professors, George M. Wrong and H.H. Langton, for which she authored three titles.

At the same time as a number of women achieved increasing recognition in the secular public realm as educators and as individual authorities on plant life, education, and history, others used print to advance causes that were more ideological in nature, from religious conservatism to women's suffrage. Some of these advocates, like Agnes Maule Machar and Nellie McClung, were at least as well known as Traill, Hoodless, Derick, Hind, Saunders, Curzon, Carnochan, and Laut; the next chapter situates these more prominent figures within the context of the many others who toiled behind the scenes to issue the mass of printed materials that supported the work of missionaries, temperance workers, social reformers, and campaigners for women's rights.

EIGHT

From Religion to Reform

Women and Denominational Publishing

AFTER 1875, THE YEARBOOKS, reports, newsletters, and periodicals generated by Canada's expanding religious print culture documented a steady stream of activities led and recorded by women. While women's growing comfort with public print is frequently associated with feminist advancement, the establishment of women's organizations with their own executives and newsletters just as often served a conservative ideological agenda. In the words of American historian Candy Gunther Brown, "in recovering women's religious fiction, it is all too easy to confuse the adoption of imaginative styles for doctrinal liberalization [and] the narration of secular experience for secularization."[1] Nonetheless, church activity of any sort could provide a beachhead in advancing the status of women, as illustrated by an 1876 incident involving Agnes Maule Machar, who was already well on her way to becoming one of the country's major public intellectuals. The lively narrative style adopted by the unidentified secretary for the Second General Assembly of the Presbyterian Church in Canada betrays his own amusement as he dutifully recorded the events preserved in the *Presbyterian Record* under the title "Women's Rights." "It is curious to notice how debates sometimes arise in the most unexpected manner, from small beginnings," he opens, "and the readiness with which members spring to their feet on the slightest deviation being proposed from their preconceived ideas of propriety." He then recounts that when "[t]he name of Miss Machar of Kingston was read as the Secretary-Treasurer of the Juvenile Mission to India ... Mr. Laing, Dundas, objected stoutly to the name of any lady appearing in the Assembly Records. He maintained it would be establishing a precedent wholly unwarranted by scripture, and the practice of the Church. It was not to be tolerated." Numerous indignant delegates (all male) leapt to Machar's defence by citing women who played important roles in the Bible: "By whom did St. Paul send his epistle to the Romans? Was it by Titus or any *man*? No, it was by a *lady*.... Let us beware that we do not despise our Phoebes and Susannahs.... Women were found last at the cross and first at the grave.... Had the Assembly not already appointed female missionaries and were their reports not before us?" In the face of such massive opposition from men who recognized their indebtedness to the handmaidens of their denomination, the obnoxious Mr. Laing withdrew his objection, "provided it was not regarded as a precedent." Machar's nomination was then "sustained by acclamation,"[2] and the frequent appearance of her name in print would become one of the hallmarks of the intellectual life of Victorian Canada. A similar spirit of assertion against narrow-minded men informs L.M. Montgomery's oft-reprinted comic story, "The Strike at Putney" (1903). Without overt reference to classical precedent, the women of a small-town Presbyterian auxiliary become lesser Lysistratas when they exercise their previously unacknowledged power by withdrawing their regular services for the church (running socials and Sunday school, playing the organ, and singing in the choir) until the men permit a visiting female missionary to speak from the pulpit.[3]

The massive involvement of women in church-based printing and publishing can be projected from a few tip-of-the-iceberg examples of initiatives in the realm of periodicals that addressed the major Protestant denominations of late nineteenth-century Canada. In 1878, sisters Margaret and Jane Buchan launched the Baptist serial, *Canadian Missionary Link* (Toronto), which Jane managed until she died in 1901.[4] Equally dedicated was Charlotte Geddie Harrington, who edited the *Message* (Halifax) for the Presbyterian Women's Foreign Missionary Society from 1895 until her death in 1906.[5] In 1886, a female associate editor joined the management of the *Outlook*, the official missionary organ of the Methodist Church in Canada. This was followed by Miss S.E. Smith's founding of the *Palm Branch* (St. John, New Brunswick), a publication of the Methodists' Woman's Missionary Society, which was aimed at "Sunday Schools as well as Circles and Bands" and continued under female editorship as its circulation grew to 6,330 in 1916.[6] In the early 1890s Florence Ada Kinton was associate editor of the Salvation Army's Canadian edition of the *War Cry* (Toronto).[7]

While periodicals are often noted in church histories, we know much less about the many individual women who put their efforts into more ephemeral publications such as pamphlets and tracts, most of which have escaped bibliographic control. Bertha-Carr Harris offers a case in point. At the back of her 1892 book describing her urban mission work in Ottawa appears a notice announcing the availability of several tracts at "5 cents per dozen or 35 cents per 100,"[8] two of which she authored. Neither title appears among the items reproduced by the Canadian Institute for Historical Microreproductions, but that collection does include her undated three-page disintegrating text, which was obviously issued as part of an evangelical series of tracts: "Appeal No. IV. To the Young Men and Boys of Kingston" (CIHM 47159).

Early in the twentieth century, Clara Rothwell Anderson developed a lighter vein of church-related literary activity when the first of her comic skits, *An Old Time Ladies' Aid Business Meeting at Mohawk Crossroads*, proved such a hit at a fundraising event for the Ladies' Aid Society of her husband's Presbyterian congregation in Shelburne, Ontario, that it was remounted many times by similar organizations. Anderson cleverly circumvented conservative distrust of the theatre by replacing the objectionable word "play" with the vaguer term "character sketch entertainment" as she self-published more than a dozen separate titles from 1912 into the 1920s. Strict control over her copyrights and royalties brought significant profits, which she donated to charity during wartime.[9] Theatre historian Kym Bird characterizes Anderson's clever plays as "domestic feminist comedy" written in the language of "Christian responsibility" and based on the principles of the Social Gospel.[10]

More serious were the publications that burgeoned from women's two major fields of activity: the missionary movement and the Sunday school movement. According to historian Mary Anne MacFarlane, "of the more than 33,000 volunteers who worked in Methodist Sunday schools in 1902, four-fifths were women," yet despite their numbers, women remained in subordinate positions within the schools' management.[11] Sunday schools' ongoing need for pedagogical material generated scores of sectarian periodicals for teachers and different age groups of children; their contents, often unsigned, ranged from Bible lessons to original fiction. As well as being the primary users of these magazines, women were also involved in many levels of their production. For example, in 1898 Jane Wells Fraser became her father's general assistant when he was appointed editor and business manager of Sunday school publications for the Presbyterian Church of Canada, and went on to become managing editor of *East and West: A Paper for Young Canadians* upon its founding in 1902.[12] This periodical published one of the first pieces written by Nellie McClung, whose career began in 1904 with stories, anecdotes, and poems in a variety of Methodist and Presbyterian Sunday school periodicals, including *Happy Days, Onward: A Paper for Young People,* and *Playmate.*

By the time McClung picked up her pen at the beginning of the twentieth century, Canadian women had been writing Sunday school material for many decades. Before their immigration to Montreal in the 1840s, the Boston-based Foster sisters, Harriet Vaughan Cheney and Eliza Lanesford Cushing, had collaborated on *The Sunday School or Village Sketches,* published in Andover in 1820 "for the Sabbath readings of children."[13] The first such book written in Canada may well be Eliza Field Jones's *Memoir of Elizabeth Jones, a Little Indian Girl Who Lived at the River-Credit Mission, Upper Canada,* an account of the death of her pious niece that was published in London in 1838. Agnes Maule Machar became one of the country's most prominent authors of Sunday school fiction, beginning with *Katie Johnstone's Cross: A Canadian Tale* (1870), which won a publisher's competition for "the book best suited to the needs of the Sunday School library."[14] As the Sunday school movement expanded toward the end of the nineteenth century, so too did the list of Canadian women who contributed to American and Canadian Sunday school periodicals or to publishers' series of Sunday school fiction. While most who wrote solely for this audience remain obscure, the size and stability of the Sunday school market provided a firm starting ground for a number of recognized novelists, including Margaret Murray Robertson, Marian Keith, and L.M. Montgomery.

Especially dramatic was the growth of women's missionary societies, "the first great national organisations to develop among women in Canada," whose membership, in all denominations, was estimated in 1916 to be "not under 200,000."[15] Once the mission field identified "heathen women and children" as a significant target, it mobilized dedicated Canadian women to join foreign efforts and other "women and children of the Church" to support their endeavours with "prayers and free-will offerings."[16] The numbers of women involved abroad as well as at home were astonishing. According to historian Ruth Compton Brouwer, "single women missionaries and missionary wives outnumbered their male colleagues in many overseas fields."[17] The same was true of Anglican missions to Canada's North, even though "[m]issionary work was ... thought of as men's work."[18] Throughout the English-speaking world, missionary accounts became popular reading because "they combined a sense of the exotic with notions of benevolent evangelism, which was connected to the romanticization of mission work."[19] Publications supporting missionary movements recognized the emotional power of eyewitness "word-pictures"[20] from individual authors, for whom such writing was an important component of their calling. One notable example was Hannah Maria Norris Armstrong, a Nova Scotian Baptist who documented her forty years in Burma and India in letters that were published in a number of Canadian and American missionary journals.[21]

From its inception in 1876, the Women's Foreign Mission Society of the Presbyterian Church in Canada gave prominence to "the circulation of missionary intelligence" and quickly proceeded from painstaking dissemination in manuscript to efficient distribution in print:

> At first letters from missionaries were copied by hand and sent out, and in the second year duplicates were reproduced by members of the Society in Toronto and a copy sent to each Auxiliary secretary, to be read at the monthly meetings. These letters were a most effective means of arousing interest. To the majority who heard them their contents were nothing less than a revelation, so little was then known of the condition of heathen women. The *Monthly Letter Leaflet* first appeared under that name in 1884. The cost was 12 cents per year.

In 1901, the total number of Presbyterian *Letter Leaflets, Foreign Missionary Tidings*, and various pamphlets issued since 1881 was reported to be 2,348,557, which generated nearly $5,000 in profits for the "general fund."[22] By 1914, the monthly circulation of *Foreign Missionary Tidings* was over 27,000, "a figure, its editor claimed, that exceeded the circulation of any comparable publication in Britain or the United States."[23] Other denominations similarly stressed dissemination through print. In 1917, retrospectively assessing the history of the Woman's Missionary Society of the Methodist Church in Canada, Mrs. E.S. Strachan identified its Literature and Publication Department as "the great grand-trunk nerve system of the organization, sending out life-currents to its remotest parts."[24] Such examples indicate that in Canada, Protestant women's expansion into print followed the pattern of American missionary women outlined in Sarah Robbins' analysis of a three-stage evolution: from personal handwritten letters, to small-scale manuscript and print dissemination, to "far more ambitious business enterprises with some professional paid staffs." Technological development was accompanied by a shift in the writers' mode of address, with "much of the writing produced by missionaries stationed abroad [...] prepared, from its very first drafting, with the idea that it would be quickly seen in print by many readers."[25]

In Canada, this mass of sectarian print yielded relatively few books. As with earlier non-fiction, most of the late nineteenth-century religious volumes written by women derived from their authors' personal experiences.

Widows composed memoirs of their deceased clerical husbands, daughters wrote biographies of their pioneer preacher fathers, and Katherine Hughes paid tribute to her uncle, Cornelius O'Brien, who had been archbishop of Halifax.[26] Other women memorialized beloved pastors or composed histories of their own parishes or religious orders.[27] Central to Jane Agar Hopper's researched history of *Old-Time Primitive Methodism in Canada* (1904) were her own recollections of revival meetings and of specific individuals ranging from colourful local preachers, who sometimes invented Biblical texts to suit their purpose, to her own godly mother. Most dramatic were her childhood memories: "I felt myself from my earliest days a terribly wicked sinner. [...] I have never wanted to be a child again to wrestle day and night with such mental turmoil. These thoughts embittered my childhood. I had a strong imagination, and the terrors of the law were never shown forth, that my mind did not improve upon the statement."[28] Several women wrote religious history that was less directly connected with their personal experience, as when Janet Carnochan published the story of a Niagara church that was not the one she attended (the Anglican St. Mark's) before turning to her own (the Presbyterian St. Andrew's),[29] and Katherine Hughes drew on her journalistic and archival experience to pen a lively biography of Father Albert Lacombe, the Oblate missionary whom she characterized as "the black-robe voyageur."[30]

Only a small proportion of these woman-authored historical and biographical texts told stories of female religious figures. Those in the Protestant tradition featured extraordinary women active on the outskirts of the established denominations, such as Methodist folk healer Ann Preston and Salvation Army activist Ada Kinton, whose memoirs were posthumously edited by her sister.[31] Stories of Catholic women sometimes bridged the two languages, as with Mary Margaret Drummond's life of Marguerite Bourgeoys, which appeared in both English and French.[32] More complex interaction underscored the work of Mother Ste-Croix (Josephine Holmes), who published anonymously as "Member of the Community." Her first book, the *Life of Madame de La Peltrie* (1859), founder of the Ursulines, was written for the convent's pupils, followed by several volumes on the history of the order. Her account in English, based on the earlier French-language history by mères Saint-Thomas (Catherine Burke) and Sainte-Marie (Adèle Cimon), was written "to correct many erroneous statements" and to "revive and refresh" former students' "sweetest reminiscences."[33] A different "Member of the Community," identified only as "a Sister of Loretto Abbey," issued the *Life and Letters of Rev. Mother Theresa Dease* (1916).

Most novel and appealing in the decades surrounding the turn of the nineteenth century were several volumes of letters and memoirs by women whose missionary zeal sent them overseas. Aptly characterized by Ruth Compton Brouwer as "New Women for God," they recounted their own agency in pursuing their goals, which often included advanced training in medicine and languages in preparation for their mission work. Their narratives of travel and adventure, which reached a huge audience, could be as exotic and exciting as the exploits of secular New Women like Sara Jeannette Duncan, and often documented greater personal risk. For example, one copy of Matilda Faulkner Churchill's *Letters from My Home in India* (1916) was placed in every Baptist Sunday school, even though its depiction of extreme poverty, the restricted lives of upper-caste women, and the missionaries' minimal success in making converts were not the usual fare for young readers. First-hand accounts of women's activity in home missions were less frequently published as books; a rare example is Bertha Carr-Harris's 1892 description of evangelical work with children, the elderly, and prisoners in Ottawa, including the founding of a Home for Friendless Women.[34]

Some of these missionary women encountered great danger and endured terrible losses, primarily from the poor sanitation and lethal diseases that threatened their health and the lives of their children. Three of Churchill's four children died in India, and Susie Carson Rijnhart buried her toddler son in the mountains near Tibet. Born in Chatham, Ontario, Susanna Carson was one of the first women to obtain an MD in Canada before she married Petrus Rijnhart, a Dutch-born charismatic enthusiast of dubious credentials who was determined to preach the gospel in Lhasa. Susie Rijnhart's low-key, often scholarly style in *With the Tibetans in Tent and Temple* (1901) draws on previous books about the region and downplays the extraordinary nature of her four years' sojourn in northwestern China, where she saved many more lives than souls. Her medical knowledge was put to unexpected use when the Rijnharts found themselves in the midst of a violent conflict between Muslims and Chinese, which cost about 100,000 lives. With the eye of the ethnographer, she determined to correct previous accounts of Tibetan religious and cultural customs, which she recorded in great detail. Despite her disparagement of "heathen" practices, Rijnhart argued that Christian missionaries "need to recognize and rejoice in the great underlying truths of all religions."[35] The final part of her book, which describes her harrowing return journey after expulsion from Tibet, desertion by her guides, and the murder of her husband, becomes increasingly compelling and demonstrates a literary talent that might well have been further exercised if Susie Rijnhart had lived past the age of forty.

Advocacy and Reform

In her study of the Anglo-American literature of social reform, Amanda Claybaugh points out that the medium of print was essential to the ability of nineteenth-century reform movements to make their case, as "social problems must be represented before they can be solved."[36] We have already seen the effectiveness of such representation in missionary writing and in the stories of abused animals that garnered support for the humane movement. The larger the social cause, the more print it generated, and one of the biggest was the prohibition of alcohol.

Most of the women who mobilized under the banner of religious commitment also shared a strong allegiance to the temperance movement. Canadians of both sexes wrote literary texts about the evils of strong drink many decades before the establishment of the first Canadian branch of the Women's Christian Temperance Union (WCTU) in Ontario in December 1874, just one month after the founding conference of the Americans' National WCTU in Cleveland.[37] For example, pre-Confederation readers in Nova Scotia had several opportunities to read Sarah Herbert's story, "Agnes Maitland. A Temperance Tale," which appeared both serially and as a pamphlet after it won a fiction contest sponsored by the *Olive Branch* (Halifax) in 1843. Pamelia Vining Yule's poem, "The Drunkard's Child" (1863), typifies the genre of temperance literature in its emotional description of the agony of a little girl who freezes to death after being abandoned by her alcoholic father. Such fiction and verse demonstrate temperance advocates' skilful deployment of sentimentality to illustrate the victimization of women and children by drinking men. While sometimes viewed as a women's issue, the movement also attracted many men; in his anthology of *Selections from Canadian Poets* (1864), editor Rev. E.H. Dewart represented the subject with a poem by Montreal author, Isidore Ascher, titled simply "Drink." The temperance cause became a particular rallying point for women at the end of the nineteenth century because of the way it dovetailed with the suffrage movement and other reform issues in what historian Sharon Anne Cook describes as the "liberated climate for women that some scholars have termed 'evangelical feminism.'"[38]

As the WCTU mushroomed in Canada, by 1882 boasting a base of ninety-six branches and 2500 members in Ontario alone,[39] its leaders quickly identified the need for a national "paper or periodical." Addie Chisholm, second president of the Ontario WCTU, declared that "We have gifted ones in our societies, who have it in their power to make its pages interesting and instructive, but we lack the necessary funds." She noted the value for the Maritimes of the *Telephone*, founded in 1884 by Mrs. J.S. Cowie of Moncton, New Brunswick, "a woman self-taught in the art of printing,"[40] and suggested that elsewhere in the country, one woman in each county might advance the cause by contributing WCTU material to local newspapers. Miss Mary McKay Scott soon founded the *Woman's Journal*, the first national organ of the WCTU, which was subsequently edited and published by Chisholm in Ottawa. By 1900 the *Woman's Journal* was being run by Mrs. Rutherford in Toronto, with a circulation of more than four thousand.[41] After its demise in 1903, it was succeeded by the *Canadian White Ribbon Tidings*, which became the signature periodical of the Ontario WCTU, and *Canada's White Ribbon Bulletin*, which operated at the national level. According to Cook, for both women and youth groups these locally produced periodicals proved a more effective "educational channel" than the many series of imported pamphlets also distributed by the WCTU because they featured fiction and advice columns, some written by members, as well as news of local branches.[42] Canada's temperance movement acquired a valuable foundational text with the appearance of *Campaign Echoes: The Autobiography of Mrs. Letitia Youmans, the Pioneer of the White Ribbon Movement in Canada* (1893), with an introduction by the major American reformer Frances E. Willard. A well-known speaker and organizer, Youmans was elected as honorary president of the federal WCTU in 1889 before she sat down to write her book, which enjoyed at least three editions.[43]

As temperance became identified as largely a woman's cause, it quickly aligned with other women's reform movements of the late nineteenth century. For example, the *Canada Citizen and Temperance Herald*, an important Toronto temperance weekly, added a woman's rights column that was associated with Sarah Anne Curzon in the 1880s; the newspaper itself was edited by suffragist Huldah Rockwell at the time of its demise in 1895.[44] Temperance reformers like Rockwell became advocates of women's suffrage because they felt that the right to vote would give women sufficient influence to promote legislation restricting the availability of alcohol. Linking the two causes was advantageous to both. Carol Lee Bacchi explains that in Canada, an alliance with prohibition benefited the suffrage movement by both broadening its base of support and enhancing its aura of respectability due to the popularity of temperance among male reformers and reform politicians. The affiliation also expanded the range of commitment by creating a link between the middle-class urbanites who were active in suffrage societies and the large rural population that supported temperance. As a result, the generally conservative ideology underlying the temperance movement had a "taming effect"[45] on Canada's suffragists, who eschewed the militancy of the British campaigners.

The convergence of suffrage and temperance is nicely illustrated in *Clipped Wings* (1899), a novel by Lottie McAlister, who was a member of the Canadian Women's Press Club, editor of *White Ribbon Tidings* from 1912 to 1914, and a suffrage activist. The first edition of her only book was introduced by Rev. W.H. Withrow, editor of the *Canadian Methodist Magazine*, who praised the story as a "tremendous indictment of the liquor traffic" that "sets forth the mission and power of woman to ennoble and bless society."[46] McAlister's narrative interweaves the causes of temperance, suffrage, and women's need for broader horizons with other areas of social reform, such as the overwork of trained nurses and the plight of underpaid female factory employees, described as "white slaves."[47] McAlister envisaged the current New Woman as a maternal feminist who "proposes not only to rock the cradle for the world but to rock the world for the cradle." While seeking public platforms, positions on school boards, and the right to earn her living, this New Woman needs to acknowledge that "[i]n the mothers were stored capabilities that the chilling breath of prejudice nipped in the bud."[48] Not a "clinging vine," the mother of Agnes Hill, the novel's heroine, is a "marvellous compound of baker, seamstress, laundress, tailoress, barber, gardener, nurse, man servant, maid servant, and had found time to be a Sunday-school teacher,"[49] yet she is disinherited by her husband's determination to amass property for their dissolute alcoholic son. McAlister deftly resolves these issues within a conservative Christian framework by marrying the occasionally radical Agnes to an evangelical minister after he is converted by her argument that women's suffrage is the route to social reform through regulation of the liquor trade. At the end, it is the Rev. Horace Harding who is writing an address on woman suffrage, while Agnes is "tenderly caring for her little ones."[50]

Locally produced suffrage fiction like *Clipped Wings* was rare in Canada, as were local suffrage periodicals. Foreign suffrage periodicals such as the *Revolution* (New York, 1868–70), the *Woman's Journal* (Boston, 1870–90), and Sylvia Pankhurst's *Votes for Women* (London, 1907–18) circulated widely; their authors and editors were warmly greeted when events such as the annual congress of the American Society for the

Advancement of Women, which met in Toronto in 1890 and in Saint John in 1896, brought international suffrage leaders to Canada.[51] Because Canada lacked the population to support the volume of independent suffrage newspapers that arose in the US,[52] the Canadian suffrage press was largely entwined with the mass of temperance publications that supported the female ballot. One of the few separate ventures was the *Champion*, issued monthly from August 1912 to April 1914 in British Columbia by the Victoria branch of the Political Equality League under the guidance of Dorothy Davis and Maria Grant.[53] Pamphlets from England and the US were widely read, but in this genre too, Canadian production was sparse.[54] Most common was the appearance of suffrage advocacy in the mainstream press, from Ethelwyn Wetherald's writing for *Wives and Daughters* in the 1890s to Flora MacDonald Denison's strenuous column, which ran from 1909 to 1913 in the *Sunday World,* Toronto's largest illustrated weekly.[55] This pattern dovetails with Marjory Lang's finding that "Journalists and writers were strongly represented in the suffrage societies, constituting nearly one-quarter of the leadership."[56] Her study of the Canadian Women's Press Club documents the substantial role played by the country's major female journalists in many of the era's causes, including suffrage: "Presswomen ... did more than join existing societies; they used their public role in the press to act as agents of organization and recruitment for women's clubs."[57] Newspaper and magazine editors, in turn, competed for "prominent reform activists in order to build subscriptions among a female readership,"[58] with the result that women's suffrage was a consistent topic in the general press. Indicative is the suffrage petition that circulated in 1912 through the *Grain Grower's Guide,* a populist newspaper widely read across the Prairies, whose women's editor was activist Francis Marion Beynon.

This integration of the suffrage cause with Canada's general print culture may account for the movement's relatively smooth, albeit less than swift, acceptance in English-speaking Canada,[59] where the most outrageous action of the suffrage campaigners was their frequent staging of mock parliaments to dramatize the absurdity of refusing to give women the vote. Kym Bird has found evidence of "nine different plays and at least thirteen different performances—four in Manitoba, seven in Ontario, and two in British Columbia" mounted from February 1893 until 1914 by various suffrage groups, usually in collaboration with the WCTU. Unlike similar American and British plays that were individually authored, Bird notes that "those in Canada were collective creations."[60] Because of this collaborative process, these plays' textual records are fragmentary and Bird's history is culled from materials scattered in archives and newspapers. Nellie McClung was the only participant to provide detailed documentation, largely based on her involvement in the Walker Theatre production of the Women's Parliament in Winnipeg in 1914. Lightly fictionalized in her novel, *Purple Springs* (1921), this event reappears in her memoir, *The Stream Runs Fast* (1945), which also reprints two lengthy newspaper reviews. The cast list of this production, provided by the Winnipeg *Telegram*, demonstrates the prevalence of local newspaperwomen in the Winnipeg Political Equality League.[61]

McClung and Machar: Two Outstanding Voices

The story of Nellie McClung's entrance into print, leading to the publication of her now classic feminist statement, *In Times Like These* (1915) after three highly successful books of fiction, demonstrates the convergence of many of the streams of Canadian women's print culture that we have been following: Sunday school writing, the temperance movement, and the campaign for women's suffrage. In her memoirs, McClung recalled that her professional writing career was initiated by a story contest in the New York magazine, *Collier's*, probably in November 1902. While her first draft of *Sowing Seeds in Danny* didn't win a prize, the magazine's positive response encouraged her to continue.[62] As she began to supplement her family income by selling her writing, McClung did not emulate L.M. Montgomery's example of pursuing the American magazine market. Instead, she turned to more familiar publications such as *Canada West*, the *Farmer's Advocate*, and the *Canadian Magazine*. Most fruitful was her recourse to the Methodist print culture in which she had been raised, beginning with the material she sent to W.H. Withrow, editor of the *Canadian Methodist Magazine*, for inclusion in the Sunday school magazines that he also edited. For her anecdotes, limericks, and comments, which appeared sporadically in *East and West*, *Onward*, *Happy Days*, and *Playmate* from 1904 to 1908, she received "some encouragement, and some small cheques."[63]

Most significant was Withrow's decision to bring her story, "Sowing Seeds in Danny," to the attention of E.S. Caswell at the Methodist Book and Publishing House. In his role as McClung's advocate, Caswell was in effect "pioneering the business of literary agency in Canada."[64] Following Caswell's advice to "get [her] name favourably known to the public" by contributing to major magazines,[65] McClung sent her first story of the engaging Watson family to the *Canadian Magazine* where it appeared in December 1905. Six months later a second story, "The Live Wire," offered the same magazine's readers another glimpse of the Watsons and their lively eldest daughter, Pearlie. In the meantime, under Caswell's guidance McClung wrote additional chapters and completed her manuscript in June 1906. As detailed in Chapter 4, the exigencies of both the Methodist publishing house and general Canadian publication practice necessitated partnership with an American firm in order to produce the book. This requirement brought Agnes Laut into McClung's story. As a young apprentice teacher, McClung had met and admired Laut when she observed her classroom in Winnipeg.[66] After both had left teaching for writing, Laut intervened in the fate of *Danny* by persuading "a New York publisher" that the manuscript was not "too evangelical" for his list.[67] Caswell's quest ended when a contract was finally signed with Doubleday, Page in April 1907. While the book was in production, Doubleday, Page created additional American exposure by arranging for a portion to be serialized in the *Ladies' Home Companion* and placed another story by McClung, "The Wedding March," in the *Delineator* where it eventually appeared in January 1909.

Far from being "too evangelical," *Sowing Seeds in Danny* proved an instant hit with the same North American readership that had warmly embraced the muscular Christianity of Ralph Connor's bestselling Glengarry novels.[68] The influential E. Cora Hind (who didn't let her friendship with McClung influence her literary judgment, and later voiced her dislike of *Painted Fires*) praised *Danny* as "the sweetest, the sanest, and the most accurate picture of the ordinary everyday life of the farms and villages of the whole West that has been written or is ever likely to be written."[69] Following publication in March 1908, *Danny* topped both *Anne of Green Gables* and *Anne of Avonlea* on the Canadian bestseller list of 1909.[70] In 1910, Grosset and Dunlap of New York reprinted 10,000 copies; in 1911 they did the same with McClung's sequel, *The Second Chance* (1910). *Danny* was into its fourteenth printing in 1922, its seventeenth in 1947, and was reissued for the last time in 1965. Translations and subsequent serializations further enhanced McClung's income.

Danny not only launched McClung career as a writer but also propelled her onto the public platform as a social activist. In her fiction, McClung lightly mocks overwrought moral earnestness and treats excessive idealism with irony; her characteristic mode is not satire but rather the humour of conviction. Principles of temperance and the Social Gospel pervade her stories, which consistently demonstrate the evils of alcohol, the moral benefit of helping others, and the ethos of maternal feminism. Her ability to combine didacticism with entertainment led to her first public appearances early in 1910, when she was hired to read her

FIGURE 8.1
Nellie McClung, c. 1914
(Cyril Jessop, Library and
Archives Canada, PA-030212)

stories to raise funds for the WCTU and the YMCA. McClung quickly discovered that her gift for public life blended fortuitously with her own
commitment to the combined causes of temperance and suffrage. That
fall she advertised herself as "Elocutionist, Entertainer, and Reader"[71] and
her initial fee of twenty dollars for a single evening's reading was quickly
met.[72] As McClung honed her platform skills, she learned that the bene-
fits of the speaking circuit were material as well as moral. After the publication of *In Times Like These*, she received two hundred dollars per week,
plus expenses, for her 1916 speaking tour for the National American
Women's Suffrage Association.[73]

In Times Like These, McClung's banner text of first-wave feminism, was
polished from lectures she delivered in Manitoba on behalf of the Political Equality League and further seasoned with her strong feelings about
the outbreak of the Great War. First published in 1915 by McLeod and
Allen in Toronto and by Appleton in New York, the book generated suffi-

cient interest to merit reprints in New York in 1916 and in Toronto in
1917 and 1919.[74] It also aroused the ire of conservatives such as Stephen
Leacock, whose acidly humorous essay "The Woman Question" implicitly
acknowledged that his opposition to first-wave feminism (and the dismal
temperance prospect of drinking nothing but water) was a lost cause.[75] In
the view of historian Veronica Strong-Boag, the book's "potent mixture of
wit, satire, good humour, and down-to-earth common sense" renders it
"the best feminist writing Canada has yet produced," notwithstanding
McClung's view that "drink was as much an enemy of Canadian manhood
as the Kaiser's legions."[76]

For nearly a century, McClung has occupied centre-stage in Canadian
women's history, due to the significance of the causes she espoused
(including her role in the persons case of 1929), to her energetic charisma
during her lifetime, and, in recent years, to controversies aroused by her
promotion of eugenics. While she inevitably subscribed to the normative
racism of her time, some of her fiction presents a more inclusive social
vision. Her novels about the Watsons legitimate a family of Irish origin, an
ethnicity then often caricatured as inferior to the English and Scots, and
Painted Fires (1925) does the same for Finnish-Canadians. Despite the
endurance of her fame, McClung was not the first prominent Canadian
woman to use literary genres to advocate women's rights and the reforms
of the Social Gospel, and she would not have wanted her predecessors like
Agnes Maule Machar to suffer the underacknowledgment that has been
their fate in the common narrative of Canadian social history.

Neither a platform speaker nor the author of a bestseller,[77] Machar
was an avid member of the National Council of Women and pursued an
extensive range of reform interests that touched on most areas of
women's print activity in nineteenth-century Canada. I have already
described her advocacy of women's rights within organized Christianity,
her authorship of Sunday school fiction, her concern about animal welfare, and her promotion of liberal-minded nationalist history. During the
post-Confederation decades she was admired as a poet and garnered
deep respect for maintaining a consistent intelligent presence in the
prose she contributed to the country's major periodicals such as the
Canadian Monthly and National Review and the *Week.* Her scores of thought-
ful and often lengthy articles dealt with topics ranging from higher education for women to addressing the needs of the poor. Self-effacing in
person but confident and indefatigable in print, Machar is described by
historian Ramsay Cook as "a brilliant woman" who was "one of the most
gifted intellectuals and social critics in late nineteenth-century Canada."[78]

Buoyed by a strong conviction that social action was a necessary component of Christian salvation,[79] she evinced no hesitation about using print media to engage in public debate with the major male thinkers of her time; if she had been born a little later, she would have joined the first generation of Canadian women to attend university. Because she had the good fortune to be "blessed with more ample means and leisure than most of the literary guild in Canada possess,"[80] she was free to pursue her interests without the worry of earning an income from her writing.

In addition to her distinction as Victorian Canada's outstanding female public intellectual, Machar was also the first Canadian to author a novel about labour relations during the decades when the topic occupied many writers of both sexes in Britain and the US. Despite her strongly Canadian outlook, Machar did not set *Roland Graeme: Knight* (1892) in rapidly industrializing Ontario but across the border, in the fictional American mill town of Minton, where her idealistic Canadian-born hero attempts to solve the tension between workers and management. This displacement reflected the difficulty of publishing in Canada; as she explained to a fellow author, "There was nothing apparently Canadian about it except the nationality of the hero. I regretted this but it could not be helped, and it certainly does not pay to publish books in Canada...."[81] As well, the setting may reflect her sense that such fiction was primarily an Anglo-American genre, as outlined in Amanda Claybaugh's analysis of the international print culture of reform.[82] Machar reserved her major critique of Canada's ills for her non-fiction, such as her call for improvement of the unhealthy factory conditions documented by the 1887 report of the Royal Commission on the Relations of Labour and Capital.[83]

Roland Graeme, which Machar regarded as her best novel, complements the writings of Marie Joussaye, the major nineteenth-century female literary voice from Canada's working class, who worked as a servant from the age of ten. It may be a particularly Canadian phenomenon that two women from such different backgrounds were among the country's most outspoken literary advocates of workers' rights and social reform. There is no evidence that they ever met in person, although an encounter would have been possible, given that for many years Joussaye resided not far from Machar's lifelong hometown of Kingston, first in Belleville and then in Toronto. Her involvement in the Toronto branch of the Working Women's Protective Association in the early 1890s represented a cause that interested Machar, who advocated reduced working hours for female factory workers. They also shared an ardent faith in the ideals of the British Empire. Despite their contrasting class origins, both writers approached labour relations from the perspective of *noblesse oblige*, calling on the goodwill of factory owners to improve the lot of their employees, while also supporting the organization of workers in the Knights of Labor. For Machar, such appeals arose directly from her goal to awaken the spirit of Christian benevolence embodied by the Social Gospel. Joussaye's use of Christian doctrine invoked a more radical image of Christ as a fellow worker who "had to toil for bread," with whom she forged a common class identity in her signature poem, "Only a Working Girl."[84] In another poem, "Labor's Greeting,"[85] Joussaye presented her solution to social and economic inequality by imploring British royalty to unseat the greedy capitalists (such as railroad magnates) who profit from the impoverishment of labourers.

For Machar, the route to a radical social analysis began with a fairly simplistic faith in the ability of do-gooders to redeem erring youth. She concluded her first novel, *Katie Johnstone's Cross* (1870), with the exhortation that "It only needs a little watchful but patient care, and some trouble and active kindness, to awaken [delinquent boys'] better nature, and turn them into useful citizens.... Perhaps every reader of this tale might be able to do something towards reclaiming one such; and were every one to try who could, it would more advance the prosperity of Canada than any development of merely material resources."[86] By the time she came to write *Roland Graeme*, she had developed a fuller understanding of the relationship between wealth and the abuse of power, the role of poverty in undermining personal morale and social well-being, and the need for a more equitable distribution of wealth in order to improve health, housing, education, social behaviour, and the conditions of women. This novel links three major areas of concern: the Social Gospel, the labour question, and the woman question. Through the spiritual crisis of the hero, Machar argues that social reform finds its best foundation in the "spirit of Christian socialism,"[87] which underpins the Knights of Labor. Fearing disorder, she refrains from challenging the social structure, seeking instead to "wake each class up as to what lies in its own power to reform."[88] Machar invokes the ideology of maternal feminism by showing that middle-class women have an important role to play in aiding the poor, and she empowers working women by giving Lizzie Mason the role of spokesperson for the factory workers. Their opportunities remain unequal, however. Middle-class Nora Blanchard utters the novel's last lines, which express a degree of optimism about the future, but Lizzie's health is broken by overwork in unsanitary conditions. The end of the novel finds her anticipating a premature death, while the novel's other working woman, showy Nelly Grove, seems to be on her way to prostitution.

FIGURE 8.2 Agnes Maule Machar distributing Humane Society literature, c. 1912 (CWPC, Library and Archives Canada, PA-125682)

Whereas Machar focused on the plight of female factory workers and on the need for middle-class women to find meaningful activity outside the home, Joussaye entered the work force as a domestic servant. Employed from the age of ten, she began to contribute poetry to the Canadian and American labour press in 1886, followed by her first book, *The Songs That Quinté Sang*, issued at her own expense in Belleville in 1895. Her sporadic publications included some journalism—most notably, an interview with Mark Twain—and occasional newspaper or broadside poetry as she moved from Ontario to Vancouver and then headed north, supposedly on her way to London, a destination she never reached. Her second book, *Selections from Anglo-Saxon Songs*, printed by the Dawson News Company sometime between 1916 and 1918, seems to have been the first volume of verse produced in the Yukon. Strategic in her activities that proclaimed the worth of the working class, Joussaye consciously challenged class boundaries, whether campaigning for Sunday streetcars in Toronto, using verse to convey her pro-union and pro-royalist sentiments, or sending her letters and poems to Canadian and British heads of state. At one point she boldly informed Prime Minister Wilfrid Laurier that "you are the head of the people and have a right to listen to one of us."[89] Her pungent personality and chequered life, which included several jail sentences, did not link her to any kind of literary community. Dominated by middle-class interests, the mainstream of Canadian literary history includes many more writers like Machar, who wrote about the working class from the outside, than authors like Joussaye, who arose from within.

NINE

The New Woman

TOWARD THE END OF THE NINETEENTH CENTURY, the rise of the New Woman[1] marked the arrival of one of the most complex and transgressive characters to inhabit the Anglo-American cultural arena. Middle-class and assertive, she challenged marriage and conventional domesticity while claiming the right to higher education, the ballot, unescorted travel, sexual freedom, and a professional career. Her material symbols of independence were the bicycle, sensible clothing, the latchkey, and sometimes the cigarette. Talia Schaffer has pointed out that the figure we now identify as the New Woman was in many ways a fictional construct who served as a focal point for anxieties about first-wave feminism, and was often far removed from the daily realities of the working and activist women who spearheaded social change.[2] In Britain and the US, novels that engaged with some or all of the issues that constellated around the New Woman were sufficiently numerous to form a distinct sub-genre. Ann Ardis has identified over one hundred titles published in England between 1880 and 1920 on different sides of the woman question, two-thirds of them written by women, although many of the best-known titles were by men: Grant Allen's *The Woman Who Did*, Thomas Hardy's *Tess of the d'Urbervilles* and *Jude the Obscure*, H.G. Wells' *Ann Veronica*, and George Gissing's *The Odd Women*.[3] Canada, in contrast, produced only a handful of novels that overtly reflect concerns associated with the New Woman.

A highlight in Canada's relatively slender contribution to the genre is the social critique that animates Joanna Wood's *The Untempered Wind* (1894), a defence of an unwed mother penned by an admirer of Thomas Hardy. Wood makes a sympathetic case for Myron Holder, resident of the sniping village of Jamestown, who refuses to divulge the name of her child's unfaithful father and marries him only when on her deathbed. Myron's pregnancy is presented as the outcome of her response to the "voice of nature." In her own eyes and those of her author, her promise to her lover, made "under no more sacred canopy than the topaz of a summer sky—with no other bridal hymn than the choral of the wind among the trees,"[4] is as valid as a formal marriage. On the whole, the power of Wood's writing generated a positive reception in Canada and the US; *Current Opinion* of New York described the book as "the strongest and best American novel of the year," and placed Wood in the company of Thomas Hardy, George Moore, George Meredith, George Eliot, Charlotte Brontë, and Charles Dickens.[5] However, exception was taken by the Toronto *Globe*, which took Wood to task for "magnifying the littleness of village life to the dimensions of an improbable malignity."[6] *The Untempered Wind* was not the first book by a Canadian woman to command attention for its anti-romantic representation of social behaviour; Mary Leslie's novel, *The Cromaboo Mail Carrier* (1878), published under the pseudonym of James Thomas Jones, was reputedly banned (or "withdrawn from circulation")[7] by her fellow citizens of Erin, Ontario, for its thinly disguised depiction of their community as "the most blackguard village in Canada."[8] Such books were exceptions to the normal practice of nineteenth-century Canadian

FIGURE 9.1
Sara Jeannette Duncan, 1890s
(Johnston and Hoffman, Library
and Archives Canada, C-046447)

fiction writers, who tended to handle social criticism with kid gloves. Similar to the way that Agnes Maule Machar took pains to sanitize Canada by setting *Roland Graeme* in the US, Wood used her second novel to correct the unflattering representation of rural Ontario in her first. *Judith Moore; or, Fashioning a Pipe* (1898), takes place in a lushly pastoral community and does an about-face in its representation of social norms by rejecting independence for the woman artist when the soprano heroine chooses marriage to a Canadian farmer over a career on the concert stage. Misao Dean finds that both of Wood's novels conform to a pattern that she sees as typical of Canadian New Woman fiction, in which "an identification between womanhood and the natural world" serves to "reconfine the New Woman within the bounds of a biologically defined femininity."[9]

Canada's most prominent author of New Woman fiction was Sara Jeannette Duncan, who cheekily dedicated her first book to Mrs. Grundy. As a journalist, Duncan had explored a wide range of options for Canadian women, from an interview with an unidentified woman doctor to an account of a visit to a Carmelite convent. She was thus well prepared to engage with New Woman issues of choice and independence in her fiction; however, nearly all her stories and novels are set abroad, in places that reflect both her foreign experience and her reliance on the international market for English-language fiction. She could allow a young Canadian woman to travel freely in a comic novel (*A Social Departure: How Orthodocia and I Went round the World by Ourselves*, 1891), but not to test her independence more seriously at home. In Duncan's oeuvre, Advena Murchison of *The Imperialist* (1904) is her closest approximation to a Canadian New Woman. A bookish and undomestic schoolteacher living in small-town Ontario, Advena remains in the position that Duncan had quickly abandoned in her own life when she left the classroom for journalism and literature. Duncan wrote this book when she was contemplating a return to Canada after living in India for many years, and may have felt that she could not place a more intrepid New Woman in her home region without alienating her potential readership. The independent women who populate some of her Anglo-Indian novels—Hilda Howe of *The Path of a Star* (1899), the unnamed, unmaternal narrator of "A Mother in India" (1903), and Dr. Ruth Pearce of *Set in Authority* (1906)—assert their individuality more directly than Advena, enacting the New Woman's struggle against larger social institutions.

Few other Canadian novels of the 1880–1920 period directly address New Woman issues. Most negative is Lily Dougall's *Madonna of a Day* (1891), which creates a smoking and drinking female journalist—

described by the *Canadian Magazine* as "most distressingly vulgar"—in order to attack the egotism and selfishness that Dougall attributes to the New Woman. To quote the *Canadian Magazine* again: "[t]he moral, of course, is that women can do nothing worse for their sex than to mock at faith and deride sentiment."[10] Any feminism attributable to the presence of strong female characters in Dougall's subsequent novel, *What Necessity Knows* (1893), is of the maternal kind. Novels that argue in favour of women's independence and advancement, such as Maria Amelia Fytche's *Kerchiefs to Hunt Souls* (1895) and Lottie McAlister's *Clipped Wings* (1899), display a tension between serious discussion of the woman question and overdetermination by romantic plot conventions. The same pattern shapes Susan Morrow Jones's *A Detached Pirate* (1904), which daringly allows a woman to disguise herself in men's clothing in order to enjoy the freedom of the streets of London, then resolves with a romantic reconciliation in the author's hometown of Halifax. L.M. Montgomery's Anne Shirley of Green Gables, in some ways Advena's successor, begins as an incipient New Woman when she follows Marilla's advice that every woman should be able to earn her own living and sets her sights on higher education; that it takes three books to marry off Anne suggests Montgomery's own sympathy with female independence. Reading the internal dynamics of such novels against their endings, as suggested by Rachel Blau Duplessis, highlights their feminist content despite their conventional conclusions.[11]

If New Women were rare in Canadian fiction, rarer still were female characters who were also authors. Before Montgomery's Emily books of the early 1920s, few Canadian novels dealt overtly with women writers. In *Beth Woodburn* (1897), Maud Petitt's titular heroine starts out wanting to emulate George Eliot, only to be chastised: "George Eliot certainly had a grand intellect, but had she only been a consecrated Christian woman how infinitely greater she might have been!"[12] Persuaded to repress her ambition, Beth burns her manuscript and dedicates her talent to missionary fiction. While she then produces novels that are "among the most successful of the day,"[13] they are much less interesting than her infant son. When Duncan's Elfrida Bell of *A Daughter of Today* (1894) exclaims, "Fancy being the author of babies, when one could be the author of books!"[14] she poses a dilemma that exemplifies the conflictual linking of female creativity and physical motherhood. The complex dynamics of these Canadian books are illuminated by Lyn Pykett's discussion of how New Woman novels that make "writing women and women's writing their subject" also "foreground the problems of their own production." The woman writer or artist "is repeatedly used as a way of figuring the lack of fit between women's desire, the socially prescribed norms of the woman's lot, and the actuality of women's lives."[15] Pykett also notes that "It is one of the many paradoxes and contradictions of New Woman fiction of the 1890s, that at a time in which women writers were so numerous, commercially successful, and much discussed in the newspaper and periodical press, their books should have focussed so frequently and minutely on the conflicts, frustrations, and the compromised or thwarted careers and/or vocations of the professional woman writer and the aspiring woman artist."[16] This disjunction hearkens back to Fanny Fern's declaration in *Ruth Hall*, her bestselling novel of 1854, that "No happy women ever writes," a claim belied by her own success.[17] Olive Schreiner offered later insight into this apparent inconsistency when she described women's fiction writing as a default. In *Woman and Labor* (1911), Schreiner argues that women achieve success in fiction because it represents one of their few sanctioned activities in a society that allowed them no opportunity to engage in the significant work done by legislators, architects, scientists, or judges: "Both the creative writer and the typist, in their respective spheres, are merely finding outlets for their powers in the direction of least mental resistance."[18] Schreiner's analysis underscores the general frustration experienced even by successful New Women, and substantiates the comment made by Nellie McClung's son, long after her death, that his mother "would have been a humdinger of a clergyman."[19] The pulpit was a professional locale that a number of Canadian women writers would have liked to occupy. McClung herself revelled in the accusation that some of her stories were "sermons in disguise," claiming "my earnest hope is that the disguise did not obscure the sermon."[20] While L.M. Montgomery disliked writing fiction like McClung's, with "an insidious moral hidden away in it like a spoonful of jam,"[21] she felt that she "would have made a good *preacher*,"[22] and opined that "women would make splendid ministers" through Anne Shirley's declaration, "If I were a man I think I'd be a minister."[23]

Lyn Pykett's point that New Women could be complicit in undermining their own agency as authors is well demonstrated by Sara Jeannette Duncan's *A Daughter of Today*, a title that Pykett mentions but does not analyze further. Duncan complicated her novel's national implications by making her heroine American and by setting most of Elfrida Bell's story in Paris and London, where she directly challenges the cultural hegemony of the Imperial centre. Misao Dean reads this configuration as Duncan's advocacy of a Canadian norm, between the extremes of American individualism and British rectitude.[24] It may also be symptomatic of Duncan's position as an expatriate trying to write her way back to Canada and therefore taking care not to offend Canadian propriety. Moreover, as a professional author she well knew that in the wake of Henry James, there was a much larger market for fiction about young American women abroad than for stories of overseas Canadians. From Duncan's perspective, an American in London was more out of place and therefore more capable of outrageous behaviour than any Canadian girl. In contrast to Mary Trent of *Cousin Cinderella: A Canadian Girl in London* (1908), who comments ironically on British behaviour but always remains within the bounds of decorum, Elfrida's performance of iconoclasm takes her onto the vaudeville stage where, in tights, she both literally and figuratively kicks up her heels at British social conventions.

Elfrida attempts to enter the London literary establishment by attaching herself to Janet Cardiff, a well-connected young writer on her way to respectable professionalism under the tutelage of her professorial father, hence a career woman whose newness is sanctioned by patriarchy. However, this friendship founders on Elfrida's uncompromising ambition: "I want George Meredith to ask to be introduced to me!"[25] she declares, after she has completed the manuscript of her book. But a series of personal rejections leads to Elfrida's suicide and her last word is the inscription on her tombstone, "Pas femme—artist." This articulation of the gender restrictions forced on the New Woman by the limited construction of selfhood available to her anticipates Virginia Woolf's ideology of ungendered (androgynous) art. Elfrida's entrapment and destruction by limitations of gender are overdetermined by the tone of the novel itself, which seems to disapprove of female egotism and ambition specifically because they are female, in contrast to the social approval of masculine ambition enjoyed by the man Elfrida loves, painter John Kendal. When we remember that Duncan's original christened name was Sara Janet, we can speculate that her self-projection into the interstices of the story further problematizes her fictional presentation of the New Woman. In the complex relationship between her two female characters, one inculcating the values of the Imperial centre, the other the rebelliousness of a former colony, there is little space for a Canadian position except to identify with the narrator's ironic view of Janet, living "an idyllic life in Devonshire" as the wife of Kendal, the artist who humiliated Elfrida, but sometimes troubled by memories of her former friend and of "a loyalty she could not hold."[26]

Notwithstanding the sparseness of New Woman fiction in Canada, covert challenges to patriarchy can be found within several apparently conventional earlier books. Pioneer chroniclers Susanna Moodie and

Catharine Parr Traill sometimes describe survival techniques they learned from Native women whose strength and bravery they admired. Their personal narratives suggest that during the middle years of the nineteenth century, despite the material hardships they endured, settler women found that emigration to a New World offered empowerment by relaxing Old World constructions of class and gender. This subtext breaks through the surface narrative of Traill's *Canadian Crusoes* (1852), written as a juvenile fictionalized survival guide. Set in the 1770s, this Robinsonnade recounts the adventures of three Canadian adolescents—a Scots brother and sister and their half-French cousin—who survive quite handily while lost in the woods for several years, largely due to the assistance of a Mohawk girl who performs the Friday role. The European children name her Indiana after saving her life, and she in turn saves them with her woodlore and hunting skills. The overt didacticism expressed in Traill's unsubtle imparting of facts, and her advocacy of a highly gendered social code for the settler children, are subverted in her presentation of Native characters. While Catharine, the young White heroine, learns to be a model housewife, Aboriginal women present strong countervailing images of knowledge and power in the complications and resolution of the novel's plot. Moreover, in an intriguing gesture toward the mid-Victorian cause of dress reform, Traill describes how Catharine and Indiana invent "blanket dresses" for themselves that closely resemble the radical Bloomer dress: "the full, short, plaited skirts reached a little below the knee; light vests bordered with fur completed the upper part, and leggings, terminated at the ankles by knotted fringes of the doe-skin, with mocassins turned over with a band of squirrel fur, completed the novel but not very unbecoming costume."[27] Without evidence to the contrary, we can speculate that Traill may have deliberately modelled this style on Amelia Bloomer's recently publicized prototype, news of which most likely reached denizens of rural Upper Canada.

Rosanna Leprohon's *Antoinette de Mirecourt* (1864) also harbours a counter-narrative that challenges its veneer of social control. Although the novel is set in eighteenth-century Montreal, an environment nominally dominated by powerful fathers and the Catholic Church, its male authority figures are curiously absent (in contrast to their visible power in Laure Conan's *Angéline de Montbrun*, written a few decades later). Following the Treaty of Paris in 1763, which ceded New France to England, the heads of French Canada's households have retired to their libraries, leaving the women to socialize with the newly arrived British army officers. In the milieu of Catholic Quebec, it is surprising to meet no priests, not even a confessor for pious Antoinette. As Antoinette negotiates between her archetypal three suitors and the frivolities of her irresponsible guardian aunt, Lucille D'Aulnay, she more closely resembles a solitary Bunyanesque pilgrim picking her way through an unfamiliar landscape than a protected daughter of a highly structured church. Her errors in judgment and consequent suffering could lead to tragedy (as in *Angéline de Montbrun*), yet Leprohon's novel terminates instead on the sprightly note of Antoinette's marriage to her faithful British lover, "[d]espite the opinion of friends and acquaintances, who had obligingly decided that Antoinette should at once enter a convent, or retire immediately to [her father's home at] Valmont, there to live and die in the strictest seclusion."[28] This happy ending is consistent with Misao Dean's view that the political nature of Leprohon's marriage plot, which unites French and English Canada, empowers women "within the economics of heterosexual exchange" because Leprohon represents "issues of political tension as problems of individual moral behaviour and thus under the authority of feminine power to restrain and guide."[29] Leprohon critiques misuse of that power through her condemnation of Lucille D'Aulnay's dangerous frivolity, yet she needs this headstrong character, whose independence is represented by her unladylike practice of driving her own horses, to pose important questions. Thus it is Lucille who issues the novel's challenge to the power of Antoinette's father: "What right has he to dispose of you to Louis Beauchesne as if you were a farm or field he wished to get rid of?"[30] And it is Lucille who has the privilege of closing the novel, having learned "a prudent horror of secret marriages."[31]

Travellers and Explorers

Intrinsically an urban genre, the New Woman novel was not easily written in Canada, where the New Woman was more prominent as a biographical identity than as a literary character. In the two volumes of short fiction edited by Sandra Campbell and Lorraine McMullen titled *Aspiring Women (1880–1900)* and *New Women (1900–1920)*,[32] the challenges overcome by women seeking social, educational, and economic advancement are less apparent in the contents of the stories than in the biographical sketches of their authors. While these writers' fiction tended to be overdetermined by romantic plot conventions, the term "New Woman" can be fittingly applied to their journalism and travel writing, which documents their independent adventures and self-created literary careers. Lily Dougall's identification of the travelling journalist as the intrinsic New Woman, in her novel

Madonna of a Day (1895), was spot-on for Canada, where newspapers and general periodicals such as the *Canadian Magazine* often featured women's accounts of overseas adventures.[33] Dougall may have been thinking of the well-publicized journey around the world recently completed by Sara Jeannette Duncan and Lily Lewis, who quickly published their adventures as both journalism and fiction. Notable future examples would include Faith Fenton, whose stories of the Klondike appeared on the front page of the *Globe* in 1898; Kit Coleman, who wrote about the Spanish-American War; Agnes Deans Cameron, who published a book about her travels in the North; and Mina Hubbard, who did the same following her unprecedented canoe trip through Labrador. Across Canada, female readers of newspapers and magazines saw how the lives and writings of the feisty journalists of the Canadian Women's Press Club provided cogent examples of courage and advancement. On the more literary side, the panorama of Canada's mobile New Women included single self-supporting writers like Pauline Johnson and Marshall Saunders, both of whom travelled extensively, engaged with their audiences in public performances or lectures, and developed distinctive profiles as social advocates.

These late nineteenth-century travellers were preceded by Anna Jameson, the first female visitor to publish a significant book about Canada. Jameson arrived in Toronto in the winter of 1836 as a recognized British bluestocking and author of both travel writing and cultural criticism. In her preface to *Winter Studies and Summer Rambles in Canada* (1838), she quickly claimed the novelty and daring requisite of the travel genre: "While in Canada, I was thrown into scenes and regions hitherto undescribed by any traveller ... and into relations with the Indian tribes, such as few European women of refined and civilised habits have ever risked, and none have recorded."[34] Her sojourn in the New World, although undertaken reluctantly (to arrange a separation agreement with her estranged husband, then Attorney General for Upper Canada), brought both mental and physical liberation. When trapped indoors by winter, she exercised her intellect by studying German writers, and when freed by the coming of spring, she embarked on a "wild expedition,"[35] largely by water, that took her across Lake Huron to Sault Ste. Marie. Despite her claim to have travelled alone, she was never entirely by herself and was protected by her identity as "the 'chancellor's lady.'"[36] However, the unescorted nature of her journey attracted the attention of reviewers, who commended her for being the intrepid yet feminine figure she had deliberately constructed.

Ever the urbane cosmopolitan on the lookout for both adequate bookshops and noble savages, Jameson discovered that first-hand experience of frontier North America, in its various stages of settlement, produced "inconsistent and apparently contradictory emotions and impressions."[37] She achieved some resolution by identifying both the sublime and the picturesque in the terrain and its inhabitants. When she reached Mackinaw, she became good friends with the American Indian agent, ethnologist Henry Schoolcraft, and especially with his half-Native wife Jane, whose writings are discussed in the following chapter. Jameson's feminist interest in Native women led to her concern about their status and her delight in making the acquaintance of the cultivated mixed-race McMurray and Schoolcraft sisters, whose mother honoured Jameson with "adoption" and a Chippewa name for being the first European woman to shoot the local rapids, albeit while a passenger in a Native-steered canoe.

In Jameson's wake[38] there were few publications about the country by female travellers (as distinct from immigrants' narratives of settlement) until the 1880s, when the completion of the Canadian Pacific Railway (CPR) in 1886 coincided with the advent of the New Woman. Quick to take advantage of the novelty was Ellen Spragge, whose "through return ticket to Victoria" was "the first one probably issued from the office at Toronto."[39] In Winnipeg she transferred to the first through-train from Montreal, an adventure recounted in a series of articles in the *Week* that were soon reissued in her book, *From Ontario to the Pacific by the CPR* (1887). Others who published their accounts of the same transcontinental journey included Lady Aberdeen, whose affection for the newly portable camera yielded *Through Canada with a Kodak* (1893), and a cluster of British visitors, some touring for pleasure and others travelling with a purpose. The cross-Canada train trip offered a comfortably exotic adventure for well-to-do sightseers such as Mrs. Algernon St. Maur, who published her condescending account as *Impressions of a Tenderfoot during a Journey in Search of Sport in the Far West* (1890). Mrs. Humphrey Ward's journey in a private first-class carriage, courtesy of Sir William Van Horne,[40] generated her novel, *Canadian Born* (1910), published in North America under the more accurate title of *Lady Merton, Colonist*.[41] Several visiting social activists issued books whose goals coincided with the development agenda of the CPR by promoting the emigration of surplus British women in order to correct the gender imbalance on the Prairies, along the lines of Jessie Saxby's *West-Nor'-west* (1890) and Marion Cran's *A Woman in Canada* (1908).

Scarcely qualifying as Canadian travel writers are a handful of women who published books about exotic foreign experiences that preceded their residence in Canada, notably Anna Leonowens's popular accounts of her five years as governess to the sixty-seven children of the King of Siam, and Harriet Boomer's description of her travels in South Africa.[42] Women who recounted journeys taken with their husbands, as in Minnie Forsyth Grant's *Life in the Sandwich Islands* (1888) and Emily Murphy's *The Impressions of Janey Canuck Abroad* (1902), or who followed conventional tourist routes to Europe, broke little new ground. On the other hand, unescorted or solo travel, or ventures into unconventional locales, were hallmarks of the New Woman. Sara Jeannette Duncan's Elfrida Bell is advised to situate her first book in this genre: "There's no end of a market for anything new in travels. Go on a walking tour through Spain by yourself, disguised as a nun or something, and write about what you see."[43] In this vein, the novelty of Grace Denison's 1890 European tour was not only her "fairly unorthodox itinerary through the Netherlands, Germany, Austria, Hungary, Switzerland, and France"[44] but also her ability to limit her baggage to a single carryall, "as elastic as a Congressman's conscience, and as neat as a Quaker's bonnet."[45] Like Denison, many independent Canadian female travellers were journalists who entertained readers of the mainstream press, as in Kit Coleman's weekly columns in the *Mail and Empire* describing her 1892 trip to London, Paris, and Dublin, and Alice Jones' essays on Italy in the *Week*. Lively Canadian women also wrote about their enjoyment of outdoor recreation. In the 1890s, New York's *Outing Magazine* published Denison's articles on cycling, including a series about her recent bicycle tour of Ireland (the combination of travel and cycling accentuating her New Woman persona), as well as Pauline Johnson's accounts of canoe trips and regular columns advocating sports for women. However, all were preceded and upstaged by Sara Jeannette Duncan and Lily Lewis.

In September 1888 these unescorted young women were just twenty-six and twenty-two years of age when they embarked on an eight-month journey around the world that Marjory Lang aptly describes as a "prefabricated news event by which the two journalists and their newspapers intended to create public interest."[46] Lewis dispatched her stories to the *Week* and Duncan sent hers to the Montreal *Daily Star*, possibly with support from Joseph Pulitzer, the owner of the New York *World* who well knew how to boost to circulation by highlighting the stunts and sensational stories of women journalists. Careful to avoid impropriety, Duncan and Lewis happily took on the arch sophistication of the New Woman, exemplified in Duncan's dedication of her resulting novel, *A Social Departure*, to Mrs. Grundy. The pair relished the notion of "going round the world the wrong way"[47] journeying by train (the CPR, coyly written as "the Seepiar") from Montreal to Vancouver and then sailing to Japan, Ceylon, India, and

FIGURE 9.2
Agnes C. Laut (Library and
Archives Canada, C-051921)

Egypt. Dignified daring was the order of the day, from whisking through
the Rockies on the cow-catcher of the steam engine following the much-
publicized example of Lady Macdonald, to riding on the backs of don-
keys, camels, and elephants. For the novel, Duncan transformed
Montreal-born Lewis into the faux-naive, English-born character of
Orthodocia, a canny choice that contributed to the book's success in the
international English-language marketplace.[48] While the author seems to
recast her own nationality when her unnamed narrator allows herself to
be described as "that American young lady,"[49] Duncan's Canadian identity
occasionally pokes through. Readers of her political columns would have
recognized Duncan's characteristic irony when her narrator describes the
CPR as both "the most masterly stroke of internal economy a Government
ever had the courage to carry out, and the most lunatic enterprise a Government was ever foolhardy enough to hazard."[50]

In the following decades, Canada's most innovative women travel writers conquered new fields on the ground and in print by pursuing direc-
tions that differed from the well-worn routes to Europe or Asia. They
proclaimed the significance of their journeys in the familiar trope of firstness, a convention mocked by Emily Murphy when she claimed that on a
winter sleigh journey to a remote Saskatchewan lumber camp managed

by her husband, "I was the first woman—white, black, or red—to traverse this part of Canada."[51] In many instances, the sense of adventure that sent women northward to the Arctic, or upward into the Rocky Mountains, or into the sparsely mapped interior of Labrador, was inspired by the "See America First" ethos that Agnes Laut helped to promote. Not limiting "America" to the portion of the continent belonging to the United States, Laut's many magazine articles published in the US included "Unclimbed Peaks of the Rockies," which depicted Canada as more challenging than Switzerland, and an account of her own adventurous canoe trip, "Fifteen Hundred Miles down the Saskatchewan."[52] On this occasion, Laut was accompanied by a niece of George Simpson, one of the first Hudson's Bay officials to travel the same route. This link to the past prompted Laut to reverse the usual claim to firstness with the notion that their adventure took them back in history and marked, instead, "the last trek to the last frontier of the last West."[53]

Like Denison, Laut, Duncan, and Lewis, Agnes Deans Cameron was a self-conscious journalist who embarked on an unusual journey in order to write about it. Accompanied by her niece, Jessie Cameron Brown, who acted as secretary and photographer, Cameron revelled in the technology of 1908, carrying a camera and an Underwood typewriter from Chicago to the Arctic Ocean. The two women claimed the primacy of being "the first white women to reach the Arctic Circle overland"[54] and "the first white women who have penetrated to Fort Rae."[55] They also brought the first typewriter to Great Slave Lake, documented in *The New North*'s three outdoor photographs of Brown typing to Cameron's dictation. In the book's many photos, Cameron is consistently attired as a New Woman, her full-length skirt always topped by a uniform-like jacket and hat that confer a masculine aura. This image of intrepidity is emphasized by the frontispiece photograph captioned "A Magnificent Trophy," in which Cameron displays the severed head of a moose, holding its antlers in her bare hands. The photo that records the hunt itself, titled "My Premier Moose," also documents the two women's technical skills: with a rifle firmly in her hands Cameron stands over the body of the still intact moose, while a smiling (and decidedly more feminine-looking) Jessie Brown stands close by, firmly clasping her portable Underwood. As well as documenting her own achievements, Cameron's text celebrates the work of northern women, from the two female missionaries who operated "the farthest north printing-press"[56] in order to produce hymns in Cree, to the Indigenous "Mrs. Chipewyan," characterized as "the New Red Woman" for being "the essential head of the household."[57]

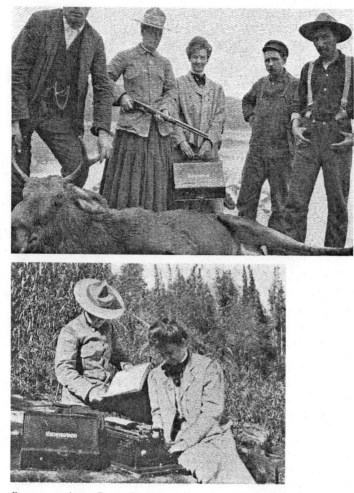

FIGURE 9.3 Agnes Deans Cameron, "My Premier Moose" and "The First Type-writer on Great Slave Lake,"1908 (Agnes Deans Cameron, *The New North*, 1910)

Cameron was a teacher who had turned to full-time journalism after running afoul of the bureaucracy of the public education system in Victoria, B.C., and she devised her trip in line with her subsequent position with the Western Canada Immigration Association. The double title of her resulting book, *The New North: Being Some Account of a Woman's Journey through Canada to the Arctic* (1910), demonstrates her dual perspective. While the major title's highlighting of the word "new" suggests an assessment of the North's potential for development, the subtitle proclaims her personal achievement as a female traveller. Cameron's uncritical allegiance to the institutions of the British Empire—the Hudson's Bay Company, the RCMP, and "the Great Churches of England and Rome"[58]—didn't prevent her from catering to American readers by describing Fourth of July festivities at Fort Smith. Her meeting with the people then referred to as Eskimos, whom she found "probably the most admirable, certainly the most interesting, and by circumstances certainly the most misunderstood and most misrepresented of all the native races of America,"[59] yielded insights into the limits of White culture and a sobering of her often flippant tone: "The intrusion of the whites has changed the whole horizon here; we can scarcely call it the coming of civilisation, but call it rather the coming of commerce."[60] Upon her return to southern Canada, Cameron built an audience for her forthcoming book with illustrated lectures and magazine articles. The unidentified author of the write-up in the Toronto *Globe* not only declared her trip "without doubt the most remarkable journey ever accomplished by a woman of this country," but went even further: "We know of no one, man or woman, who heretofore in the one season between ice and ice has been able to accomplish what these two women have done; that is, to follow the Mackenzie to the sea, and to return against current by the Peace and so out to civilization again by the route of the Lesser Slave."[61] Cameron was feted at a banquet of the Toronto Suffrage Association[62] and honoured at a civic reception in Victoria, but her celebrity was cut short by her death in 1912, at the age of forty-eight, of pneumonia following an appendectomy.

By the early twentieth century, women travel writers—especially travelling journalists—were familiar figures, but Euro-Canadian female explorers remained as rare as unicorns. While exploration writing has long been recognized as an important cornerstone of Canadian historical and literary studies, the genre remained resolutely masculine until the end of the nineteenth century. The first decade of the twentieth saw publications by two women who were the first to record their agency in visiting, mapping, and naming Canadian terrain within the general model of exploration discourse: Mary Schaffer Warren and Mina Benson Hubbard. Both were launched into the wilderness by early widowhood, but they had little else in common.

Mary Sharples Schaffer was an American who regularly visited the Rockies while assisting her botanist husband, Dr. Charles Schaffer, with the research that led to her completion of his book, *Alpine Flora of the Canadian Rockies* (1907), four years after his death. Captivated by the ruggedness of the landscape, she spent many summers camping in the mountains and photographing the land and its Aboriginal inhabitants. In

1915, after marrying her wilderness guide, William Warren, she moved permanently to Banff. An occasional contributor to periodicals, she recounted her experiences in *Old Indian Trails* (1911), which celebrates a challenging wilderness and its original Aboriginal population. It was in relation to Maligne Lake that Schaffer was recognized as an explorer, although she always attributed the success of her expedition to her guides and claimed that she had "only RE-FOUND it as it had long been a famous hunting ground for Stonies from Morley and the Crees of the Athabaska."[63] Known as Chaba Imne (Beaver Lake) to the Stoney, who had ceased to visit the site following the decline of its beaver stock, the lake was briefly noted in 1875 by Henry MacLeod, a CPR surveyor who hadn't actually reached it.[64] Schaffer's determination to find the somewhat mythical body of water has become a benchmark in the larger historical context of the rise of women's mountaineering and the growth of wilderness tourism in Canada's National Parks. After obtaining an approximate map from her Stoney friend, Sampson Beaver, Schaffer and her party reached and photographed the site in the summer of 1908. The publication of her account in the *Canadian Alpine Journal* led to an invitation to survey the region for the Geological Survey of Canada.

Schaffer's single exploit as an explorer was a sidebar to her enduring identity as an Alberta photographer and a pioneer of women's recreation in the Rockies. In contrast, when Ontario-born Mina Benson married American adventure writer Leonidas Hubbard in 1901, she had no intention of becoming a public figure and no notion that she would soon produce a book documenting her achievement as the first accurate mapper of the Labrador interior. A trained nurse, Mina was captivated by Hubbard's romantic fascination with "about the only part of the continent that hasn't been explored."[65] She fully supported his 1903 expedition and, after he died of starvation because he had followed the wrong river, took up his mission herself. Engaging three of her husband's guides, Mina collected ample supplies and equipment. In 1905, with little fanfare, she embarked on the right river and, during the course of her journey, corrected the faulty map that had misled the previous expedition. Her party enjoyed favourable weather, ample fish and game, and interesting encounters with the Indigenous population. They reached their destination of Ungava a good six weeks before the arrival of the rival expedition of Dillon Wallace, sponsor of the first ill-fated journey who was now trying to rehabilitate his reputation.

By December 1905, Mina was giving the first of many lantern-slide lectures describing her adventure. She issued several magazine accounts

FIGURE 9.4 Mina Hubbard, "In the Heart of the Wilderness," "With the Nascaupee Women," and "On the Trail," 1905 (Mrs. Leonidas Hubbard Jr., *A Woman's Way through Unknown Labrador,* 1909)

before she published *A Woman's Way through Unknown Labrador* (1908)[66] to counter Wallace's version of the tragedy that had claimed her husband's life. Illustrated with many photographs, Mina's volume includes an image titled "On the Trail," which depicts her as the archetypal New Woman traveller. She confidently strides across the tundra with a smile on her face and a rifle in her hand, wearing streamlined sensible clothing comprising a plain shirt, a flared ankle-length skirt, and a functional hat (similar to those worn by her guides) with a mosquito-veil, with several leather bags slung over her shoulder. Only the careful reader of her narrative will realize that her guides did the hunting and her rifle was seldom used. In another photo, "In the Heart of the Wilderness," she sits on the floor of a canoe, clearly a passenger and not a paddler, with an open book on her lap that may well be the expedition diary that served as the basis of the published account. Other photos show her doing her own washing and sharing in the cooking, although here again the text recounts that meal preparation was usually done by her guides. Notable also is a picture of Mina talking to a group of Nascaupee women. While her position is heightened by standing on a rock, we can see that the length of her skirt is similar to theirs, and she too is wearing moccasins. The book includes many photos of the landscape and of her three (male) Native guides, but just one ("Stormbound") depicts Mina in their company, perhaps a way of declaring distance in a situation that could have been viewed as compromising.

For a woman of Mina Hubbard's generation with literary ambitions, the Labrador trip and the success of the resulting book would have provided the perfect springboard into a writing career. Yet, like the two women who reluctantly wrote up their two months in the camp of Big Bear in 1885 (see Chapter 3), Mina preferred to conclude her experience of accidental authorship by subsiding into private life. While lecturing in England and arranging for publication of her book, she met Harold Ellis, whom she soon married. The social milieu of a landed Yorkshire family and the quick arrival of three children, followed by the breakup of her marriage, did not encourage Mina Hubbard to pick up her pen again.

TEN

Addressing the Margins of Race

IN CONTRAST TO THEIR OUTSPOKEN concern about the welfare of women and children, and their interest in improving the working and living conditions of workers and immigrants, Canada's late nineteenth-century social reformers did not often deplore discrimination against non-Whites, whether Indigenous, Black, or "Oriental." Under the growing influence of new theories of race and eugenics, as well as the perceived economic threat of Asian immigrant labour, most Euro-Canadians accepted the prevailing belief in the superiority of White, British-based culture and promoted an Anglo-Saxon identity for Canada. Non-White immigration was actively discouraged, and it was assumed that Aboriginal peoples were destined to be absorbed into the general population. In Britain and the United States, early first-wave feminism was linked with the anti-slavery movement, which also had strong advocates among women in Canada. Abolitionists assisted many fleeing Black Americans to cross the border into the British colonies; however, after the American Civil War, most Canadians expected Black American refugees to return to the US and White social reformers paid little attention to the plight of those who settled in Atlantic and Central Canada. With each of Canada's visible minorities, it was therefore up to members of these communities to speak up on their own behalf. Some audible early voices belonged to women.

Black Women Writers

The research of Afua Cooper, George Elliott Clarke and Wayde Compton has made it possible to trace a slender strain of Black Canadian women's writing that begins with a single letter by Susana Smith, an American-born

177

ex-slave who arrived in Nova Scotia with other Black Loyalists in 1783 and joined the group of some twelve hundred Black North Americans who emigrated to Sierra Leone in 1792. Smith's cornerstone position in the documentary record illustrates the serendipity of history; we know her name only because of the efficiency of a colonial administration that preserved the letter she wrote to request soap in order to wash her family's clothes.[1] Living through similarly diasporic circumstances, most of Canada's early Black women writers were transient and transnational, and spent much of their lives in the United States. Those known to be active in the second half of the nineteenth century include immigrant Priscilla Stewart, who composed a poem in 1858 upon leaving California for British Columbia, where she believed "all live free and well" in Queen Victoria's domain.[2] Others reversed the journey. Cincinnati-born, Toronto-educated Mollie E. Lewis (b.1842) became a recognized author following her return to the United States upon her marriage to Toussaint L'Ouverture Lambert in 1867. In Detroit, Mollie Lambert edited her church's journal and published journalism, poetry, and fiction, little of which can now be found.[3] Two Canadian-born Black women followed a similar pattern in becoming known as American writers. In 1874, the family of Montreal-educated Amelia E. Hall[4] (1858–1922) relocated in Baltimore, where she met and married Harvey Johnson, a prominent Baptist minister. Here she founded *The Joy* (1887–?) a monthly literary magazine for Black writers and readers, followed by the first of her three juvenile novels, *Clarence and Corinne* (1890), which was the first manuscript by a woman to be issued by the American Baptist Publication Society. Lucretia Newman Coleman, born in Canada West, sought a similar readership with her novel, *Poor Ben*, published by the AME Sunday School Union in Tennessee in 1890.[5] One of the few Black women to publish in Canada was Rebecca Gibbs, who resided in the gold rush town of Barkerville, B.C., in the 1860s, where she contributed verse to the *Cariboo Sentinel.*

More distinctive and substantial was the career of Mary Ann Shadd (later Cary). Although she spent most of her life in the US, Shadd lived in the Windsor area for sixteen crucial years, from 1851 to 1867, during which she established her presence as Canada's first female newspaper editor and first major Black female writer. She had entered the public sphere before moving north. Opposing the dominance of the Black clergy in the US, she published her views in Frederick Douglass's paper, the *North Star*, where she issued a characteristic call to action: "We should do more, and talk less." She also published *Hints to the Colored People of the North* (1849), a twelve-page pamphlet now known only from extracts pub-

lished in the *North Star*, in which she advocated education, moral refine-
ment, and economic self-sufficiency.[6] Described by her biographer as "not
so much a black nationalist but a black activist searching for a safe home
for blacks,"[7] the freeborn Shadd entered Canada and the country's cultural history following the Americans' passing of the Fugitive Slave Law in
1850. This measure, which forced Northern free states to arrest alleged
runaway slaves, vastly accentuated the appeal of the British sections of
North America to Black Americans, whether escaped slaves or legally free.
The resulting influx of Black settlers, particularly into the Windsor area,
generated its own print culture, which included some of the first women's
reading groups in Ontario.[8] Illiterate members of this community were
given voice by the American abolitionist movement in Benjamin Drew's
The Refugee: Narratives of Fugitive Slaves in Canada. Related by Themselves ...
(Boston, 1856), which included over a hundred personal accounts, of
which seventeen were from women.

Most visible were the competing newspapers of Henry Bibb, who in
1851 founded *Voice of the Fugitive* (now believed to be largely the work of
his more literate wife, Mary),[9] and Mary Ann Shadd, who established the
Provincial Freeman in 1853 to counter the Bibbs' segregationist approach
to Black settlement and education. The Bibbs' paper lasted less than
three years, its office destroyed by fire in October 1853, nine months
before Henry's death at the age of thirty-nine. Shadd's paper was more
feminist and provocative in style, advocating women's rights as well as the
abolition of slavery. In testimony to her fierce dedication, it managed to
survive for six precarious years of uncertain financing and erratic production. Whereas the title of the Bibbs' paper represented the perspective
that its audience was in exile, "awaiting the time when they might return
to a United States cleansed of slavery,"[10] Shadd encouraged American
Black immigrants to think of Canada as their permanent home. This
vision maintained the position first established in her pamphlet, *A Plea for
Emigration: or, Notes of Canada West ...* (1852). While literature advocating
British immigration to Canada abounded during the pre-Confederation
period, Shadd's booklet is the only example known to have been
authored by a woman, and also the only one to address Black settlers. In
her eagerness to present the British colonies as a haven for "colored"
Americans, Shadd overstated the country's welcome to non-Whites and
the ease with which they could establish themselves, having little experience of the social and economic discrimination that flourished in Canada
West despite the legal equality nominally guaranteed by Her Majesty's
prohibition of slavery.[11]

Aboriginal Women Writers

Indicative of the Canadian colonies' racism is the extent to which its early Black literary culture operated in isolation, with a little external support from abolitionist circles. Writing by Aboriginal women, on the other hand, meshed more easily with the Euro-Canadian mainstream, in part because such writers fit within the framework of the Noble Savage and their culture was of ethnographic interest. Like Pauline Johnson, Canada's best-known Native writer from the 1890s to the present, a number of women of mixed Indigenous and European heritage who were educated in the Anglo-American literary tradition became authors themselves and served as intermediaries between the two cultures. This pattern began with Jane Johnston Schoolcraft (Bamewawagezhikaquay, 1800–42), daughter of John Johnston,[12] a Scots-Irish independent fur trader who secured his position by marrying into an elite Ojibwe family. At Sault Ste. Marie, Jane grew up in a hybrid border environment that interwove strands of Indigenous, French, and British culture. Although the book-filled Johnston home was on the American side of the St. Mary's River, John Johnston retained his status as a British subject and his family, "like the whites, Indians and métis around them, identified with the British, not the Americans."[13]

Taught mostly at home, the Johnston children were also each briefly sent away to further their education; when she turned ten, Jane spent a difficult year with her father's relatives in Ireland and England. She began to write poetry at the age of fifteen, and continued to do so after her marriage to the American Indian agent and ethnographer Henry Rowe Schoolcraft, who took pride in his own aptitude for literature. Little of Jane's writing was recognized before her death in 1842, other than a selection that appeared in a manuscript newspaper edited by Henry during the winter of 1826–27.[14] In 1836, Anna Jameson's westward travels enabled her to meet three Johnston women with whom she felt a strong cultural and emotional affinity due to their blending of Indigenous dignity and European gentility: Jane; her mother, Ozhaguscodaywayquay, known as Susan; and her sister, Charlotte Johnston McMurray. Jameson commended the women's manners and admired Susan, "a woman of pure Indian blood," who not only "did the honours of her house with unembarrassed, unaffected propriety"[15] but also warmly adopted Jameson into her family. However, it was Jane, the most literary of the trio, with whom Jameson identified most closely. She found Jane's "choice of language pure and remarkably elegant"[16] and on bidding them farewell, she exclaimed, "I am sorry to leave these kind, excellent people, but most I regret Mrs. Schoolcraft."[17] Jameson was sufficiently intrigued with Aboriginal culture to include in her own travel narrative, *Winter Studies and Summer Rambles in Canada* (1838), the first print publication of several Ojibwe songs and stories "from Mrs. Schoolcraft's translation." Her rationale was more ethnographic than literary in that she found these texts to "have at least the merit of being genuine. Their very wildness and childishness, and dissimilarity to all other fictions, will recommend them...."[18]

Preserved in collections of her husband's papers, Jane Schoolcraft's surviving manuscripts, in English and Ojibwe, were published in 2007 in Dale Parker's scholarly edition, which includes over three dozen original poems (some with many variants), ten English stories based on Ojibwe culture, and another dozen texts that are direct translations, mostly of traditional Ojibwe songs. Her original poetry in English reflects the prevailing Anglo-romantic themes of her time, emphasizing nature as a source or reflection of private emotion, and valuing home and friendship. Her female identity underscores the verses that refer to her sisters or her father, and especially the poems that mourn the death of her young son. Specific Ojibwe references appear in an English poem to her maternal grandfather and in her use of Ojibwe words to title the four poems within the suite "Absence," written to her husband. Otherwise, Jane seems to have written entirely in one language or the other, with her bilingualism serving as a linguistic bridge when she prepared translations of her own poems or of traditional material.

Other than Pauline Johnson, who shared Jane Schoolcraft's penchant for poetry, the mixed-race women who found their way into print were informative rather than creative writers and are closely identified with frontier environments across the country. On the East Coast, Labrador Métis Lydia Campbell (1818–1905), who had no formal schooling, recorded her memories at the behest of a clergyman who arranged for their publication as a newspaper series in 1894–95. Later reissued as a book titled *Sketches of Labrador Life,* they have acquired the status of a local classic as "the first published writings of a native Labrador resident."[19]

Two western women of mixed-race descent present a more complex relationship between their heritage and the subjects of their writing, in that they avoided front-page acknowledgment of their Aboriginal lineage, yet were inspired to write about Native cultures that, for the most part, were not their own. In Victoria, Martha Douglas Harris (1854–1933), the well-educated youngest daughter of part-Black Sir James Douglas (second governor of Vancouver Island) and half-Cree Amelia Connolly Douglas, collected stories from two Indigenous cultures for her only book, *History and Folklore of the Cowichan Indians* (1901), which she presented as "a memento of British Columbia" and "a contribution towards [the] preservation" of the people on whose land she resided.[20] As evidence of her ability to do her own translations, Harris included one story written entirely in the Cowichan language, followed by a version in English. Into this volume of relatively impersonal material, Harris tucked six Cree legends received from her mother and obliquely acknowledged her First Nation lineage in her accompanying introduction: "As a little girl, I used to listen to these legends with the greatest delight, and in order not to lose them, I have written down what I can remember of them." In so doing, she recognized their value as oral culture: "When written down they lose their charm which was in the telling. They need the quaint songs and the sweet voice that told them, the winter gloaming and the bright fire as the only light—then were these legends beautiful."[21]

Oral culture also underpins Amelia McLean Paget's *People of the Plains* (1909), which presents a description of the Saskatchewan Cree that was so sympathetic that it elicited some correction in the preface written by Duncan Campbell Scott, deputy superintendent of Indian Affairs, the government department that had commissioned the book. Paget was born in 1867 in Fort Simpson, Northwest Territories, into a fur trade family that subsequently moved to Saskatchewan. Fluent in Cree and Saulteaux (Ojibwe), she behaved quite fearlessly during the period of unrest in 1885 when members of her family travelled for two months with Big Bear as rumoured captives (along with two Ontario women, Theresa Delaney and Theresa Gowanlock, who later issued their own account, described in Chapter 3). An elite Hudson's Bay family, the McLeans did not openly acknowledge their Aboriginal lineage derived from the unidentified Native wife of Amelia's great-great-grandfather, and historian Sarah Carter notes that Amelia likely acquired her knowledge of Native peoples and languages through the family's servants and nursemaids.[22] This lack of overt personal identification with the people she studied renders Paget's positive approach all the more unexpected. Like Martha Douglas Harris, Paget saw herself as a preserver of an inevitably disappearing people and their culture, and presented stories and information obtained through direct conversation with informants in their own tongues. She travelled extensively during the summer of 1906 to interview Cree elders about their beliefs and customs, recording the religious and social practices of both men and women, including details of family and domestic life. Like Pauline Johnson's juvenile stories about the banned potlatch and the white dog feast, and her magazine articles about

FIGURE 10.1
E. Pauline Johnson, c. 1895
(Library and Archives Canada,
C-085125)

Indian mothers and family life published during the same decade, Paget's book implicitly sought to correct common pejorative notions about Indigenous culture, including the women's mothering and housekeeping skills, which were criticized in government publications in order to justify the residential school system.[23]

Whereas the writing of Black women like Mary Ann Shadd was little known beyond Black communities until a surge of recent scholarly interest, Pauline Johnson (1861–1913) always sought a broad English-speaking audience in Canada and abroad. Daughter of an English-born mother and a mostly Mohawk father, she and her siblings were raised to respect the cultures of both parents. After the death of her father in 1884, Pauline followed the common path taken by many impecunious English-speaking women when she turned to writing to help maintain the reduced household of her mother and her sister. Never hesitant about living by her pen, she embarked on a lifelong career as an independent writer/performer while self-consciously playing up her double heritage, both onstage and off. Her part-Mohawk ethnicity enhanced her appeal to her readers and audiences as she increasingly turned to Native life for material and developed her public profile as spokesperson for Native rights and values. There is no evidence that she knew of Jane Schoolcraft, although both wrote poems of tribute to their Native grandfathers, or any of the other part-Native women discussed above. Johnson occasionally cited Tennyson, Keats, and Walter Scott as favourite authors and recommended John Richardson's *Wacousta* as a Canadian novel that, in her eyes, portrayed Aboriginals in a positive manner. She also admired "Hiawatha," Longfellow's popular narrative poem based on Iroquois history, whose character of Minnehaha inspired the construction of her own performance costume.[24] Although American author William Dean Howells was her mother's first cousin, the connection was of no benefit to Pauline.

Beautiful and charming, Johnson deployed her charisma strategically, whether quietly seeking favours in letters to patrons or thrilling audiences by denouncing the dispossession of the Cree in "The Cattle Thief," one of her most effective performance pieces. Her appearances on the stage and in print worked in tandem to maintain her celebrity; central to her fame was her insistence on performing original material. In all she wrote about 160 poems and 200 pieces of prose, selections of which were issued in three volumes of poetry and three books of stories. While Johnson sold some of her poems and much of her later prose to American periodicals, all her books were issued solely in Canada with the exception of the first, which was published in England. Unlike the writers discussed in Chapter 5, who made their living from American markets, Johnson's primary audience was Canadian. During the course of her career, she broke new ground in three principal areas: as a rare example of a successful self-supporting female author and performer, as Canada's first significant writer of First Nations heritage (of either sex), and as the country's most explicit early woman author of erotic love poetry presented from a female perspective, a feature of her work that still remains underacknowledged.

During the first stage of her career, from 1883 until 1892, Johnson's name frequently appeared in Canadian newspapers and magazines, especially Toronto's major weekly serials, the *Week* and *Saturday Night*, where she published lyric poetry about nature and love, and lively prose columns recounting her canoeing and camping adventures. Her growing literary status was highlighted by the inclusion of two of her poems in W.D. Lighthall's landmark anthology, *Songs of the Great Dominion* (1889). In print, Johnson's presence as a distinctive female voice was at first stronger than her Mohawk identity. She almost always wrote under the signature "E. Pauline Johnson," whether describing love and disappointment from a woman's perspective in such lyrics as "The Idlers" (1890) and "Re-Voyage" (1891), or jauntily recounting canoe trips enjoyed by a capable outdoorswoman. Her feminine identity and her prowess as a canoeist combined to reverse the normal gender roles in Victorian poetry. In "Wave-Won," for example, the poem is controlled by the female narrator who steers the canoe while she blatantly objectifies her passive male lover:

> Your splendid eye aflame
> Put heaven's stars to shame,
> Your god-like head so near my lap was laid—
> My hand is burning where
> It touched your wind-blown hair,
> As sweeping to the rapids' verge, I changed my paddle blade.[25]

Johnson's combination of independence, sexual honesty, and athleticism established her presence as an intrepid New Woman. Previously attuned to amateur theatricals, she became a professional performer in 1892 once she realized that audiences would pay to attend her recitations. After her first season, she decided to emphasize the Native aspects of her writing by assembling a costume that was not the dress of any one tribe, but rather a collage of various artifacts that represented Aboriginal identity. She wore a necklace of bears' teeth and ornamented her asymmetrical buckskin dress with evocative objects, including Iroquois silverwork, a Sioux scalp, and her father's hunting knife. The image created by this costume dovetailed with the tremendous popularity of such attractions of the 1880s and 1890s as Buffalo Bill Cody's Wild West Show and ethnological Aboriginal exhibits at large-scale expositions. To maintain her middle-class audience and her social status at a time when the morals of actresses were often suspect, Johnson took pains to assert her respectability. She usually toured with a male partner, the most enduring being Walter McRaye, twelve years her junior, who joined her in 1901 and remained her faithful advocate long after her death. The fact that she never married, despite one broken public engagement and many rumoured broken hearts, enhanced her mystique.

On stage, Johnson normally divided her program into two sections representing her dual identity. The opening half featured her Native poems and stories, performed in her buckskin costume with her long hair streaming down her back. After intermission she returned wearing an elegant evening gown, with her hair pinned up in the fashion of a Victorian lady, a change that effectively contained the potential disruptiveness of her Native material. In addition to the poems and stories that found their way into print, she and her partner performed topical comic skits that are now lost except for the descriptions recorded in newspaper reviews. From 1892 until 1909 Johnson maintained a rigorous touring schedule that included many one-night stands in small towns across Canada, as well as occasional ventures into the United States (including Chautauqua appearances in 1907–08) and three trips to England.

On her first visit to London, during the spring and summer of 1894, Johnson enjoyed a triumphant season of society performances in drawing rooms and similar venues, and arranged for publication of her first book of poems. *The White Wampum* was issued in 1895 in an elegant compact edition from John Lane in London and was well reviewed in both Britain and Canada. The front cover of this little book prominently featured the name "Tekahionwake" (Double Wampum), adapted from her grandfather. Tekahionwake subsequently became Johnson's regular pseudonym, used primarily in her professional life. Her letters show that in private she was "Pauline" to her friends and "Paul" to her siblings.

Despite her public identity as a poet, Johnson's output of new verse diminished through the 1890s in favour of the more marketable genres of fiction and journalism. Her second book of poems, *Canadian Born*, was a modest production, issued in Toronto in 1903 to fewer and cooler reviews. As she wearied of the stage, she sought new outlets for prose. From 1906 to 1912 her major venues were two Chicago periodicals, *Boys' World* and *Mother's Magazine*, for which she wrote stories and articles on various topics, including many that presented positive images of First Nations culture. In 1909, suffering from the first stages of breast cancer, Johnson retired to Vancouver and renewed her acquaintance with Joe Capilano (Su-à-pu-luck), a Salish chief whom she had met during her second visit to London in 1906. In 1910 and 1911, Vancouver's *Daily Province Magazine* published her versions of the traditional stories she had received from Joe and Mary Capilano (Líxwelut). Some were collected as *Legends of Vancouver*, issued in 1911 by the Vancouver branch of the Women's Canadian Club to raise money to support Johnson during her final illness. This book proved extremely popular across Canada, and has always remained in print. That same year, Toronto's Musson Book Company published her final collection of verse, *Flint and Feather*, later misleadingly described as her "Complete Poems."[26] Shortly after her death in 1913, McRaye arranged for the publication of two prose collections: *The Moccasin Maker*, a selection of stories about women, some of which were first published in *Mother's Magazine*, and *The Shagganappi*, a book of stories for boys, many from *Boys' World*. Most of her periodical prose remains uncollected. So admired was Pauline Johnson that she received a civic funeral from the city of Vancouver, which declared a half-holiday in her honour and permitted her to be buried in Stanley Park near Siwash Rock, the subject of one of her best-known stories. In 1961, the centenary of her birth was celebrated with a commemorative stamp bearing her image, making her the first woman (other than the Queen), the first author, and the first Native Canadian to be thus distinguished.

Johnson's singularity as a Native woman poet garnered superlative notices from major cultural commentators of her day. In Canada, Hector Charlesworth admired her as a "unique figure on the border-land between the worlds of ancient tradition and modern art" and proclaimed her not only "the greatest living poetess" but also one of the "greatest woman poets of all time."[27] In England, Theodore Watts-Dunton was entranced by "the most interesting English poetess now living" who struck "a new note—the note of the Red Man's Canada," while the reviewer for London's *Magnet Magazine* found her "the most unique fixture in the literary world of today."[28] Such comments show that her reception was shaped by her intrepidity as a female writer/performer and her novelty as an accomplished Native voice in the lofty realm of poetry. Yet her distinction as a "daughter of decadence," to borrow Elaine Showalter's term,[29] was met with silence. Elaine Showalter notes that poetry was not a genre generally deployed by New Women to advance their causes, and identifies Ella Wheeler Wilcox as the American "spokeswoman for female sexuality."[30] However Johnson's verses were far more explicit than Wilcox's best-selling *Poems of Passion* (1883) and *Poems of Pleasure* (1888), and her overt eroticism must have resonated with those who paid money to see her display her ankles and loose hair on stage, or those who read such poems as "The Idlers." This poem is particularly effective in the way it builds up the sensual atmosphere of a hot day in "a Canadian July," only to close with the fracturing of the lovers' relationship. All of nature seems to be erotically charged and as the details unfold, the moment of "perfect langour" is ripe with anticipation. Most overt is the sensuality of the fifth stanza, in which the woman gazes longingly at the body of her lover, whose open shirt reveals his "might/Of muscle" and "splendid sunburnt throat." After she says "Your hand just touches mine" the seduction intensifies as they make eye contact in the seventh stanza and kiss chastely in the eighth: "So perfect is the single kiss your lips lay on my hand." But then something happens between the two final stanzas: the unspecified event could be consummation, or violation, or something less definable. This silence creates the poem's shift in mood expressed in the last stanza's negative language: "disused," "abused," "no after-blow." The lovers have lost something as intangible as the now dead "homeward blowing wind," something for which "hearts will pay the cost."

The reticence of Johnson's audience about such poems poses intriguing questions. Did her contemporaries disregard her eroticism because her reception was so thoroughly overdetermined by race and gender? Did they lack the language to encompass simultaneously her elevated status as an exotic "princess" figure and her voicing of female desire? Or did they implicitly accept the sensuality of her love poetry as an expected component of her performance of Aboriginality, an identity that constructed Native women as sexually available? Race continues to overdetermine Johnson's profile in the twenty-first century. In *Poets in the Public Sphere* (2003), her study of race and eroticism in the poetry of nineteenth-century American women, critic Paula Bennett includes Johnson as an important Native voice yet omits her entirely from her chapter on the literary representation of female desire, despite Johnson's many poems that expressed love and passion from a woman's perspective at a time when most love poetry enacted the male gaze.

Pauline Johnson's prominence in Canada's cultural milieu was unmatched by any other woman writer during the entire pre-1918 period. She masterfully deployed her position on the racial margin by envisioning an inclusive society in which "French and English and Red men" stand "shoulder-to-shoulder"[31] while also reprimanding that same nation for its mistreatment of its First Nations in such poems as "The Cattle Thief" and "The Corn Husker." The latter deftly transforms the literal scene of an old Native woman husking corn into the figurative image of a disinherited people. The subject recalls classic depictions of harvesters in European art, but whereas those canvases celebrated plenty, this word-painting depicts "might's injustice," a brilliantly managed phrase that highlights the powerful word "injustice" while assigning blame only to the impersonal notion of "might." While Johnson had to be careful not to offend those on whom she depended to publish her work, her political position resonates in this poem's final image of Native peoples "banished from their lands" and now treated as if they were as insignificant as "dead husks" of corn. By limiting her sphere of action to the performance venues of the stage and the page, Pauline Johnson could utter political statements without threatening to alienate her readers and her audience.

The Asian Eaton Sisters

More transnational were the literary careers of the Eaton sisters, whose peripatetic parents settled their growing family in Montreal in 1873. Their British-born father, Edward Eaton, was a merchant who became an ineffectual painter. Their Chinese mother, Grace Trefusius Eaton, was educated in England and was described in her obituary as "a woman of considerable intellectual and literary attainments" who will be remembered for "a serial story she wrote in the *Montreal Witness* which depicted the life of China as she knew it."[32] Of their fourteen children, four daughters are known to have become involved in writing: London-born Edith Maud (1865–1914), Jersey City-born Grace Helen (1867–1957) and Sara (1868–1940), and Montreal-born Winnifred (1875–1954). Grace, who never publicly acknowledged her racial identity, occasionally contributed to newspapers before she married journalist and editor Walter Blackburn Harte and moved to Boston. During the 1890s she assisted with his literary enterprises, which included a series of editorial positions with general interest periodicals, daily newspapers, and fin-de-siècle literary magazines. After her husband's early death she studied law and in 1947 published the first history of women lawyers in the United States.[33] Sara, who married artist Karl Bosse, was for a time Winnifred's collaborator and the nominal author of four articles on Chinese cuisine published in 1913 in American periodicals. The sisters' partnership became visible on the title page of their *Chinese-Japanese Cookbook* (Chicago, 1914) by Sara Bosse and Onoto Watanna.[34]

Rather than following Grace's example of merging with the North American mainstream, her better-known sisters created distinctive public profiles by selecting pseudonyms that proclaimed an Asian identity. Edith remained faithful to her origins by publishing under the Chinese name "Sui Sin Far" (meaning "water fragrant flower, or narcissus")[35] while Winnifred adopted a pseudo-Japanese identity as Onoto Watanna, a choice that reflected North Americans' elevated view of Japan at the end of the nineteenth century. In addition to negotiating their unusual lineage, Edith and Winnifred each did a stint of journalism in Jamaica and moved back and forth across the Canadian–American border, writing mostly for the American market. Winnifred, who outlived her delicate sister by forty years, enjoyed a period of prosperity when she worked as a Hollywood scriptwriter in the 1920s, described in Chapter 5. Like Pauline Johnson, the Eaton sisters displayed complex responses to their mixed heritage, which they chose to perform to a White audience in a fashion that simultaneously fulfilled stereotypes and challenged prejudices. Edith's approach was more serious: her realistic fiction and journalism visited the Chinatowns of the American West Coast in order to document the discrimination that she had experienced personally. Winnifred was more boldly inventive, both in her romantic stories and in her transformation of her Chinese heritage into an exotic Japanese identity that enabled her

ONOTO WATANNA
[Fac-simile of author's autograph in Japanese]

FIGURE 10.2
Winnifred Eaton ("Onoto Watanna"),
c. 1902 (Onoto Watanna, *The Wooing of
Wistaria*, 1902)

to pose in elegant kimonos and occasionally claim to have been born in a land that she never even visited. Initially viewed by scholars as less "authentic" than Edith in dealing with racial discrimination, Winnifred is now being recuperated as "the first writer of Asian descent to publish a novel in the United States."[36] As with Pauline Johnson, criticism of her writing has been overdetermined by race, an imbalance corrected by Jean Lee Cole in her analysis of the variant voices that shaped Winnifred's entire career.

Like Mary Ann Shadd, the Eaton sisters have interested many more scholars in the US than in Canada. These historians and critics tend to construct the sisters as American writers despite their allegiance to Canada, where both are buried. While Edith spent much of her adult life in the US and used San Francisco or Seattle as the setting for most of the stories collected in her only book, *Mrs. Spring Fragrance* (Chicago, 1912), her first articles were published in Montreal newspapers and criticized Canadian treatment of the Chinese. Her 1896 letter to the editor of the Montreal *Daily Star*, published as "A Plea for the Chinaman," constituted a rare challenge to government policy, arguing against the proposed increase in the head tax on the grounds that "the Chinaman is as much a human being as those who now presume to judge him."[37] In her 1909 essay, "Leaves from the Mental Portfolio of a Eurasian," Edith presented a highly personal account of encountering discrimination wherever she lived or travelled, and mocked the route taken by her sister: "They tell me that if I wish to succeed in literature in America, I should dress in Chinese costume, carry a fan in my hand, wear a pair of scarlet beaded slippers, live in New York, and come of high birth." She felt she inhabited a no man's land, a racial alien regardless of her locale: "So I roam backward and forward across the continent. When I am East, my heart is West. When I am West, my heart is East…. After all I have no nationality and am not anxious to claim any."[38]

Much more at home in North America, Winnifred produced a best-selling romantic novel nearly every year from 1899 to 1910, supplemented by well-researched articles on Japanese culture and daily life. She then shed her Asian identity when it no longer served her purpose. After she settled in Calgary following her 1917 marriage to businessman Frank Reeve, mention of her mixed parentage disappeared. In two extensive articles about Winnifred written in 1922 by Elizabeth Bailey Price upon the publication of *Sunny San*, Winnifred's last "Japanese" novel, Onoto Watanna is represented as the pen name of an Alberta rancher's wife who was born in Montreal and learned about Asia through the stories of her adventuresome Oxford-educated merchant father. Claiming that despite her recent residency in the United States she was "desirous to be known henceforth as a Canadian,"[39] Winnifred provided her interviewer with substantial information about her father's English family and remained silent about her mother. The following year, she enhanced her renewed identity with an address to the Canadian Club of Calgary titled "The Canadian Spirit in Our Literature" in which she teasingly denounced the popular image of Canada as continually snowbound. She endorsed the "campaign to coax superior immigration to our land," argued for the need to support Canadian writers, and called for nationalistic fiction that celebrated the romance of the West.[40] Her specific reference to "our immense cattle lands" suggests that she was consciously grooming her audience for her new identity as an Alberta writer. Titled *Cattle* (1924), her next novel appeared under the name "Winnifred Eaton." Her last book, set in the same ranching landscape, was *His Royal Nibs* (1925) by "Winifred Eaton Reeve," the name under which she pursued her next career as a Hollywood screenwriter until the film industry was devastated by the Depression.

Winnifred Eaton's variable self-constructions highlight the fluidity of identity that some mixed-race women writers successfully deployed during an era when exoticism was at times a useful commodity. Early in the twentieth century, publishers of Pauline Johnson and Onoto Watanna enhanced their books with frontispiece photographs of the authors in costumes that appeared to authenticate their difference (Pauline in her buckskin performance dress and Winnifred in a kimono) while also confirming the women's adherence to mainstream standards of feminine beauty. This imagery was often transferred from the body of the author to the design of her book: volumes of Johnson's writings enjoyed the artistry of some of Canada's major book designers, such as J.E.H. MacDonald's renditions of First Nations art in McClelland and Stewart's editions of *Legends of Vancouver* issued in the 1920s and 1930s, while Eaton's pseudo-Japanese books were issued by Harper in New York with beautiful covers, full-colour illustrations, and pages decorated with Asian images. During the early twentieth century, marginality could be advantageous for both author and publisher when it dovetailed with the majority culture's desire for unthreatening novelty.

CONCLUSION

Oberservations on the Canon

As WOMEN WRITERS BECAME INCREASINGLY prominent toward the end of the nineteenth century, they received frequent coverage in general and literary magazines: sometimes in inclusive articles about Canadian authors, and sometimes in articles dedicated solely to female writers. Most widely read was Thomas O'Hagan's "Some Canadian Women Writers," an inventory that was published three times, its first appearance in *Catholic World* in 1896, quickly followed by condensed versions in the *Week* and in J. Castell Hopkins' *Canada: An Encyclopedia of the Country*.[1] Most such studies were written by men;[2] their tone was always laudatory and usually refrained from being excessively patronizing, for women were seen as important contributors to the growing promise of a strong cultural identity to accompany Canada's political destiny. In 1899, writing on "Recent Canadian Fiction" for the New York *Forum*, Laurence Burpee commented: "It will be observed that in fiction, as in verse, Canadian women are marching apace with the members of the opposite sex; and this applies as well to the quality as to the quantity of their productions."[3]

While the selection of named authors in these articles often reflected the critic's own circle of acquaintances, when reviewed as an ensemble, they offer a distinct canon. Articles with an historical focus recognized Susanna Moodie, Catharine Parr Traill, Anna Jameson, Rosanna Leprohon, and Isabella Valancy Crawford. Commentators looking at the present and future listed the most promising living writers as Sara Jeannette Duncan, Susie Frances Harrison, Pauline Johnson, Blanche Macdonnell, Agnes Maule Machar, Jean McIlwraith, Marshall Saunders, and Ethelwyn Wetherald. To some degree, therefore, nineteenth-century women writers identified as Canadian were spared the exclusion from the gendered

193

definition of authorship that marginalized vast numbers of British and American women who competed with professional male writers in the commercial marketplace.[4]

Despite such attention, the stakes were loaded against women when it came to elite accolades such as membership in the Royal Society of Canada, founded in 1882, which admitted the first woman to its flourishing literary section with the election of Gabrielle Roy in 1947. The contrasting fate of two late nineteenth-century writers illuminates the role of gender in the shifting construction of reputation in Canada. Sara Jeannette Duncan, quickly recognized as a major critic and author while she was active from the mid-1880s through the 1910s, subsided into nearly total eclipse after her death in 1922. The perspicacity of Malcolm Ross in reissuing *The Imperialist* in the New Canadian Library in 1961 led to renewed interest in the 1970s from a fresh generation of scholars, operating under a variety of theoretical perspectives from new criticism to feminism and post-colonialism. Over the past thirty years, Duncan has been the subject of many articles, theses, and books, and much of her writing has been brought back into print. On the other hand, now banished for its implicit racism is the dialect *habitant* writing, once canonized as the authentic voice of Canada, which was best known in the verse of William Henry Drummond.[5]

Underlying these canonical shifts are not only changing assessments of content, style, and ideology, but also institutional factors relating to gender. Duncan, whose education stopped at teacher training and whose only claim to significance was her writing, possessed no external cultural capital to buttress her reputation. In contrast, Drummond's professional status as a medical doctor and his social acquaintance with cultural power brokers earned him election to Britain's Royal Society of Literature in 1898 and to the Royal Society of Canada in 1899, followed by honorary degrees from the University of Toronto in 1902 and Bishop's College in 1905. So divergent has been their later status that scholarly writings about Duncan, as recorded in the MLA database, outnumber those about Drummond by a factor of ten (in July 2009, there were seventy-four items on Duncan and seven on Drummond).

The recuperation of Duncan and other early Canadian women writers that began in the 1970s has led to one of our favourite cultural myths: the notion that "the number of excellent women writers in Canada is remarkable."[6] In a spirit of smugness, naiveté, or optimism, or perhaps in accordance with Canadians' proverbial "niceness"[7] or what one writer has called "the national desire to please,"[8] we continue to embrace the view expressed in 1984 by an editor of several anthologies that "Canada has produced an unusual, even a predominant, number of women writers."[9] So prevalent is this myth that in 2000 Russell Smith blithely claimed that "In this country, our most famous writers are about 70 per cent women."[10] Similar examples abound in the first decade of the twenty-first century. In March 2002, Martin Levin, books editor at the *Globe and Mail*, congratulated Canadian women for their prominence as fiction writers and his own Books Section for reviewing them, yet whoever had prepared the same newspaper's "Holiday Fiction Special" ten weeks earlier was not similarly informed and only selected texts by men.[11] When literary authorities regard such notions as facts, it is not surprising to see them echoed by scholars in other fields, such as the economist who stated in 2003 that ever since Frances Brooke's publication of the first novel about North America, "Women writers have always held their own in Canada."[12]

The writers themselves are less sanguine. Margaret Atwood's claim that "the percentage of prominent and admittedly accomplished women writers, in both prose and poetry, is higher in Canada than it is in any of the other English-speaking countries"[13] was balanced by her knowledge that the actual figure was less than half of Russell Smith's "70 per cent." In a 1976 interview, Atwood responded impatiently when asked "How do you account for the fact that the majority of the best contemporary Canadian literature is indeed being written by women?" Answering "That's a question like are you still beating your wife," she noted that when examined directly, "many" turned into "some," typified by women getting about a third of the space in current literary anthologies. In Atwood's view, the question really being asked was "How come women can write"?[14] The same question—"Why so many Canadian women?"—remained in the air two decades later when Carol Shields addressed an audience at Harvard in a speech carefully titled "A View from the Edge of the Edge." She responded, "Part of me resents this question, since no one would ever think to ask, 'Why are there so many male writers?'" and noted that statistics demonstrate a preponderance of men. Her musings as to why the misperception should prevail then settled on women representing 70 percent of novel readers, who buy books by women because they choose to "hear other women's voices."[15] As Margaret Atwood succinctly noted, "Whether the glass is two-thirds empty or a third full depends upon how thirsty you are."[16]

A potent explanation for this pattern appears in references to Samuel Johnson's oft-cited comparison of a woman preacher to a dancing dog: "Sir, a woman preaching is like a dog's walking on his hind legs. It is not done well; but you are surprised to find it done at all."[17] In 1824, Margaret Blennerhassett's request for leniency from her reviewers echoed Johnson in her plea: "That it is some merit also, for a female to write verses at all."[18] A century and a half later, defending her privacy against those who felt entitled to ask what she was writing about, Ethel Wilson told inquisitive friends, "You'd never ask a woman at a cocktail party if she was pregnant, and if you did, she wouldn't tell you. It's really the same thing and I shall not tell you either." Then she mused, "Is it perhaps that a writing woman is like a preaching dog—abnormal?"[19] This unacknowledged sense of abnormality, I would argue, accounts for our distorted notion of the presence of women in Canada's literary history. The few dogs teetering on their hind legs, above the many who stand normally on four, are briefly more visible and seem more abundant than their actual numbers. Thus in 1987, it appeared to George Bowering that "the late sixties and early seventies saw a remarkable rise to prominence of our women writers, especially among the fiction writers. In fact they took over."[20]

In fact, the opposite is true, as Atwood and Shields both attest. While it may seem that a surprising number of Canadian women have achieved celebrity, as borne out in Lorraine York's selection of five women (Johnson, Montgomery, de la Roche, Shields, and Atwood) and just two men (Leacock and Ondaatje) for her recent study of *Literary Celebrity in Canada*,[21] achieving celebrity is not the same as enjoying canonicity. Despite current illusions of female literary dominance, it remains difficult to restructure mainstream perceptions of early Canadian writing even though the recuperative impulse of the last three decades has produced reprints of many books by women, as well as new anthologies dedicated solely to early women poets and short story writers.[22] However, this work remains ghettoized; while recuperative efforts have altered the canon of Canadian women writers, they have scarcely touched the primary canon of Canadian literature. For evidence, we have only to compare the surge of new omnibus teaching anthologies that appeared in the first decade of the twenty-first century with the earlier wave of such publications that marked the 1970s. In the new tomes, the sole substantial expansion of the canon of early women writers has been in the realm of racial representation: Pauline Johnson now receives more attention than in the past, and Edith Eaton and Mary Ann Shadd are occasionally included. Symptomatic of this lack of deep change is Oxford University Press's disingenuous reissue in 2008 of its 1966 selection of *Canadian Short Stories*, edited by Robert Weaver, with publicity claiming this to be "one of the finest anthologies of Canadian short fiction ever published" because it "includes enduring classics by such giants of Canadian literature as Frederick Philip Grove, Morley Callaghan, and Sinclair Ross."[23] Of Weaver's twenty-seven selected authors, just six are women (Ethel Wilson, Joyce Marshall, P.K. Page, Anne Hébert, Mavis Gallant, and Alice Munro). The period before 1920 is represented by E.W. Thompson, Charles G.D. Roberts, Duncan Campbell Scott, and Stephen Leacock. Lacking any acknowledgment of the existence of "enduring classics" by Susanna Moodie, Pauline Johnson, L.M. Montgomery, Marjorie Pickthall, Susie Frances Harrison, and Nellie McClung, to name half a dozen significant early female contributors to the genre, the book disavows the recuperative work of the last four decades and leaves readers to infer that Canada's first noteworthy women writers of short stories appeared in the 1940s.

It is difficult to find consistent and accurate quantitative data describing the presence of women in Canada's literary history. However, the studies that are available indicate that the measurable presence of women on the English-Canadian literary scene has altered much less over time than our current myth of female literary dominance would lead us to expect, and support Atwood's general perception that women have accounted for about one-third of the published literary writing in English. For 1984–85, an analysis of all books published in Canada and listed in *Quill & Quire* showed that 31 percent of the authors were women; they comprised 57 percent of the writers for children and young adults, 29 percent of the poets, and 26 percent of the novelists.[24] From Watters' *Checklist of Canadian Literature in English* (which does not distinguish between adult and juvenile literature), a count of works published up to and including 1905 reveals that women represented about 30.5 percent of the total number of authors of monographs of poetry and fiction, and produced about 31 percent of the titles. There was a clear distinction by genre: women were 24 percent of the poets and wrote 19 percent of the poetry titles, but were 41 percent of the fiction writers and produced 45 percent of the titles of fiction books.[25] Women were much less active in all other categories such as religion, history, biography, and travel. Robert Lecker's quantitative analysis of the presence of women in Canadian fiction anthologies from the 1920s to the early 1990s shows that while the gender gap noticeably diminished in the 1980s, stories by women stalled at an inclusion rate below 40 percent.[26]

Canadian women may seem to "predominate" in literature because writing is one of the few areas in which women have made a consistent public impact, as evidenced in the online *Dictionary of Canadian Biography,* which currently (December 2009) includes 503 women and 7,923 men. More than 28 percent (147) of these historically significant women are identified as authors, in contrast to 11.5 percent (916) of the men. Authorship is the largest identification category for women, followed by education and religion.[27] This pattern is exemplified in Alice Munro's *Lives of Girls and Women*, where the only remarkable woman in the history of her fictional Wawanosh County is one "whose poems used to be published in newspapers throughout Canada and the United States,"[28] albeit her significance does not extend to mention of her name. Hence it is not surprising that in *Maclean's* magazine's 1986 national poll, more than twice as many women as men chose writing as a field in which they would like to achieve success.[29] In more recent exercises such as *Maclean's* compilation of the "100 Most Important Canadians in History" (1998), which included seventeen women,[30] or its later list of "25 Canadians Who Inspired the World" (2000), which named five,[31] the majority of notable women were identified with the arts, and writing was the most prominent activity. While it is true that second-wave feminism has produced a shift in this pattern with the recognition of women's impact in other areas of public life such as politics, business, and sports,[32] I would argue that the correct question is not why Canada produces so many women writers, but why writing remains the area in which women have most commonly achieved recognition.

And yet, as this book demonstrates, that recognition has been partial and limited. While it is not possible to alter the historical record and claim that female poets or fiction writers outnumbered or outperformed men, it is possible to reconfigure the literary field so that the areas in which women achieved a presence receive greater acknowledgment. This is a slow and arduous effort. There is promise in new books such as Janice Fiamengo's *The Woman's Page: Journalism and Rhetoric in Early Canada* (2008), whose studies of six specific writers demonstrate that journalism is worthy of careful study, and Dean Irvine's analysis of women's essential participation in the infrastructure of Canadian modernism in *Editing Modernity: Women and Little-Magazine Cultures in Canada, 1916–1956* (2008). *Canadian Women in Print* is one more contribution to this process.

NOTES

꧁꧂

INTRODUCTION

1 Robert Darnton, "What Is the History of Books?" in *The Kiss of Lamourette: Reflections in Cultural History* (New York: Norton, 1990), 107–35; Thomas R. Adams and Nicolas Barker, "A New Model for the Study of the Book," in *The Potencie of Life: Books in Society: The Clark Lectures, 1986–1987*, ed. Nicolas Barker (London: British Library, 1993), 5–43.

2 Leslie Howsam, "In My View: Women and Book History," *SHARP News* 7, no. 4 (Autumn 1998): 1–2; Simone Murray, "Introduction," in *Mixed Media: Feminist Presses and Publishing Politics* (London: Pluto Press, 2004), 1–28; Howsam is cited by Trysh Travis, "The Women in Print Movement," *Book History* 11 (2008): 275.

3 Pierre Bourdieu, *The Field of Cultural Production* (New York: Columbia University Press, 1993).

4 See Carole Gerson, "Writers without Borders: The Global Framework of Canada's Early Literary History," *Canadian Literature* 201 (Summer 2009): 15–33.

5 Linda Hutcheon, "Rethinking the National Model," in *Rethinking Literary History*, ed. Linda Hutcheon and Mario J. Valdés (New York: Oxford University Press, 2002), 3–49.

6 Carrie MacMillan, Lorraine McMullen, and Elizabeth Waterston, *Silenced Sextet: Six Nineteenth-Century Canadian Women Novelists* (Montreal/Kingston: McGill-Queen's University Press, 1992); Janice Fiamengo, *The Woman's Page: Journalism and Rhetoric in Early Canada* (Toronto: University of Toronto Press, 2008).

7 Separate studies of individual authors also prevail in edited collections of essays about early Canadian women writers, such as Lorraine McMullen's *Re(dis)covering Our Foremothers* (Ottawa: University of Ottawa Press, 1990) and Jennifer Chambers' *Diversity and Change in Early Canadian Women's Writing* (Newcastle upon Tyne: Cambridge Scholars Publishing, 2008).

8 Edward Hartley Dewart, "Introduction," in *Selections from Canadian Poets* (Montreal: Lovell, 1864), viii.

9 Howsam, "In My View," 1.

CHAPTER 1

1 See Leslie Howsam, "Women in Publishing and the Book Trades in Britain, 1830–1914," *Leipziger Jahrbuch zur Buchgeschichte* 6 (1996): 67–79.

2 Leona M. Hudak, *Early American Women Printers and Publishers, 1639–1820* (Metuchen/London: Scarecrow Press, 1978), 210–19.

3 C. Galarneau, "Mesplet, Fleury," *Dictionary of Canadian Biography* (hereafter *DCB*) 4, online; H. Pearson Gundy, *Early Printers and Printing in the Canadas* (Toronto: Bibliographical Society of Canada, 1957), 17; Aegidius Fauteux, *The Introduction of Printing into Canada* (Montreal: Rolland Paper Co., 1957), Chapter 4, 16.

4 Margaret Lane Ford, "Types and Gender: Ann Franklin, Colonial Printer," in *A Living of Words: American Women in Print Culture*, ed. Susan Albertine (Knoxville: University of Tennessee Press, 1995), 1.

5 I.R. Dalton, "Simms, Sophia (Dalton)," *DCB* 8, online; for Ann Mott and Elizabeth Gay, see Patricia Fleming, *Atlantic Canadian Imprints, 1801–1820: A Bibliography* (Toronto: University of Toronto Press, 1991), 25, 75; for Anne Lovell, see Elizabeth Hulse, *A Dictionary of Toronto Printers, Publishers, etc.* (Toronto: Anson-Cartright, 1982), 150–51.

6 Jean-Marie Lebel, "Lefrançois, Charles," *DCB* 6, online.

7 Éric Leroux, "Printers: From Shop to Industry," *History of the Book in Canada* (hereafter *HBC*) 2: 77.

8 Christina Burr, "Defending 'The Art Preservative': Class and Gender Relations in the Printing Trades Unions, 1850–1914," *Labour/Le Travail* 31 (Spring 1993): 73.

9 Leroux, "Printers," 83.

10 Patricia Fleming, "The Binding Trades," *HBC* 2: 104.

11 Christina Burr and Éric Leroux, "Working in the Printing Trades," *HBC* 3: 364–65.

12 Burr, "Defending," 67–69.

13 Leroux, "Printers," 83, 104.

14 Burr, "Defending," 70.

15 Fleming, "The Binding Trades, 104.

16 "Some Women Workers in Victoria," Victoria *Daily Times*, 27 May 1895, 6.

17 Marian Tidcombe, *Women Bookbinders, 1880–1920* (New Castle/London: Oak Knoll Press/British Library, 1996), 18.

18 Ibid., 26.

19 Gwendolyn Davies, "The Elephant and the Primrose: The Prat Sisters in New York," *Journal of Pre-Raphaelite Studies* 6/7 (1998): 129–44.

20 Tidcombe, *Women Bookbinders*, 219, cites an exhibition in Vancouver in 1912 by Anna Macy, about whom nothing further has been found.

21 "A Chapter on Lady Editors," *Canadian Son of Temperance* 4, no. 1 (7 January 1854): 2. Edinburgh was one of the few cities where women achieved an effective presence, following a strike in 1873; by 1910 they numbered 850 compositors, as opposed to about a thousand men. See Sian Reynolds, "Women Compositors," *Edinburgh History of the Book in Scotland* 4: 133–35.

22 Chris Raible, *The Power of the Press: The Story of Early Canadian Printers and Publishers* (Toronto: Lorimer, 2007), 60 In the US, there was similar resistance to

the "petticoat invasion" when publishers tried to hire female compositors in the 1860s–1870s. See Ava Baron, "Women and the Making of the American Working Class: A Study of the Proletarianization of Printers," *Review of Radical Political Economics* 14, no. 3 (1982): 23–42.

23 Burr, "Defending," 62.

24 Dorothy W. Rungeling, *Life and Works of Ethelwyn Wetherald, 1857–1940* (Ridgeville: Rungeling, 2004), 41–42.

25 Victoria *Daily Times*, 27 May 1895, 6.

26 National Council of Women of Canada, *Women of Canada, Their Life and Work*, compiled for distribution at the Paris National Exhibition, 1900; rpt. 1975 (hereafter *WoC*), 77.

27 Lauren Pringle De La Vars, "Victoria Press," in *British Literary Publishing Houses, Dictionary of Literary Biography*, vol. 106, ed. Patricia J. Anderson and Jonathan Rose (Detroit: Gale, 1991), 311–14.

28 According to Howsam, "Women in Publishing," 71–72, the press produced at least 112 individual works, but they are difficult to identify.

29 Patricia Okker, *Our Sister Editors: Sarah J. Hale and the Tradition of Nineteenth-Century American Women Editors* (Athens: University of Georgia Press, 1995), 19.

30 In "Henrietta Muir Edwards: The Journey of a Canadian Feminist" (dissertation, Simon Fraser University, 1996), Patricia Roome cites a reference to *Women's Work in Canada* that appeared in the *Christian Helper* in 1881 (83), as well as a reference in the *Canadian Missionary Link* (1883) to a piece for a Christmas entertainment "titled 'A Teluga Girl's Story,' ... produced by the Montreal Women's Printing Office, illustrated by Henrietta and sold privately" (85).

31 Roome, "Henrietta Muir Edwards," 83. Into the early 1880s, Montreal's city directory listed the Working Girls' Association at 73 Bleury and the Young Women's Reading Room next door at 75, but there is no reference to the Montreal Women's Printing Office at that address or under "Printers."

32 These can be found as CIHM microfiche 86581-6, and 9-91734.

33 Elizabeth Driver, *Culinary Landmarks: A Bibliography of Canadian Cookbooks, 1825–1949* (Toronto: University of Toronto Press, 2008), 145, 463.

34 Mary Lu MacDonald, *Literature and Society in the Canadas, 1824–1850* (Lewiston: Edwin Mellen, 1992), 25.

35 Yvan Lamonde and Andrea Rotundo, "The Book Trade and Bookstores," *HBC* 1: 136.

36 Frances Stewart, *Our Forest Home: Being Extracts from the Correspondence of the Late Frances Stewart* (Montreal: Gazette, 1902), 25.

37 Heather Murray, *Come, Bright Improvement! The Literary Societies of Nineteenth-Century Ontario* (Toronto: University of Toronto Press, 2002), 26–28.

38 *Langton Records: Journals and Letters from Canada, 1837–1846* (Edinburgh: R. and R. Clark, 1904), 322; reprinted in Barbara Williams, ed., *A Gentlewoman in Upper Canada: The Journals, Letters, and Art of Anne Langton* (Toronto: University of Toronto Press, 2008), 355.

39 Murray, *Come*, 27.

40 Ibid., 98.

41 Ibid., 71.

42 Heather Murray, "Literary Societies," *HBC* 2: 475.

43 Another fifteen towns are named where "similar societies are known to exist" (*WoC* 398); the lack of significant overlap with Murray's list of eighteen Ontario women's literary societies (Murray, *Come*, 190) indicates that a national inventory would be quite extensive.

44 Gwendolyn Davies, "Murray, Frances Elizabeth," *DCB* 13, online.

45 Lois K. Yorke, "Edwards, Anna Harriette," *DCB* 14, online.

46 Loren Lerner, "William Notman's Portrait Photographs of Girls Reading from the 1860s to 1880s: A Pictorial Analysis Based on Contemporary Writings," *Papers of the Bibliographic Society of Canada* 47, no. 1 (2009): 45–73.

47 Agnes Maule Machar, *Roland Graeme: Knight* (1892; Ottawa: Tecumseh, 1996), 174.

48 S.H. Frost, "Report of Evangelistic Hall and Girls' Reading Room" (Montreal, 1905) 6, 10 (CIHM 66106); *WoC*, 405.

49 Jean Cogswell, "Case Study: Women's Institute Libraries," *HBC* 3, 498–500; Linda M. Ambrose, *For Home and Country: The Centennial History of the Women's Institutes in Ontario* (Erin: Boston Mills Press, 1996), 57–58.

50 Beth Milne, *Medicine Hat Public Library: The First Eighty Years* (Medicine Hat: Friends of the Medicine Hat Public Library, 1998), 1–2; Women's Literary Club fonds, Esplanade Archives, Medicine Hat, Alberta.

51 Chantal Savoie, "Des salons aux annales: Les réseaux et associations des femmes des lettres à Montréal au tournant du xxe siècle," *Voix et Images* 27, no. 2 (2002): 248.

52 Reproduced in *HBC* 1: 369.

53 Sophie Montreuil, "Joséphine Marchand-Dandurand: Readings in the Feminine," *HBC* 2: 461–65.

54 Lady Schultz, *How to Provide Good Reading for Children* (Toronto: Bryant Press, 1895).

55 National Council of Women of Canada, "Report of Sub-committee on Literature," adopted by the executive for submission to the National Council, 1896; CIHM 93412.

56 Madge Merton and John A. Cooper, "Our Children and Their Reading," *Canadian Magazine* 8 (January 1896): 286.

57 Angers to Soeur Saint François-Xavier, 26 September 1883, in Laure Conan, *J'ai tant de sujets de désespoir*, ed. Jean-Noël Dion (Montreal: Éditions Varia, 2002), 159.

58 Emily P. Weaver, A.E. Weaver, and E.C. Weaver, eds., *Canadian Women's Annual and Social Service Directory* (Toronto: McClelland, Goodchild, and Stewart, 1915), 209.

59 *WoC*, 173.

60 Yvan Lamonde, Peter F. McNally, and Andrea Rotundo, "Public Libraries and the Emergence of a Public Culture," *HBC* 2: 268.

61 Julie Roy, "Le réseau épistolaire comme horizon d'écriture au tournant du xixe siècle: Des « protoscriptrices » canadiennes en quête de visibilité," http://egodoc.revues.org/octobre2002/docs/D987612/VS987712.htm

62 Colin M. Coates and Cecilia Morgan, *Heroines and History: Representations of Madeleine de Verchères and Laura Secord* (Toronto: University of Toronto Press, 2002), 41–67.

63 Julie Roy, "Des réseaux en convergence: Les Éspaces de la sociabilité littéraire aud féminin dans la première moitié du xixe siècle," *Globe: Revue Internationale d'Études Québécoises* 7, no. 1 (2004): 95.

64 The manuscript volume, "Deborah How Cottnam. 'Precious Relics. A Collection of Original Pieces,'" compiled by Grizelda Tonge, is now in the Scott Library at UCLA.

65 Barbara Williams, "Introduction," in *A Gentlewoman in Upper Canada: The Journals, Letters, and Art of Anne Langton* (Toronto: University of Toronto Press, 2008), 83.

66 Patricia Godsell, ed., *Diary of Jane Ellice* (Toronto: Oberon, 1975), 7.

67 Ibid., 50.

68 Patricia Godsell, ed., *Letters & Diaries of Lady Durham* (Toronto: Oberon, 1979), 44.

69 Lady Dufferin, *My Canadian Journal, 1872–1878* (New York: Appleton, 1891), vii.

70 Kathryn Carter, "Neither Here Nor There: Mary Gapper O'Brien Writes 'Home,' 1828–1838," in *Diversity and Change in Early Canadian Women's Writing*, ed. Jennifer Chambers (Cambridge: Cambridge Scholars Press, 2008), 8–21.

71 See J.I. Little, ed., *Love Strong as Death: Lucy Peel's Canadian Journal, 1833–1836* (Waterloo: Wilfrid Laurier University Press, 2001).

72 *Langton Records*, 62–63; reprinted in Williams, *A Gentlewoman*, 175–77.

73 Anne Langton, *The Story of Our Family* (Manchester: Thomas Sowler and Co., 1881), iii.

74 *Langton Records*, 93; reprinted in Williams, *A Gentlewoman*, 200. The family records in the Archives of Ontario contain some manuscripts of Anne's poems, which seem to have remained unpublished.

75 Benjamin Drew, *The Refugee: Narratives of Fugitive Slaves in Canada. Related by Themselves* ... (Boston: John P. Jewett, 1856), 30, 31.

76 Jodi Aoki, "Private to Public: Frances Stewart, Ellen Dunlop, and the Production of *Our Forest Home*," MA thesis, Trent University, 2007, 2, 34, 61.

77 Cecily Devereux and Kathleen Venema, eds., *Women Writing Home, 1700–1920, Female Correspondence across the British Empire*, vol. 3, Canada (London: Pickering and Chatto, 2006), xxx–xxxi.

78 Kathleen Venema, "Letitia Mactavish Hargrave and Hudson's Bay Company Domestic Politics," in *ReCalling Early Canada*, ed. Jennifer Blair et al. (Edmonton: University of Alberta Press, 2005), 153–55.

79 Carl Ballstadt, Elizabeth Hopkins, and Michael A. Peterman, eds., *Letters of Love and Duty: The Correspondence of Susanna and John Moodie* (Toronto: University of Toronto Press, 1993), 147.

80 Henriette Dessaules, *Journal, premier cahier, 1874–1876*, ed. Jean-Louis Major (Montreal: Bibliothèque Québécoise, 1999), 51.

81 Jean-Louis Major, "Inventaire et invention d'une littérature: Le Corpus d'éditions critiques," in *Challenges, Projects, Texts: Canadian Editing*, ed. John Lennox and Janet M. Patterson (New York: AMS Press, 1993), 83–85.

82 Rev. William Chipman, "Preface," in *Memoir of Mrs. Eliza Ann Chipman* (Wolfville, 1855), 3.

83 "Edited, with introductory notes of her life, by her son, Francis E. Clark" (Boston: United Society of Christian Endeavor, 1911).

84 Carole Gerson and Jacques Michon, "Editors' Introduction," *HBC* 3: 4–6.

85 Driver, *Culinary Landmarks*, 93.

86 Ibid., 526.

87 Driver cites a few Canadian editions of early cookbooks translated into Ukrainian (1046) and German (358), in both instances written by men.

88 Kirsten Wolf, "Þorsteinsdóttir, Torfhildur (Holm)," *DCB* 14, online.

89 Emily P. Weaver, A.E. Weaver, and E.C. Weaver, eds., *The Canadian Women's Annual and Social Services Directory* (Toronto: McClelland, Goodchild, and Stewart, 1915), 201.

90 Florence Randal Livesay, "Note by Translator," in *Songs of Ukraina, with Ruthenian Poems* (London: Dent, 1916), 20.

CHAPTER 2

1 See the charts of the growth of print in *History of the Book in Canada* (hereafter *HBC*) 1: "Imprints by Decade," 89; "Newspapers Founded Pre-1801 and 1801–20," 230; "Newspapers Founded in the Atlantic Colonies," 231; "Newspapers Founded in Lower and Upper Canada, 1821–1840," 232.

2 Susanna Moodie, "Editor's Table," *Victoria Magazine* 1 (June 1848): 240.

3 Mrs. [Anna Sophia] Stephens, "Literary Ladies of America," *Amaranth* 3, no. 5 (May 1843): 129–36. Elaine Showalter's *A Jury of Her Peers* (2009) outlines the nationalist impulse that inspired many American women writers in the 1820s and 1830s, leading to three anthologies of American women's poetry in the late 1840s; see especially pp. 32–34 and 60–63.

4 Marie Tremaine, *A Bibliography of Canadian Imprints, 1751–1800* (Toronto: University of Toronto Press, 1952) includes *A Sermon Occasioned by the Death of the Honorable Mrs. Abigail Belcher* (Halifax: A. Henry, 1771), 75–76; *Death: The Way to the Believer's Compleat Happiness. Illustrated and Improved, in a Sermon, Occasioned by the Death of Mrs. Jane Chipman* (Halifax: A. Henry, 1775), 96–97.

5 Michel Verrette, *L'alphabétisation au Québec, 1660–1900* (Quebec: Septentrion, 2002), 92.

6 Alison Prentice et al., *Canadian Women: A History* (Toronto: Harcourt Brace Jovanovich, 1988), 57; *Formulaire de prieures, a L'usage des pensionnaires des religieuses ursulines* (Montreal: Fleury Mesplet and Charles Berger, 1777); Tremaine, *A Bibliography*, 122.

7 Kathleen Rochefort Murray, "Sainte Anne as Symbol of Literacy in Quebec Culture," *Quebec Studies* 30 (2000): 73.

8 Elizabeth Jane Errington, *Wives and Mothers, Schoolmistresses and Scullery Maids: Working Women in Upper Canada, 1790–1840* (Montreal: McGill-Queen's University Press, 1995), 210.

9 Tremaine, *A Bibliography*, 140.

10 Nancy Towle, *Some of the Writings, and Last Sentences of Adolphus Dewey, Executed at Montreal, Aug 30th, 1833* (Montreal: J.A. Hoisington, Printer, 1833).

11 Donald Chaput, "Charlotte de Rocheblave, Métisse Teacher of the Teachers," *Beaver* (Autumn 1977): 55–58.

12 Christiana Brant is the Mohawk "princess" who was working on Biblical translations in 1824: see *Faith of Our Fathers: A Century of Victory* ([Toronto?]: Methodist Missionary Society, 1924), 6.

13 Donald Chaput, "The 'Misses Nolin' of Red River," *Beaver* (Winter 1975): 14–17.

14 Bruce Peel, "Thomas, Sophia (Mason)," *Dictionary of Canadian Biography* (hereafter *DCB*) 9, online.

15 *Quebec Herald*, 8–29 December 1788, cited by Tremaine, *A Bibliography*, 273–74.

16 Patricia Fleming, *Upper Canadian Imprints, 1801–1841: A Bibliography* (Toronto: University of Toronto Press, 1988), 175.

17 Tremaine, *A Bibliography*, 269, 289.

18 Elizabeth Driver, *Culinary Landmarks: A Bibliography of Canadian Cookbooks, 1825–1949* (Toronto: University of Toronto Press, 2008), 82–83, 286–87, 287–88.

19 Mary Lu MacDonald, "Reading between the Lines: An Analysis of Canadian Literary Prefaces and Prospectuses in the First Half of the Nineteenth Century," in *Prefaces and Literary Manifestoes/Préfaces et manifestes littéraires*, ed. E.D. Blodgett and A.G. Purdy (Edmonton: Research Institute for Comparative Literature, 1990), 40.

20 Marie-Emmanuel Chabot, "Guyart, Marie, dite Marie de l'Incarnation," *DCB* 1, online; Hélène Bernier, "Morin, Marie," *DCB* 2, online; Jean-Pierre Asselin, "Regnard Duplessis, Marie-Andrée," *DCB* 2, online; Burke and Cimon are in Gabrielle Lapointe, "Les Ursulines de Québec," *Dictionnaire des oeuvres littéraires du Québec* (hereafter *DOLQ*) 1, 743–45; Mme de Gomez is in John Hare and Jean-Pierre Wallot, *Les imprimés dans le Bas-Canada, 1801–40: Bibliographie analytique* (Montreal: PUM, 1967), 246.

21 Patricia Okker notes a distinct rise in American female editors in the 1820s: *Our Sister Editors: Sara J. Hale and the Tradition of Nineteenth-Century American Women Editors* (Athens: University of Georgia Press, 1995), 8.

22 Mary Lu MacDonald, "The *Montreal Museum*, 1832–1834: The Presence and Absence of Literary Women," in *Women's Writing and the Literary Institution/L'écriture au féminin et l'institution littéraire*, ed. C. Potvin and J. Williamson (Edmonton: University of Alberta Research Institute for Comparative Literature, 1992), 139–50.

23 Mary Lu MacDonald, *Literature and Society in the Canadas, 1817–1850* (Lewiston: Edwin Mellen Press, 1992), 303, 307; Mary Markham Brown, *An Index to the* Literary Garland (Toronto: Bibliographical Society of Canada, 1962).

24 MacDonald, *Literature and Society in the Canadas*, 281.

25 Patty's comment about having "altered my style" suggests that there may have been more than one hand involved. *Novascotian*, 13 July 1826, 257.

26 Candidates include Mary Heaviside (Lady Love), who may have done the illustrations based on the work of Captain G.F. Lyon (Phyllis Creighton, "Heaviside, Mary," *DCB* 9, online), and Lucy Lyon, the captain's young wife (Ann Savours, *The Search for the North West Passage* [New York: St. Martin's Press, 1999], 12).

27 *Poems* (Southampton: Forbes and Pittman, 1857).

28 Driver, *Culinary Landmarks*, 288.

29 Pierre Gérin, "Une ecrivaine acadienne à la fin du XIXe siècle: Marichette," *Atlantis* 10, no. 1 (1984): 38–45.

30 Carl Ballstadt, Elizabeth Hopkins, and Michael A. Peterman, eds., *I Bless You in My Heart: Selected Correspondence of Catharine Parr Traill* (Toronto: University of Toronto Press, 1996), 267.

31 "Address to the Public," Widow Fleck, *Poems on Various Subjects*, 2nd ed. (Montreal: A. Bowman, 1835); M. Ethelind Sawtell, "Preface," in *The Mourner's Tribute; or Effusions of Melancholy Hours* (Montreal: Armour and Ramsay, 1840); "Our Table," *Literary Garland* 2 (1840): 123.

32 A similar entreaty to "Buy the life of the worthy but persecuted widow; and give what you please above sixpence-halfpenny, for a temporary relief" concludes Sophie Berthelette Chaureth's *Sketches of the Life, Troubles, and Grievances of a French Canadian Lady* (Toronto: n.p., 1857), 32.

33 "Our Table," *Literary Garland* 3 (1845): 576.

34 William Barker, "Books and Reading in Newfoundland and in Labrador," *HBC* 1: 362–64.

35 Gwendolyn Davies, "Researching Eighteenth-Century Maritime Women Writers: Deborah How Cottnam—A Case Study," in *Working in Women's Archives*, ed. Helen M. Buss and Marlene Kadar (Waterloo: Wilfrid Laurier University Press, 2001), 35.

36 The manuscript "Deborah How Cottnam. 'Precious Relics. A Collection of Original Pieces,'" [Nova Scotia, c. 1820], compiled by Grizelda Tonge, is now at the Scott Library, UCLA.

37 Gwendolyn Davies, "'Dearer Than His Dog': Literary Women in Pre-Confederation Nova Scotia," *Studies in Maritime Literary History* (Fredericton: Acadiensis, 1991), 71–87.

38 Sally Kirby Padelford, according to WorldCat.

39 Email from Gwendolyn Davies, 6 April 2007.

40 Gwendolyn Davies, "Private Education for Women in Early Nova Scotia: 1784–1894," *Acadiensis* 20, no. 1 (1995): 14.

41 Gwendolyn Davies, "'In the Garden of Christ': Methodist Literary Women in Nineteenth-Century Maritime Canada," in *The Contribution of Methodism to Atlantic Canada*, ed. Charles H.H. Scobie and John Webster Grant (Montreal/Kingston: McGill-Queen's University Press, 1992), 206, 215.

42 *Narrative of the Life and Christian Experience of Mrs. Mary Bradley* (Boston: Strong and Brodhe, 1849), 150

43 Gwendolyn Davies, "Herbert, Sarah (1824–46) and Mary Eliza Herbert (1829–72), *Oxford Companion to Canadian Literature* (Toronto: Oxford University Press, 1997), 531.

44 Handwritten attributions to Herbert appear in the bound volume in the Baldwin Room, Metro Toronto Library, microfilmed by McLaren Micropublishing.

45 Davies, "'Dearer Than His Dog,'" 83–85.

46 Driver, *Culinary Landmarks*, 13.

47 Davies, "'Dearer Than His Dog,'" 85.

48 Manon Brunet, "Les femmes dans la production de la littérature francophone du début de XIXᵉ siècle québécois," in *Livre et lecture au Québec (1800–1850)*, ed. Claude Galarneau and Maurice Lemire (Quebec: Institut Québécois de Recherche sur la Culture, 1988), 167–80.

49 *Les textes poétiques du Canada français*, vol. 2, ed. Jeanne d'Arc Lortie avec la collaboration de Pierre Savard et Paul Wyczynski (Montreal: Fides), 89–90.

50 *La vie littéraire au Québec*, vol. 2, ed. Denis Saint-Jacques and Maurice Lemire (Sainte-Foy: Les Presses de l'Université Laval, 2005), 91.

51 Julie Roy, "Le 'genre' prétexte: Récit de soi et critique sociale dans les correspondences 'féminines' au tournant du XIXᵉ siècle," in *Portrait des arts, des letters de de l'éloquence au Québec (1760–1840)*, ed. Bernard Andrès and Marc André Bernier (Quebec: Les Presses de l'Université Laval, 2002), 187.

52 Her poems have since been published in volumes 2–5 of *Les textes poétiques du Canada français, 1606–1867*, ed. Jeanne d'Arc Lortie avec la collaboration de Pierre Savard, Paul Wyczynski (Montreal:.Fides, 1987). See also Louise-Amélie Parent, *Quelques traits particuliers aux saisons du bas Canada ...*, ed. Roger LeMoine (Orléans: Editions David, 2000).

53 Julie Roy, "Voyages en pays de re-connaissance: Paysages et mémoires dans l'oeuvre de Louise-Amélie Panet-Berczy (1789–1865)," in *Intercultural Journeys/Parcours interculturels*, ed. Natasha Dagenais, Joanna Daxell, and Roxanne Rimstead (Sherbrooke: l'Université de Sherbrooke, 2003), 166–67.

54 Lortie et al., *Les textes poétiques*, vol. 4.

55 Mary Lu MacDonald, "The *Montreal Museum, 1832–1834*: The Presence and Absence of Literary Women," in *Women's Writing and the Literary Institution/L'écriture au féminin et l'institution littéraire*, ed. C. Potvin et al. (Edmonton: University of Alberta Press, 1992), 139.

56 Ibid., 140.

57 The poems were likely brought to Canada by an acquaintance of Moodie's brother, Samuel Strickland, who had emigrated in 1825; *Susanna Moodie: Letters of a Lifetime*, ed. Carl Ballstadt, Elizabeth Hopkins, and Michael A. Peterman (Toronto: University of Toronto Press, 1985), 73–74.

58 "Editor's Table," *Victoria Magazine* 1, no. 12 (August 1848): 287.

59 Ibid., 288.

60 In 1942, Edwin Guillet transcribed the poems from a copy that has since disappeared. Copies of his typescript are to be found in several libraries and in his papers at Trent University.

61 Philippe Sylvain, "Monk, Maria," *DCB* 7, online.

62 Normand Lester, *Le livre noir du Canada anglais* (Montreal: Intouchables, 2001), 125–29.

63 Edward Hartley Dewart, *Selections from Canadian Poets* (Montreal: Lovell, 1864), xi.

64 Davies, "'Dearer Than His Dog,'" 87.

65 Benjamine Sulte, "Préface," in *Fleurs du printemps* by Mme Duval-Thibault (Fall River: Société de publication de l'Indépendant, 1892), viii.

CHAPTER 3

1 *Catholic World* 63 (September 1896): 779–95; condensed in the *Week* 13 (25 September 1896): 1050–53.

2 W.D. Lighthall, *Songs of the Great Dominion* (London: Walter Scott, 1889), xxxii.

3 J.E. Wetherell, *Later Canadian Poems* (Toronto: Copp Clark, 1893); rev. *Canadian Magazine* 1 (August 1893): 507–08.

4 Gérard Genette, *Paratexts: Thresholds of Interpretation*, trans. Jane E. Lewin (New York: Cambridge University Press, 1997), 263.

5 Rosanna Leprohon, *Antoinette de Mirecourt* (1864; Ottawa: Carleton University Press 1989), 1.

6 Gayatri Spivak, "Translator's Preface," in *Of Grammatology* by Jacques Derrida (Baltimore: Johns Hopkins University Press, 1976), ix–xiii.

7 Anne Innis Dagg, "Canadian Voices of Authority: Non-fiction and Early Women Writers," *Journal of Canadian Studies* 27, no. 2 (Summer 1992): 111–13.

8   Theresa Delaney and Theresa Gowanlock, *Two Months in the Camp of Big Bear* (1885; Regina: Canadian Plains Research Centre, 1999), 3–4, 51.

9   Jennet Roy, *History of Canada for the Use of Schools and Families* (Montreal: Armour and Ramsay, 1847), [iii].

10   Mary Lu Macdonald, "Reading between the Lines: An Analysis of Canadian Literary Prefaces and Prospectuses in the First Half of the Nineteenth Century," in *Prefaces and Literary Manifestoes/Préfaces et manifestes littéraires*, ed. E.D. Blodgett and A.G. Purdy (Edmonton: Research Institute for Comparative Literature, 1990), 30–32.

11   Julia Catherine Beckwith Hart, *St. Ursula's Convent or the Nun of Canada* (1824; Ottawa: Carleton University Press, 1991), 3.

12   MacDonald, "Reading," 40.

13   Ibid., 34.

14   Ibid., 35.

15   Carole Gerson, *A Purer Taste: The Writing and Reading of Fiction in English in Nineteenth-Century Canada* (Toronto: University of Toronto Press, 1989), 18–19.

16   Rebecca Gould Gibson, "'My Want of Skill': Apologias of British Women Poets, 1660–1800," in *Eighteenth-Century Women and the Arts*, ed. Frederick M. Keener and Susan E. Lorsch (New York: Greenwood Press, 1988), 79–86.

17   Elizabeth N. Lockerby ("E.N.L."), *The Wild Brier: or, Lays by an Untaught Minstrel* (Charlottetown: Excelsior, 1866), vii; Janet C. Conger, *A Daughter of St. Peter's* (New York: Lovell, 1888), [i]; Caroline Hayward, *The Battles of the Crimea, with Other Poems* (Port Hope: Ansley, 1855), [7].

18   Mrs. Mary Norton, *The Ministry of Flowers and Other Poems* (Toronto: Briggs, 1890), [vii]; Margaret Gill Currie, *Gabriel West and Other Poems* (Fredericton: Cropley, 1866), [v]; Kate Simpson Hayes ("Mary Markwell") *Aweena* (Winnipeg: Hart, 1906), [ix]; Lockerby, *The Wild Brier*, viii; Augusta Baldwyn, *Poems* (Montreal: Lovell, 1859), [ix]; Ethel Ursula Foran, *Poems* (Montreal: Beauchemin, 1921), 7.

19   Margaret Blennerhasset, *The Widow of the Rock, and Other Poems* (Montreal: Sparhawk, 1824), [iii].

20   Elizabeth Gaskell, *The Life of Charlotte Brontë* (Harmondsworth: Penguin, 1981), 173.

21   Suzanne Juhasz, *Naked and Fiery Forms: Modern American Poetry by Women, a New Tradition* (New York: Harper, 1976). Ireland was similarly described as a country "where the word *woman* and the word *poet* were almost magnetically opposed" by Eavan Boland, *Object Lessons* (New York: Norton, 1995), xi.

22   Baldwyn, *Poems*, [ix]; Sarah E. Sherwood Faulkner, *Sea Murmurs and Woodland Songs* (Toronto: Briggs, 1903), [iii]; Ethel Ursula Foran, *Springtime Fancies* (Montreal: Gazette, 1935), [ix].

23   Julie Roy, "Le 'genre' prétexte: Récit de soi et critique sociale danes les correspondences 'féminines' au tournant du XIXᵉ siècle," in *Portrait des arts, des lettres et de l'éloquence au Québec (1760–1840)*, ed. Bernard Andrès and Marc André Bernier (Quebec: Laval University Press, 2002), 181–201, 186–87.

24   Léonise Valois ("Atala"), *Fleurs sauvages* (Montreal: Beauchemin, 1910), 7.

25   Wendy Wall, *The Imprint of Gender* (Ithaca: Cornell University Press, 1993), 175; E.R. Curtius, "Affected Modesty," In *European Literature and the Latin Middle Ages*, trans. W.R. Trask (London: Routledge, 1953), 83–85.

26 William Thomas Carroll Ryan, *Oscar: and Other Poems* (Hamilton: Franklin, 1857), [5].

27 Mary Anne McIver, *Poems* (Ottawa: Taylor), n.p.

28 Edward Hartley Dewart, *Songs of Life: A Collection of Poems* (Toronto: Dudley and Burns, 1869), iii–v; Isidore Ascher, *Voices from the Hearth. A Collection of Verses* (Montreal: Lovell, 1863), 9–14.

29 George E. Merkley, *Canadian Melodies and Poems* (Toronto: Hart and Riddell, 1893), v.

30 Dewart, *Songs of Life*, iv; Merkley, *Canadian Melodies and Poems*, v; Ryan, *Oscar*, viii–ix; Joseph Kearney Foran, *Poems and Canadian Lyrics* (Montreal: Sadlier, 1895), [iii].

31 Mrs. E.S. Macleod, *Carols of Canada* (Charlottetown: Coombs, 1893), v.

32 Pamelia Vining Yule, *Poems of the Heart and Home* (Toronto: Bengough Moore, 1881), iv.

33 Steven Totosy de Zepetnek, *The Social Dimensions of Fiction* (Wiesbaden: Vieweg, 1993), 64.

34 Anne Finch, "The Introduction," *The Poems of Ann Countess of Winchilsea*, ed. Myra Reynolds (Chicago: University of Chicago Press, 1903), 4.

35 Annie Louisa Walker, *Leaves from the Backwoods* (Montreal: Lovell, 1861), 107.

36 Carole Gerson, "Annie Louisa Walker Coghill," *Canadian Notes and Queries*, 37 (1987): 9–10.

37 Sandra M. Gilbert and Susan Gubar, *The Madwoman in the Attic* (New Haven: Yale University Press, 1979), 49.

38 Currie, *Gabriel West*, [v]; Conger, *A Daughter of St. Peter's*, [i]; McIver, *Poems*, n.p.

39 Conger, *A Daughter of St. Peter's*, [i].

40 Clotida Jennings ("Maude"), *Linden Rhymes* (Halifax: Fuller, 1854), [v].

41 Jeanne-Lydia Branda ("Marie Sylvia"), *Vers le bien* (Ottawa, 1916), [3].

42 Carrie Leonard, *Gems for the Home Circle* (London: Cameron, 1869); Margaret E. Tennant, *The Golden Chord* (Almonte: McLeod and McEwen, 1899), [v].

43 Clara Mountcastle, *Is Marriage a Failure? Lost! And Many Gems of Verse* (Toronto: Imrie Graham, 1899), [iv].

44 Hayward, *The Battles of the Crimea*, [i, iii].

45 Joséphine Dandurand, *Nos travers* (Montreal: Beauchemin, 1901), [5].

46 Mrs. W.W. Rodd, "Introduction," in *Sunbeams: A Collection of Original Poems* (Charlottetown, 1898), [3].

47 Hart, *St. Ursula's*, 3–4.

48 Robertine Barry, *Fleurs champêtres* (Montreal: Desaulniers, 1895), i.

49 Anna-Marie Duval-Thibault, *Deux testaments: Esquisse de moeurs canadiennes* (Fall River: Imprimere de L'Independent, 1888), 2.

50 Sarah Anne Curzon, *Laura Secord, the Heroine of 1812: A Drama, and Other Poems* (Toronto: Robinson, 1887), n.p.

51 Thomas O'Hagan, "Some Canadian Women Writers," *Catholic World* 63 (September 1896), 784.

52 Mrs. John Crawford, *Songs of All Seasons, Climes, and Times, a Motley Jingle of Jumbled Rhymes* (Toronto: Rose, 1890), [iii].

53 Clara Mountcastle ("Caris Sima"), *The Mission of Love; Lost; and Other Poems* (Toronto: Hunter Rose, 1882), [v].

54 Gaetane de Montreuil, "Préface," in *Contes et légendes* by Madame A.B. Lacert (Ottawa: Beauregard, 1915), [4].

55 W.H. Withrow, "Introduction," in *Sowing and Reaping* by Pamelia Vining Yule (Toronto: Briggs, 1889), iii.

56 Elaine Showalter, *A Literature of Their Own* (Princeton: Princeton University Press, 1977), 73.

57 W.H. Withrow, "Introduction," in *Clipped Wings* by Lottie McAlister (Toronto: Briggs, 1899), [iii].

58 John Reade, "Introduction," in *Poetical Works of Mrs. Leprohon* by Mrs. [Rosanna] Leprohon (Montreal: Lovell, 1881), 4, 8.

59 Judge W.D. Prowse, "Introduction," in *The Victorian Triumph and Other Poems* by Isabella Whiteford Rogerson (Toronto: Briggs, 1898), vii; Constance Fairbanks and Harry Piers, "Biographical Sketch" in *Frankincense and Myrrh* by Mary Jane Katzmann Lawson (Halifax: Morton, 1893), vi; Rev. William Stephenson, "Preface," in *Wayside Flowers* by Harriette Annie Wilkins (Toronto: Hunter Rose, 1876), v.

60 John Garvin, "A Word from the Editor," in *Collected Poems* by Isabella Valancy Crawford (Toronto: Briggs, 1905), 1.

61 Laura Durand, "Memoir," in *Elise Le Beau* ... by Evelyn Durand (Toronto: University of Toronto Press, 1921), xiv; Ethelwyn Wetherald, "Introduction," in Crawford, *Collected Poems*, 19.

62 Virginia Woolf, *A Room of One's Own* (1929; London: Grafton, 1985), 71.

63 Garvin in Crawford, *Collected Poems*, 1; Wetherald in Crawford, *Collected Poems*, 27.

64 Andrée Levesque, *La norme et les déviantes* (Montreal: Remue-ménage, 1989), 7. I prefer her original invocation of "le discours" to the translation's use of "theory": "There is theory and then there is real life."

65 Susie Frances Harrison, *Crowded out! and Other Sketches* (Ottawa: Evening Journal Office, 1886), [iii].

66 Sara Jeannette Duncan, *A Social Departure* (New York: Appleton, 1890), v.

67 Mrs. Jameson, *Winter Studies and Summer Rambles in Canada*, 3 vols. (London: Saunders and Otley, 1838), vol. 1, vi (NCL ed., 9).

68 Catharine Parr Traill, "Introduction," in *The Backwoods of Canada* (1836; Ottawa: Carleton University Press, 1997), 1.

69 Leprohon, *Antoinette*, 1.

70 Ibid., 3.

71 Misao Dean, *Practising Femininity: Domestic Realism and the Performance of Gender in Early Canadian Fiction* (Toronto: University of Toronto Press, 1998), 42–56. This topic is taken up again in Chapter 4.

72 Susanna Moodie, *Life in the Clearings versus the Bush* (1853; Toronto: McClelland and Stewart, 1989), 65.

73 Susanna Moodie, *Roughing It in the Bush* (1852; Ottawa: Carleton University Press, 1988), 215.

74 Moodie, *Life in the Clearings*, 20.

75 Dean, *Practising Femininity*, 41. Dean discusses Moodie's style in relation to Patricia Meyer Spacks' *Gossip*, 36–41.

76 Moodie, *Life in the Clearings*, 59.

77 Ibid., 252.

78 See Carole Gerson, "L.M. Montgomery and the Conflictedness of a Woman Writer," in *Storm and Dissonance: L.M. Montgomery and Conflict*, ed. Jean Mitchell (Newcastle: Cambridge Scholars Publishing, 2008), 67–80

CHAPTER 4

1   http://cufts2.lib.sfu.ca/CRDB/BVAS/resource/5724

2   Anne Innis Dagg, *The Feminine Gaze* (Waterloo: Wilfrid Laurier University Press, 2001).

3   Micheline Cambron and Carole Gerson, "Literary Authorship," *History of the Book in Canada* (hereafter *HBC*) 2, 131.

4   "Échantillon des acteurs de la vie littéraire (1895–1918)—les hommes," "Échantillon des acteurs de la vie littéraire (1895–1918)—les femmes," *Histoire de la vie littéraire au Québec* (hereafter *VLQ*) 5, 150–75.

5   Robertine Barry, "French Canadian Women in Literature," in *Women of Canada, Their Life and Work* (hereafter *WoC*), compiled by the National Council of Women of Canada for distribution at the Paris National Exhibition, 1900 (rpt. 1975), 190–91.

6   Mary Jean Green, "The 'Literary' Feminists and the Fight for Women's Writing in Quebec," *Journal of Canadian Studies* 21, no. 1 (1986): 128–43.

7   Chantal Savoie, "'Moins de dentelles, plus de psychologie' et une heure à soi: les *Lettres* de Fadette et la chronique féminine au tournant du xxᵉ siècle," in *Tendances actuelles en histoire littéraire canadienne*, ed. Denis Saint-Jacques (Quebec: Nota Bene, 2003), 185.

8   *VLQ* 5: 285, 288–92.

9   "The Impressions of Janey Canuck Abroad" ran in the *National Monthly of Canada* from June 1902 until May 1903, and "The Impressions of Janey Canuck at Home" from June to November, 1903. My thanks to Tracy Kulba for this information.

10 Donna Coates, "Emily Murphy," in *Canadian Writers before 1890: Dictionary of Literary Biography* (hereafter *DLB*) 99, ed. W.H. New (Detroit: Gale, 1990), 257.

11 Isabel Bassett, "Introduction," in *Janey Canuck in the West* by Emily Ferguson Murphy (Toronto: McClelland and Stewart, 1975), xxii.

12 John Brewer, *The Pleasures of the Imagination: English Culture in the Eighteenth Century* (London: HarperCollins, 1997), 190

13 See Ernest Curtius, "The Book as Symbol," Chapter 16 of his *European Literature and the Latin Middle Ages* (1948; trans. 1953); Jesse M. Gellrich, *The Idea of the Book in the Middle Ages* (Ithaca: Cornell University Press, 1985).

14 Alison Adburgham, *Women in Print: Writing Women and Women's Magazines from the Restoration to the Accession of Victoria* (London: Allen and Unwin, 1972).

15 Mary Kelley, *Private Woman, Public Stage: Literary Domesticity in Nineteenth-Century America* (New York: Oxford University Press, 1984), 28–29.

16 Margaret Atwood, "A Thing or Two about Nationalism," *Vancouver Sun*, 20 August 1973, 5; Susanna Moodie, *Life in the Clearings versus the Bush,* first published in 1853, reprinted in the New Canadian Library edition (Toronto: McClelland and Stewart, 1989), 65; Susanna Moodie, *Roughing It in the Bush: or, Life in Canada*, ed. Carl Ballstadt (Ottawa: Carleton University Press, 1986), 215.

17 Mary Poovey, *The Proper Lady and the Woman Writer: Ideology as Style in the Works of Mary Wollstonecraft, Mary Shelley, and Jane Austen* (Chicago: University of Chicago Press, 1984), xv.

18 Virginia Woolf, *A Room of One's Own* (1929; London: Grafton, 1985), 62.

19 *Susanna Moodie: Letters of a Lifetime*, ed. Carl Ballstadt, Elizabeth Hopkins, and Michael A. Peterman (Toronto: University of Toronto Press, 1985), 99.

20 Curzon to Kirby, 14 October 1892, Kirby papers, AO.

21 Louisa Murray, "An Appeal to Patriotic Canadians," *Week* 6, 10 May 1889, 362.

22 Barbara Godard, "Murray, Louisa Annie," *Dictionary of Canadian Biography* (hereafter *DCB*) 12, online.

23 While circulation figures provided by magazines for publicity purposes are not reliable, indicative is that in 1915 the Montreal *Family Herald*, which published much fiction, reported 169,000 subscriptions. K.S. Fenwick, "The Magazine and Farm Paper Situation," *Economic Advertising* 8, no. 6 (June 1915): 23–27.

24 Florence Sherk, *The Workshop and Other Poems* (Fort William: Times-Journal, 1919), [ix].

25 Mrs. Nobody to MacMechan [1918–], MacMechan papers, no. 874, 729, Dalhousie University Archives.

26 "Introduction," in *The Poetical Works of Mrs. Leprohon* (Montreal: Lovell, 1881), 4.

27 Although posthumous books are usually graced with informative prefaces, the only clue regarding Miss Campbell is that some of the poems were written at Zorra (near Woodstock, Ontario).

28 To cite four examples from the many that abound: an unidentified friend prepared *Memorials of Margaret Elizabeth, Only Daughter of Rev. Albert Des Brisay of the Province of New Brunswick* (New York: Carlton and Phillips, 1856) shortly after the young author died of consumption at the age of nineteen. Jane McKenzie Arkley's *A Book of Verse* (Sherbrooke, 1912) appeared nearly two decades after her death in 1894. More than twenty years after Evelyn Durand died in 1900, her sister edited her collected poems (*Elise Le Beau: A Dramatic Idyll, and Lyrics and Sonnets* [Toronto: University of Toronto Press, 1921], while it was Mary Stewart Durie Gibson's mourning husband who brought out his wife's *Stories and Verses* (Toronto: Briggs, 1913).

29 Samantha Matthews, *Poetical Remains: Poets' Graves, Bodies, and Books in the Nineteenth Century* (Oxford/New York: Oxford University Press, 2004), 4, 5.

30 Margaret J.M. Ezell, "The Posthumous Publication of Women's Manuscripts and the History of Authorship," in *Women's Writing and the Circulation of Ideas: Manuscript Publication in England, 1550–1800*, ed. George Justice and Nathan Tinker (New York: Cambridge University Press, 2002), 128–29.

31 Line Gosselin, "Marmette, Marie-Louise," *DCB* 15, online.

32 E. Cora Hind, *Tales of the Road*, no. III (Winnipeg, 1913).

33 Wilfred Eggleston, *Literary Friends* (Ottawa: Borealis, 1980), 112.

34 S. Squire Spriggs, *The Methods of Publishing*, 2nd ed. (London: Incorporated Society of Authors, 1891), 63.

35 Caswell to McClung, 31 July 1905, McClung fonds, PABC.

36 Caswell to McClung, 12 September 1905, McClung fonds, PABC. The success of this arrangement is discussed further in Chapter 8.

37 Among Canadian poets published by Briggs during this period, there were a few variations. Amelia Garvin's *Grey Knitting* (1914), a fifteen-page booklet selling for twenty-five cents that was issued for the first Christmas of the Great War, had sufficient topical appeal to earn her a royalty of 10 percent without any apparent authorial contribution. With his 1905 *Collected Poems*, in exchange for guaranteeing the sale of at least four hundred copies at $1.50 apiece, Wilfred Campbell received a royalty of 10 percent on the first four hundred and an additional thirty-five cents on each subsequent copy ordered by or through him. Ryerson Archive, boxes 6–9, William Briggs Agreements, United Church Archives.

38 Hannah Isabel Graham to Henry Morgan, 7 February 1905, Morgan papers, MG29 D61, vol. 9, LAC.

39 Harrison to W.D. Lighthall, 20 May 1890, Lighthall papers, Box 1 f6, McGill.

40 Graeme Mercer Adam, "Canadian Literature," *Week* 7 (4 July 1890), 486.

41 Ballstadt et al., eds., *Letters of a Lifetime*, 234, 245.

42 Jack Brown, "'The Adopted Daughter' Identified," *Canadian Notes & Queries* 15 (1975): 11–12.

43 Jamieson to Belcher, 11 February 1918, 7 January 1919, Belcher papers, AO.

44 "Keeps Secret 70 Years Then Tells," *Edmonton Journal*, 3 February 1960, 25.

45 Elizabeth Driver, *Culinary Landmarks* (Toronto: University of Toronto Press, 2008), 322–34; Elizabeth Hulse, "The Hunter Rose Company: A Brief History," *The Devil's Artisan* 18 (1986): 6.

46 Marjorie McDowell, "Children's Books," in *Literary History of Canada*, ed. Carl F. Klinck (Toronto: University of Toronto Press, 1967), 624. See Elizabeth Waterston, "Diana Bayley: A Grandmama's Tale," *Canadian Children's Literature* 27, no. 2 [102] (2001): 60–66.

47 *Macmillans in Canada Present This List of Books by Canadian Authors* (Toronto: Macmillan, 1929).

48 Anne Innis Dagg, *The 50% Solution: Why Should Women Pay for Men's Culture?* (Waterloo: Otter Press, 1986), 30.

49 Claude Potvin, *Le Canada français et sa littérature de jeunesse* (Moncton: Éditions CRP, 1981). There is no similar historical inventory for English-Canadian children's literature.

50 Françoise Lepage, Judith Saltman, and Gail Edwards, "Children's Authors and Their Markets," *HBC* 3: 148.

51 M. Goodman, *Mrs. Goodman's First Step in History, Dedicated to the Young Ladies of Canada* (Montreal: Lane, 1827), iii, iv, 22.

52 Susan Mann Trofimenkoff, "Rae, Ann Cuthbert (Knight; Fleming)," *DCB* 8, online.

53 "Editor's Table," *Victoria Magazine* 1 (September 1847): 24. It was also praised in the *Literary Garland* as "a very excellent School Book." "Our Table," *Literary Garland*, n.s. 5 (1847), 387.

54 During the 1840s, Cheney published two religious children's books in Boston, where she may have then resided (*DLB* 99: 71). These texts have nothing to do with Canada, in contrast with Charlotte Tonna's *The Newfoundland Fishermen* (1835; 1846, 1853), a children's religious chapbook making interesting use of its author's earlier experience in a colony that would later join Canada.

55 See Carole Gerson, "*The Snow Drop* and *The Maple Leaf:* Canada's First Periodicals for Children," *Canadian Children's Literature* no. 18/19 (1980): 10–23.

56 Moodie, "The Foundling of the Storm," *Maple Leaf* 1 (1852): 13.

57 Barbara T. Gates and Ann B. Shteir, "Introduction," in *Natural Eloquence: Women Reinscribe Science* (Madison: University of Wisconsin Press, 1999), 8–9. Traill's nature writing receives further attention in Chapter 7.

58 Rupert Schieder, "Editor's Preface," in *Canadian Crusoes: A Tale of the Rice Lake Plains* by Catharine Parr Traill (Ottawa: Carleton University Press, 1986), xiii. Further discussion of this book appears in Chapter 9.

59 Catharine Parr Traill, *Narratives of Nature* (London: Edward Lacey, n.d.), v.

60 See Judith St. John, "A Peep at the Esquimaux through Early Children's Books," *The Beaver* (Winter 1965): 38–44.

61 Mrs. A. Campbell, *Rough and Smooth: or, Ho! for an Australian Gold Field* (Quebec: Hunter Rose, 1865), [1].

62 Sheila Egoff and Judith Saltman, *The New Republic of Childhood: A Critical Guide to Canadian Children's Literature in English* (Toronto: Oxford University Press, 1990), 133–34.

63 Candy Gunther Brown, *Word in the World: Evangelical Writing, Publishing, and Reading in America 1789–1880* (Chapel Hill: University of North Carolina Press, 2004), 105–06.

64 Gwendolyn Davies, *Marshall Saunders and Beautiful Joe: Education through Fiction* (Truro: Nova Scotia Teachers College, 1995), 9.

65 R.G. Moyles, "Young Canada: An Index to Canadian Materials in Major British and American Periodicals," *Canadian Children's Literature* 78 (1995): 8. Moyles argues that Wetherald deserves better recognition: "Ethelwyn Wetherald: An Early, Popular, and Prolific Poet," *Canadian Children's Literature* 59 (1990): 6–16.

66 Elizabeth Gaskell, *The Life of Charlotte Brontë* (1857; Penguin, 1981), 173; Caroline Ticknor, *Hawthorne and His Publisher* (Boston: Houghton Mifflin, 1913), 141.

67 Manon Brunet, "Angers, Félicité," *DCB* 15, online.

68 Abbé Henri-Raymond Casgrain to Pierre-Joseph-Olivier Chauveau, 8 October 1883, in Laure Conan, *J'ai tant de sujets de désespoir: Correspondance, 1878–1924,* ed. Jean-Noël Dion (Montreal: Éditions Varia, 2002), 161.

69 "In spite of your kind words, I feel the need to justify to have tried to write. I must say that it is entirely or almost entirely, due to circumstances. My will, I assure you, had little to do with it. Only necessity has given me the extraordinary courage to have my work published." Angers to Casgrain, 9 December 1882, in ibid., 139.

70 "I am already ashamed to have had my work published. Perhaps, sir, you do not understand this feeling—men are made for publicity—But believe me, I am saying this without affectation; it is a sentiment as deep as it is sincere." Angers to Casgrain, 1 October 1883, in ibid., 160.

71 "I never gave you permission to link my real name with my pseudonym," Angers to Casgrain, 14 January 1884, in ibid., 173.

72 "If I were a man, I would be treated very differently." Angers to Laurier, 6 April 1904, in ibid., 286.

73 Michael A. Peterman, "In Search of Agnes Strickland's Sisters," *Canadian Literature* 121 (Summer 1989): 116; "Reconstructing the *Palladium of British Amer-*

ica: How the Rebellion of 1837 and Charles Fothergill Helped to Establish Susanna Moodie as a Writer in Canada," *Papers of the Bibliographical Society of Canada* 40, no. 1 (2002): 7–36.

74 Moodie, *Roughing It in the Bush*, 441; Ballstadt et al., eds., *Letters of a Lifetime*, 97, 99, 110.

75 Susan Coultrap-McQuinn, *Doing Literary Business: American Women Writers in the Nineteenth Century* (Chapel Hill: University of North Carolina Press, 1990), 28–32.

76 Clara Thomas, *Love and Work Enough: The Life of Anna Jameson* (Ottawa: Carleton University Press, 1967), 163–64.

77 Carl Ballstadt, "Editor's Introduction," in *Roughing It in the Bush: or, Life in Canada* by Susanna Moodie (Toronto: McClelland and Stewart, 1989), xxix, xxx, xxxv.

78 Richard A. Davies, ed., *Letters of Thomas Chandler Haliburton* (Ottawa: Carleton University Press, 1988), 160.

79 Ballstadt et al., eds., *Letters of a Lifetime*, 111, 126–27, 136; Ballstadt, "Editor's Introduction," xxxiii.

80 Ballstadt et al., eds., *Letters of a Lifetime*, 224, 229, 299. In 1865 Moodie received £60 as a beneficiary of the Royal Literary Fund. Lovell paid $100 for "Dorothy Chance," printed in the Montreal *Daily News* in 1867.

81 Carrie Macmillan, Lorraine McMullen, and Elizabeth Waterston, *Silenced Sextet: Six Nineteenth-Century Canadian Women Novelists* (Montreal/Kingston: McGill-Queen's University Press, 1992), 69.

82 George L. Parker, *Beginnings of the Book Trade in Canada* (Toronto: University of Toronto Press, 1985), 232–34

83 Review of Mrs. J. Kerr Lawson, "Doctor Bruno's Wife: A Toronto Society Story," *Canadian Magazine* 2 (1894): 204.

84 Francis E. Vaughan, *Andrew C. Lawson, Scientist, Teacher, Philosopher* (Glendale: Arthur H. Clark, 1970), 26. This biography of her son is the major source for Lawson.

85 Bernard McEvoy, "The Canadian Society of Authors," *Canadian Magazine* 12 (April 1899): 563.

86 "Notes," *Canadian Magazine* 13 (July 1899): 292; "Canadian Society of Authors," James Mavor papers, Box 34, Fisher Library, University of Toronto.

87 *Canadian Magazine*, contributors' ledger, MU 2123, AO.

88 Arthur Stringer, "Wild Poets I've Known: Marjorie Pickthall," *Saturday Night* (14 June 1941): 41.

89 Pickthall papers, Lorne Pierce Collection, Queen's University Archives, 2001b Box 59, file 10; Box 68, f3.

90 L.M. Montgomery, *The Selected Journals of L.M. Montgomery*, vol. 2, ed. Mary Rubio and Elizabeth Waterston (Toronto: Oxford University Press, 1984–2004), 1 March 1919, 308. In February 1896 her first money was actually a five-dollar prize for a poem entered in a contest by the *Evening Mail* on "Which has the more patience under the ordinary cares and trials of life—man or woman?" followed five days later by a cheque from *Golden Days* (Philadelphia) for a story, "Our Charivari." The three-dollar cheque that she often cited as her first earnings arrived two months later, from the same magazine, for a poem, "The Apple Picking Time," *Selected Journals*, vol. 1, 157–59.

91 L.M. Montgomery to G.B. MacMillan, 29 December 1903, in *My Dear Mr. M.: Letters to G.B. MacMillan from L.M. Montgomery*, ed. Francis W.P. Bolger and Elizabeth R. Epperly (Toronto: Oxford University Press, 1992), 3.

92 Ibid., 3.

93 Montgomery, *Selected Journals* 1, 290.

94 Ibid., 310.

95 Ibid., 358.

96 Montgomery, *My Dear Mr. M.*, 3.

97 Ibid., 5.

98 L.M. Montgomery to Ephraim Weber, 7 March 1905, in *The Green Gables Letters*, ed. Wilfred Eggleston (Ottawa: Borealis, 1981), 26.

99 R.W. Russell, D.W. Russell, and Rea Wilmshurst, *Lucy Maud Montgomery: A Preliminary Bibliography* (Waterloo: University of Waterloo Library, 1986).

100 L.M. Montgomery to Ephraim Weber, 22 December 1908, *Green Gables Letters*, 81.

101 In 1924, 45 percent of the more than eight hundred English-speaking members of the CAA were women, and 16 percent of the seventy-four members of the French section. By 1933, women were 58 percent of some 730 English-speaking members, and 24 percent of the French. Canadian Authors Association, "Membership Roll of the Association," *Canadian Bookman* (1924): 120–22, 146–47; Canadian Authors Association, "Directory of Members," *Canadian Author* 11 (1933): 16–23.

102 See Peggy Lynn Kelly, "Introduction to Macbeth," in *Shackles* by Madge MacBeth (Ottawa: Tecumseh, 2005), 1–58.

103 Mildred Low to Macbeth, 23 January 1918, Macbeth papers, NAC, MG30, D52, vol. 1.

104 See Terry Lovell, *Consuming Fiction* (New York: Verso, 1987), 132, 159–61, on the exclusion of "woman to woman" writing from the canon.

CHAPTER 5

1 Catherine Helen Spence, *Mr. Hogarth's Will* (1865; Victoria: Penguin, 1988), 40–41.

2 Susan Coultrap-McQuin, *Doing Literary Business: American Women Writers in the Nineteenth Century* (Chapel Hill: University of North Carolina Press, 1990), 2.

3 Elaine Showalter, *A Jury of Her Peers: American Women Writers from Anne Bradstreet to Annie Proulx* (New York: Knopf, 2009), 107.

4 Millicent Lenz, "Harriet Beecher Stowe"; Marilyn H. Karrenbrock, "Mary Mapes Dodge," in *American Writers for Children before 1900: Dictionary of Literary Biography* (hereafter *DLB*, vol. 42, ed. Glen Estes (Detroit: Gale, 1985), 345, 150.

5 Martha Saxton, *Louisa May: A Modern Biography of Louisa May Alcott* (Boston: Houghton Mifflin, 1977), 296, 300.

6 Angela Woollacott, *To Try Her Fortune in London: Australian Women, Colonialism, and Modernity* (New York: Oxford University Press, 2001), 3.

7 Sara Jeannette Duncan, "American Influence on Canadian Thought," the *Week*, 7 July 1887, 518.

8 Lampman's first book, *Among the Millet, and Other Poems* (1888), was financed by his wife's money. His second, *Lyrics of Earth* (1895), was brought out in a small

edition of 550 copies with the Boston literary publisher Copeland and Day, while the publication of his third, *Alcyone*, was to be privately subsidized (Bruce Nesbitt, "Archibald Lampman," *DLB*, vol. 92, *Canadian Writers, 1890–1920*, 173, 177). As noted in Chapter 4, in 1944 Scott claimed "he had published all of his books at his own expense," Wilfred Eggleston, *Literary Friends* (Ottawa: Borealis, 1980), 112.

9   Len Early and Michael A. Peterman, "Introduction," in *Winona; or, the Foster-Sisters* by Isabella Valancy Crawford (Peterborough: Broadview, 2007), 15–16, 20–21, 62–63.

10 "Toboggan," *Outing*, March 1887, 546.

11 Micheline Cambron and Carole Gerson, "Literary Authorship," *History of the Book in Canada* (hereafter *HBC*) 2: 129.

12 Misao Dean, "Researching Sara Jeannette Duncan in the Papers of A.P. Watt and Company," *Canadian Literature* 178 (Autumn 2003): 181–86.

13 Charlotte Gray, *Flint and Feather: The Life and Times of E. Pauline Johnson, Tekahion-wake* (Toronto: HarperFlamingo Canada), 98–103.

14 Joanna E. Wood, "Algernon Charles Swinburne: An Appreciation," *Canadian Magazine* 17 (May 1901): 2–11; "Presentation at Court," *Canadian Magazine* 17 (October 1901): 506–10.

15 Richmond Reference Library, Douglas Sladen Collection, Letterbook sla. 16, Agnes M Machar to Sladen, Kingston, Canada, 23 March 1893. Cited by Gwendolyn Davies, "Publishing Abroad," in *History of the Book in Canada*, vol. 2, *1840–1918*, ed. Yvan Lamonde, Patricia Lockhart Fleming, and Fiona A. Black (Toronto: University of Toronto Press, 2005), 145–46.

16 See Marion Marzolf, *Up from the Footnote: A History of Women Journalists* (New York: Hastings House, 1977), 18–29.

17 Nick Mount, *When Canadian Literature Moved to New York* (Toronto: University of Toronto Press, 2005), 38.

18 Walter Blackburn Harte, cited in the *Week*, 12 February 1892, 172.

19 Mary Temple Bayard, "Eve Brodlique," *Canadian Magazine* 7 (1896): 517.

20 Nick Mount, "Exodus: When Canadian Literature Moved to New York," Ph.D. dissertation, Dalhousie University, 2001. Appendix A shows that nineteen returned, including eleven of the thirty-one women.

21 Ethelwyn Wetherald, *Lyrics and Sonnets* (Toronto: Nelson, 1931), xvii.

22 Her obituary claims she had written twelve. Anne Elizabeth Wilson, "Beloved Friend," *Saturday Night* (17 December 1930): 28.

23 Gertrude Pringle, "Miss Jean MacIlwraith, Canadian Authoress," *Saturday Night* 41 (30 January 1926): 21, 28.

24 Mount, "Exodus," 54–55.

25 Constance Lindsay Skinner, "Foreword," in *Songs of the Coast Dwellers* (New York: Coward-McCann, 1930), viii.

26 Skinner to Snowden Dunn Scott, 8 January 1920, Scott papers, UBC archives.

27 While letters mention several offers of $200 and £50, no figure is attached to their publication of *Geoffrey Moncton*, which they seem to have purchased from her directly. Carl Ballstadt, Elizabeth Hopkins, and Michael A. Peterman, eds., *Susanna Moodie: Letters of a Lifetime* (Toronto: University of Toronto Press, 1985), 132, 144, 150, 154, 162–63.

28 Ibid., 126–27; Carl Ballstadt, "Editor's Introduction," in *Roughing It in the Bush* by Susanna Moodie (Ottawa: Carleton University Press, 1988), xxxiii.

29 Carrie MacMillan, Lorraine McMullen, and Elizabeth Waterston, *Silenced Sextet: Six Nineteenth-Century Canadian Women Novelists* (Montreal/Kingston: McGill-Queen's University Press, 1992), 64, 69.

30 Archibald MacMechan to McTavish, 23 November 1906, Newton McTavish papers, North York Public Library.

31 Marjorie Pickthall to McTavish, 22 May 1907, 7 November 1908, McTavish papers.

32 Andrew Macphail papers, NAC MG30 D150, vol. 3.

33 Arthur Stringer, "Wild Poets I've Known: Marjorie Pickthall," *Saturday Night* (14 June 1941): 41; Pickthall papers, Lorne Pierce Collection, Queen's University Archives, 2001b Box 59, f10; Box 68, f3.

34 Stringer, "Wild Poets," 41.

35 Frank Packard papers, Record of income, NAC MG 30 D114, vol. 1.

36 "Bought and Sold Book," Montgomery papers, University of Guelph Archives, XZIMSA098042.

37 Pierre Berton, *Hollywood's Canada: The Americanization of Our National Image* (Toronto: McClelland and Stewart, 1975), 20, 44.

38 L.M. Montgomery, *Selected Journals of L.M. Montgomery*, vol. 2, ed. Mary Rubio and Elizabeth Waterston (Toronto: Oxford University Press, 1987), 18 December 1919, 358.

39 A claim in her publicity material that has not been verified: Diana Birchall, *Onoto Watanna: The Story of Winnifred Eaton* (Urbana: University of Illinois Press, 2001), 127.

40 Reeve papers, University of Calgary, Box 1, f5. Letters regarding her movie work are in Box 1, f6; see also Elizabeth Bailey Price, "Onoto Watanna Has Written a New Book," *Canadian Bookman* 4 (22 April 1922): 123–25, and "Onoto Watanna, an Amazing Author," *MacLean's* 35 (15 October 1922): 64–65; Birchall, *Onoto Watanna*, 117–28.

41 "Sets Credit Rating by Day, Gets Book Plot in Sleep," *Toronto Daily Star*, 15 October 1938, 13.

CHAPTER 6

1 Margaret Beetham, "Towards a Theory of the Periodical as Publishing Genre," in *Investigating Victorian Journalism*, ed. Laurel Brake, Aled Jones, and Lionel Madden (London: Macmillan 1990), 19–32.

2 See, for example, Kay Boardman, "The Ideology of Domesticity: The Regulation of the Household Economy in Victorian Women's Magazines," *Victorian Periodicals Review* 33, no. 2 (Summer 2000): 150–64.

3 Margaret Fuller, "American Literature: Its Position in the Present Time, and Prospects for the Future," in *Papers on Literature and Art, Part II* (London: Wiley and Putnam, 1846), 138.

4 Iona Italia, *The Rise of Literary Journalism in the Eighteenth Century: Anxious Employment* (London/New York: Routledge, 2005), 49–65.

5 Kirsten T. Saxton, "Introduction," in *The Passionate Fictions of Eliza Haywood: Essays on Her Life and Work*, ed. Kirsten T. Saxon and Rebecca P. Bocchicchio (Lexington: University of Kentucky Press, 2000), 2.

6   Anna Miegon, "*The Ladies' Diary* and the Emergence of the Almanac for Women, 1704–1753," dissertation, Simon Fraser University, 2008.

7   Italia, *The Rise of Literary Journalism*, 178.

8   E.M. Palmegiano, *Women and British Periodicals, 1832–1867: A Bibliography* (New York/London: Garland, 1976), 24–26; Barbara Onslow, *Women of the Press in Nineteenth-Century Britain* (London: Macmillan, 2000), 214–39.

9   Judith Johnston and Hillary Fraser, "The Professionalization of Women's Writing: Extending the Canon," in *Women and Literature in Britain, 1800–1900*, ed. Joanne Shattock (Cambridge: Cambridge University Press, 2001), 231–50, 243.

10 Patricia Okker, *Our Sister Editors: Sara J. Hale and the Tradition of Nineteenth-Century American Women Editors* (Athens/London: University of Georgia Press, 1995), 167–220.

11 "Whittelsey, Abigail Goodrich," *Encyclopedia Britannica*, Britannica Online, 15 June 2009, http://search.eb.com.proxy.lib.sfu.ca/article-9126043.

12 Kristin Mapel Bloomberg, "Cultural Critique and Consciousness Raising: Clara Bewick Colby's *Woman's Tribune* and Late-Nineteenth-Century Radical Feminism," in *Women in Print: Essays on the Print Culture of American Women from the Nineteenth and Twentieth Centuries*, ed. James P. Danky and Wayne A. Wiegand (Madison: University of Wisconsin Press, 2006), 34.

13 Georges Bellerive, *Brèves apologies de nos auteurs féminins* (Quebec: Librairie Garneau, 1920).

14 *La vie littéraire au Québec* (hereafter *VLQ*), vol. 5, 90.

15 Carole Gerson, "Anthologies and the Canon of Early Canadian Women Writers," in *Re(dis)covering Our Foremothers*, ed. Lorraine McMullen (Ottawa: University of Ottawa Press, 1989), 58.

16 Walter Blackburn Harte, "Canadian Journalists and Journalism," *New England Magazine* 5, no. 4 (December 1891): 433.

17 Mary Temple Bayard, "Eve Brodlique," *Canadian Magazine* 7 (1896): 517. By 1886, there were reportedly over two hundred women competing for stories in New York City alone, according to Margery Lang, *Women Who Made the News: Female Journalists in Canada, 1880–1945* (Montreal/Kingston: McGill-Queen's University Press, 1999), 38.

18 Lang, *Women Who Made the News*, 60.

19 Ibid., 34. In his obituary of Sheppard, Hector Charlesworth also lists Kate Westlake Yeigh, Madge Merton (Mrs. J.E. Atkinson), Jean Graham, and Marjorie MacMurchy among Sheppard's protégées. Hector Charlesworth, "The Late E.E. Sheppard," *Saturday Night* (22 November 1924): 2.

20 "The Editor at Leisure," *Canadian Queen* 3, no. 4 (April 1891): 154. Its publisher, William Gardner Osgoodby, "was arrested on charge of conspiring to defraud arising from 'fake prize-guessing contests,'" according to Elizabeth Hulse, *A Dictionary of Toronto Printers, Publishers, Booksellers, and the Allied Trade, 1798–1900* (Toronto: Anson-Cartwright, 1982), 197. In 1926, top sales of Canadian magazines were 82,013 for *MacLean's Magazine* and 68,054 for the *Canadian Home Journal*, according to Mary Vipond, "Canadian Nationalism and the Plight of Canadian Magazines in the 1920s," *Canadian Historical Review* 58, no. 1 (1977): 44.

21 At this early stage, Montgomery wrote under pseudonyms. In the *Ladies' Journal*, she was Maud Eglington for the poem "On the Gulf Shore" (Feb 1895), and

Maud Cavendish for the poem "When the Apple-Blossoms Blow" (June 1895) and the story "A Baking of Gingersnaps" (July 1895); R.W. Russell, D.W. Russell, and Rea Wilmshurst, *Lucy Maud Montgomery: A Preliminary Bibliography* (Waterloo: University of Waterloo Library, 1986).

22 *Women of Canada: Their Life and Work* (hereafter *WoC*), compiled for distribution at the Paris National Exhibition by the National Council of Women of Canada (1900; rpt. 1975), 76.

23 E.W. Thomson to Ethelwyn Wetherald, 24 April 1893, M.O. Hammond Papers, Series 10-J, MU 3386, AO.

24 Hulse cites Henry Watson Fox, 101; William Osgoodby, 197; George A. Walton, 272; and Squire Frank Wilson, 283 in Hulse, *A Dictionary*.

25 Brian Clarke, "English-Speaking Canada from 1854," in *A Concise History of Christianity in Canada*, ed. Terence Murphy (Toronto: Oxford University Press, 1996), 287–90.

26 Ruth Compton Brouwer, *New Women for God: Canadian Presbyterian Women and India Missions, 1876–1914* (Toronto: University of Toronto Press, 1990), 7.

27 Sharon Anne Cook, *"Through Sunshine and Shadow": The Woman's Christian Temperance Union, Evangelicalism, and Reform in Ontario, 1874–1930* (Montreal/Kingston: McGill-Queen's University Press, 1995), 138.

28 *WoC*, 74–76.

29 Lang, *Women Who Made the News*, 138.

30 Ibid., 135.

31 Emily P. Weaver, A.E. Weaver, and E.C. Weaver, *The Canadian Women's Annual and Social Service Directory* (Toronto: McClelland, Goodchild, and Stewart, 1915), 200.

32 These appeared in January and March 1896.

33 "Women Workers," *Ladies' Journal* (May 1895): 8.

34 "Staff of the Women's *Globe*," *Globe*, 18 April 1895, 4.

35 Lang, *Women Who Made the News*, 254.

36 Ann Colbert, "Philanthropy in the Newsroom: Women's Editions of Newspapers, 1894–1896," *Journalism History* 22, no. 3 (1996), online. See also Ann Mauger Colbert, "Literary and Commercial Aspects of Women's Editions of Newspapers, 1894–1896," in *Blue Pencils and Hidden Hands: Women Editing Periodicals, 1830–1910*, ed. Sharon M. Harris and Ellen Gruber Garvey (Boston: Northeastern University Press, 2004), 20–35. Thanks to Mary Chapman for this source.

37 20 July 1895, 8.

38 The poem that appeared, "Keepsakes," had been published in 1888 and was not "Written for the *Halifax Herald Woman's Extra*" as claimed (1 October 1895, 9).

39 A. Marion Donovan, "The Evolution of the Colored Woman," Halifax *Herald Woman's Extra*, 1 October 1895, 10.

40 M. Grant [probably Maria Heathfield Grant], "The Suffrage Question," Victoria *Daily Times*, 27 May 1895, 8.

41 See Veronica Strong-Boag, *The Parliament of Women: The National Council of Women of Canada, 1893–1929* (Ottawa: National Museums of Canada, 1976).

42 Marjory MacMurchy, *The Woman—Bless Her* (Toronto: Gundy, 1916), 11.

43 *Woman's Century* 3, no. 3 (September 1915): [1].

44 "Annual meeting, Woman's Century," *Woman's Century*, March 1917, 12.

45 "Our New Year," *Woman's Century*, May 1917, 6.

46 Lang, *Women Who Made the News*, 6–14.

47 *WoC*, 73–77.

48 Lang, *Women Who Made the News*, 29.

49 C. Pelham Mulvany, *Toronto: Past and Present* (Toronto: W.E. Caiger, 1884), 80.

50 Paul Rutherford, *A Victorian Authority: The Daily Press in Late Nineteenth-Century Canada* (Toronto: University of Toronto Press, 1982), 81.

51 L.M. Montgomery, *The Selected Journals of L.M. Montgomery*, vol. 1, ed. Mary Rubio and Elizabeth Waterston (Toronto: Oxford University Press, 1985), 267.

52 Lang, *Women Who Made the News*, 48–51.

53 See Janice Fiamengo's chapter on Duncan in *The Woman's Page: Journalism and Rhetoric in Early Canada* (Toronto: University of Toronto Press, 2008), 59–87.

54 See Fiamengo's chapter on Coleman in ibid., 121–52.

55 Lang, *Women Who Made the News*, 43.

56 Ibid., 59–60.

57 Chantal Savoie, "Persister et signer: Les signatures féminines et l'évolution de le reconnaissance sociale de l'écrivaine (1893–1929)," *Voix et Images* 30, no. 1 (August 2004): 67–79.

58 "Borrowed Light," *True Flag*, 9 April 1853, in Fanny Fern, *Ruth Hall and Other Writings*, ed. Joyce W. Warren (New Brunswick: Rutgers University Press, 1986), 252.

59 Lang, *Women Who Made the News*, 67.

60 These are enumerated in Elizabeth V. Burt, ed., *Women's Press Organizations, 1881–1999* (Westport: Greenwood Press, 2000).

61 Lang, *Women Who Made the News*, 71.

62 Ibid., 23.

63 Marjory Lang, "Shortt, Emily Ann McCausland (Cummings)," *Dictionary of Canadian Biography* (hereafter *DCB*) 15, online.

64 Nellie McClung, *Nellie McClung, the Complete Autobiography: Clearing in the West and The stream Runs Fast*, ed. Veronica Strong-Boag and Michelle Lynn Rosa (Peterborough: Broadview, 2003), 337–41.

65 Madge Macbeth, *Boulevard Career* (Toronto: Kingswood House, 1957), 108–12.

66 Weaver et al., *The Canadian Women's Annual*, 200

67 *Canadian Days: Selections for Every Day in the Year from the Works of Canadian Authors*, compiled by the Toronto Women's Press Club (Toronto: Musson, [1911]).

68 Isabel Ecclestone Mackay, "Prefatory Notes," in *Verse and Reverse* by Members of the Toronto Women's Press Club (Toronto: Goodchild, 1922), [3].

69 Wilfred Campbell, "Mermaid Inn," *Globe*, 22 October 1892, 177.

70 Lang, *Women Who Made the News*, 43–47.

71 Mary Markwell [Hayes], "Canadian Women Writers—Have They Yet Arrived?" *Canadian Bookman* 2, no. 4 (April 1910): 52.

72 Chantal Savoie, "La page féminie des grands quotidiens montréalais comme lieu de sociabilité littéraire au tournant de xxᵉ siècle," *Tangence* 80 (hiver 2006): 125–42, 126.

73 Ibid., 132–33, 134–35.

74 Pharos [Laura Durand], "The Saturday Book Club," *Globe*, 11 February 1905, 9.
75 "Women in Journalism," *Week*, 23 June 1893, 712.
76 Lang, *Women Who Made the News*, 144–45.
77 Danielle Hamelin, "Nurturing Canadian Letters: Four Studies in the Publishing and Promotion of English-Canadian Writing, 1890–1920," dissertation, Toronto, 1994, 244–48. Thanks to Janet Friskney for researching the contributors to the *Saturday Magazine*.
78 Ibid., 255–57.

CHAPTER 7

1 Anne Innis Dagg, "Canadian Voices of Authority: Non-fiction and Early Women Writers," *Journal of Canadian Studies* 27, no. 2 (Summer 1992): 110. This article preceded her book, which offers more information on individual authors: *The Feminine Gaze: A Canadian Compendium of Non-fiction Women Authors and Their Books, 1836–1945* (Waterloo: Wilfrid Laurier University Press, 2001).
2 Clara M. Chu and Bertrum H. MacDonald, "The Public Record: An Analysis of Women's Contributions to Canadian Science and Technology before the First World War," in *Despite the Odds: Essays on Canadian Women and Science*, ed. Marianne Gosztonyi Ainley (Montreal: Véhicule Press, 1990), 71.
3 Chu and MacDonald, "The Public Record," 70.
4 These terms are taken from Susan Staves, *A Literary History of Women's Writing in Britain, 1660–1789* (Cambridge/New York: Cambridge University Press, 2006), 243–44.
5 Elizabeth M. Smyth, "Lawler (Lawlor), Elizabeth Gertrude," *Dictionary of Canadian Biography* (hereafter *DCB*) 15, online.
6 Issued in Morang's Literature Series, with title pages that chart her progress. *The Merchant of Venice* (1906) describes her as "Gertrude Lawler, M.A., English Specialist, Harbord Collegiate Institute, Toronto" while *A Midsummer Night's Dream* (1909) identifies her as "Gertrude Lawler, MA, Head of the English Department, Harbord Collegiate Institute, Toronto; and Critic and Instructor in Methods in English in the Faculty of Education, University of Toronto."
7 Dagg, *The Feminine Gaze*, 196.
8 Linda Ambrose, *For Home and Country: The Centennial History of the Women's Institutes in Ontario* (Erin: Boston Mills Press, 1996), 41.
9 Ibid., 21–22.
10 Ibid., 20.
11 The earliest example cited by Elizabeth Driver in *Culinary Landmarks* is *Our Own Cook Book* (Fenelon Falls: Victoria Women's Institute, 1905), 445.
12 Louise Fradet, "Anctil, Jeanne," *DCB* 15, online.
13 Judith Johnston and Hilary Fraser, "The Professionalization of Women's Writing: Extending the Canon," in *Women and Literature in Britain, 1800–1900*, ed. Joanne Shattock (Cambridge/New York: Cambridge University Press), 231–50.
14 Catharine Parr Traill, *The Backwoods of Canada*, ed. Michael A. Peterman (Ottawa: Carleton University Press, 1997), 112.
15 Ibid., 179.

16 Carl Ballstadt, Elizabeth Hopkins, and Michael A. Peterman, eds., *I Bless You in My Heart: Selected Correspondence of Catharine Parr Traill* (Toronto: University of Toronto Press, 1996), 135.

17 Traill, *The Backwoods*, 104.

18 Traill, "A Glance within the Forest," in *Forest and Other Gleanings: The Fugitive Writings of Catharine Parr Traill*, ed. Michael A. Peterman and Carl Ballstadt (Ottawa: University of Ottawa Press, 1994), 250.

19 Michael A. Peterman, "'Splendid Anachronism': The Record of Catharine Parr Traill's Struggles as an Amateur Botanist in Nineteenth-Century Canada," in *Re(dis)covering Our Foremothers*, ed. Lorraine McMullen (Ottawa: University of Ottawa Press, 1990), 173, 183.

20 Margaret Steffler and Neil Steffler, "'If We Would Read It Aright': Traill's 'Ladder to Heaven,'" *Journal of Canadian Studies* 38, no. 3 (2004): 126.

21 Marianne Gosztonyi Ainley, "Science in Canada's Backwoods: Catharine Parr Traill," in *Natural Eloquence: Women Reinscribe Science*, ed. Barbara T. Gates and Ann B. Shteir (Madison: University of Wisconsin Press, 1997), 92.

22 Between 1877 and 1911 she published twenty-nine journal articles on horticulture; Chu and Macdonald, "The Public Record," 68.

23 Margaret Gillett, "Carrie Derick (1862–1941) and the Chair of Botany at McGill," in *Despite the Odds: Essays on Canadian Women and Science*, ed. Marianne Gosztonyi Ainley (Montreal: Véhicule, 1990), 74–87.

24 Gwendolyn Davies, "Publishing Abroad," *History of the Book in Canada* (hereafter *HBC*) vol. 2, *1840–1918*, ed. Yvan Lamonde, Patricia Lockhart Fleming, and Fiona A. Black (Toronto: University of Toronto Press, 2005), 145.

25 Eliza M. Jones, *Lecture on Co-operative Dairying and Winter Dairying* (Montreal: Lovell, 1893), 1.

26 Tami Adilman, "Evlyn Farris and the University Women's Club," in *In Her Own Right: Selected Essays on Women's History in BC*, ed. Barbara Latham and Cathy Kess (Victoria: Camosun College, 1980), 155.

27 *The Women's Canadian Historical Society of Toronto* [Toronto? 1896?] CIHM 29461; *Women of Canada*, complied for distribution at the Paris National Exhibition by the National Council of Women of Canada, 395.

28 *WoC*, 394–96. In 1915, E.P. Weaver, A.E. Weaver, and E.C. Weaver's *Canadian Women's Annual and Social Service Directory* listed twenty-nine local and specialized associations affiliated with the Ontario History Society (219). Boutilier cautions that in mixed societies, "female members by no means took an equal share in the governance or work of the society," "Women's Rights and Duties: Sarah Anne Curzon and the Politics of Canadian History," in *Creating Historical Memory*, ed. Beverly Boutilier and Alison Prentice (Vancouver: UBC Press, 1977), 66.

29 Kenneth N. Windsor, "Historical Writing in Canada to 1920," in *Literary History of Canada*, ed. Carl F. Klinck (Toronto: University of Toronto Press, 1967), 238–39. The only women he mentions are the Lizars sisters and Machar.

30 See Elizabeth Smyth, "'Writing Teaches Us Our Mysteries': Women Religious Recording and Writing History," in *Creating Historical Memory*, ed. Beverly Boutilier and Alison Prentice (Vancouver: UBC Press, 1977): 101–28.

31 *Dictionnaire des oeuvres littéraires du Québec* 1, 743–45.

32 Mrs. C.M. Day, *Pioneers of the Eastern Townships* (Montreal: Lovell, 1863), viii.

33 Marion L. Phelps, *Biography, Mrs. Catherine Matilda (Townsend) Day* (Knowlton: Marion L. Phelps, 1988), 65–66.

34 Evelyn MacLeod, "Owen, Elizabeth Lee (Macdonald)," *DCB* 13, online.

35 Jean Barman, "'I Walk My Own Track in Life and No Mere Male Can Bump Me off It': Constance Lindsay Skinner and the Work of History," in *Creating Historical Memory*, ed. Beverly Boutilier and Alison Prentice (Vancouver: UBC Press, 1997), 132.

36 Janice Fiamengo, "'Abundantly Worthy of Its Past': Agnes Maule Machar and Early Canadian Historical Fiction," *Studies in Canadian Literature* 27, no. 1 (2002): 15.

37 Robina and Kathleen MacFarlane Lizars, *In the Days of the Canada Company: The Story of the Settlement of the Huron Tract and a View of the Social Life of the Period 1825–1850* (Toronto: Briggs, 1896), [xi].

38 Cecilia Morgan, "Carnochan, Janet," *DCB* 15, online.

39 Colin M. Coates and Cecilia Morgan, *Heroines and History: Representations of Madeleine de Verchères and Laura Secord* (Toronto: University of Toronto Press, 2002), 236.

40 Beverly Boutilier, "Women's Rights and Duties: Sarah Anne Curzon and the Politics of Canadian History," in Boutilier and Prentice, *Creating Historical Memory*, 51–74; 51–52.

41 Ibid., 64–65.

42 Cecilia Morgan, "'Of Slender Frame and Delicate Appearance': The Placing of Laura Secord in the Narratives of Canadian Loyalist History," in *Gender and History in Canada*, ed. Joy Parr and Mark Rosenfeld (Mississauga: Copp Clark), 104.

43 Boutilier, "Women's Rights and Duties," 63.

44 Sarah Anne Curzon, *Laura Secord: The Heroine of 1812 and Other Poems* (Toronto: C.B. Robinson, 1887), Preface, n.p.

45 Coates and Morgan, *Heroines and History*, 19.

46 Ibid., 62.

47 Maria J.I. Thorburn, *The Orphans' Home of the City of Ottawa. Sketch of the First Forty Years, 1864–1904* (Toronto: Briggs, 1904), vi.

48 Mary Markwell [Kate Simpson Hayes], "Agnes Laut as a Writer and as a Woman," Winnipeg *Free Press*, 31 October 1908, 17.

CHAPTER 8

1 Candy Gunther Brown, *The Word in the World: Evangelical Writing, Publishing, and Reading in America 1789–1880* (Chapel Hill: University of North Carolina Press, 2004), 99.

2 "Women's Rights," *Presbyterian Record for the Dominion of Canada* (July 1876): 190.

3 First published in *Western Christian Advocate* (16 September 1903): 14–15.

4 Paul R. Dekar, "Buchan, Jane," *Dictionary of Canadian Biography* (hereafter *DCB*) 13, online.

5 Bonnie Huskins, "Geddie, Charlotte Anne (Harrington)," *DCB* 13, online.

6 H.L. [Harriet Louise] Platt, *The Story of the Years: A History of the Woman's Missionary Society of the Methodist Church, Canada, from 1881 to 1906*, vol. 1 (n.p., n.d.),

137–38; Mrs. E. S. Strachan, *The Story of the Years ... 1906–1916*, vol. 3 (Toronto: Women's Missionary Society, Methodist Church Canada, 1917), 314.

7 Marianne Valverde, "Kinton, Ada Florence," *DCB* 13, online.

8 Bertha Carr-Harris, *Lights and Shades of Mission Work; or, Leaves from a Worker's Note Book* (Ottawa: Free Press, 1892), n.p.

9 "Canadian Women in the Public Eye: Mrs. P.W. Anderson," *Saturday Night* (10 September 1921): 22, 31.

10 Kym Bird, *Redressing the Past: The Politics of Early English-Canadian Women's Drama, 1880–1920* (Montreal/Kingston: McGill-Queen's University Press, 2004), 158.

11 Cited by Brian Clarke, "English-Speaking Canada from 1854," in *A Concise History of Religion in Canada*, ed. Terence Murphy and Roberto Perin (Toronto: Oxford University Press, 1996), 287.

12 Lorne Pierce, *The Chronicle of a Century* (Toronto: Ryerson, [1929]), 151–59.

13 Anton Wagner, "Eliza Lanesford Cushing," in *Canadian Writers before 1890: Dictionary of Literary Biography* (hereafter *DLB*), vol. 99, ed. W.H. New, 85.

14 Carole Gerson, "Agnes Maule Machar," in *Canadian Writers, 1890–1920*, *DLB* 92, ed. W.H. New, 221.

15 Marjory MacMurchy, *The Woman—Bless Her* (Toronto: S.B. Gundy, 1916), 12.

16 Agnes F. Robinson, *A Quarter of a Century* (Toronto: Women's Foreign Missionary Society of the Presbyterian Church in Canada, 1901), 2.

17 Ruth Compton Brouwer, *New Women for God: Canadian Presbyterian Women and India Missions* (Toronto: University of Toronto Press, 1990), 5.

18 Myra Rutherdale, *Women and the White Man's God: Gender and Race in the Canadian Mission Field* (Vancouver: UBC Press 2002), 4.

19 Ibid., xxi.

20 Mary Cramp, *Retrospects: A History of the Formation and Progress of the Women's Missionary Aid Societies of the Maritime Provinces* (Halifax: Holloway Brothers, 1892), 4.

21 Allen B. Robertson, "Norris, Hannah Maria (Armstrong)," *DCB* 14, online.

22 Robinson, *A Quarter of a Century*, 8.

23 Brouwer, *New Women for God*, 29.

24 Strachan, *The Story of the Years*, vol. 3, 312.

25 Sarah Robbins, "Woman's Work for Woman: Gendered Print Culture in American Mission Movement Narratives," in *Women in Print: Essays on the Print Culture of American Women from the Nineteenth and Twentieth Centuries*, ed. James P. Danky and Wayne A. Wiegand (Madison: University of Wisconsin Press, 2006), 251–52.

26 For example: Blanche Read, *The Life of John Read* (Toronto: Salvation Army, 1899); Mary J. Shenton, *A Biographical Sketch of the Late Rev. Job Shenton by His Widow with Some of His Sermons and Lectures* (St. John: McMillan, 1902); Camilla Sanderson, *John Sanderson the First; or A Pioneer Preacher at Home* (Toronto: Briggs, 1910); Katherine Hughes, *Archbishop O'Brien: Man and Churchman* (Ottawa: Crain, 1906).

27 For example: M.A. Nannary, *Memoir of the Life of Rev. E.J. Dumphy* (St. John: Weekly Herald, 1877); Mary Hoskin, *History of St. Basil's Parish, St. Joseph Street* (Toronto: Catholic Register and Canadian Extension, 1912); May Harvey Drummond, *The Grand Old Man of Dudswell Being the Memoirs of the Rev. Thos. Shaw Chapman, M.A.* (Quebec: Telegraph, 1916).

28 Mrs. R.P. Hopper, *Old-Time Primitive Methodism in Canada (1829–1884)*, (Toronto: Briggs, 1904), 107–09.

29 The two histories developed from an invited paper, "Two Frontier Churches," read to the Canadian Institute in 1890, according to John L. Field, *Janet Carnochan* (Markham: Fitzhenry and Whiteside, 1985), 24.

30 Katherine Hughes, *Father Lacombe: The Black-Robe Voyageur* (Toronto: Briggs, 1911).

31 Helen E. Bingham, *An Irish Saint: The Life of Ann Preston Known as "Holy Ann"* (Toronto: Briggs, 1907); Ada Kinton, *Just One Blue Bonnet: The Life Story of Ada Florence Kinton, Artist and Salvationist* (Toronto: Briggs, 1907).

32 Margaret Mary Drummond, *The Life and Times of Margaret Bourgeoys (the Venerable)* (Boston: Angel Guardian Press, 1907); *La vénérable mère Marguerite Bourgeoys*, traduit de l'anglais par Joseph Bruneau (Montréal: Soeurs de la Congrégation de Notre-Dame, [1910–]).

33 Mother Ste-Croix, *Glimpses of the Monastery* (Quebec: Darveau, 1872), 5–8.

34 Bertha Carr-Harris, *Lights and Shades of Mission Work; or, Leaves from a Worker's Note Book* (Ottawa: Free Press, 1892).

35 Susie Carson Rijnhart, *With the Tibetans in Tent and Temple: Narrative of Four Years' Residence on the Tibetan Border, and of a Journey into the Far Interior* (Chicago/New York/Toronto: Fleming H. Revell, 1901), 111.

36 Amanda Claybaugh, *The Novel of Purpose: Literature and Social Reform in the Anglo-American World* (Ithaca: Cornell University Press, 2007), 2.

37 Sharon Anne Cook, *"Through Sunshine and Shadow": The Woman's Christian Temperance Union, Evangelicalism, and Reform in Ontario, 1874–1930* (Montreal/Kingston: McGill-Queen's University Press, 1995), 15.

38 Ibid., 7.

39 Ibid., 61.

40 Mrs. Addie Chisholm, *Why and How: A Hand-book for the Use of the WCT Unions in Canada* (Montreal: Witness Printing House, 1884), 39.

41 National Council of Women of Canada, *Women of Canada: Their Life and Work* (1900; rpt. 1975), 76, 259; Sharon Anne Cook, "Davis, Adeline (Chisholm; Foster, Lady Foster)," *DCB* 14, online.

42 Cook, *"Through Sunshine and Shadow,"* 144–47.

43 T.A. Crowly, "Creighton, Letitia (Youmans), *DCB* 12, online.

44 Lorraine McMullen, "Vincent, Sarah Anne (Curzon)," *DCB* 12, online; Alison Prentice, Beth Light, Paula Bourne, Wendy Mitchinson, and Gail Cuthbert Brandt, *Canadian Women: A History* (Toronto: Harcourt Brace, 1988), 175.

45 Carol Lee Bacchi, *Liberation Deferred? The Ideas of the English-Canadian Suffragists, 1877–1918* (Toronto: University of Toronto Press, 1983), 70.

46 W.H. Withrow, "Introduction," in *Clipped Wings* by Lottie McAlister (Toronto: Briggs, 1899). This preface was omitted from the second edition.

47 McAlister, *Clipped Wings*, 156.

48 Ibid., 25.

49 Ibid., 22.

50 Ibid., 184.

51 Edith M. Luke, "Woman Suffrage in Canada," *Canadian Magazine* 5 (August 1895): 334; Catherine L. Cleverdon, *The Woman Suffrage Movement in Canada* (1950; Toronto: University of Toronto Press, 1974), 180.

52 Thirty-three American suffrage papers appeared between 1870 and 1890, according to E. Claire Jerry, "The Role of Newspapers in the Nineteenth-Century Woman's Movement," in *A Voice of Their Own: The Woman Suffrage Press, 1840–1910*, ed. Martha M. Solomon (Tuscaloosa/London: University of Alabama Press, 1991), 24.

53 Gloria Whelen, "Maria Grant," in *In Her Own Right: Selected Essays on Women's History in BC*, ed. Barbara Latham and Cathy Kess (Victoria: Camosun College, 1980), 125–46, 141.

54 Cleverdon, *The Woman Suffrage Movement*, 291. Writing is notably absent from Bacchi's list of strategies: "Canadian suffragists staged mock parliaments, sponsored plays, arranged exhibits, sold postcards, and generally used more subtle methods of persuasion"; Bacchi, *Liberation Deferred*, 34.

55 See Janice Fiamengo's analysis of Denison's suffrage rhetoric in *The Woman's Page: Journalism and Rhetoric in Early Canada* (Toronto: University of Toronto Press, 2008), 152–76. Denison's suffrage perspective also infused her Whitmanesque personal little magazine, the *Sunset of Bon Echo*; see Dean Irvine, *Editing Modernity: Women and Little-Magazine Cultures in Canada, 1916–1956* (Toronto: University of Toronto Press, 2008), 185–94.

56 Margery Lang, *Women Who Made the News: Female Journalists in Canada, 1880–1945* (Montreal/Kingston: McGill-Queen's University Press, 1999), 225.

57 Ibid., 224.

58 Ibid., 223.

59 Most municipalities granted female property owners the vote before 1900. At the provincial level, full suffrage was achieved in Manitoba, Alberta, Saskatchewan, and British Columbia in 1916, followed by Ontario in 1917, Nova Scotia in 1918, New Brunswick in 1919, Prince Edward Island in 1922, and Quebec in 1940. Full franchise was achieved at the federal level in 1918.

60 Bird, *Redressing the Past*, 69.

61 Lang, *Women Who Made the News*, 226. Less influential was Lucile Vessot Galley's *Famous Women* (1916), a little-known play, "imbued with the feminist buoyancy of the age" that was published for the use of women's societies (Bird, *Redressing the Past*, 197).

62 Nellie McClung, *Clearing in the West and The Stream Runs Fast*, ed. Veronica Strong-Boag and Michelle Lynn Rosa (Peterborough: Broadview, 2003), 369.

63 Ibid., 370.

64 Michael A. Peterman and Janet B. Friskney, "'Booming' the Canuck Book: Edward Caswell and the Promotion of Canadian Writing," *Journal of Canadian Studies* 30, no. 3 (Fall 1995): 82.

65 Ibid., 77.

66 Mary Hallett and Marilyn Davis, *Firing the Heather: The Life and Times of Nellie McClung* (Saskatoon: Fifth House, 1994), 42

67 Mary Markwell [Kate Simpson Hayes], "Agnes Laut as a Writer and as Woman," Winnipeg *Free Press*, 31 October 1908, 17.

68 Eli MacLaren analyzes the international copyright situation that enabled Connor's massive popularity in "The Magnification of Ralph Connor: *Black Rock* and the North American Copyright Divide," *Papers of the Bibliographical Society of America* 101, no. 4 (2007): 507–31.

69 Kennethe M. Haig, *Brave Harvest: The Life Story of E. Cora Hind, LL.D.* (Toronto: Thomas Allen, 1945), 130.

70 Mary Vipond, "Best Sellers in English Canada, 1899–1918: An Overview," *Journal of Canadian Fiction* 24 (1978): 115.

71 Clarence Karr, *Authors and Audiences: Popular Canadian Fiction in the Early Twentieth Century* (Montreal/Kingston: McGill-Queen's University Press, 2000), 111.

72 McClung, *Clearing in the West*, 371.

73 Hallett and Davis, *Firing the Heather*, 156.

74 See Fiamengo, *The Woman's Page*, for an analysis of McClung's rhetoric in her speeches and in print.

75 Stephen Leacock, "The Woman Question," *Maclean's Magazine* (October 1915): 7–9; reprinted in *Canadian Literature in English: Texts and Contexts*, vol. 1, ed. Cynthia Sugars and Laura Moss (Toronto: Pearson Longman, 2009), 510–14.

76 Veronica Strong-Boag, "'Ever a Crusader': Nellie McClung, First-Wave Feminist," in *Rethinking Canada*, ed. Veronica Strong-Boag and Anita Claire Fellman (Toronto: Copp Clark, 1986), 179; Strong-Boag, "Introduction," in *In Times Like These* by Nellie McClung (Toronto: University of Toronto Press, 1972), xiv, xix.

77 Machar attended literary events such as the "Evening with Canadian Authors" of 16 January 1892 at which Pauline Johnson made her "debut," but she claimed that her voice was too soft for the stage and her poems were read aloud by someone else ("Canadian Literature," *Globe*, 18 January 1892), 5.

78 Ramsay Cook, *The Regenerators: Social Criticism in Late Victorian English Canada* (Toronto: University of Toronto Press, 1985), 186.

79 See Janice Fiamengo's chapter on Machar in *The Woman's Page*.

80 Walter Blackburn Harte, "Some Canadian Writers of Today," *New England Magazine* 9, no. 1 (September 1890): 35.

81 Agnes Maule Machar to Douglas Sladen, 23 March 1893, Richmond Reference Library, Douglas Sladen Collection, Letter book Sla. 16; cited by Gwendolyn Davies, "Publishing Abroad," in *History of the Book in Canada*, vol. 2, *1840–1918*, ed. Yvan Lamonde, Patricia Lockhart Fleming, and Fiona A. Black (Toronto: University of Toronto Press, 2005).

82 Amanda Claybaugh, *The Novel of Purpose: Literature and Social Reform in the Anglo-American World* (Ithaca: Cornell University Press, 2007).

83 Fidelis [Agnes Maule Machar], "Unhealthy Conditions of Women's Work in Factories," *The Week*, 8 May 1896, 566–69.

84 Carole Gerson, "Only a Working Girl: The Story of Marie Joussaye Fotheringham," *Northern Review* 19 (Winter 1998): 141–60.

85 Carole Gerson, "Marie Joussaye's *Labor's Greeting*," *Canadian Poetry* no. 53 (Fall 2003): 87–95.

86 Agnes Maule Machar, *Katie Johnstone's Cross: A Canadian Tale* (Toronto: Campbell, 1870), 204–05.

87 Agnes Maule Machar, *Roland Graeme: Knight* (1892; Ottawa: Tecumseh, 1996), 10.

88 Ibid., 148.

89 Marie Joussaye to Wilfrid Laurier, Vancouver [n.d.], Laurier papers, LAC, 584–79.

CHAPTER 9

1   I follow Martha H. Patterson's example of capitalizing the term "New Woman" "to emphasize its constructed nature"; Martha H. Patterson, *Beyond the Gibson Girl: Reimagining the American New Woman, 1895–1915* (Urbana: University of Illinois Press, 2005), 187.

2   Talia Schaffer, "'Nothing but Foolscap and Ink': Inventing the New Woman," in *The New Woman in Fiction and in Fact: Fin de Siècle Feminisms*, ed. Angélique Richardson and Chris Willis (London: Palgrave, 2001), 39–52.

3   Ann Ardis, *New Women, New Novels: Feminism and Early Modernism* (New Brunswick: Rutgers University Press, 1990).

4   Joanna E. Wood, *The Untempered Wind* (1894; Ottawa: Tecumseh, 1994), 6.

5   "General Gossip of Authors and Writers," *Current Opinion* 16 (October 1894): 338; cited by Klay Dyer, "Introduction," in Wood, *The Untempered Wind*, xiv–xv.

6   "Of the Making of Books There Is No End," *Globe*, 10 November 1894, 9.

7   Andrea Austin, "(Un)building the Nation: Mary Leslie's *The Cromaboo Mail Carrier*, *Victorian Review* 21, no. 1 (Summer 1995): 50.

8   James Thomas Jones [Mary Leslie], *The Cromaboo Mail Carrier: A Canadian Love Story* (Guelph: Hacking, 1878), 3.

9   Misao Dean, *Practising Femininity: Domestic Realism and the Performance of Gender in Early Canadian Fiction* (Toronto: University of Toronto Press, 1998), 63.

10 *Canadian Magazine* 7 (August 1896): 394.

11 Rachel Blau Duplessis, *Writing beyond the Ending: Narrative Strategies of Twentieth-Century Women Writers* (Bloomington: Indiana University Press, 1985).

12 Maud Petitt, *Beth Woodburn* (Toronto: Briggs, 1897), 40.

13 Ibid., 156.

14 Sara Jeannette Duncan, *A Daughter of Today* (1894; Ottawa: Tecumseh, 1988), 157.

15 Lyn Pykett, *The 'Improper' Feminine: The Women's Sensation Novel and the New Woman Writing* (London/New York: Routledge, 1992), 177.

16 Lyn Pykett, "Portraits of the Artist as a Young Woman: Representations of the Female Artist in the New Woman Fiction of the 1890s," in *Victorian Women Writers and the Woman Question*, ed. Nicola Diane Thompson (Cambridge: Cambridge University Press, 1999), 136.

17 Elaine Showalter, *A Jury of Her Peers: American Women Writers from Anne Bradstreet to Annie Proulx* (New York: Knopf, 2009), 86.

18 Olive Schreiner, *Woman and Labor* (New York: Stokes, 1911), 163.

19 Candace Savage, *Our Nell: A Scrapbook Biography of Nellie McClung* (Saskatoon: Western Producer Prairie Books, 1979), 181.

20 Nellie McClung, *Nellie McClung, the Complete Autobiography: Clearing in the West and The Stream Runs Fast*, ed. Veronica Strong-Boag and Michelle Lynn Rosa (Peterborough: Broadview, 2003), 364.

21 L.M. Montgomery, *The Selected Journals of L.M. Montgomery*, vol. 1, ed. Mary Rubio and Elizabeth Waterston (Toronto: Oxford University Press, 1984), 263.

22 L.M. Montgomery to G.B. MacMillan, 3 December 1905, in *My Dear Mr. M.: Letters to G.B. MacMillan from L.M. Montgomery*, ed. Francis W.P. Bolger and Elizabeth R. Epperly (Toronto: Oxford University Press, 1992), 17.

23   L.M. Montgomery, *Anne of Green Gables* (1908; New York: Norton, 2007), 202.

24   Misao Dean, "The Process of Definition: Nationality in Sara Jeannette Duncan's Early International Novels," *Journal of Canadian Studies* 20, no. 2 (Summer 1985): 132–49.

25   Duncan, *A Daughter of Today*, 254.

26   Ibid., 281.

27   Catharine Parr Traill, *Canadian Crusoes* (1852; Ottawa: Carleton University Press, 1986), 124.

28   Rosanna Leprohon, *Antoinette de Mirecourt: or, Secret Marrying and Secret Sorrowing* (1864; Ottawa: Carleton University Press, 1989), 237.

29   Dean, *Practising Femininity*, 43.

30   Leprohon, *Antoinette*, 73.

31   Ibid., 238.

32   Lorraine McMullen and Sandra Campbell, eds., *Aspiring Women: Short Stories by Canadian Women, 1880–1890* (Ottawa: University of Ottawa Press, 1993); Sandra Campbell and Lorraine McMullen, eds., *New Women: Short Stories by Canadian Women, 1900–1920* (Ottawa: University of Ottawa Press, 1991).

33   Some of these are noted by Cecilia Morgan in *'A Happy Holiday': English Canadians and Transatlantic Tourism, 1870–1930* (Toronto: University of Toronto Press, 2008), 27–28, 378.

34   Anna Jameson, *Winter Studies and Summer Rambles in Canada*, vol. 1 (London: Saunders and Otley, 1838; Toronto: McClelland and Stewart, 1990), vi (NCL ed., p. 9).

35   Ibid., vol. 3, 356 (NCL ed., 542).

36   Ibid., vol. 2, 160 (NCL ed., 262).

37   Ibid., 237 (NCL ed., 303).

38   The Canadian portion of her book was reissued as *Sketches in Canada; and Rambles among the Red Men* (London: Longman, Brown, Green, and Longmans, 1852).

39   Ellen Spragge, "Jottings along the CPR," *Week*, 8 July 1886, 508. The series ran until 9 September 1886.

40   John Sutherland, *Mrs. Humphrey Ward: Eminent Victorian, Pre-eminent Edwardian* (New York: Oxford University Press, 1990), 289–92.

41   This title was the sixth top-selling book on the Canadian bestseller list for 1910; Mary Vipond, "Best Sellers in English Canada 1899–1918: An Overview," *Journal of Canadian Fiction* 24: 116.

42   Anna Harriette Leonowens, *The English Governess at the Siamese Court: Being Recollections of Six Years in the Royal Palace at Bangkok* (London: Trubner, 1870); Anna Harriette Leonowens, *The Romance of the Harem* (Boston: Osgood, 1873); Harriet A. Roche, *On Trek in the Transvaal: or, Over Berg and Veldt in South Africa* (London: Sampson Low, 1878).

43   Duncan, *A Daughter of Today*, 187.

44   Eva-Marie Kroller, *Canadian Travellers in Europe, 1851–1900* (Vancouver: UBC Press, 1987), 76.

45   Grace E. Denison, *A Happy Holiday* (Toronto, 1893), n.p.

46   Marjory Lang, *Women Who Made the News: Female Journalists in Canada, 1880–1945* (Montreal/Kingston: McGill-Queen's University Press, 1999), 27.

47 Sara Jeannette Duncan, *A Social Departure: How Orthodocia and I Went round the World by Ourselves* (New York: Appleton, 1890), 182.

48 After her newspaper accounts entertained the thirty thousand readers of the Montreal *Daily Star*, the book version was her best-known volume in her lifetime, selling more than sixteen thousand copies by 1904. Linda Quirk, "The Place of Bibliography in the Academy Today: Reassessing Sara Jeannette Duncan," *PBSC/CSBC* 46, no. 1 (Spring 2008): 83–84.

49 Duncan, *Social Departure*, 2.

50 Duncan, *Social Departure*, 10. A later Canadian reference appears in her recollection of "the scratched paint on the back of a Presbyterian pew in Canada, and my own small boot" (372).

51 Emily Murphy, *Janey Canuck in the West* (1917; Toronto: McClelland and Stewart, 1975), 58.

52 Valerie Legge, "'Why Go Abroad?' Agnes Laut in *Wonderland*," in *Literary Environments: Canada and the Old World*, ed. Britta Olinder (Brussels: Peter Lang, 2006), 61–73.

53 Agnes Laut, "Fifteen Hundred Miles down the Saskatchewan," *Scribner's* 45 (1909): 459.

54 Linda L. Hale, "Cameron, Agnes Deans," *Dictionary of Canadian Biography* (hereafter *DCB*) 14, online.

55 Agnes Deans Cameron, *The New North: Being Some Account of a Woman's Journey through Canada to the Arctic* (New York: Appleton, 1910), 309.

56 Ibid., 39.

57 Ibid., 132.

58 Ibid., 185.

59 Ibid., 221.

60 Ibid., 225–26.

61 "Remarkable Journey of Two Women to the Arctic Ocean," *Globe*, Saturday Magazine Section, 6 February 1909, 6.

62 "Dinner to Miss Deans Cameron," *Globe*, 28 April 1909, 8.

63 Janice Sanford Beck, *No Ordinary Woman: The Story of Mary Schaffer Warren* (Calgary: Rocky Mountain Books, 2002), 72; Canada, Energy Mines and Resources Canada, Permanent Committee on Geographical Names, Jasper Park File 0241, Mabel B. Williams to R. Douglas, 23 September 1929, citing a letter from Mary Schaffer, quoted by Pearlann Reichwein and Lisa McDermott, "Opening the Secret Garden: Mary Schaffer, Jasper Park Conservation, and the Survey of Maligne Lake, 1911," in *Culturing Wilderness in Jasper Park*, ed. I.S. MacLaren (Edmonton: University of Alberta Press, 2007), 163.

64 Ibid., 65.

65 Roberta Buchanan, Anne Harte, and Bryan Greene, *The Woman Who Mapped Labrador: The Life and Expedition Diary of Mina Hubbard* (Montreal/Kingston: McGill-Queen's University Press, 2005), 71.

66 Sherrill Grace's scholarly edition was published by McGill-Queen's University Press in 2004; Hubbard's travel writing receives critical attention in Wendy Roy's *Maps of Difference: Canada, Women, and Travel* (Montreal/Kingston: McGill-Queen's University Press, 2005).

CHAPTER 10

1 Susana Smith, 12 May 1792, in *"Our Children Free and Happy': Letters from Black Settlers in Africa in the 1790s*, ed. Christopher Fyfe (Edinburgh: University of Edinburgh Press, 1991), 24.

2 Priscilla Stewart, "A Voice from the Oppressed to the Friends of Humanity," in *bluesprint: Black British Columbian Literature and Orature*, ed. Wade Compton (Vancouver: Arsenal Pulp Press, 2001), 49–50.

3 Mistakenly cited in some sources as Toronto-born "M.E. Lampert," she has been documented in Janet Gray, "Passing as Fact: Mollie E. Lambert and Mary Eliza Tucker Lambert Meet as Racial Modernity Dawns," *Representations* 64 (Autumn 1998): 41–75.

4 George Elliott Clarke, *Odysseys Home: Mapping African-Canadian Literature* (Toronto: University of Toronto Press, 2002), 250, 330, 381; Wendy Wagner, "Mrs. A.E. Johnson (Amelia Johnson)," in *American Women Prose Writers, 1870–1920, Dictionary of Literary Biography* 221, ed. Sharon M. Harris, Heidi L. Jacobs, and Jennifer M. Putzi (Detroit: Gale, 2000), 230–37.

5 Ibid., 338, 357.

6 Jane Rhodes, *Mary Ann Shadd Cary: The Black Press and Protest in the Nineteenth Century* (Bloomington: Indiana University Press, 1998), 21–22.

7 Ibid., 6.

8 Heather Murray, *Come, Bright Improvement! The Literary Societies of Nineteenth-Century Ontario* (Toronto: University of Toronto Press, 2002), 71.

9 Afua P. Cooper, "Black Women and Work in Nineteenth-Century Canada West: Black Woman Teacher Mary Bibb," in *"We're Rooted Here and They Can't Pull Us Up": Essays in African Canadian Women's History*, ed. Peggy Bristow et al. (Toronto: University of Toronto Press, 1994), 164, n30.

10 Robin Winks, *The Blacks in Canada: A History* (Montreal/Kingston: McGill-Queen's University Press, 1997), 395.

11 See Afua P. Cooper's *The Hanging of Angélique* (Toronto: HarperCollins, 2006) for Canada's history of slavery.

12 David A. Armour's entry on John Johnston in *Dictionary of Canadian Biography* (hereafter *DCB*) 6 barely mentions his wife and gives no information about his children.

13 Robert Dale Parker, ed., *The Sound the Stars Make Rushing through the Sky: The Writings of Jane Johnston Schoolcraft* (Philadelphia: University of Pennsylvania Press, 2007), 12.

14 Henry Rowe Schoolcraft, *The Literary Voyager; or, Muzzeniegun*, ed. Philip A. Mason (1962; Westport: Greenwood Press, 1974).

15 Mrs. [Anna] Jameson, *Winter Studies and Summer Rambles in Canada*, vol. 3 (London: Saunders and Otley, 1838), 183–86 (NCL 454–55).

16 Ibid., 36 (NCL 378).

17 Ibid., 244 (NCL 485).

18 Ibid., 88 (NCL 403). Jameson's selections closely follow the versions that Jane had prepared for Schoolcraft's manuscript newspaper, *The Literary Voyager*.

19 Tony Williams, "Preface," in *Sketches of Labrador Life* by Lydia Campbell (St. John's: Killick Press, 2000), vii.

20 Martha Douglas Harris, *History and Folklore of the Cowichan Indians* (Victoria: Colonist Printing and Publishing, 1901), preface [4].

21 Ibid., 57.

22 Sarah Carter, "Introduction," in *People of the Plains* by Amelia Paget (Regina: Canadian Plains Research Centre, 2004), ix, xiii.

23 Ibid., xxvi.

24 Veronica Strong-Boag and Carole Gerson, *Paddling Her Own Canoe* (Toronto: University of Toronto Press, 2000), 110.

25 Johnson, "Wave-Won," in *E. Pauline Johnson: Collected Poetry and Selected Prose*, ed. Carole Gerson and Veronica Strong-Boag (Toronto: University of Toronto Press, 2002), 86.

26 Frequently reissued for many decades, it has now been superseded by *E. Pauline Johnson: Collected Poetry and Selected Prose*, ed. Carole Gerson and Veronica Strong-Boag.

27 Hector Charlesworth, "Baton and Buckskin," Vancouver *Province*, 6 October 1894, 436; Hector Charlesworth, "The Indian Poetess," *Lake Magazine* (September 1892): 86.

28 Theodore Watts-Dunton, rev. of *Songs of the Great Dominion*, *Athenaeum*, 28 September 1889, 412; *Magnet Magazine* (6 January 1897), Johnson fonds, McMaster.

29 Elaine Showalter, ed., *Daughters of Decadence: Women Writers of the Fin-de-Siècle* (London: Virago, 1993).

30 Elaine Showalter, *A Jury of Her Peers: American Women Writers from Anne Bradstreet to Annie Proulx* (New York: Knopf, 2009), 211–12.

31 Pauline Johnson, "The Good Old N.P." (1896), in Gerson and Strong-Boag, eds., *E. Pauline Johnson*, 119.

32 "Anglo-Chinese Woman's Career," Montreal *Gazette*, 9 May 1922, 5. This story has not been found.

33 James Doyle, "Law, Legislation, and Literature: The Life of Grace H. Harte," *Biography* 17, no. 4 (1994): 367–85.

34 Diana Birchall, *Onoto Watanna: The Story of Winnifred Eaton* (Urbana: University of Illinois Press, 2001), 107–10.

35 Lorraine McMullen, "Eaton, Edith," *DCB* 14, online.

36 Jean Lee Cole, *The Literary Voices of Winnifred Eaton: Redefining Ethnicity and Authenticity* (New Brunswick: Rutgers University Press, 2002), 3.

37 Edith Eaton ["E.E."], "A Plea for the Chinaman," Montreal *Daily Star*, 21 September 1896, 5. Several negative letters led to Eaton's powerful rebuttal, signed "Edith Eaton" and published under the title "The Chinese Defended," 29 September 1896, 5. Thanks to Mary Chapman for information about the latter.

38 Sui Sin Far, "Leaves from the Mental Portfolio of a Eurasian," *Independent*, 21 January 1909, 132.

39 Elizabeth Bailey Price, "Onoto Watanna, an Amazing Author," *Maclean's Magazine* 35 (15 October 1922): 64.

40 Winnifred Reeve, "The Canadian Spirit in Our Literature," Calgary *Daily Herald*, 24 March 1923, 11.

CONCLUSION

1   Thomas O'Hagan, "Some Canadian Women Writers," *Catholic World* 63 (September 1896): 779–85; *Week*, 25 September 1896, 1050–53; J. Castell Hopkins, *Canada: An Encyclopedia of the Country*, vol. 5 (Toronto: Linscott, 1899), 170–76.

2   Contributions by women included Ethelwyn Wetherald's four articles in the *Week* in 1888 on S. Frances Harrison, Agnes Maule Machar, Louisa Murray, and Annie Rothwell; M. Bourchier Sanford, "Some Women Writers of Canada," *Godey's Magazine* 135 (July 1897): 13–21, and Winnifred Lee Wendell, "The Modern School of Canadian Writers," *Bookman* 11 (1900): 515–26.

3   Laurence Burpee, "Recent Canadian Fiction," *Forum* (August 1899): 755.

4   For a useful summary, see Christine Haynes, "Reassessing 'Genius' in Studies of Authorship," *Book History* 8 (2005): 299–303, 311. For an account of the voluminous historical presence of American women, see Elaine Showalter, *A Jury of Her Peers: American Women Writers from Anne Bradstreet to Annie Proulx* (New York: Knopf, 2009).

5   A selection of Drummond's poetry appeared as title no. 11 in the New Canadian Library in 1959. Similar use of dialect in E.W. Thomson's *Old Man Savarin Stories* was praised by Archibald Lampman as "particularly apt to a Canadian ear," *Week*, 12 August 1885, 800–01.

6   Blanche Gelfant, *Women Writing in America: Voices in Collage* (Hanover: University Press of New England, 1984), 146.

7   Marian Botsford Fraser, *Walking the Line: Travels along the Canadian/American Border* (Vancouver: Douglas and McIntyre, 1989), 16.

8   Jane Barker Wright, *The Understanding* (Erin: Porcupine's Quill, 2002), 114.

9   Rosemary Sullivan, "Introduction," *Stories by Canadian Women* (Toronto: Oxford University Press, 1984), ix.

10   Russell Smith, "Real Men Don't Read Fiction ...," *Globe and Mail*, 4 March 2000, R5.

11   Martin Levin, "Ladies' Day in CanLit," *Globe and Mail*, 2 March 2002, D12; "Holiday Fiction Special," *Globe and Mail*, 22 December 2001, R1–R6. The five chosen male writers were Michael Crummey, Brian Doyle, Andrew Pyper, Eric Wright, and George Elliott Clarke.

12   Katherine L. Morrison, *Canadians Are Not Americans* (Toronto: Second Story Press, 2003), xvi.

13   Margaret Atwood, "Introduction," in *Roughing It in the Bush* by Susanna Moodie (London: Virago, 1986), xiv.

14   J.R. (Tim) Struthers, "An Interview with Margaret Atwood," *Essays on Canadian Writing* 6 (1976): 26.

15   Carol Shields, "A View from the Edge of the Edge" [1997] in *Carol Shields and the Extra-ordinary*, ed. Marta Dvorak and Manina Jones (Montreal: McGill-Queen's University Press, 2007), 27.

16   Margaret Atwood, "Introduction," in *New Oxford Book of Canadian Verse* (Toronto: Oxford University Press, 1983), xxix.

17   James Boswell, *Life of Samuel Johnson*, vol. 2 (London: Charles Dilly, 1791), Chapter 9.

18   Margaret Blennerhassett, *The Widow of the Rock, and Other Poems* (Montreal: Sparhawk, 1824), iii.

19 Ethel Wilson, *Stories, Essays, Letters*, ed. David Stouck (Vancouver: UBC Press, 1987), 109. The source is undated, but likely 1962–63.

20 George Bowering, "Language Women," in *Imaginary Hand: Essays by George Bowering* (Edmonton: NeWest Press, 1988)., 100. This statement was critiqued by Jennifer Henderson, "Gender in the Discourse of Canadian Literary Criticism," *Open Letter* 8th series, no. 3 (Spring 1992): 47–57, 49.

21 She excluded Leonard Cohen because of the role of the recording industry in shaping his celebrity; see Lorraine York, *Literary Celebrity in Canada* (Toronto: University of Toronto Press, 2007), 7.

22 We have yet to establish the Canadian equivalent of the Society for the Study of American Women Writers, founded in 1998.

23 Publicity email from Oxford University Press Canada, 27 October 2008; the same language appears on their website, http://www.oupcanada.com/catalog/9780195401318.html, 10 July 2009.

24 Anne Innis Dagg, *The 50% Solution: Why Should Women Pay for Men's Culture?* (Waterloo: Otter Press, 1986), 30.

25 Carole Gerson, "Anthologies and the Canon of Early Canadian Women Writers," in *Re(dis)covering Our Foremothers*, ed. Lorraine McMullen (Ottawa: University of Ottawa Press, 1989), 56–57.

26 Robert Lecker, "Anthologizing English-Canadian Fiction: Some Canonical Trends," *Open Letter* 9th series, no. 1 (Fall 1994): 44–46.

27 These categories are not absolute: many of the writers also show up as teachers, and a number of the women known for their religious work are also classified as authors.

28 Alice Munro, *Lives of Girls and Women* (New York: Signet, 1974), 27.

29 The breakdown was: Acting (M: 10.4 percent W: 12.4 percent), Sports (M: 29.4 percent W: 12.6 percent), Politics (M: 7.1 percent W: 4.4 percent), Business (M: 36.5 percent W: 33.8 percent), Writing (M: 16.2 percent W: 36 percent). Tables courtesy of Maclean Hunter.

30 *Maclean's Magazine* (1 July 1998): "The 100 Most Important Canadians in History" is the theme of the entire issue.

31 "Canadians Who Inspired the World," *Maclean's Magazine* (4 September 2000): 26–48.

32 This pattern, which pertains to retrospective analysis, shifted somewhat with the *Globe and Mail*'s "50 Nation Builders," 1 June 2002, F4–F5, whose 14.5 women included four in public life, four in the arts, and a few in sports and science, and altered further with forward-looking summaries such as *Maclean's* "50 Canadians to Watch in 2003" (20 January 2003) whose eight women spread across music, sports, public life, and religion.

Archival Sources

ARCHIVES OF ONTARIO (AO)
F18, Alexander Emerson Belcher fonds
F 1076, William Kirby fonds
MU 2123, *Canadian Magazine*, contributors' ledger
RG 8-5, M.O. Hammond fonds

BRITISH COLUMBIA ARCHIVES
MS-0010, Nellie McClung fonds

DALHOUSIE UNIVERSITY ARCHIVES
MS 2-82, Archibald MacMechan fonds

ESPLANADE ARCHIVES, MEDICINE HAT, ALBERTA
Women's Literary Club fonds

LIBRARY AND ARCHIVES CANADA (LAC)
MG26-G, R10811-0-X-E, Wilfrid Laurier fonds
MG29-D61, R7531-0-8-E, Henry Morgan fonds
MG30-D52, R2057-0-2-E, Madge Macbeth fonds
MG30-D114, R1916-0-4-E, Frank Packard fonds
MG30-D150, R2364-0-6-E, Andrew MacPhail fonds

McGILL UNIVERSITY LIBRARIES, RARE BOOKS AND
SPECIAL COLLECTIONS DIVISION
William Douw Lighthall papers

McMaster University Library, William Ready Division of Archives and Research Collections
E. Pauline Johnson fonds

North York Central Library
Newton MacTavish papers

Queen's University Archives
Lorne Pierce fonds

Thomas Fisher Rare Book Library, University of Toronto
MS collection 119, James Mavor fonds

University of British Columbia Library, Special Collections
Snowden Dunn Scott fonds

University of Calgary Library, Special Collections
Winnifred Eaton Reeve fonds

University of Guelph, Archival and Special Collections
L.M. Montgomery collection

Online Source

The *Dictionary of Canadian Biography*, the source of many note citations, is available online at http://www.biographi.ca/.

Published Sources

"A Chapter on Lady Editors." *Canadian Son of Temperance* 4, no. 1 (7 January 1854): 2.

Adam, Graeme Mercer. "Canadian Literature." *The Week*, 4 July 1890, 486.

Adams, Thomas R., and Nicolas Barker. "A New Model for the Study of the Book." In *The Potencie of Life: Books in Society: The Clark Lectures, 1986–1987*, edited by Nicolas Barker, 5–43. London: British Library, 1993.

Adburgham, Alison. *Women in Print: Writing Women and Women's Magazines from the Restoration to the Accession of Victoria*. London: Allen and Unwin, 1972.

Adilman, Tami. "Evlyn Farris and the University Women's Club." In *In Her Own Right: Selected Essays on Women's History in BC*, edited by Barbara Latham and Cathy Kess, 147–66. Victoria: Camosun College, 1980.

Ainley, Marianne Gosztonyi. "Science in Canada's Backwoods: Catharine Parr Traill." In *Natural Eloquence: Women Reinscribe Science*, edited by Barbara T. Gates and Ann B. Shteir, 79–97. Madison: University of Wisconsin Press, 1997.

Ambrose, Linda M. *For Home and Country: The Centennial History of the Women's Institutes in Ontario*. Erin: Boston Mills Press, 1996.

"Annual Meeting, Woman's Century." *Woman's Century*, March 1917, 12.

Aoki, Jodi. "Private to Public: Frances Stewart, Ellen Dunlop, and the Production of *Our Forest Home.*" MA thesis, Trent University, 2007.

Ardis, Ann. *New Women, New Novels: Feminism and Early Modernism.* New Brunswick, NJ: Rutgers University Press, 1990.

Ascher, Isidore. *Voices from the Hearth. A Collection of Verses.* Montreal: Lovell, 1863.

Atwood, Margaret. "A Thing or Two about Nationalism." *Vancouver Sun,* 20 August 1973, 5.

———. "Introduction." In *New Oxford Book of Canadian Verse,* edited by Margaret Atwood and Robert Weaver, xxix. Toronto: Oxford University Press, 1984.

———. "Introduction." In *Roughing It in the Bush* by Susanna Moodie. London: Virago, 1986.

Austin, Andrea. "(Un)building the Nation: Mary Leslie's *The Cromaboo Mail Carrier.*" *Victorian Review* 21, no. 1 (Summer 1995): 36–52.

Bacchi, Carol Lee. *Liberation Deferred? The Ideas of the English-Canadian Suffragists, 1877–1918.* Toronto: University of Toronto Press, 1983.

Baldwyn, Augusta. *Poems.* Montreal: Lovell, 1859.

Ballstadt, Carl. "Editor's Introduction." In *Roughing It in the Bush or Life in Canada* by Susanna Moodie, xxxiii. Ottawa: Carleton University Press, 1988.

———, Elizabeth Hopkins, and Michael A. Peterman, eds. *I Bless You in My Heart: Selected Correspondence of Catharine Parr Traill.* Toronto: University of Toronto Press, 1996.

Ballstadt, Carl, Elizabeth Hopkins, and Michael Peterman, eds. *Susanna Moodie: Letters of a Lifetime.* Toronto: University of Toronto Press, 1985.

Ballstadt, Carl, Elizabeth Hopkins, and Michael A. Peterman, eds. *Letters of Love and Duty: The Correspondence of Susanna and John Moodie.* Toronto: University of Toronto Press, 1993.

Barker, William. "Books and Reading in Newfoundland and in Labrador." In *History of the Book in Canada,* vol. 1, *Beginnings to 1840,* edited by Patricia Lockhart Fleming, Gilles Gallichan, and Yvan Lamonde, 362–64. Toronto: University of Toronto Press, 2004.

Barman, Jean. "'I Walk My Own Track in Life and No Mere Male Can Bump Me Off It': Constance Lindsay Skinner and the Work of History." In *Creating Historical Memory: English-Canadian Women and the Work of History,* edited by Beverly Boutilier and Alison Prentice, 129–63. Vancouver: UBC Press, 1997.

Baron, Ava. "Women and the Making of the American Working Class: A Study of the Proletarianization of Printers." *Review of Radical Political Economics* 14, no. 3 (1982): 23–42.

Barry, Robertine. *Fleurs champêtres.* Montreal: Desaulniers, 1895.

———. "French Canadian Women in Literature." In *Women of Canada: Their Life and Work,* compiled by the National Council of Women of Canada, 190–91. National Council of Women of Canada [1900], 1975.

Bassett, Isabel. "Introduction." In *Janey Canuck in the West* by Emily Ferguson Murphy, xxii. Toronto: McClelland and Stewart, 1975.

Bayard, Mary Temple. "Eve Brodlique." *Canadian Magazine* 7 (1896): 515–18.

Beetham, Margaret. "Towards a Theory of the Periodical as Publishing Genre." In *Investigating Victorian Journalism*, edited by Laurel Brake, Aled Jones, and Lionel Madden, 19–32. London: Macmillan, 1990.

Bellerive, Georges. *Brèves apologies de nos auteurs féminins.* Quebec: Librairie Garneau, 1920.

Berton, Pierre. *Hollywood's Canada: The Americanization of Our National Image.* Toronto: McClelland and Stewart, 1975.

Bingham, Helen E. *An Irish Saint: The Life of Ann Preston Known as "Holy Ann."* Toronto: Briggs, 1907.

Birchall, Diana. *Onoto Watanna: The Story of Winnifred Eaton.* Urbana: University of Illinois Press, 2001.

Bird, Kym. *Redressing the Past: The Politics of Early English-Canadian Women's Drama, 1880–1920.* Montreal/Kingston: McGill-Queen's University Press, 2004.

Blennerhassett, Margaret. *The Widow of the Rock, and Other Poems.* Montreal: Sparhawk, 1824.

Bloomberg, Kristin Mapel. "Cultural Critique and Consciousness Raising: Clara Bewick Colby's *Woman's Tribune* and Late Nineteenth-Century Radical Feminism." In *Women in Print: Essays on the Print Culture of American Women from the Nineteenth and Twentieth Centuries*, edited by James P. Danky and Wayne A. Wiegand, 27–63. Madison: University of Wisconsin Press, 2006.

Boardman, Kay. "The Ideology of Domesticity: The Regulation of the Household Economy in Victorian Women's Magazines." *Victorian Periodicals Review* 33, no. 2 (Summer 2000): 150–64.

Boland, Eavan. *Object Lessons: The Life of the Woman and the Poet in Our Time.* New York: Norton, 1995.

Bolger, Francis W.P., and Elizabeth R. Epperly, eds. *My Dear Mr. M.: Letters to G.B. MacMillan from L.M. Montgomery.* Toronto: Oxford University Press, 1992.

Boswell, James. *Life of Samuel Johnson*, vol. 2, Chapter 9. London: Charles Dilly, 1791.

Bourdieu, Pierre. *The Field of Cultural Production: Essays on Art and Literature*, edited by Randal Johnson. New York: Columbia University Press, 1993.

Boutilier, Beverly. "Women's Rights and Duties: Sarah Anne Curzon and the Politics of Canadian History." In *Creating Historical Memory: English-Canadian Women and the Work of History*, edited by Beverly Boutilier and Alison Prentice, 51–74. Vancouver: UBC Press, 1997.

Boutilier, Beverly, and Alison Prentice, eds. *Creating Historical Memory: English-Canadian Women and the Work of History.* Vancouver: UBC Press, 1997.

Bowering, George. "Language Women." In *Imaginary Hand: Essays by George Bowering*, 99–109. Edmonton: NeWest Press, 1988.

Bradley, Mary. *Narrative of the Life and Christian Experience of Mrs. Mary Bradley of Saint John, New Brunswick.* Boston: Strong and Brodhead, 1849.

Branda, Jeanne-Lydia [pseud. Marie Sylvia]. *Vers le bien.* [Ottawa?], 1916.

Brewer, John. *The Pleasures of the Imagination: English Culture in the Eighteenth Century.* London: HarperCollins, 1997.

Brouwer, Ruth Compton. *New Women for God: Canadian Presbyterian Women and India Missions, 1876–1914.* Toronto: University of Toronto Press, 1990.

Brown, Candy Gunther. *The Word in the World: Evangelical Writing, Publishing, and Reading in America 1789–1880.* Chapel Hill: University of North Carolina Press, 2004.

Brown, Jack. "'The Adopted Daughter' Identified." *Canadian Notes & Queries* 15 (1975): 11–12.

Brown, Mary Markham. *An Index to the Literary Garland.* Toronto: Bibliographical Society of Canada, 1962.

Brunet, Manon. "Les femmes dans la production de la littérature francophone du début de XIXe siècle québécois." In *Livre et lecture au Québec (1800–1850),* edited by Claude Galarneau and Maurice Lemire, 167–80. Quebec: Institut Québécois de Recherche sur la Culture, 1988.

Buchanan, Roberta, Anne Harte, and Bryan Greene, eds. *The Woman Who Mapped Labrador: The Life and Expedition Diary of Mina Hubbard.* Montreal/Kingston: McGill-Queen's University Press, 2005.

Burpee, Laurence. "Recent Canadian Fiction." *Forum* (August 1899): 752–60.

Burr, Christina. "Defending 'The Art Preservative': Class and Gender Relations in the Printing Trades Unions, 1850–1914." *Labour/Le Travail* 31 (Spring 1993): 47–73.

Burr, Christina, and Eric Leroux. "Working in the Printing Trades." In *History of the Book in Canada,* vol. 3, *1918–1980,* edited by Carole Gerson and Jacques Michon, 358–68. Toronto: University of Toronto Press, 2007.

Burt, Elizabeth V., ed. *Women's Press Organizations, 1881–1999.* Westport: Greenwood Press, 2000.

Cambron, Micheline, and Carole Gerson. "Literary Authorship." In *History of the Book in Canada,* vol. 2, *1840–1918,* edited by Yvan Lamonde, Patricia Lockhart Fleming, and Fiona A. Black, 119–34. Toronto: University of Toronto Press, 2005.

Cameron, Agnes Deans. *The New North: Being Some Account of a Woman's Journey through Canada to the Arctic.* New York: Appleton, 1910.

Campbell, Mrs. A. *Rough and Smooth: or, Ho! for an Australian Gold Field.* Quebec: Hunter Rose, 1865.

Campbell, Lydia. *Sketches of Labrador Life.* Preface by Tony Williams. St. John's: Killick Press, 2000.

Campbell, Sandra, and Lorraine McMullen, eds. *New Women: Short Stories by Canadian Women, 1900–1920.* Ottawa: University of Ottawa Press, 1991.

Campbell, Wilfred. "At the Mermaid Inn." *Globe,* 22 October 1892, 177.

"Canada's Early Women Writers," http://cufts2.lib.sfu.ca/CRDB/BVAS/resource/5724.

Canadian Authors Association. "Directory of Members." *Canadian Author* 11 (1933): 16–23.

———. "Membership Roll of the Association." *Canadian Bookman* (May): 120–22; (June 1924): 146–47.

Canadian Days: Selections for Every Day in the Year from the Works of Canadian Authors. Compiled by the Toronto Women's Press Club. Toronto: Musson, 1911.

"Canadians Who Inspired the World." *Maclean's Magazine* (4 September 2000): 26–48.

"Canadian Women in the Public Eye: Mrs. P.W. Anderson." *Saturday Night* (10 September 1921): 22, 31.

Carr-Harris, Bertha. *Lights and Shades of Mission Work; or, Leaves from a Worker's Note Book.* Ottawa: Free Press, 1892.

Carter, Kathryn. "Neither Here Nor There: Mary Gapper O'Brien Writes 'Home,' 1828–1838." In *Diversity and Change in Early Canadian Women's Writing,* edited by Jennifer Chambers, 8–21. Newcastle upon Tyne: Cambridge Scholars Publishing, 2008.

Chaput, Donald. "Charlotte de Rocheblave, Métisse Teacher of the Teachers." *Beaver* (Autumn 1977): 55–85.

———. "The 'Misses Nolin' of Red River." *Beaver* (Winter 1975): 14–17.

Charlesworth, Hector. "Baton and Buckskin." *Vancouver Province,* 6 October 1894, 436.

———. "The Indian Poetess: A Study." *Lake Magazine* (September 1892): 81–87.

———. "The Late E.E. Sheppard." *Saturday Night,* 22 November 1924, 2.

Chaureth, Sophie Berthelette. *Sketches of the Life, Troubles, and Grievances of a French Canadian Lady.* Toronto, 1857.

Chipman, Ann. *Memoir of Mrs. Eliza Ann Chipman.* Wolfville, 1855.

Chisholm, Mrs. Addie. *Why and How: A Hand-book for the Use of the* WCT *Unions in Canada.* Montreal: Witness Printing House, 1884.

Chu, Clara M., and Bertrum H. MacDonald. "The Public Record: An Analysis of Women's Contributions to Canadian Science and Technology before the First World War." In *Despite the Odds: Essays on Canadian Women and Science,* edited by Marianne Gosztonyi Ainley, 63–73. Montreal: Véhicule Press, 1990.

Clarke, Brian. "English-Speaking Canada from 1854." In *A Concise History of Christianity in Canada,* edited by Terence Murphy and Roberto Perin, 287–90. Toronto: Oxford University Press, 1996.

Clarke, George Elliott. *Odysseys Home: Mapping African-Canadian Literature.* Toronto: University of Toronto Press, 2002.

Claybaugh, Amanda. *The Novel of Purpose: Literature and Social Reform in the Anglo-American World.* Ithaca: Cornell University Press, 2007.

Cleverdon, Catherine L. *The Woman Suffrage Movement in Canada.* First published in 1950. Reprint, Toronto: University of Toronto Press, 1974.

Coates, Colin M., and Cecilia Morgan. *Heroines and History: Representations of Madeleine de Verchères and Laura Secord.* Toronto: University of Toronto Press, 2002.

Coates, Donna. "Emily Murphy." In *Canadian Writers before 1890: Dictionary of Literary Biography*, vol. 99, edited by W.H. New, 255–58. Detroit: Gale, 1990.

Cogswell, Jean. "Case Study: Women's Institute Libraries." In *History of the Book in Canada*, vol. 3, *1918–1980*, edited by Carole Gerson and Jacques Michon, 498–500. Toronto: University of Toronto Press, 2007.

Colbert, Ann. "Philanthropy in the Newsroom: Women's Editions of Newspapers, 1894–1896." *Journalism History* 22, no. 3 (Autumn 1996): 90–99.

Colbert, Ann Mauger. "Literary and Commercial Aspects of Women's Editions of Newspapers, 1894–1896." In *Blue Pencils and Hidden Hands: Women Editing Periodicals, 1830–1910*, edited by Sharon M. Harris and Ellen Gruber Garvey, 20–35. Boston: Northeastern University Press, 2004.

Cole, Jean Lee. *The Literary Voices of Winnifred Eaton: Redefining Ethnicity and Authenticity.* New Brunswick: Rutgers University Press, 2002.

Compton, Waded, ed. *bluesprint: Black British Columbian Literature and Orature.* Vancouver: Arsenal Pulp Press, 2001.

Conan, Laure. *J'ai tant de sujets de désespoir: Correspondence, 1878–1924*, edited by Jean-Noël Dion. Montreal: Éditions Varia, 2002.

Conger, Janet C. *A Daughter of St. Peter's.* New York: Lovell, 1888.

Cook, Ramsay. *The Regenerators: Social Criticism in Late Victorian English Canada.* Toronto: University of Toronto Press, 1985.

Cook, Sharon Ann. *"Through Sunshine and Shadow": The Woman's Christian Temperance Union, Evangelicalism, and Reform in Ontario, 1874–1930.* Montreal/Kingston: McGill-Queen's University Press, 1995.

Cooper, Afua P. "Black Women and Work in Nineteenth-Century Canada West: Black Woman Teacher Mary Bibb." In *"We're Rooted Here and They Can't Pull Us up": Essays in African Canadian Women's History*, edited by Peggy Bristow et al., 70, 143. Toronto: University of Toronto Press, 1994.

———. *The Hanging of Angélique.* Toronto: HarperCollins, 2006.

Coultrap-McQuin, Susan. *Doing Literary Business: American Women Writers in the Nineteenth Century.* Chapel Hill: University of North Carolina Press, 1990.

Cramp, Mary. *Retrospects: A History of the Formation and Progress of the Women's Missionary Aid Societies of the Maritime Provinces.* Halifax: Holloway Brothers, 1892.

Crawford, Isabella Valancy. "Toboggan." *Outing* (March 1887): 546.

Crawford, Mrs. John [Isabella Valancy]. *Songs of All Season, Climes, and Times, a Motley Jingle of Jumbled Rhymes.* Toronto: Rose, 1890.

Currie, Margaret Gill. *Gabriel West and Other Poems.* Fredericton: Cropley, 1866.

Curtius, Ernest. *European Literature and the Latin Middle Ages*, translated by W.R. Rask. New York: Pantheon, 1953.

Curtius, E.R. "Affected Modesty." In *European Literature and the Latin Middle Ages*, translated by W.R. Trask, 83–85. London: Routledge, 1979.

Curzon, Sarah Anne. *Laura Secord, the Heroine of 1812: A Drama: and Other Poems.* Toronto: C.B. Robinson, 1887.

Dagg, Anne Innis. "Canadian Voices of Authority: Non-fiction and Early Women Writers." *Journal of Canadian Studies* 27, no. 2 (Summer 1992): 107–22.

————. *The Feminine Gaze: A Canadian Compendium of Non-fiction Women Authors and Their Books, 1836–1945*. Waterloo: Wilfrid Laurier University Press, 2001.

————. *The 50% Solution: Why Should Women Pay for Men's Culture?* Waterloo: Otter Press, 1986.

Dandurand, Josephine. *Nos travers*. Montreal: Beauchemin, 1901.

Darnton, Robert. "What Is the History of Books?" In *The Kiss of Lamourette: Reflections in Cultural History*, 107–35. New York: Norton, 1990.

Davies, Gwendolyn. "'Dearer Than His Dog': Literary Women in Pre-Confederation Nova Scotia." In *Studies in Maritime Literary History*, 71–87. Fredericton: Acadiensis, 1991.

————. "Herbert, Sarah (1824–46) and Mary Eliza Herbert (1829–72)." In *The Oxford Companion to Canadian Literature*, 2nd ed., edited by Eugene Benson and William Toye, 531. Toronto: Oxford University Press, 1997.

————. "'In the Garden of Christ': Methodist Literary Women in Nineteenth-Century Maritime Canada." In *The Contribution of Methodism to Atlantic Canada*, edited by Charles H.H. Scobie and John Webster Grant, 205–17. Montreal/Kingston: McGill-Queen's University Press, 1992.

————. *Marshall Saunders and Beautiful Joe: Education through Fiction*. Truro: Nova Scotia Teachers College, 1995.

————. "Private Education for Women in Early Nova Scotia: 1784–1894." *Acadiensis* 20, no. 1 (1995): 9–19.

————. "Publishing Abroad," In *History of the Book in Canada*, vol. 2, *1840–1918*, edited by Yvan Lamonde, Patricia Lockhart Fleming, and Fiona A. Black, 139–46. Toronto: University of Toronto Press, 2005.

————. "Researching Eighteenth-Century Maritime Women Writers: Deborah How Cottnam–a Case Study." In *Working in Women's Archives: Researching Women's Private Literature and Archival Documents*, edited by Helen M. Buss and Marlene Kadar, 35–50. Waterloo: Wilfrid Laurier University Press, 2001.

————. "The Elephant and the Primrose: The Prat Sisters in New York." *Journal of Pre-Raphaelite Studies* 6, no. 7 (1998): 129–44.

Davies, Richard A., ed. *Letters of Thomas Chandler Haliburton*. Toronto: University of Toronto Press, 1988.

Day, Mrs. C.M. *Pioneers of the Eastern Townships*. Montreal: Lovell, 1863.

de Montreuil, Gaetane. "Préface." In *Contes et légendes* by Madame A.B. Lacert, n.p. Ottawa: Beauregard, 1915.

Dean, Misao. *Practising Femininity: Domestic Realism and the Performance of Gender in Early Canadian Fiction*. Toronto: University of Toronto Press, 1998.

————. "Researching Sara Jeannette Duncan in the Papers of A.P. Watt and Company." *Canadian Literature* 178 (Autumn 2003): 181–86.

————. "The Process of Definition: Nationality in Sara Jeannette Duncan's Early International Novels." *Journal of Canadian Studies* 20, no. 2 (Summer 1985): 132–49.

Delaney, Theresa, and Theresa Gowanlock. *Two Months in the Camp of Big Bear*. First published in 1885. Reprinted with a scholarly introduction by Sarah Carter. Regina: Canadian Plains Research Center, 1999.

Denison, Grace E. *A Happy Holiday*. Toronto, 1893.

Dessaules, Henriette. *Journal, premier cahier, 1874–1876*, edited by Jean-Louis Major. Montreal: Bibliothèque Québécoise, 1999.

Devereux, Cecily, and Kathleen Venema, eds. *Women Writing Home, 1700–1920, Female Correspondence across the British Empire*, vol. 3, *Canada*. London: Pickering and Chatto, 2006.

Dewart, Edward Hartley. *Selections from Canadian Poets: With Occasional Biographical Notes, and an Introductory Essay on Canadian Poetry*. Montreal: J. Lovell, 1864.

———. *Songs of Life: A Collection of Poems*. Toronto: Dudley and Burns, 1869.

"Dinner to Miss Deans Cameron." *Globe*, 28 April 1909, 8.

Donovan, A. Marion. "The Evolution of the Colored Woman." *Halifax Herald Woman's Extra*, 1 October 1895, 10.

Doyle, James. "Law, Legislation, and Literature: The Life of Grace H. Harte." *Biography* 17, no. 4 (1994): 367–85.

Drew, Benjamin. *The Refugee: Narratives of Fugitive Slaves in Canada. Related by Themselves, with an Account of the History and Condition of the Colored Population in Upper Canada*. Boston: John P. Jewett, 1856.

Driver, Elizabeth. *Culinary Landmarks: A Bibliography of Canadian Cookbooks, 1825–1949*. Toronto: University of Toronto Press, 2008.

Drummond, Margaret Mary. *The Life and Times of Margaret Bourgeoys (the Venerable)*. Boston: Angel Guardian Press, 1907.

Drummond, May Harvey. *The Grand Old Man of Dudswell Being the Memoirs of the Rev. Thos. Shaw Chapman, M.A.* Quebec: Telegraph, 1916.

Dufferin, Lady. *My Canadian Journal, 1872–1878*. New York: Appleton, 1891.

Duncan, Sara Jeannette. *A Daughter of Today*. First published in 1894. Reprint, Ottawa: Tecumseh, 1988.

———. *A Social Departure: How Orthodocia and I Went round the World by Ourselves.* New York: Appleton, 1890.

———. "American Influence on Canadian Thought." *Week*, 7 July 1887, 518.

Duplessis, Rachel Blau. *Writing beyond the Ending: Narrative Strategies of Twentieth-Century Women Writers*. Bloomington: Indiana University Press, 1985.

Durand, Laura. "Memoir." In *Elise Le Beau: A Dramatic Idyll, and Lyrics and Sonnets* by Evelyn Durand, xiii–xxi. Toronto: University of Toronto Press, 1921.

Duval-Thibault, Anna-Marie. *Deux testaments: Esquisse de moeurs canadiennes*. Fall River: Imprimere de L'Indépendent, 1888.

Eaton, Edith [E.E.]. "A Plea for the Chinaman." Montreal *Daily Star*, 21 September 1896, 5.

———. [Sui Sin Far]. "Leaves from the Mental Portfolio of a Eurasian." *Independent*, 21 January 1909, 125–32.

"The Editor at Leisure." *Canadian Queen* 3, no. 4 (April 1891): 154.

Eggleston, Wilfrid. *Literary Friends*. Ottawa: Borealis Press, 1980.

Egoff, Sheila, and Judith Saltman. *The New Republic of Childhood: A Critical Guide to Canadian Children's Literature in English*. Toronto: Oxford University Press, 1990.

Errington, Elizabeth Jane. 1995. *Wives and Mothers, Schoolmistresses, and Scullery Maids: Working Women in Upper Canada, 1790–1840.* Montreal/Kingston: McGill-Queen's University Press, 1995.

Ezell, Margaret J.M. "The Posthumous Publication of Women's Manuscripts and the History of Authorship." In *Women's Writing and the Circulation of Ideas: Manuscript Publication in England, 1550–1800,* edited by George Justice and Nathan Tinker, 121–36. New York: Cambridge University Press, 2002.

Fairbanks, Constance, and Harry Piers. "Biographical Sketch." In *Frankincense and Myrrh: Selections from the Poems of the Late Mrs. William Lawson,* edited by Harry Piers and Constance Fairbanks, vi. Halifax: Morton, 1893.

Faith of Our Fathers: A Century of Victory, 1824–1924. [Toronto–]: Methodist Missionary Society, 1924.

Faulkner, Sarah E. Sherwood. *Sea Murmurs and Woodland Songs.* Toronto: Briggs, 1903.

Fauteux, Aegidius. *The Introduction of Printing into Canada.* Montreal: Rolland Paper, 1957.

Fenwick, K.S. "The Magazine and Farm Paper Situation." *Economic Advertising* 8, no. 6 (June 1915): 23–27.

Fern, Fanny. *Ruth Hall and Other Writings,* edited by Joyce W. Warren. New Brunswick, NJ: Rutgers University Press, 1986.

Fiamengo, Janice. "'Abundantly Worthy of Its Past': Agnes Maule Machar and Early Canadian Historical Fiction." *Studies in Canadian Literature* 27, no. 1 (2002): 15–31.

———. *The Woman's Page: Journalism and Rhetoric in Early Canada.* Toronto: University of Toronto Press, 2008.

Field, John L. *Janet Carnochan.* Markham: Fitzhenry and Whiteside, 1985.

"50 Canadians to Watch in 2003." *Macleans's,* 20 January 2003: 24–31.

"50 Nation Builders." *Globe and Mail,* 1 June 2002, F4–F5.

Finch, Anne. "The Introduction." In *The Poems of Ann Countess of Winchilsea,* edited by Myra Reynolds, 4–6. Chicago: University of Chicago Press, 1903.

Fleck, Widow. "Address to the Public." *Poems on Various Subjects,* 2nd ed. Montreal: A. Bowman, 1835.

Fleming, Patricia. *Atlantic Canadian Imprints, 1801–1820: A Bibliography.* Toronto: University of Toronto Press, 1991.

———. "The Binding Trades." In *History of the Book in Canada,* vol. 2, *1840–1918,* edited by Yvan Lamonde, Patricia Lockhart Fleming, and Fiona A. Black, 101–06. Toronto: University of Toronto Press, 2005.

———. *Upper Canadian Imprints, 1801–1841: A Bibliography.* Toronto: University of Toronto Press, 1988.

Foran, Ethel Ursula. *Poems.* Montreal: Beauchemin, 1921.

———. *Springtime Fancies.* Montreal: Gazette, 1935.

Foran, Joseph Kearney. *Poems and Canadian Lyrics.* Montreal: Sadlier, 1895.

Ford, Margaret Lane. "Types and Gender: Ann Franklin, Colonial Printer." In *A Living of Words: American Women in Print Culture*, edited by Susan Albertine, 1–16. Knoxville: University of Tennessee Press, 1995.

Fraser, Marian Botsford. *Walking the Line: Travels along the Canadian/American Border*. Vancouver: Douglas and McIntyre, 1989.

Frost, S.H. "Report of Evangelistic Hall and Girls' Reading Room." Montreal, 1905.

Fuller, Margaret. "American Literature; Its Position in the Present Time, and Prospects for the Future." *Papers on Literature and Art, Part II*. London: Wiley and Putnam, 1846.

Garvin, John. "A Word from the Editor." In *The Collected Poems of Isabella Valancy Crawford* by Isabella Valancy Crawford, 1–4. Toronto: Briggs, 1905.

Gaskell, Elizabeth. *The Life of Charlotte Bronte*. First published in 1857. Reprint, Harmondsworth: Penguin, 1975.

Gaskell, Elizabeth. *The Life of Charlotte Brontë*. First published in 1857. Reprint, Harmondsworth: Penguin, 1981.

Gates, Barbara T., and Ann B. Shteir. "Introduction: Charting the Tradition." In *Natural Eloquence: Women Reinscribe Science*, edited by Barbara T. Gates and Ann B. Shteir, 3–26. Madison: University of Wisconsin Press, 1999.

Gelfant, Blanche. *Women Writing in America: Voices in Collage*. Hanover: University Press of New England, 1984.

Gellrich, Jesse M. *The Idea of the Book in the Middle Ages: Language, Theory, Mythology, and Fiction*. Ithaca: Cornell University Press, 1985.

"General Gossip of Authors and Writers." *Current Opinion* 16 (October 1894): 338. Cited by Klay Dyer, "Introduction." In *The Untempered Wind*, edited by Joanne E. Wood, xiv–xv. Ottawa: Tecumseh, 1994.

Genette, Gérard. *Paratexts: Thresholds of Interpretation*. Translated by Jane E. Lewin. New York: Cambridge University Press, 1997.

Gérin, Pierre. "Une ecrivaine acadienne à la fin du XIXᵉ siècle: Marichette." *Atlantis* 10, no. 1 (1984): 38–45.

Gerson, Carole. *A Purer Taste: The Writing and Reading of Fiction in English in Nineteenth-Century Canada*. Toronto: University of Toronto Press, 1989.

———. "Agnes Maule Machar." In *Canadian Writers, 1890–1920, Dictionary of Literary Biography*, vol. 92, edited by W.H. New, 220–21. Detroit: Gale, 1990.

———. "Annie Louisa Walker Coghill." *Canadian Notes and Queries* 37 (1987): 9–10.

———. "Anthologies and the Canon of Early Canadian Women Writers." In *Re(dis)covering Our Foremothers*, edited by Lorraine McMullen, 55–76. Ottawa: University of Ottawa Press, 1989.

———. "L.M. Montgomery and the Conflictedness of a Woman Writer." In *Storm and Dissonance: L.M. Montgomery and Conflict*, edited by Jean Mitchell, 67–80. Newcastle: Cambridge Scholars Publishing, 2008.

———. "Marie Joussaye's *Labor's Greeting*." *Canadian Poetry* 53 (Fall 2003): 87–95.

———. "Only a Working Girl: The Story of Marie Joussaye Fotheringham." *Northern Review* 19 (Winter 1998): 141–60.

———. "*The Snow Drop* and *The Maple Leaf:* Canada's First Periodicals for Children." *Canadian Children's Literature* 18/19 (1980): 10–23.

———. "Writers without Borders: The Global Framework of Canada's Early Literary History." *Canadian Literature* 201 (Summer 2009): 15–33.

Gerson, Carole, and Jacques Michon. "Editors' Introduction." In *History of the Book in Canada*, vol. 3, *1918–1980*, edited by Carole Gerson and Jacques Michon, 3–9. Toronto: University of Toronto Press, 2007.

Gibson, Rebecca Gould. "'My Want of Skill': Apologias of British Women Poets, 1660–1800." In *Eighteenth-Century Women and the Arts*, edited by Frederick M. Keener and Susan E. Lorsch, 79–86. New York: Greenwood Press, 1988.

Gilbert, Sandra M., and Susan Gubar. *The Madwoman in the Attic.* New Haven: Yale University Press, 1979.

Gillett, Margaret. "Carrie Derick (1862–1941) and the Chair of Botany at McGill." In *Despite the Odds: Essays on Canadian Women and Science,* edited by Marianne Gosztonyi Ainley, 74–87. Montreal: Véhicule, 1990.

Godsell, Patricia, ed. *Diary of Jane Ellice* by Jane Ellice. Toronto: Oberon, 1975.

———. *Letters & Diaries of Lady Durham.* Toronto: Oberon, 1979.

Goodman, M. *Mrs. Goodman's First Step in History, Dedicated to the Young Ladies of Canada.* Montreal: Lane, 1827.

Grant, M. [probably Maria Heathfield Grant]. "The Suffrage Question. Two Views: Fairly Stated from Both Standpoints." *Victoria Daily Times,* 27 May 1895, 8.

Gray, Charlotte. *Flint and Feather: The Life and Times of E. Pauline Johnson, Tekahionwake.* Toronto: Harperflamingo Canada, 2002.

Gray, Janet. "Passing as Fact: Mollie E. Lambert and Mary Eliza Tucker Lambert Meet as Racial Modernity Dawns." *Representations* 64 (Autumn 1998): 41–75.

Green, Mary Jean. "The 'Literary' Feminists and the Fight for Women's Writing in Quebec." *Journal of Canadian Studies* 21, no. 1 (1986): 128–43.

Gundy, H. Pearson. *Early Printers and Printing in the Canadas.* Toronto: Bibliographical Society of Canada, 1957.

Haig, Kennethe M. *Brave Harvest: The Life Story of E. Cora Hind, LL.D.* Toronto: Thomas Allen, 1945.

Hallett, Mary, and Marilyn Davis. *Firing the Heather: The Life and Times of Nellie McClung.* Saskatoon: Fifth House, 1994.

Hamelin, Danielle. "Nurturing Canadian Letters: Four Studies in the Publishing and Promotion of English-Canadian Writing, 1890–1920." Ph.D. dissertation, University of Toronto, 1994.

Harris, Martha Douglas. *History and Folklore of the Cowichan Indians.* Victoria: Colonist Printing and Publishing, 1901.

Harrison, Susie Frances. *Crowded out! and Other Sketches.* Ottawa: Evening Journal Office, 1886.

Harte, Walter Blackburn. "Canadian Journalists and Journalism." *New England Magazine* 5, no. 4 (December 1891): 433.

————. "Some Canadian Writers of Today." *New England Magazine* 9, no. 1 (September 1890): 35.

Hayes, Kate Simpson [Mary Markwell, pseud.]. *Aweena: An Indian Story of a Christmas Tryst in the Early Days*. Winnipeg: John A. Hart, 1906.

Haynes, Christine. "Reassessing 'Genius' in Studies of Authorship." *Book History* 8 (2005): 287–320.

Hayward, Caroline. *The Battles of the Crimea, with Other Poems*. Port Hope: Ansley, 1855.

Henderson, Jennifer. "Gender in the Discourse of Canadian Literary Criticism." *Open Letter* 8th series, no. 3 (Spring 1992): 47–57.

Hind, E. Cora. *Tales of the Road*, no. 3. Winnipeg, 1913.

"Holiday Fiction Special." *Globe and Mail*, 22 December 2001, R1–R6.

Hopkins, J. Castell, ed. *Canada: An Encyclopedia of the Country*, vol. 5. Toronto: Liscott, 1899.

Hopper, Mrs. R.P. *Old-Time Primitive Methodism in Canada [1829–1884]*. Toronto: Briggs, 1904.

Hoskin, Mary. *History of St. Basil's Parish, St. Joseph Street*. Toronto: Catholic Register and Canadian Extension, 1912.

Howsam, Leslie. "In My View: Women and Book History." *SHARP News* 7, no. 4 (Autumn 1998): 1–2.

————. "Women in Publishing and the Book Trades in Britain, 1830–1914." *Leipziger Jahrbuch zur Buchgeschichte* 6 (1996): 67–79.

Hubbard, Mina Benson. *A Woman's Way through Unknown Labrador*, edited by Sherrill Grace. Montreal/Kingston: McGill-Queen's University Press, 2004.

Hudak, Leona M. *Early American Women Printers and Publishers, 1639–1820*. Metuchen/London: Scarecrow Press, 1978.

Hughes, Katherine. *Archbishop O'Brien: Man and Churchman*. Ottawa: Crain, 1906.

————. *Father Lacombe: The Black-Robe Voyageur*. Toronto: Briggs, 1911.

Hulse, Elizabeth. *A Dictionary of Toronto Printers, Publishers, Booksellers, and the Allied Trade, 1798–1900*. Toronto: Anson-Cartwright, 1982.

————. "The Hunter Rose Company: A Brief History." *The Devil's Artisan* 18 (1986): 6.

Hutcheon, Linda. "Rethinking the National Model." In *Rethinking Literary History*, edited by Linda Hutcheon and Mario J. Valdés, 3–49. New York: Oxford University Press, 2002.

Irvine, Dean. *Editing Modernity: Women and Little-Magazine Cultures in Canada, 1916–1956*. Toronto: University of Toronto Press, 2008.

Italia, Iona. *The Rise of Literary Journalism in the Eighteenth Century: Anxious Employment*. London/New York: Routledge, 2005.

Jameson, Mrs. [Anna]. *Sketches in Canada; and Rambles among the Red Men*. London: Longman, Brown, Green, and Longmans, 1852.

————. *Winter Studies and Summer Rambles in Canada*, 3 vols. London: Saunders and Otley, 1838. Page numbers are also given for the New Canadian Library edition: Toronto: McClelland and Stewart, 1990.

Jennings, Clotilda [Maude, pseud]. *Linden Rhymes*. Halifax: Fuller, 1854.

Jerry, E. Claire. "The Role of Newspapers in the Nineteenth-Century Woman's Movement." In *A Voice of Their Own: The Woman Suffrage Press, 1840–1910*, edited by Martha M. Solomon, 17–29. Tuscaloosa/London: University of Alabama Press, 1991.

Johnson, Emily Pauline. *E. Pauline Johnson: Collected Poetry and Selected Prose*, edited by Carole Gerson and Veronica Strong-Boag. Toronto: University of Toronto Press, 2002.

Johnston, Judith, and Hillary Fraser. "The Professionalization of Women's Writing: Extending the Canon." In *Women and Literature in Britain, 1800–1900*, edited by Joanne Shattock, 231–50. Cambridge/New York: Cambridge University Press, 2001.

Jones, Eliza M. *Lecture on Co-operative Dairying and Winter Dairying*. Montreal: J. Lovell, 1893.

Juhasz, Suzanne. *Naked and Fiery Forms: Modern American Poetry by Women, a New Tradition*. New York: Harper and Row, 1976.

Karr, Clarence. *Authors and Audiences: Popular Canadian Fiction in the Early Twentieth Century*. Montreal/Kingston: McGill-Queen's University Press, 2000.

Karrenbrock, Marilyn H. Karrenbrock. "Mary Mapes Dodge." In *American Writers for Children before 1900: Dictionary of Literary Biography*, vol. 42, edited by Glen Estes, 146–60. Detroit: Gale, 1985.

"Keeps Secret 70 Years Then Tells." *Edmonton Journal*, 3 February 1960, 25.

Kelley, Mary. *Private Woman, Public Stage: Literary Domesticity in Nineteenth-Century America*. New York: Oxford University Press, 1984.

Kelly, Peggy Lynn. "Introduction." In *Shackles* by Madge MacBeth, edited by Peggy Lynn Kelly, 1–58. Ottawa: Tecumseh, 2005.

Kinton, Ada. *Just One Blue Bonnet: The Life Story of Ada Florence Kinton, Artist and Salvationist*. Toronto: Briggs, 1907.

Kröller, Eva-Marie. *Canadian Travellers in Europe, 1851–1900*. Vancouver: UBC Press, 1987.

La vénérable mère Marguerite Bourgeoys. Traduit de l'anglais par Joseph Bruneau. Montreal: Soeurs de la Congrégation de Notre-Dame, [1910–].

Lamonde, Yvan, Peter F. McNally, and Andrea Rotundo. "Public Libraries and the Emergence of a Public Culture." In *History of the Book in Canada*, vol. 2, *1840–1918*, edited by Yvan Lamonde, Patricia Lockhart Fleming, and Fiona A. Black, 250–71. Toronto: University of Toronto Press, 2005.

Lamonde, Yvan, and Andrea Rotundo. "The Book Trade and Bookstores." In *History of the Book in Canada*, vol. 1, *Beginnings to 1840*, edited by Patricia Lockhart Fleming, Gilles Gallichan, and Yvan Lamonde, 124–37. Toronto: University of Toronto Press, 2004.

Lang, Marjory. *Women Who Made the News: Female Journalists in Canada, 1880–1945*. Montreal/Kingston: McGill-Queen's University Press, 1999.

Langton Records: Journals and Letters from Canada, 1837–1846. First published in Edinburgh in 1904. Reprinted in *A Gentlewoman in Upper Canada: The Journals,*

Letters, and Art of Anne Langton, edited by Barbara Williams. Toronto: University of Toronto Press, 2008.

Laut, Agnes. "Fifteen Hundred Miles down the Saskatchewan." *Scribner's* 45 (1909): 459–74.

Leacock, Stephen. "The Woman Question." *Maclean's Magazine* (October 1915): 7–9. Reprinted in *Canadian Literature in English: Texts and Contexts*, vol. 1, edited by Cynthia Sugars and Laura Moss, 510–14. Toronto: Pearson Longman, 2009.

Lecker, Robert. "Anthologizing English-Canadian Fiction: Some Canonical Trends." *Open Letter* 9th series, no. 1 (Fall 1994): 25–80.

Legge, Valerie. "'Why Go Abroad?' Agnes Laut in *Wonderland*." In *Literary Environments: Canada and the Old World*, edited by Britta Olinder, 61–73. Brussels: Peter Lang, 2006.

Lenz, Millience. "Harriet Beecher Stowe. " In *American Writers for Children before 1900: Dictionary of Literary Biography*, vol. 42, edited by Glen Estes, 338–50. Detroit: Gale, 1985.

Leonard, Carrie. *Gems for the Home Circle*. London: Cameron, 1869.

Leonowens, Anna Harriette. *The English Governess at the Siamese Court: Being Recollections of Six Years in the Royal Palace at Bangkok*. London: Trubner, 1870.

———. *The Romance of the Harem*. Boston: Osgood, 1873.

Lepage, Françoise, Judith Saltman, and Gail Edwards. "Children's Authors and Their Markets." In *History of the Book in Canada*, vol. 3, *1918–1980*, edited by Carole Gerson and Jacques Michon, 145–53. Toronto: University of Toronto Press, 2007.

Leprohon, Rosanna. *Antoinette de Mirecourt: or, Secret Marrying and Secret Sorrowing*. Montreal: Lovell, 1864. Centre for Editing Early Canadian Texts 6. Ottawa: Carleton University Press, 1989.

Lerner, Loren. "William Notman's Portrait Photographs of Girls Reading from the 1860s to 1880s: A Pictorial Analysis Based on Contemporary Writings." *Papers of the Bibliographical Society of Canada* 47, no.1 (2009): 45–73.

Leroux, Éric. "Printers: From Shop to Industry." In *History of the Book in Canada*, vol. 2, *1840–1918*, edited by Yvan Lamonde, Patricia Lockhart Fleming, and Fiona A. Black, 75–87. Toronto: University of Toronto Press, 2005.

Leslie, Mary [James Thomas Jones]. *The Cromaboo Mail Carrier: A Canadian Love Story*. Guelph: Hacking, 1878.

Lester, Normand. *Le livre noir du Canada anglais*. Montreal: Intouchables, 2001.

Levesque, Andrée. *La norme et les déviantes*. Montreal: Remue-ménage, 1989.

Levin, Martin. "Ladies' Day in CanLit." *Globe and Mail*, 2 March 2002, D12.

Lighthall, W.D. *Songs of the Great Dominion*. London: Scott, 1889.

Livesay, Florence Randal. "Note by Translator." In *Songs of Ukraina, with Ruthenian Poems*, translated by Florence Randal Livesay. London: Dent, 1916.

Lizars, Robina MacFarlane, and Kathleen MacFarlane Lizars. *In the Days of the Canada Company: The Story of the Settlement of the Huron Tract and a View of the Social Life of the Period 1825–1850*. Toronto: Briggs, 1896.

Lockerby, Elizabeth N. [E.N.L.]. *The Wild Brier: or, Lays by an Untaught Minstrel.* Charlottetown: Excelsior, 1866.

Lortie, Jeanne d'Arc, avec la collaboration de Pierre Savard et Paul Wyczynski. *Les textes poétiques du Canada français,* vol. 2–5. Montreal: Fides, 1987.

Lovell, Terry. *Consuming Fiction.* New York: Verso, 1987.

Luke, Edith M. "Woman Suffrage in Canada." *Canadian Magazine* 5 (August 1895): 328–36.

Macbeth, Madge. *Boulevard Career.* Toronto: Kingswood House, 1957.

MacDonald, Mary Lu. *Literature and Society in the Canadas, 1817–1850.* Lewiston: Edwin Mellen Press, 1992.

———. "Reading between the Lines: An Analysis of Canadian Literary Prefaces and Prospectuses in the First Half of the Nineteenth Century." In *Prefaces and Literary Manifestoes/Préfaces et manifestes littéraires,* edited by E.D. Blodgett and A.G. Purdy, 29–42. Edmonton: Research Institute for Comparative Literature, 1990.

———. "*The Montreal Museum,* 1832–1834: The Presence and Absence of Literary Women." In *Women's Writing and the Literary Institution/L'écriture au féminin et l'institution littéraire,* edited by C. Potvin and J. Williamson, 139–50. Edmonton: University of Alberta Research Institute for Comparative Literature, 1992.

Machar, Agnes Maule. *Katie Johnstone's Cross: A Canadian Tale.* Toronto: J. Campbell, 1870.

———. *Roland Graeme, Knight: A Novel of Our Time.* First published in 1892. Reprint, Ottawa: Tecumseh, 1996.

——— [Fidelis]. "Unhealthy Conditions of Women's Work in Factories." *Week,* 8 May 1896, 566–69.

MacKay, Isabel Ecclestone. "Prefatory Notes." In *Verse and Reverse* by members of the Toronto Women's Press Club. Toronto: F.D. Goodchild, 1922.

MacLaren. Eli. "The Magnification of Ralph Connor: *Black Rock* and the North American Copyright Divide." *Papers of the Bibliographical Society of America* 101, no. 4 (2007): 507–31.

Macleod, Mrs. E.S. *Carols of Canada.* Charlottetown: Coombs, 1893.

MacMillan, Carrie, Lorraine McMullen, and Elizabeth Waterston. *Silenced Sextet: Six Nineteenth-Century Canadian Women Novelists.* Montreal/Kingston: McGill-Queen's University Press, 1992.

Macmillans in Canada Present This List of Books by Canadian Authors. Toronto: Macmillan, 1929.

MacMurchy, Marjory. *The Woman–Bless Her.* Toronto: S.B. Gundy, 1916.

Major, Jean-Louis. "Inventaire et invention d'une littérature: Le Corpus d'éditions critiques." In *Challenges, Projects, Texts: Canadian Editing,* edited by John Lennox and Janet M. Patterson, 70–88. New York: AMS Press, 1993.

Markwell, Mary [Kate Simpson Hayes]. "Agnes Laut as a Writer and as Woman." *Winnipeg Free Press,* 31 October 1908, 17.

Marzolf, Marion. *Up from the Footnote: A History of Women Journalists.* New York: Hastings House, 1977.

Matthews, Samantha. *Poetical Remains: Poets' Graves, Bodies, and Books in the Nineteenth Century*. New York: Oxford University Press, 2004.

McAlister, Lottie. *Clipped Wings*. Toronto: Briggs, 1899.

McClung, Nellie. *Nellie McClung, the Complete Autobiography: Clearing in the West and The Stream Runs Fast*, edited by Veronica Strong-Boag and Michelle Lynn Rosa. Peterborough: Broadview, 2003.

McDowell, Marjorie. "Children's Books." In *Literary History of Canada: Canadian Literature in English*, edited by Carl F. Klinck. Toronto: University of Toronto Press, 1967.

McEvoy, Bernard. "The Canadian Society of Authors." *Canadian Magazine* 12 (April 1899): 561–63.

McIver, Mary Anne. *Poems*. Ottawa: I.B. Taylor, 1859.

McMullen, Lorraine. *Re(dis)covering Our Foremothers*. Ottawa: University of Ottawa Press, 1990.

McMullen, Lorraine, and Sandra Campbell, eds. *Aspiring Women: Short Stories by Canadian Women, 1880–1890*. Ottawa: University of Ottawa Press, 1993.

Merkley, George E. *Canadian Melodies and Poems*. Toronto: Hart and Riddell, 1893.

Merton, Madge, and John A. Cooper. "Our Children and Their Reading." *Canadian Magazine* 8 (January 1896): 282–87.

Miegon, Anna. "*The Ladies' Diary* and the Emergence of the Almanac for Women, 1704–1753." Ph.D. dissertation, Simon Fraser University, 2008.

Milne, Beth. *Medicine Hat Public Library: The First Eighty Years*. Medicine Hat: Friends of the Medicine Hat Public Library, 1998.

Montgomery, L.M. *Anne of Green Gables*, edited by Mary Rubio and Elizabeth Waterston. Norton Critical Editions. New York: W.W. Norton, 2007.

———. *The Selected Journals of L.M. Montgomery*, edited by Mary Rubio and Elizabeth Waterston, 5 vols. Toronto: Oxford University Press, 1984–2004.

———. "The Strike at Putney." *Western Christian Advocate*, 16 September 1903, 14–15.

Montreuil, Sophie. "Joséphine Marchand-Dandurand: Readings in the Feminine." In *History of the Book in Canada*, vol. 2, *1840–1918*, edited by Yvan Lamonde, Patricia Lockhart Fleming, and Fiona A. Black, 461–65. Toronto: University of Toronto Press, 2005.

Moodie, Susanna. "Editor's Table." *Victoria Magazine* 1 (June 1848): 240.

———. *Life in the Clearings versus the Bush*. First published in 1853. Reprint, New Canadian Library edition. Toronto: McClelland and Stewart.

———. *Roughing It in the Bush: or, Life in Canada*, edited by Carl Ballstadt. Centre for Editing Early Canadian Texts 5. Ottawa: Carleton University Press, 1986.

———. "The Foundling of the Storm." *Maple Leaf* 1 (1852): 13.

Morgan, Cecilia. "*A Happy Holiday*": *English Canadians and Transatlantic Tourism, 1870–1930*. Toronto: University of Toronto Press, 2008.

———. "'Of Slender Frame and Delicate Appearance': The Placing of Laura Secord in the Narratives of Canadian Loyalist History." In *Gender and History in Canada*, edited by Joy Parr and Mark Rosenfeld, 103–19. Mississauga: Copp Clark, 1996.

Morrison, Katherine L. *Canadians Are Not Americans.* Toronto: Second Story Press, 2003.

Mount, Nick. "Exodus: When Canadian Literature Moved to New York." Ph.D. dissertation, Dalhousie University, 2001.

———. *When Canadian Literature Moved to New York.* Toronto: University of Toronto Press, 2005.

Mountcastle, Clara [Caris Sims, pseud.]. *Is Marriage a Failure? Lost! And Many Gems of Verse.* Toronto: Imrie Graham, 1899.

———. *The Mission of Love; Lost; and Other Poems.* Toronto: Hunter Rose, 1882.

Moyles, R.G. "Ethelwyn Wetherald: An Early, Popular, and Prolific Poet." *Canadian Children's Literature* 59 (1990): 6–16.

———. "Young Canada: An Index to Canadian Materials in Major British and American Periodicals." *Canadian Children's Literature* 78 (1995): 7–63.

Mulvany, C. Pelham. *Toronto: Past and Present.* Toronto: W.E. Caiger, 1884.

Munro, Alice. *Lives of Girls and Women.* New York: Signet, 1974.

Murphy, Emily Ferguson. *Janey Canuck in the West.* First published in 1917. Reprint, Toronto: McClelland and Stewart, 1975.

Murray, Heather. *Come, Bright Improvement! The Literary Societies of Nineteenth-Century Ontario.* Toronto: University of Toronto Press, 2002.

———. "Literary Societies." In *History of the Book in Canada,* vol. 2, *1840–1918,* edited by Yvan Lamonde, Patricia Lockhart Fleming, and Fiona A. Black, 473–78. Toronto: University of Toronto Press, 2005.

Murray, Kathleen Rochefort. "Sainte Anne as Symbol of Literacy in Quebec Culture." *Quebec Studies* 30 (2000): 70–78.

Murray, Simone. *Mixed Media: Feminist Presses and Publishing Politics.* London: Pluto Press, 2004.

Nannary, M.A. *Memoir of the Life of Rev. E.J. Dumphy.* St. John: Weekly Herald, 1877.

National Council of Women of Canada. *Women of Canada: Their Life and Work.* First published in 1900. Reprint, National Council of Women of Canada, 1975.

Norton, Mrs. Mary. *The Ministry of Flowers and Other Poems.* Toronto: Briggs, 1890.

O'Hagan, Thomas. "Some Canadian Women Writers." *Catholic World* 63 (September 1896): 779–85.

"Of the Making of Books There Is No End." *Globe,* 10 November 1894, 9.

Okker, Patricia. *Our Sister Editors: Sara J. Hale and the Tradition of Nineteenth-Century American Women Editors.* Athens/London: University of Georgia Press, 1995.

Onslow, Barbara. *Women of the Press in Nineteenth-Century Britain.* London: Macmillan, 2000.

"Our New Year." *Woman's Century* (May 1917): 6.

Our Own Cook Book. Fenelon Falls: Victoria Women's Institute, 1905.

Paget, Amelia. *People of the Plains,* edited by Sarah Carter. Regina: Canadian Plains Research Centre, 2004.

Palmegiano, E.M. *Women and British Periodicals, 1832–1867: A Bibliography.* New York/London: Garland, 1976.

Parent, Louise-Amélie. *Quelques traits particuliers aux saisons du bas Canada*, edited by Roger LeMoine. Orléans: Editions David, 2000.

Parker, George L. *Beginnings of the Book Trade in Canada*. Toronto: University of Toronto Press, 1985.

Patterson, Martha H. *Beyond the Gibson Girl: Reimagining the American New Woman, 1895–1915*. Urbana: University of Illinois Press, 2005.

Peterman, Michael A. "In Search of Agnes Strickland's Sisters." *Canadian Literature* 121 (Summer 1989): 116.

———. "'Splendid Anachronism': The Record of Catharine Parr Traill's Struggles as an Amateur Botanist in Nineteenth-Century Canada." In *Re(dis)covering Our Foremothers*, edited by Lorraine McMullen, 173–85. Ottawa: University of Ottawa Press, 1990.

Peterman, Michael A., and Janet B. Friskney. "'Booming' the Canuck Book: Edward Caswell and the Promotion of Canadian Writing." *Journal of Canadian Studies* 30, no. 3 (Fall 1995): 60–90.

Petitt, Maud. *Beth Woodburn*. Toronto: Briggs, 1897.

Phelps, Marion L. *Biography, Mrs. Catherine Matilda (Townsend) Day*. Knowlton: Marion L. Phelps, 1988.

Pierce, Lorne. *The Chronicle of a Century*. Toronto: Ryerson, 1929.

Platt, H.L. [Harriet Louise]. *The Story of the Years: A History of the Woman's Missionary Society of the Methodist Church, Canada, from 1881 to 1906*, vol. 1. [n.d., n.p.].

Poovey, Mary. *The Proper Lady and the Woman Writer: Ideology as Style in the Works of Mary Wollstonecraft, Mary Shelley, and Jane Austen*. Chicago: University of Chicago Press, 1984.

Potvin, Claude. *Le Canada français et sa littérature de jeunesse*. Moncton: Éditions CRP, 1981.

Prentice, Alison, Beth Light, Paula Bourne, Wendy Mitchinson, and Gail Cuthbert Brandt. *Canadian Women: A History*. Toronto: Harcourt Brace, 1988.

Price, Elizabeth Bailey. "Onoto Watanna, an Amazing Author." *Maclean's Magazine* 35 (15 October 1922): 64–65.

Pringle, Gertrude. "Miss Jean MacIlwraith, Canadian Authoress." *Saturday Night* 41 (30 January 1926): 21, 28.

Prowse, Judge W.D. "Introduction." In *The Victorian Triumph and Other Poems* by Isabella Whiteford Rogerson. Toronto: Briggs, 1898.

Pykett, Lyn. "Portraits of the Artist as a Young Woman: Representations of the Female Artist in the New Woman Fiction of the 1890s." In *Victorian Women Writers and the Woman Question*, edited by Nicola Diane Thompson, 135–50. Cambridge: Cambridge University Press, 1999.

———. *The "Improper" Feminine: The Women's Sensation Novel and the New Woman Writing*. London/New York: Routledge, 1992.

Quirk, Linda. "The Place of Bibliography in the Academy Today: Reassessing Sara Jeannette Duncan." *PBSC/CSBC* 46, no. 1 (Spring 2008): 79–86.

Raible, Chris. *The Power of the Press: The Story of Early Canadian Printers and Publishers.* Toronto: J. Lorimer, 2007.

Read, Blanche. *The Life of John Read.* Toronto: Salvation Army, 1899.

Reade, John. "Introduction." In *Poetical Works of Mrs. Leprohon* by Mrs. [Rosanna] Leprohon. Montreal: J. Lovell, 1881.

Reeve, Winnifred. "The Canadian Spirit in Our Literature." Calgary *Daily Herald,* 24 March 1923, 11.

"Remarkable Journey of Two Women to the Arctic Ocean." *Globe,* Saturday Magazine Section, 6 February 1909, 6.

Rev. of *History of Canada, for the Use of Schools* by Jennet Roy. *Victoria Magazine* 1 (September 1847): 24.

Reynolds, Sian. "Women Compositors." In *The Edinburgh History of the Book in Scotland,* vol. 4, edited by David Finkelstein and Alistair McCleery, 133–35. Edinburgh: Edinburgh University Press, 2007.

Rhodes, Jane. *Mary Ann Shadd Cary: The Black Press and Protest in the Nineteenth Century.* Bloomington: Indiana University Press, 1998.

Rijnhart, Susie Carson. *With the Tibetans in Tent and Temple: Narrative of Four Years' Residence on the Tibetan Border, and of a Journey into the Far Interior.* Chicago: F.H. Revell, 1901.

Robbins, Sarah. "Woman's Work for Woman: Gendered Print Culture in American Mission Movement Narratives." In *Women in Print: Essays on the Print Culture of American Women from the Nineteenth and Twentieth Centuries,* edited by James P. Danky and Wayne A. Wiegand, 251–75. Madison: University of Wisconsin Press, 2006.

Robinson, Agnes F. *A Quarter of a Century.* Toronto: Women's Foreign Missionary Society of the Presbyterian Church in Canada, 1901.

Roche, Harriet A. *On Trek in the Transvaal: or, Over Berg and Veldt in South Africa.* London: Sampson Low, 1878.

Rodd, Mrs. W.W. *Sunbeams: A Collection of Original Poems.* Charlottetown, 1898.

Roome, Patricia. "Henrietta Muir Edwards: The Journey of a Canadian Feminist." Ph.D. dissertation, Simon Fraser University, 1996.

Roy, Jennet. *History of Canada for the Use of Schools and Families.* Montreal: Armour and Ramsay, 1847.

Roy, Julie. "Des réseaux en convergence: Les Éspaces de la sociabilité littéraire aud féminin dans la première moitié du xixe siècle." *Globe: Revue Internationale d'Études Québécoises* 7, no. 1 (2004): 79–105.

———. "Le 'genre' prétexte: Récit de soi et critique sociale dans les correspondences 'féminines' au tournant du xixe siècle." In *Portrait des arts, des letters de de l'éloquence au Québec (1760–1840),* edited by Bernard Andrès and Marc André Bernier, 180–201. Quebec: Laval University Press, 2002.

———. "Le réseau épistolaire comme horizon d'écriture au tournant du xixe siècle: Des 'protoscriptrices' canadiennes en quête de visibilité," http://egodoc.revues.org/octobre2002/docs/D987612/VS987712.htm.

————. "Voyages en pays de re-connaissance: Paysages et mémoires dans l'oeuvre de Louise-Amélie Panet-Berczy (1789–1865)." In *Intercultural Journeys/Parcours interculturels*, edited by Natasha Dagenais, Joanna Daxell, and Roxanne Rimstead, 157–69. Baldwin Mill's: Les Éditions Topeda Hill, 2003.

Roy, Wendy. *Maps of Difference: Canada, Women, and Travel.* Montreal/Kingston: McGill-Queen's University Press, 2005.

Rungeling, Dorothy W. *Life and Works of Ethelwyn Wetherald, 1857–1940.* [Ridgeville]: Rungeling, 2004.

Russell, R.W., D.W. Russell, and Rea Wilmshurst. *Lucy Maud Montgomery: A Preliminary Bibliography.* Waterloo: University of Waterloo Library, 1986.

Rutherdale, Myra. *Women and the White Man's God: Gender and Race in the Canadian Mission Field.* Vancouver: UBC Press, 2002.

Rutherford, Paul. *A Victorian Authority: The Daily Press in Late Nineteenth-Century Canada.* Toronto: University of Toronto Press, 1982.

Ryan, William Thomas Carroll. *Oscar: and Other Poems.* Hamilton: Franklin, 1857.

Sanderson, Camilla. *John Sanderson the First; or A Pioneer Preacher at Home.* Toronto: Briggs, 1910.

Sanford, M. Bourchier. "Some Women Writers of Canada." *Godey's Magazine* 135 (July 1897): 13–21.

Savage, Candace. *Our Nell: A Scrapbook Biography of Nellie McClung.* Saskatoon: Western Producer Prairie Books, 1979.

Savoie, Chantal. "Des salons aux annales: Les réseaux et associations des femmes des lettres à Montréal au tournant du XXᵉ siècle." *Voix et images* 27, no. 2 (2002): 238–53.

————. "La page féminie des grands quotidiens montréalais comme lieu de sociabilité littéraire au tournant de XXᵉ siècle." *Tangence* 80 (hiver 2006): 125–42.

————. "'Moins de dentelles, plus de psychologie' et une heure à soi: Les *Lettres* de Fadette et la chronique féminine au tournant du XXᵉ siècle." In *Tendances actuelles en histoire littéraire canadienne*, edited by Denis Saint-Jacques, 183–99. Quebec: Nota Bene, 2003.

————. "Persister et signer: Les signatures féminines et l'évolution de le reconnaissance sociale de l'écrivaine (1893–1929)." *Voix et images* 30, no. 1 (August 2004): 67–79.

Savours, Ann. *The Search for the North West Passage.* New York: St. Martin's Press, 1999.

Sawtell, M. Ethelind. *The Mourner's Tribute; or Effusions of Melancholy Hours.* Montreal: Armour and Ramsay, 1840.

Saxton, Kirsten T. "Introduction." In *The Passionate Fictions of Eliza Haywood: Essays on Her Life and Work*, edited by Kirsten T. Saxon and Rebecca P. Bocchicchio, 1–18. Lexington: University of Kentucky Press, 2000.

Saxton, Martha. *Louisa May: A Modern Biography of Louisa May Alcott.* Boston: Houghton Mifflin, 1977.

Schaffer, Talia. "'Nothing but Foolscap and Ink': Inventing the New Woman." In *The New Woman in Fiction and in Fact: Fin de siècle Feminisms*, edited by Angélique Richardson and Chris Willis. London: Palgrave, 2001.

Schieder, Rupert. "Editor's Preface." In *Canadian Crusoes: A Tale of the Rice Lake Plains* by Catharine Parr Traill, edited by Rupert Schieder, xiii–xvi. Centre for Editing Early Canadian Texts 2. Ottawa: Carleton University Press, 1986.

Schoolcraft, Henry Rowe. *The Literary Voyager; or, Muzzeniegun*, edited by Philip A. Mason. Westport: Greenwood Press, 1974.

Schoolcraft, Jane Johnston. *The Sound the Stars Make Rushing through the Sky: The Writings of Jane Johnston Schoolcraft*, edited by Dale Parker. Philadelphia: University of Pennsylvania Press, 2007.

Schreiner, Olive. *Woman and Labor*. New York: Stokes, 1911.

Schultz, Lady. *How to Provide Good Reading for Children*. Toronto: Bryant Press, 1895.

"Sets Credit Rating by Day, Gets Book Plot in Sleep." Toronto *Daily Star*, 15 October 1938, 13.

Shenton, Mary J. *A Biographical Sketch of the Late Rev. Job Shenton by His Widow with Some of His Sermons and Lectures*. St. John: McMillan, 1902.

Sherk, Florence. *The Workshops and Other Poems*. Fort William: Times-Journal, 1919.

Shields, Carol. "A View from the Edge of the Edge." In *Carol Shields and the Extraordinary*, edited by Marta Dvorak and Manina Jones, 17–29. Montreal/Kingston: McGill-Queen's University Press, 2007.

Showalter, Elaine. *A Jury of Her Peers: American Women Writers from Anne Bradstreet to Annie Proulx*. New York: Knopf, 2009.

———. *A Literature of Their Own*. Princeton: Princeton University Press, 1977.

———, ed. *Daughters of Decadence: Women Writers of the Fin-de-Siècle*. London: Virago, 1993.

Skinner, Constance Lindsay. *Songs of the Coast Dwellers*. New York: Coward-McCann, 1930.

Smith, Russell. "Real Men Don't Read Fiction...." *Globe and Mail*, 4 March 2000, R5.

Smyth, Elizabeth M. "'Writing Teaches Us Our Mysteries': Women Religious Recording and Writing History." In *Creating Historical Memory: English-Canadian Women and the Work of History*, edited by Beverly Boutilier and Alison Prentice, 101–28. Vancouver: UBC Press, 1997.

"Some Women Workers in Victoria." Victoria *Daily Times*, 27 May 1895, 6.

Spence, Catherine Helen. *Mr. Hogarth's Will*. First published in 1865. Reprint, Victoria: Penguin, 1988.

Spivak, Gayatri. "Translator's Preface." In *Of Grammatology* by Jacques Derrida, ix–xiii. Baltimore: Johns Hopkins University Press, 1976.

Spriggs, S. Squire. *The Methods of Publishing*, 2nd ed. London: Incorporated Society of Authors, 1891.

St. Jacques, Denis, and Maurice Lemire, eds. *La vie littéraire au Québec.* Sainte-Foy: Les Presses de l'Université Laval, 2005.

St. John, Judith. "A Peep at the Esquimaux through Early Children's Books." *The Beaver* (Winter 1965): 38–44.

"Staff of the Women's *Globe.*" *Globe,* 18 April 1895, 4.

Staves, Susan. *A Literary History of Women's Writing in Britain, 1660–1789.* Cambridge/New York: Cambridge University Press, 2006.

Ste-Croix, Mother. *Glimpses of the Monastery.* Quebec: Darveau, 1872.

Steffler, Margaret, and Neil Steffler. "'If We Would Read It Aright': Traill's 'Ladder to Heaven." *Journal of Canadian Studies* 38, no. 3 (2004): 123–52.

Stephens, Mrs. [Anna Sophia]. "Literary Ladies of America." *Amaranth* 3, no. 5 (May 1843): 129–36.

Stephenson, Rev. William. "Preface." In *Wayside Flowers* by Harriette Annie Wilkins, v. Toronto: Hunter Rose, 1876.

Stewart, Frances. *Our Forest Home: Being Extracts from the Correspondence of the Late Frances Stewart.* Montreal: Gazette, 1902.

Strachan, E.S. *The Story of the Years: A History of the Woman's Missionary Society of the Methodist Church, Canada, 1906–1916,* vol. 3. Toronto: Woman's Missionary Society, Methodist Church Canada, 1917.

Stringer, Arthur. "Wild Poets I've Known: Marjorie Pickthall." *Saturday Night* (14 June 1941): 41.

Strong-Boag, Veronica. "'Ever a crusader': Nellie McClung, First-Wave Feminist." In *Rethinking Canada,* edited by Veronica Strong-Boag and Anita Claire Fellman, 178–90. Toronto: Copp Clark, 1986.

———. "Introduction." In *In Times Like These* by Nellie McClung, xiv–xix. Toronto: University of Toronto Press, 1972.

———. *The Parliament of Women: The National Council of Women of Canada, 1893–1929.* Ottawa: National Museums of Canada, 1976.

Strong-Boag, Veronica, and Carole Gerson. *Paddling Her Own Canoe.* Toronto: University of Toronto Press, 2000.

Struthers, J.R. [Tim]. "An Interview with Margaret Atwood." *Essays on Canadian Writing,* no. 6 (1976): 18–27.

Sullivan, Rosemary. "Introduction." In *Stories by Canadian Women,* edited by Rosemary Sullivan, ix–xix. Toronto: Oxford University Press, 1984.

Sulte, Benjamine. "Préface." In *Fleurs du printemps* by Mme Duval-Thibault, vii–xi. Fall River: Société de publication de l'Indépendant, 1892.

Sutherland, John. *Mrs. Humphrey Ward: Eminent Victorian, Pre-eminent Edwardian.* New York: Oxford University Press, 1990.

Symmes, Lydia Clark. *My Mother's Journal,* edited, with introductory notes of her life, by her son, Francis E. Clark. Boston: United Society of Christian Endeavor, 1911.

Thomas, Clara. *Love and Work Enough: The Life of Anna Jameson.* Toronto: University of Toronto Press, 1967.

Thorburn, Maria J.I. *The Orphans' Home of the City of Ottawa. Sketch of the First Forty Years, 1864–1904.* Toronto: Briggs, 1904.

Ticknor, Caroline. *Hawthorne and His Publisher.* Boston: Houghton Mifflin, 1913.

Tidcombe, Marian. *Women Bookbinders, 1880–1920.* New Castle/London: Oak Knoll Press/British Library, 1996.

Totosy de Zepetnek, Steven. *The Social Dimensions of Fiction.* Wiesbaden: Vieweg, 1993.

Towle, Nancy. *Some of the Writings, and Last Sentences of Adolphus Dewey, Executed at Montreal, Aug 30th, 1833.* Montreal: J.A. Hoisington, Printer, 1833.

Traill, Catharine Parr. "A Glance within the Forest." In *Forest and Other Gleanings: The Fugitive Writings of Catharine Parr Traill,* edited by Michael A. Peterman and Carl Ballstadt. Ottawa: University of Ottawa Press, 1994.

———. *Canadian Crusoes.* First published in 1852. Reprint, First published in 1836. Centre for Editing Early Canadian Texts 2. Ottawa: Carleton University Press, 1986.

———. *Narratives of Nature.* London: Edward Lacey, n.d.

———. *The Backwoods of Canada,* edited by Michael A. Peterman. First published in 1836. Centre for Editing Early Canadian Texts 11. Ottawa: Carleton University Press, 1997.

Travis, Trysh. "The Women in Print Movement." *Book History* 11 (2008): 275–300.

Tremaine, Marie. *A Bibliography of Canadian Imprints, 1751–1800.* Toronto: University of Toronto Press, 1952.

Valois, Léonise [Atala]. *Fleurs sauvages.* Montreal: Beauchemin, 1910.

Vaughan, Francis E. *Andrew C. Lawson, Scientist, Teacher, Philosopher.* Glendale: Arthur H. Clark, 1970.

Venema, Kathleen. "Letitia Mactavish Hargrave and Hudson's Bay Company Domestic Politics." In *ReCalling Early Canada,* edited by Jennifer Blair et al., 145–72. Edmonton: University of Alberta Press, 2005.

Verrette, Michel. *L'Alphabétisation au Québec, 1660–1900.* Quebec: Septentrion, 2002.

Vipond, Mary. "Best Sellers in English Canada, 1899–1918: An Overview." *Journal of Canadian Fiction* 24 (1978): 96–119.

———. "Canadian Nationalism and the Plight of Canadian Magazines in the 1920s." *Canadian Historical Review* 58, no. 1 (1977): 43–63.

Wagner, Anton. "Eliza Lanesford Cushing." In *Canadian Writers Before 1890: Dictionary of Literary Biography,* vol. 99, edited by W.H. New, 85. Detroit: Gale, 1990.

Walker, Annie Louisa. *Leaves from the Backwoods.* Montreal: Lovell, 1861.

Wall, Wendy. *The Imprint of Gender.* Ithaca: Cornell University Press, 1993.

Waterston, Elizabeth. "Diana Bayley: A Grandmama's Tale." *Canadian Children's Literature* 27, no. 2 (2001): 60–66.

Weaver, Emily P., A.E. Weaver, and E.C. Weaver, eds. *Canadian Women's Annual and Social Service Directory.* Toronto: McClelland, Goodchild, and Stewart, 1915.

Wendell, Winnifred Lee. "The Modern School of Canadian Writers." *Bookman* 11 (1900): 515–26.

Wetherald, Ethelwyn. "Introduction." In *Collected Poems of Isabella Valancy Crawford*, edited by J.W. Garvin, 15–29. Toronto: Briggs, 1905.

———. *Lyrics and Sonnets*. Toronto: Nelson, 1931.

Wetherell, J.E. *Later Canadian Poems*. Toronto: Copp Clark, 1893.

Whelen, Gloria. "Maria Grant." In *In Her Own Right: Selected Essays on Women's History in BC*, edited by Barbara Latham and Cathy Kess, 125–46. Victoria: Camosun College, 1980.

Williams, Barbara. "Introduction." In *A Gentlewoman in Upper Canada: The Journals, Letters, and Art of Anne Langton*, 3–104. Toronto: University of Toronto Press, 2008.

Wilson, Anne Elizabeth. "Beloved Friend." *Saturday Night* (17 December 1930): 28.

Wilson, Ethel. *Stories, Essays, Letters*, edited by David Stouck. Vancouver: UBC Press, 1987.

Windsor, Kenneth N. "Historical Writing in Canada to 1920." In *Literary History of Canada*, edited by Carl F. Klinck, 208–50. Toronto: University of Toronto Press, 1967.

Winks, Robin. *The Blacks in Canada: A History*. Montreal/Kingston: McGill-Queen's University Press, 1997.

Withrow, W.H. "Introduction." In *Clipped Wings* by Lottie McAlister, [iii]. Toronto: Briggs, 1889.

———. "Introduction." In *Sowing and Reaping: or, Records of the Ellisson Family* by Pamelia Vining Yule [Mrs. J.C. Yule], iii–iv. Toronto: Briggs, 1899.

"Women in Journalism." *Week*, 23 June 1893, 712.

"Women's Rights." *Presbyterian Record for the Dominion of Canada* (July 1876): 190.

"Women Workers." *Ladies' Journal* (May 1895): 8.

Wood, Joanna E. "Algernon Charles Swinburne. An Appreciation." *Canadian Magazine* 17 (May 1901): 2–11.

———. "Presentation at Court." *Canadian Magazine* 17 (October 1901): 506–10.

———. *The Untempered Wind*. First published in 1894. Reprint, Ottawa: Tecumseh, 1994.

Woolf, Virginia. *A Room of One's Own*. First published in 1929. Reprint, London: Grafton, 1985.

Woollacott, Angela. *To Try Her Fortune in London: Australian Women, Colonialism, and Modernity*. New York: Oxford University Press, 2001.

Wright, Jane Barker. *The Understanding*. Erin: Porcupine's Quill, 2002.

York, Lorraine. *Literary Celebrity in Canada*. Toronto: University of Toronto Press, 2007.

Yule, Pamelia Vining. *Poems of the Heart and Home*. Toronto: Bengough Moore, 1881.

INDEX